Joey Kirkpatrick and Flora C. Mace

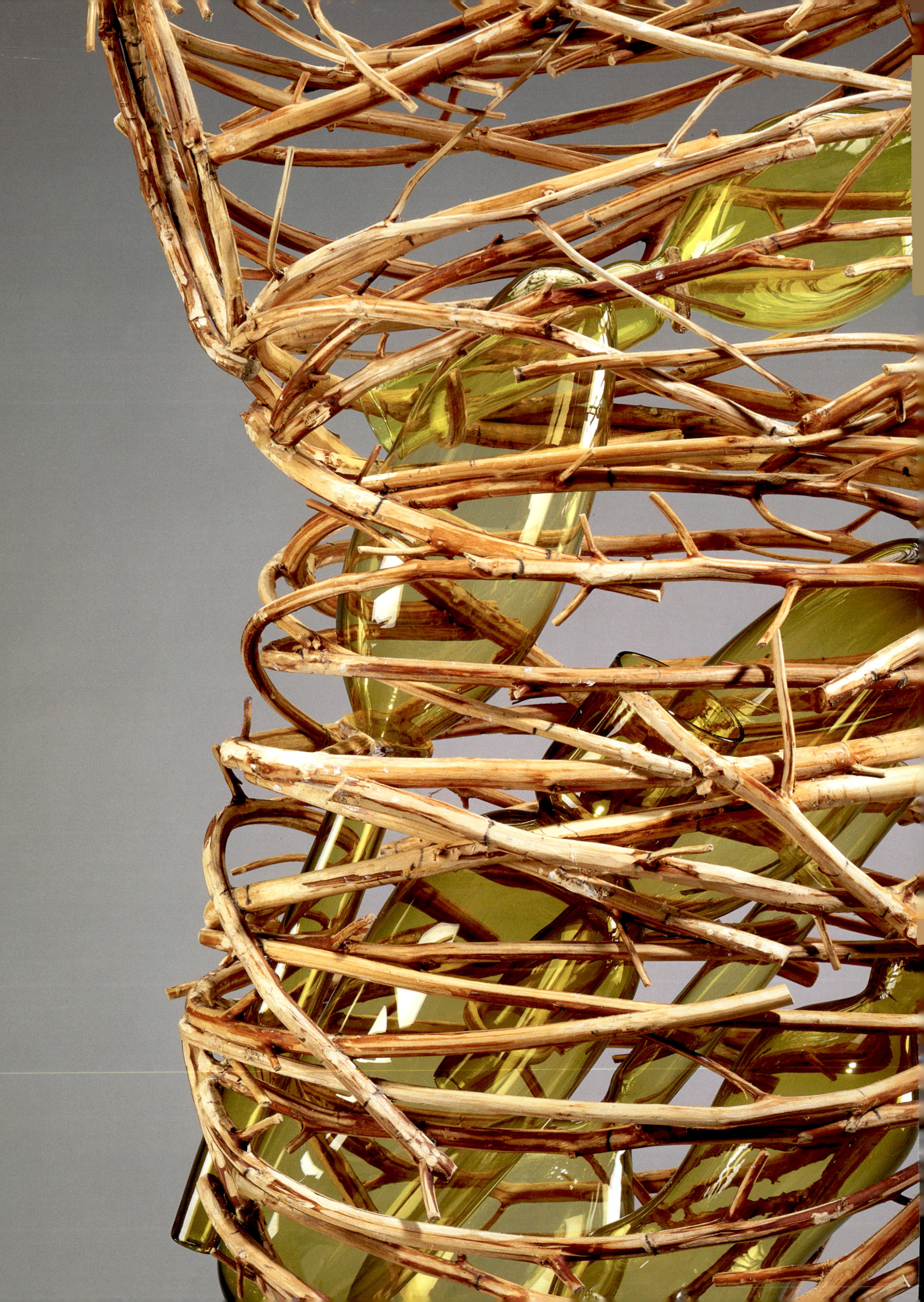

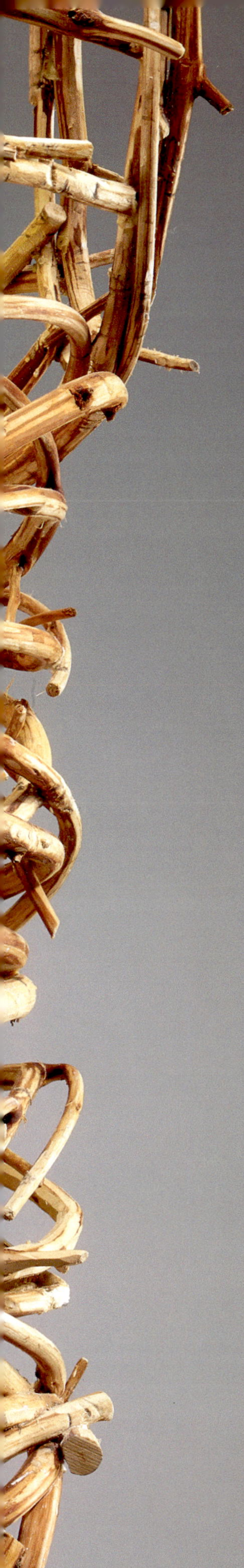

Joey Kirkpatrick and Flora C. Mace

Linda Tesner

With contributions by

Mark Doty

Daniel J. Hinkley

Patricia Kirkpatrick

Marquand Books

Seattle

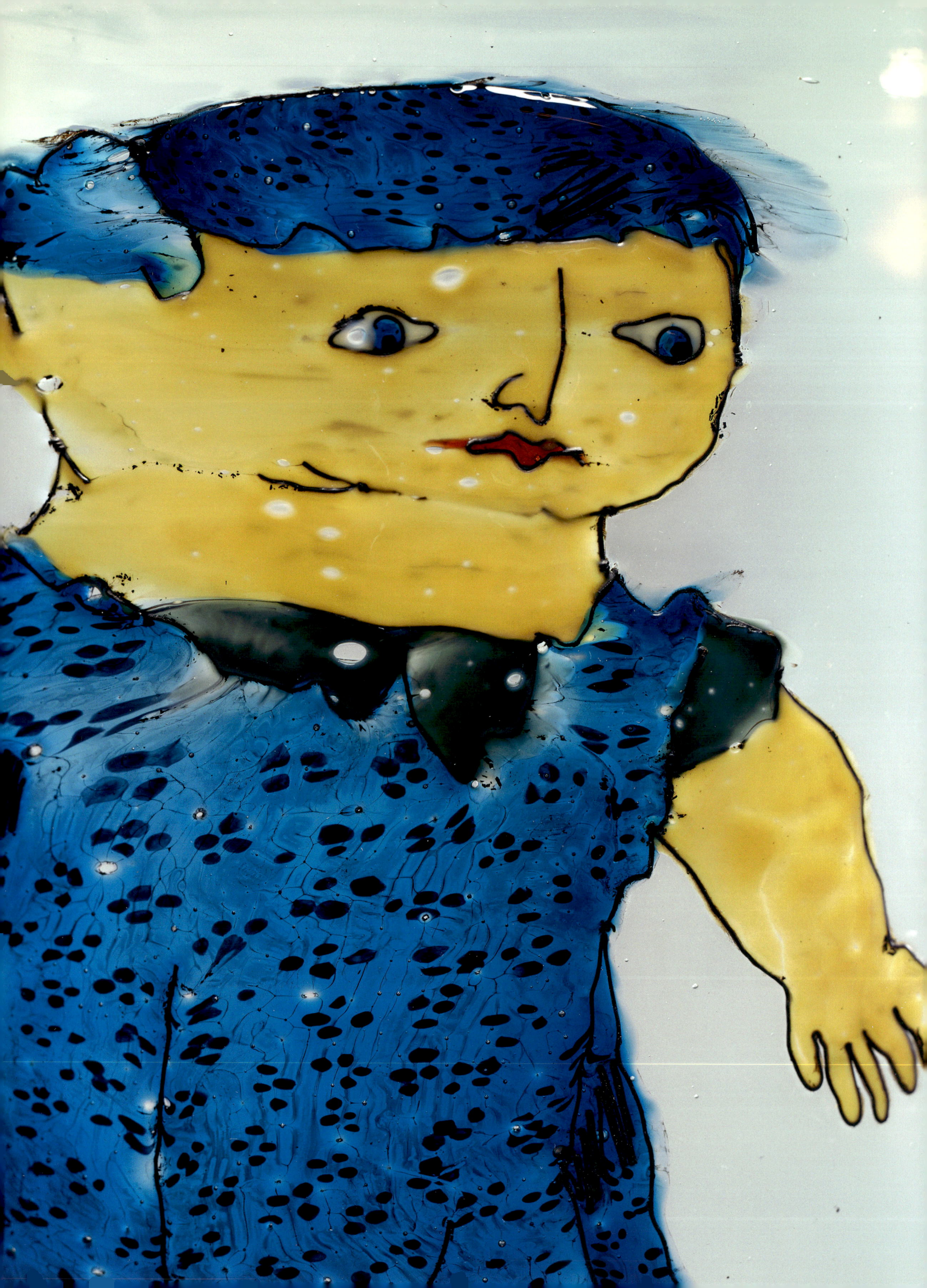

Flora and Joey are two of the most talented and creative artists with whom I have ever worked. Both of them have been working with me since they were students thirty-six years ago. Their unbelievable passion and energy have inspired my team year after year. As artists who have had a thirty-six-year relationship, they really understand the power of collaboration.

—*Dale Chihuly*

Contents

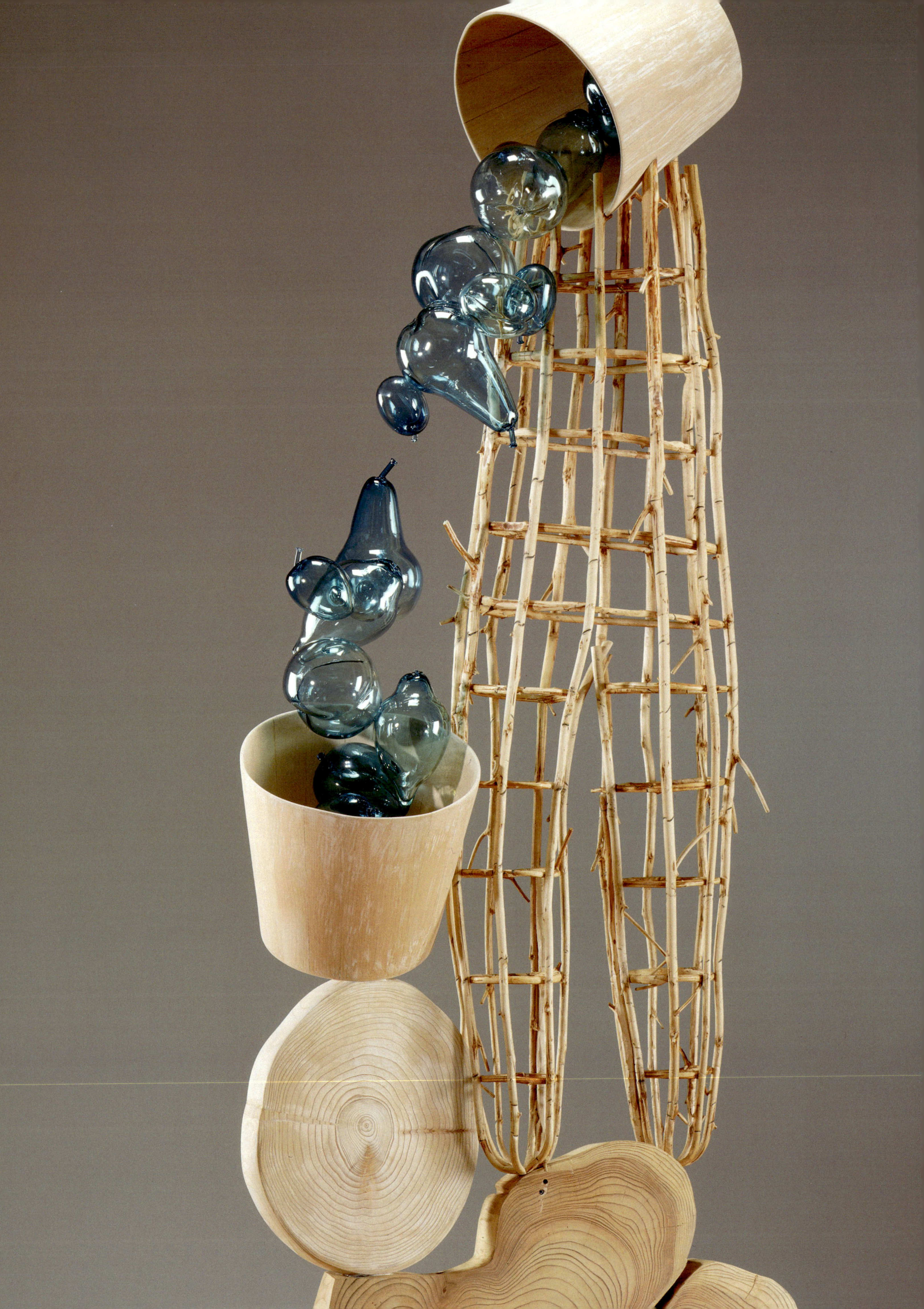

Mark Doty

"The Material Knows Everything That's Ever Happened to It"

Joey Kirkpatrick, Flora C. Mace,
and the Play of Contraries

"Glass," Joey says, "has a perfect memory. Whatever you do to it while it's being formed, the least thing, it remembers." She picks up whatever's at hand, a wooden paddle or a hand tool Flora's made, to demonstrate her meaning. "Say you touch it, when it's just out of the fire, with a metal tool—that place you touch is a little cooler than the rest then, and it will always be there. It's become part of the life of the work, because the material knows everything that's ever happened to it."

In that way, the body of a piece of glass is like a human body, a human self—every shaping stroke, every gesture in our direction, leaves some impression, some shifting either subtle or apparent. Even if we leave those experiences that give form to our temperaments and characters out of the argument and simply attend to the body, aren't we marked, as physical beings, by all that's touched us, all the ways we've been shaped? The old scar on a wrist, where a bone broke in a fall and had to be mended; the finger calloused from holding the pencil; the ridge of rougher skin in the palm, beneath the base of each finger, from lifting the rough-textured bars that hold the weight plates, the dumbbells . . . the tattoo, the discolored tooth, the vaccination mark, the knot of tension in a shoulder, the weak knee: a body's a kind of record of where it's been. Thus it's entirely sensible that in so many cosmologies the first men and women are made of clay: impressionable, permeable, capable of being marked.

It's a long way from the warmth and elasticity of human skin to the cool hardness of glass. And yet glass retains about it something of the living thing, which is perhaps the strangest of its paradoxes. It was unthinkably, frighteningly hot and now it's a cool pleasure, something restful and inviting about it. It was untouchable and now it is wonderfully tactile. It was liquid and now it at least seems solid, though molecular physics says it's not. It is incredibly durable and will last for thousands of years, even outside in the weather, yet all it takes is one blow to shatter it.

Contradiction isn't quite the right word for these paradoxes. I like William Blake's term *contraries*. Contraries, he said, are not opposites; instead, they're more like magnetic poles, those yoked forces that could not exist one without

Water's Edge, Year's Round (detail), 1994
Glass, wood, paint, and steel, 79 × 30 × 11 inches

the other; they are the wellspring of dynamic, life-giving tension. "Without contraries," Blake wrote, "there is no progression."

Such contraries are near the source of the art that Flora and Joey have produced together over thirty-five years. Seen in this light, the apparent visual disparity of their diverse production vanishes; it's all of a piece: cylinders and sculptures, fruit and paintbrushes, basket-like forms of bentwood, bronze spheres, bird pages. Everything arises out of a brilliant series of contraries, and the work of the artists is an extended, beautiful act of yoking—a bringing together.

What are the forces that are yoked here?

I'd begin with spontaneity and patience, which is right where the women's collaboration began. Joey had loopy, offhand, and vigorous drawings, many of them based upon on an old doll collection she'd inherited, images of children and women, dancing figures, and beasts. Flora wanted to help her find a way to put these images on glass, and so—as is Flora's wont—a technique was born, a process designed: wire drawings, to capture the spunky energy of Joey's hand, and then colored glass patiently filled into the spaces created between the forms. Then, after the new "drawing" was heated, a blown-glass cylinder was rolled over it, lifting the drawing onto the new form—expanding its lines, making its color radiant, making the whole thing shift in relation to the form of the vessel, so that the new "drawing" was even more alive than the first.

So what began in the freehand gesture, in a quick moment, becomes the labor of hours, of days, of seemingly infinite patience, trying, getting it wrong, trying again, till somehow the made thing emerges—yes!—and looks like the effortless product of a moment's inspiration.

Art and nature, those venerable, categorical opposites, are confounded in Flora's and Joey's work. Gorgeously naturalistic fruit turn out to be hard and permanent triumphs of the glassblower's form. Taken to increasingly larger scales, they cease to seem "natural" at all; now the gigantic pear or the very large eggplant have the presence of monumental sculpture, announcing the fact that they're made things. When the eggplant is transparent and all ashimmer with swirling Venetian rods of glass, it's as if we're looking at an eggplant's DNA, the deep mathematical structure suddenly visible.

These big wooden forms look so temporary, like a basketmaker's constructions. But the spheres and torsos of woven wood and the tall, standing bird turn out to have armatures of steel inside their peeled-alder encasements. What seems unstable is permanent. Making something as ephemeral as a piece of fruit in the lasting medium of glass, or something as fleeting as a perched bird in steel and alder—well, what is brief and what stays can no longer be readily told apart.

It would be a diminishment to call Joey and Flora "glass artists." What they do is to take an idea or a fascination through multiple stages, multiple forms, exploring the technical possibilities for bringing the idea into actuality—and, like Blake before them, inventing processes where none already exist. In this way, the two artists seem rather like poets; what compels them is the central idea, the germ of feeling and thinking that a poetic image is. And then the image is "translated," as it were. Not into language, in this case, but into a complex and continually growing vocabulary of forms.

Bird forms, for instance, move from drawing to large, flattened wood figures, stylized, to portraits on glass "pages" done with exacting accuracy. The idea, the poetic image at the core, becomes at once more clear and more elusive somehow, as many forms come to embody it, pointing to it without ever defining away its mystery.

Like art and nature, the categories of art and science have come to be mutually exclusive. (It occurs to me that Joey and Flora would have been quite happy working in the Renaissance, when those two terms were perfectly at ease with one another, if not inseparable.) Their "bird pages" refer to the illustrations in field guides—well, these heavy sheets of glass *are* a field guide, offering key information for the recognition of avian species. But this guide is expressive too; it joins that tradition of illustration interested in capturing a sense of life, and the perceiver's involvement in that life, at the juncture where art and science meet.

And, of course, we're talking about the work of *two* artists, not one. This might be the most complex yoking of all, the way that two sensibilities overlap, merge, separate, conflict, and resolve. A continuing dynamic, itself both unstable and solid, evolving, transforming materials and processes as it transforms itself.

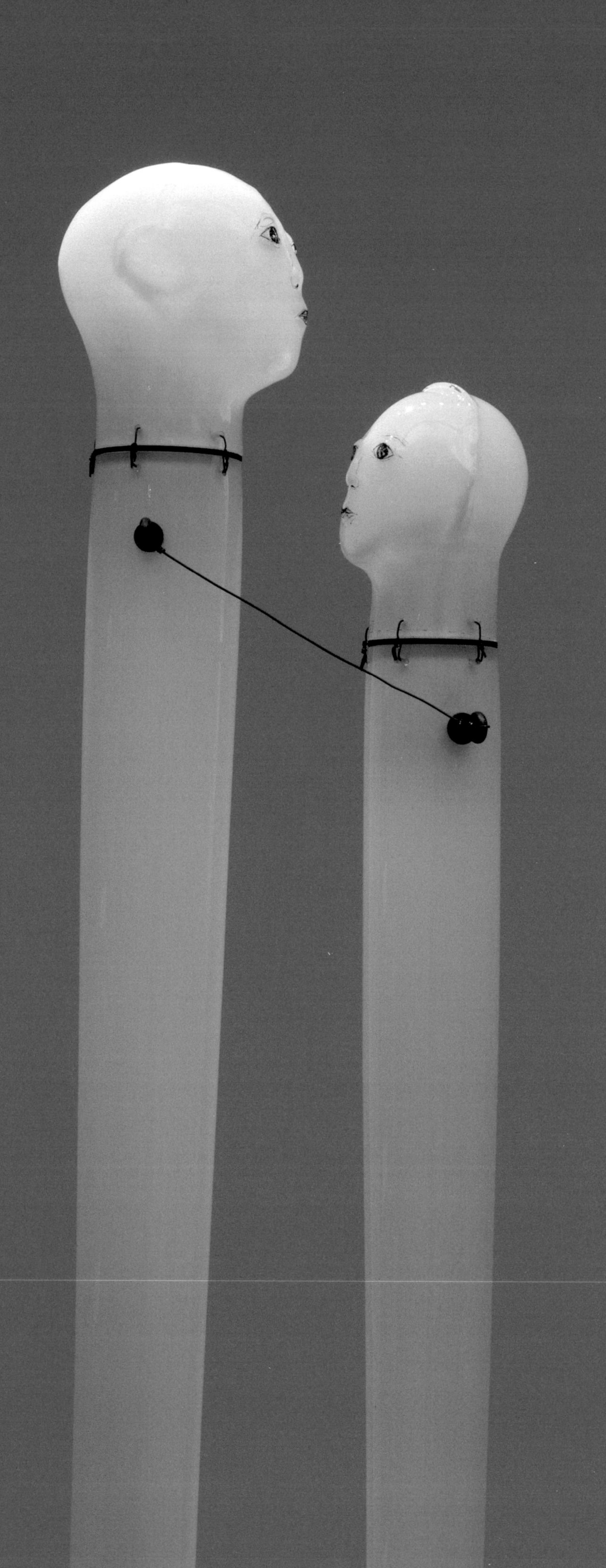

Linda Tesner

Groundings for Collaboration
Joey Kirkpatrick and Flora C. Mace

Often we are asked how two individuals can make one cohesive work of art. It's true that some of the work may represent the sentiments of one of us more than the other, and that it is conceived out of an autobiographical response to our individual condition. It is, however, fabricated to speak to an audience outside ourselves by use of a common visual language.

—Joey Kirkpatrick and Flora C. Mace

Since 1979, Joey Kirkpatrick and Flora C. Mace have been partners in life and in art, equal participants in a collaborative studio practice that has merged the disciplines of glassblowing, sculpture, drawing, printmaking, and assemblage. They are what is reverently called "artists' artists," meaning that these women make no distinction between their lives and their art, and that activities outside the studio—like bird-watching; antiquing for boat models, vintage decoys, and Inuit dolls; or fishing for salmon in Puget Sound—inform their work and vice versa. Their story began at Pilchuck Glass School in Stanwood, Washington, when they were young artists just beginning to shape their lives outside the formative and protective community of art school. Today, their light-filled studio on the canal between Puget Sound and Lake Union, near the Ballard neighborhood of Seattle, is their hot shop, technical laboratory, drawing studio, and spiritual home.

Collaboration in contemporary art is a relatively unusual occurrence, even in the twenty-first century, when anything-goes experimentation is the norm. Some notable pairs known for creating joint works are British artists Gilbert and George, German photographers Bernd and Hilla Becher, Swiss artists Peter Fischli and David Weiss, and the American twins Doug and Mike Starn—and, in the glass world, Stanislav Libenský and Jaroslava Brychtová. It goes almost without saying that successful collaborations—especially a union that flourishes for more than thirty-five years—require unique circumstances and suitably aligned personalities. It would be a fascinating investigation, though the subject of another book, to explore the qualities that are necessary for a fertile joint creative process. Art making is, after all, typically a solitary exercise. In Kirkpatrick's and Mace's instance, it would seem that

Neither Two a Stranger (detail), 1983
Glass, slate, and steel, 29 × 7 × 4½ inches

their individual upbringings, leading up to their meeting at Pilchuck, proved grounding for their lives' future work.

New England was home to Mace, who was raised on nine acres of a family farm in Hampton Beach, New Hampshire, a homestead one mile inland from the Atlantic Ocean because, as lore dictates, farmland should not be too close to the climatic vagaries of the sea. Her childhood home was multigenerational and served by a wood stove for food and warmth. Her father was a plumber and ran a clam shucking business. Her mother suffered from mental illness and spent Mace's childhood in and out of mental hospitals, before dying during Mace's high school years.

Mace's youth was filled with chores in support of the family—hunting and gathering, literally—to assist in life on the land. She speaks of hunting game with her father, fishing for flounder, harvesting clams and oysters, picking berries, felling timber with her grandfather, and tending to the maintenance of the family's fishing boats. Even as a child, she loved to build things, particularly tree houses, and early on she developed her signature adeptness with hand tools. Like many rural children, Mace became active in 4-H and, at one time, had a herd of fifty sheep, some of whom she sheared in sheep-shearing competitions. "My sheep became my sculptures," she has said, wholly without irony.

Following college at Plymouth State University, in Plymouth, New Hampshire, Mace was selected to participate in a national program called International Farm Youth Exchange (IFYE). Ultimately, the IFYE became a model for the Peace Corps, but in 1973–74 the IFYE sent 4-H students to foreign countries to represent the United States as goodwill ambassadors. Mace was sent to Norway for nearly a year, spending a month at a time in various regions of the country. There, in eerie prescience of her own future, she visited village glass factories and observed families of glassmakers at work.

When she returned to the United States, Mace enrolled in graduate school at the University of Illinois, Champaign-Urbana. From her childhood on the farm, Mace knew well how to improvise with found materials and objects at hand; she was already a skilled welder. In her MFA program, she studied sculpture.

During the 1970s, glassblowing was in its nascence in American college art departments. While the University of Illinois had a rudimentary hot shop, neighboring Illinois State University, Bloomington, had a hot shop run by Joel Philip Myers, a former designer-in-residence at Blenko Glass Company in Milton, West Virginia. Mace began to explore glass as a medium in Bloomington, while still making sculpture in Champaign.

Mace credits a glib query to her sculpture instructor, "Who's the most important artist working in glass?" as a decisive moment in her graduate school career. The resounding answer, "Dale Chihuly," spurred Mace to pick up the phone and track down Chihuly at the Rhode Island School of Design (RISD), Providence. Remarkably, Chihuly encouraged her curiosity and warmly urged Mace to join him at a workshop he was giving that summer through the University of Utah at Snowbird. Mace invited her sister to join her on a road trip to the West, where they camped for the duration of the

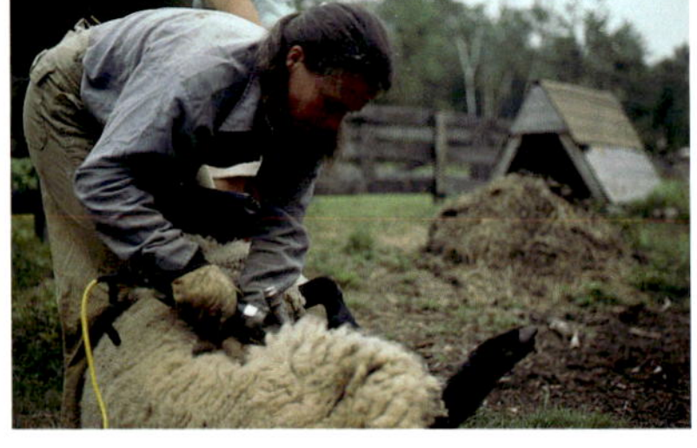

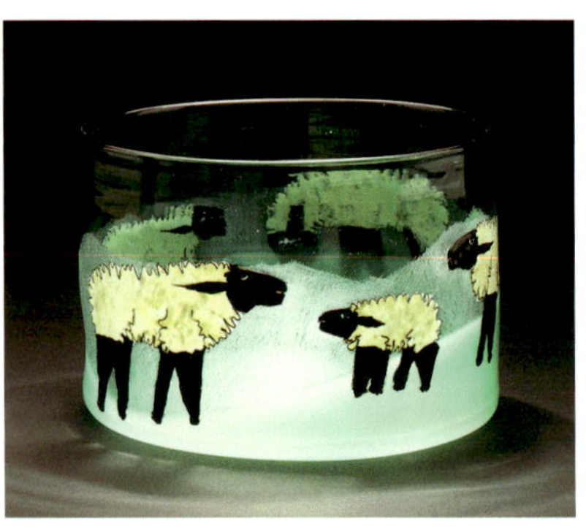

Mace shearing a sheep, 1979.

Sheep Bowl, 1982
Glass and wire, 7½ × 9 × 9 inches

 Joey Kirkpatrick and Flora C. Mace

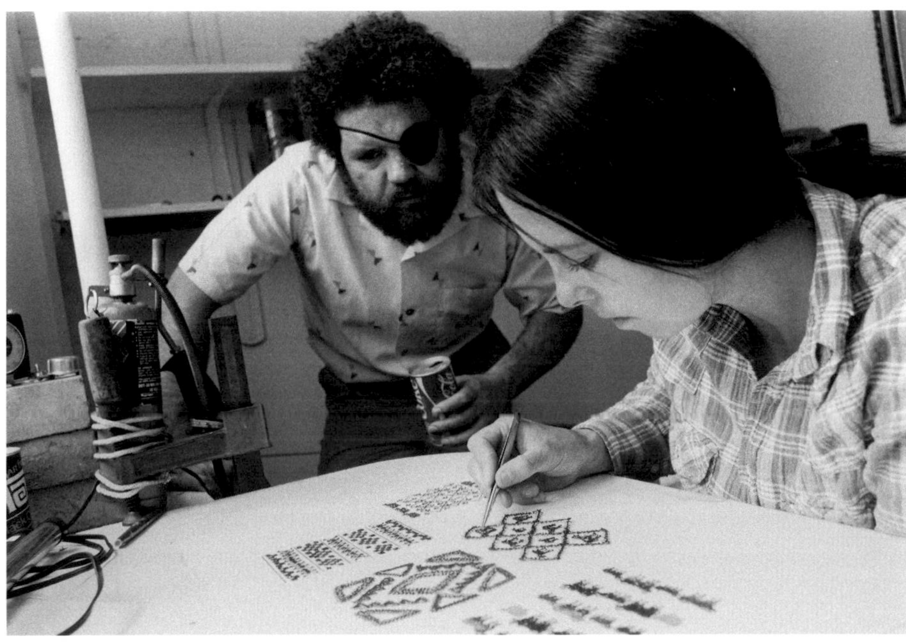

workshop because they could not afford lodging. Chihuly was leading just one of several month-long visual arts sessions—ceramic artists Peter Voulkos and Marilyn Levine were also instructors. The year was 1975.

Even though Mace had already been making glass in Illinois, when she arrived at Snowbird she quickly became swept up in Chihuly's infectious enthusiasm and zeal for innovation. In Illinois, Mace had been experimenting with using thin glass cane to make small drawings, which were picked up on the glass gather as design elements in the finished pieces. Chihuly was instantly intrigued and wondered if Mace would make drawings for his own work. Before long, Mace was an integral team member for Chihuly's early blows, traveling to Providence armed with a cache of small glass drawings.

Mace later participated at RISD in the creation of Chihuly's celebrated *Irish Cylinders* series of 1975,[1] making glass cane drawings to be picked up on the blown vessels. Propitiously begun on St. Patrick's Day, the series was completed over the Thanksgiving holiday of the same year. Noted as the last body of work made by Chihuly before his devastating car accident in England, in which he lost an eye, the *Irish Cylinders* feature details illustrating scenes from James Joyce's *Ulysses*, as well as shamrocks, Irish flags, cairns, and Dublin streetscapes.

It would be a few years before Mace joined the faculty at Pilchuck. In the meantime, she established an artists' residency program at Wheaton Village (now WheatonArts), Millville, New Jersey, and continued to assist Chihuly in projects at RISD. In 1979, he persuaded her to spend the summer in Stanwood, working with aspiring young glass artists at Pilchuck.

Kirkpatrick's youth was, in many ways, the polar opposite to Mace's. The third of four daughters, she was born and raised in a solidly middle-class home in Des Moines, Iowa. A self-described tomboy, Kirkpatrick spent her childhood playing with neighborhood kids and swimming in the municipal pool every day of summer.

In addition to Kirkpatrick's natural athleticism and love of the outdoors, she credits her mother for presenting all sorts of creative opportunities for Kirkpatrick and her siblings. At an early age, Kirkpatrick began studying art at the Des Moines Art Center, where studio classes and contemporary art exhibitions offered plenty of stimulus as well as dedicated mentors for the blossoming young artist. The center's exhibitions exposed Kirkpatrick to the work of Alexander Calder, Giorgio Morandi, and Egon Schiele, artists whose work has informed her studio practice to this day. Eventually Kirkpatrick would go on to teach at the Art Center through her high school, college, and postgraduate years.

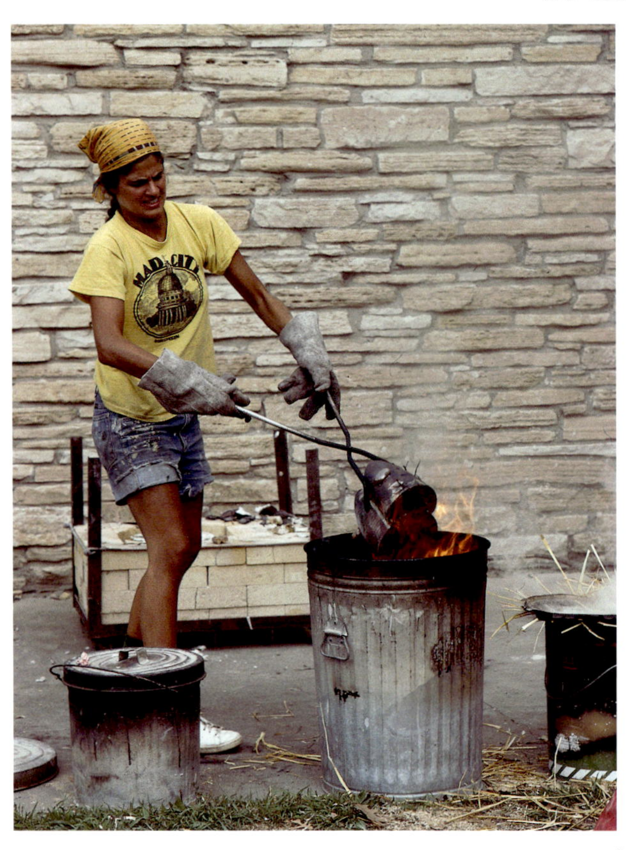

Kirkpatrick raku-firing a ceramic sculpture, Des Moines Art Center, 1976.

Trips to Chicago, to visit a beloved aunt, were also influential for the young artist. Kirkpatrick's aunt was a serious practicing artist, encouraging Kirkpatrick's interests by bringing her along to adult education classes taught at the School of the Art Institute of Chicago. In Chicago, Kirkpatrick was introduced to ground-breaking women sculptors, such as Lenore Tawney and Claire Zeisler.[2]

Kirkpatrick vividly remembers, as a child, coming across a *Saturday Evening Post* article about the sculptor Alberto Giacometti.[3] She knew instantly then that she wanted a similar creative life—not only making art but living in such a way that intellectual curiosity and visual aesthetics would be the warp and weft of daily life.

Kirkpatrick attended the University of Iowa, Iowa City, where she passionately pursued her interest in drawing, earning a BA in that discipline. Here, too, Kirkpatrick developed what would be a career-long devotion to the human figure. She recalls attending life-drawing classes three days a week for six hours a day. Following graduation, Kirkpatrick returned to Des Moines and joined the faculty at the Art Center, teaching drawing and maintaining her own committed studio practice. It was during this time that the artist acquired a collection of dolls that had been used in still life drawing practicums at the Art Center.

Kirkpatrick also had an introduction to the hot shop in college, and after returning to Des Moines following graduation, she looked for an opportunity to continue to work in glass. Fortunately, Iowa State University, in nearby Ames, had a glassblowing facility, and Kirkpatrick began to travel the thirty-or-so miles to take classes there as a continuing education student. While earning her living by teaching at the Art Center, Kirkpatrick experimented with glass in combination with other materials. She had also developed an interest in ceramics—saggar firing in particular—and tended to use blown-glass elements in combination with ceramic and fiber in integrated sculptural compositions. Despite Kirkpatrick's experimentation in other mediums, her first love of drawing remained a constant.

At a certain point, Kirkpatrick recognized the need to expand her horizons beyond the comfort of her hometown; she was ready to explore the art world at some distance from Des Moines. In the company of one of her sisters, Kirkpatrick picked up a craft magazine and fell upon an advertisement for Pilchuck Glass School that featured a photograph of one of Chihuly's baskets. "Come to the Northwest; take glass blowing," the ad read.

     Joey Kirkpatrick and Flora C. Mace

In August 1979, Kirkpatrick arrived at the Pilchuck Glass School for a two-and-a-half week residency, intrigued by Chihuly's nontraditional methods and wondering if her passion for drawing could translate into the medium of glass. Within her first hour at Pilchuck, Kirkpatrick was introduced to Dale Chihuly, Benjamin Moore, William Morris, Italo Scanga, Lino Tagliapietra—and Flora C. Mace. Perhaps, Chihuly suggested, Mace might be able to help Kirkpatrick with those drawings. The collaboration began.

The Wire Drawing Cylinders, 1979–1984

Kirkpatrick's and Mace's incomparable wire drawings inlaid into glass cylinders were the first collaborations by these artists. When they met in 1979, Mace had already been working with the challenge of placing a figurative drawing onto the surface of a blown vessel.

As Mace recounts, her undergraduate training had inculcated a sense that the ability to draw the human figure laid the foundation from which all other art forms followed.[4] She was intrigued by gestural drawing, but found that she was more adept at "drawing" in glass cane (also referred to as glass thread) than in pencil. She would heat and bend the cane to draw contours of the human body, which she placed onto a steel plate. Often Mace sprinkled glass powder within the form's outlines to evoke the volume one would normally achieve with pencil shading. She would then roll a gather of glass across the thread drawing to pick it up onto the vessel's surface. The primary technical challenges Mace addressed were how easily the figure became distorted as the glass was blown and how she could keep facial details in place. Eventually, these figurative pieces by Mace became so resolved and refined that they were featured in a solo exhibition at Heller Gallery in New York in 1977, a groundbreaking moment for such a young woman to have a single-artist exhibition at a prestigious glass gallery.

In the late 1970s, American studio glass was in its infancy. Mace notes that many of her early figurative works were made out of whatever glass was at hand—mayonnaise jars, ashtrays, candy dishes, beer bottles (in fact, many of her early figure drawings have an amber cast, most likely from repurposed bottle glass). She was making these works alternately at the University of Illinois, Champaign-Urbana, and at the Rhode Island School of Design, Providence, where she would join Dale Chihuly's experimental blows. In addition to her own work, she produced most of the line drawings featured on Chihuly's seminal *Irish Cylinders* as well as glass-cane patterns for Chihuly's *Blanket Cylinders*.

When Kirkpatrick arrived at Pilchuck Glass School during the summer of 1979, Mace had already been experimenting for several years with the merging of graphic art with glass art making—it was almost as if Mace had been readying herself to collaborate with Kirkpatrick. Kirkpatrick showed Mace the drawings from her portfolio—the animated line drawings from her days at the Des Moines Art Center and the University of Iowa.

Mace immediately began to imagine how Kirkpatrick's drawings could be applied to glass, but also innately understood that the process of drawing in

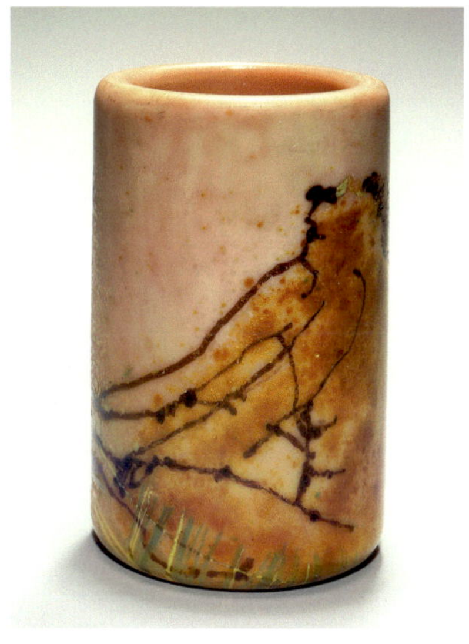

Flora C. Mace, **First Figure**, 1974
Glass, 6½ × 4 × 4 inches

glass might compromise the liveliness of Kirkpatrick's hand. Mace literally stumbled across a possible solution in the hardware store: perhaps Kirkpatrick's drawings could be translated into wire outlines, which could then be applied, referred to as *pickups* in glassblowing, onto the blown-glass vessels in the hot shop.

From this humble suggestion sprang a unique method of drawing on glass. Kirkpatrick would make a drawing in pencil, then duplicate it in steel wire, a wire thin enough for her to be able to handle it easily with pliers, defining such details as the minute crevices between a baby's toes or the particular purse of a doll's lips. The artists were interested in how much the wire drawing would be distorted after it was applied to the hot glass and then blown, so Kirkpatrick began photocopying the drawings to both preserve a record of the appliqués as well as track their distortions. Their experiments taught them that the wire could easily spark and burn away, leaving a trace of its disintegration that appeared almost like the stutter of a pencil stroke. They also found that sometimes the wire would break apart in undesirable places. A workable remedy for those unplanned breaks was to decisively snip the wires apart in places so that when the drawing expanded with the hot glass, the wire's overall contour would hold its shape. Where they created a break in the wire, that line had to be structurally continued with a cane of clear glass. This also solved the problem of the drawing "rounding out," that is, over-expanding during the blowing process and thus losing its definition.

The earliest of the collaborative cylinders feature simple outlines of female human figures, often cradling a baby or with a baby placed within the figure's womb. In retrospect, the artists acknowledge that many of these early drawings were consciously self-referential. Indeed, some of the figures look roughly like Kirkpatrick and Mace, with their long hair or ponytails. There is almost always a narrative quality to the drawings—like a mother reaching for a baby in a high chair—but at other times the images are more mysteriously metaphoric, like a figure housed in a suitcase or climbing a ladder to the top of the vessel. Sometimes babies float weightlessly in a frieze around the cylinder, punctuated by tiny safety pins. In other vessels, the artists added shards of colored glass that they picked up on the vessel prior to picking up the drawings, a technique Mace had used in her early figurative vessels. These veils of color bathe the figures like watercolor washes and further enliven the vessels' surfaces.

From the simple female figurative line drawings, Kirkpatrick and Mace began to develop a vocabulary of imagery. At the time, both young artists had sisters who were pregnant or had recently given birth, and, moving beyond the mother and child themes of the earliest cylinders, they began to explore images of Japanese wind socks, carp-shaped kites called *koinobori*. The symbolism of the *koinobori* is associated with childbirth; traditionally when a baby boy was born, the child's maternal grandmother would give a *koinobori* to the parents as a gift for the baby. During the Edo period, May 5 was designated *Kodomo no hi* (Boys' Day), an official holiday.[5] The carp as a symbol for boys evolved out of a Chinese myth that if a carp were to swim up the Yellow River and climb a waterfall, it became a dragon. The image of a carp fighting its way upstream evolved in Japan into a male symbol of strength

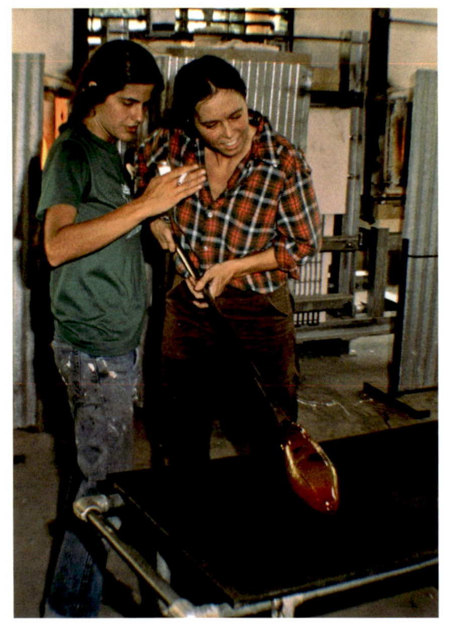

Mace and Kirkpatrick blowing their first collaborative vessels, Pilchuck Glass School, 1979.

Joey Kirkpatrick and Flora C. Mace

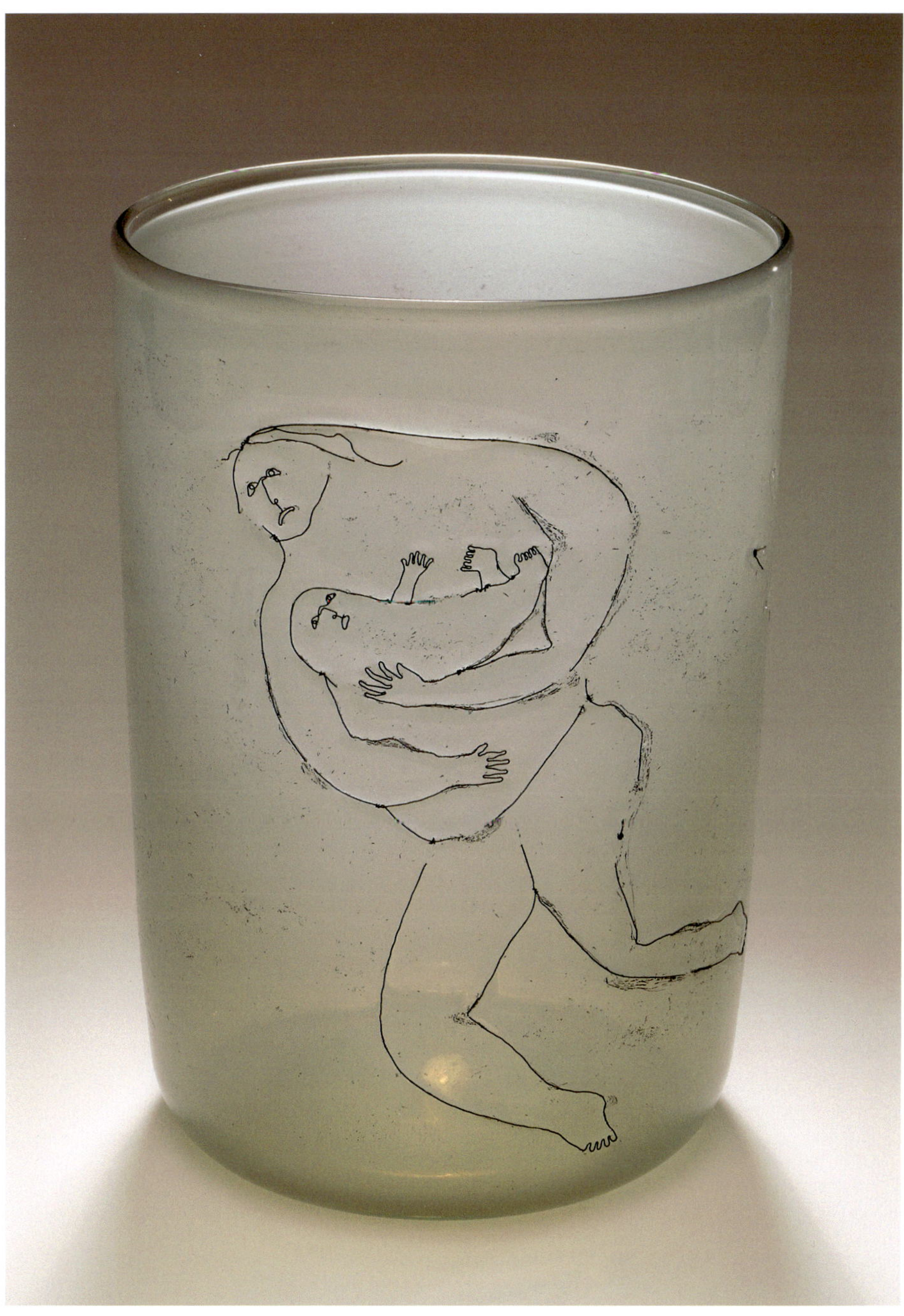

and perseverance—a poignant choice for two young women working in the predominantly male universe of glassblowing.

The wind kite imagery presented an opportunity to push the wire drawing technique in a more complex direction. First, Kirkpatrick and Mace began to use color within the contours of the wire drawing, a practice that involved Mace in the application of color to the image and thereby making each image a full collaboration between the artists. After Kirkpatrick manipulated the wire into a drawing, Mace, working on a hot plate, filled in the drawing by using a torch to melt canes of colored glass to literally "color in" the shapes created by the wire. The finished image resembled a hybrid plique-à-jour object—exceedingly thin and flat, the drawing could be picked up with tweezers.[6]

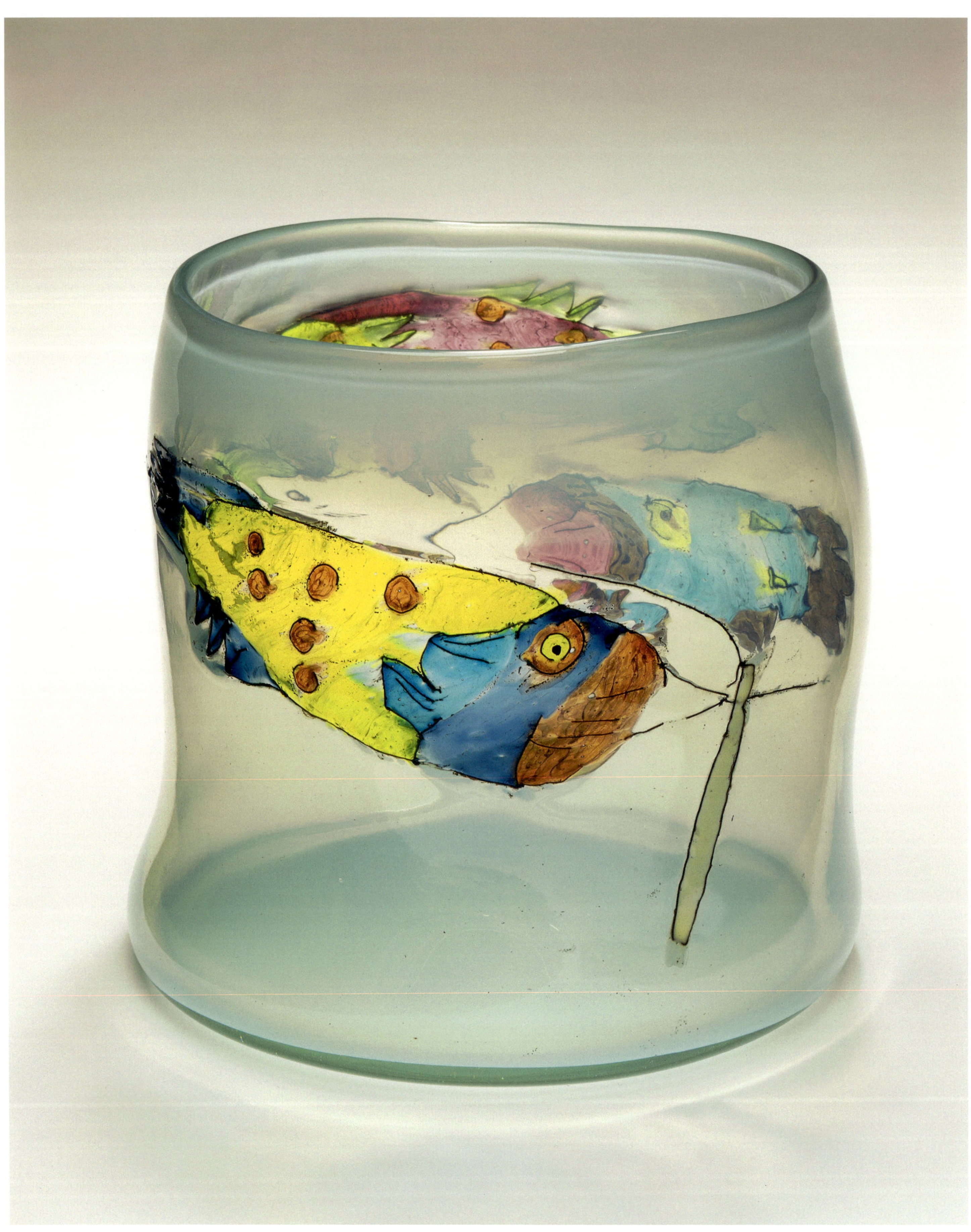

In the hot shop, these little glass designs were heated and then applied to a vessel in the early stage of blowing. The very act of blowing the glass into a cylinder created another opportunity to animate the surface. Because the colored glass expanded at a different rate than the rest of the body of the vessel, the colored segments that made up the images responded more sensitively to the breath of the glassblower. The result was that the wind kite images literally puffed out from the wall of the cylinder, as if the artist blew the wind to swell each *koinobori*.

Other whimsical drawings followed, usually inspired by anecdotal elements of the artists' lives together. They began collecting vintage Cracker Jack charms, which found their way into the cylinder imagery. Mah-jongg sticks and little Indian animal figurines inspired other images. Kirkpatrick recounts a time when she was reading about Inuit culture and came across the narwhal as a mythical beast. The artists then began playfully cutting their baby figures and fish figures in half, recombining the parts into imaginary creatures Kirkpatrick called *narwhals*. At another time, the artists crafted lion tamers and acrobats, figures one might see in a circus, or they composed fanciful animals and placed them around the edge of a cylinder to suggest a carousel. The artists' choices for surface decoration were personal icons that spoke to their joy in being together, as well as to their playfulness as artists and young adults.

In another body of imagery, Kirkpatrick and Mace turned to Kirkpatrick's doll collection and her drawings on paper of dolls from her days at the Des Moines Art Center. Kirkpatrick admits that the doll collection is anomalous with her interests as a child—she was a confirmed tomboy and never played with dolls. The collection, however, was less an assemblage of toys for gender-specific play than a carefully chosen compilation of historical and ethnic dolls, each with a distinct personality akin to the narrative female figures of Kirkpatrick's and Mace's earliest cylinder drawings in that the dolls implied a certain narrative in their postures and juxtapositions. The artists responded to the individual persona of each doll and were intrigued by the ironies associated with the traditional connotations of dolls as women's subject matter.

The doll imagery presents the apogee of Kirkpatrick's and Mace's achievement with applying wire drawings to glass cylinders. These are the most complex images the artists chose to apply to glass cylinders. For one thing, the drawings began not as dreamlike images sketched by Kirkpatrick from her imagination but as studies from actual objects. The dolls themselves were quite detailed; each had a particular facial expression and wore a

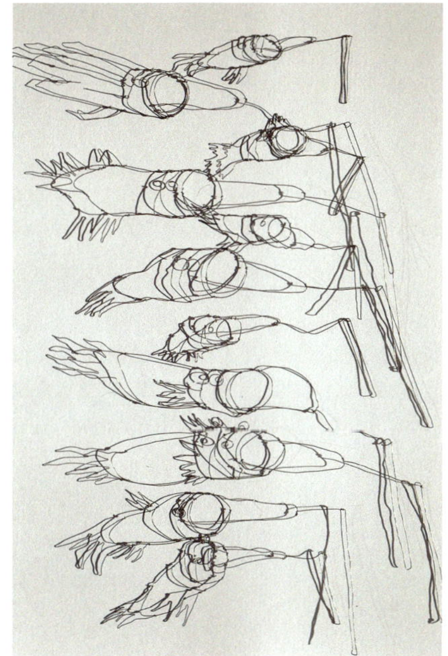

Bent-wire wind kite drawings awaiting glass thread fill-in.

Wind Kites, 1982
Glass and wire, 8 × 8 × 8 inches

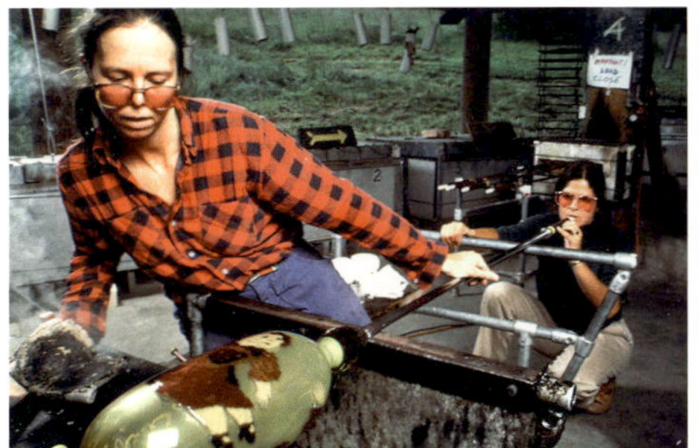
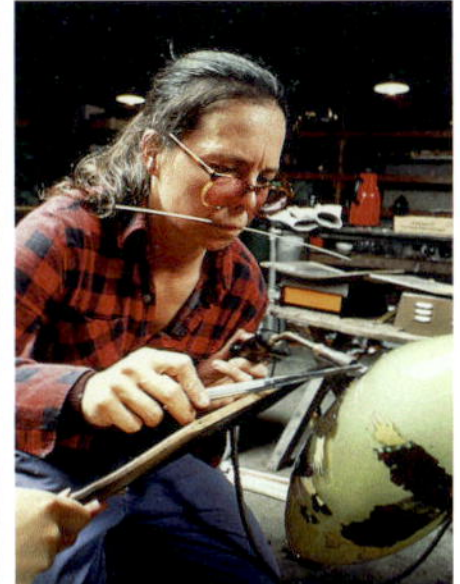
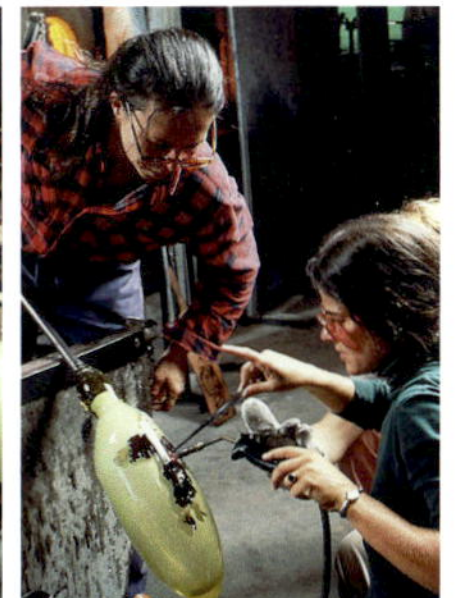

Mace and Kirkpatrick blowing *Doll Drawing Cylinders*, 1984.

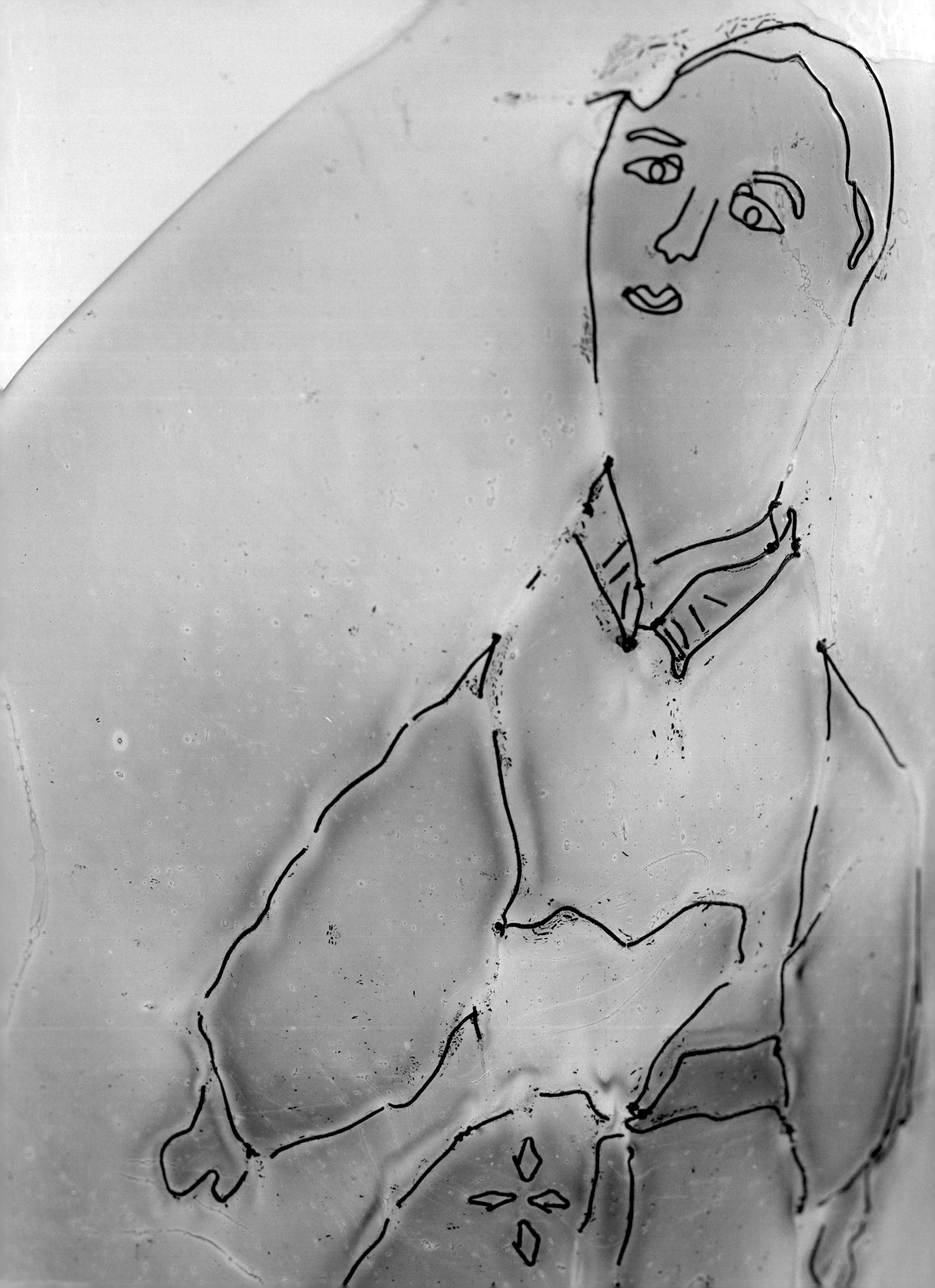

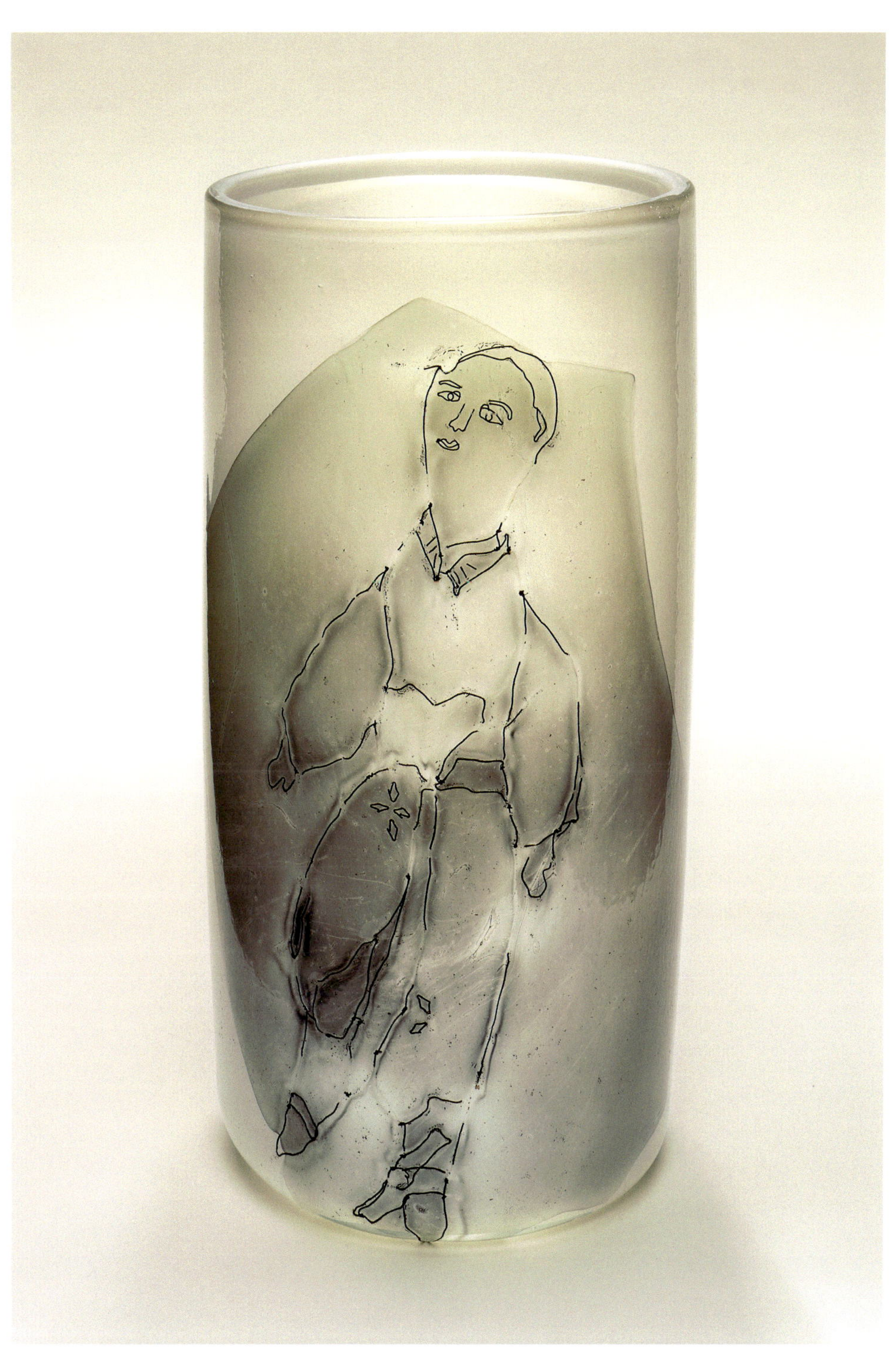

François, 1980
Glass and wire, 11½ × 6 × 6 inches

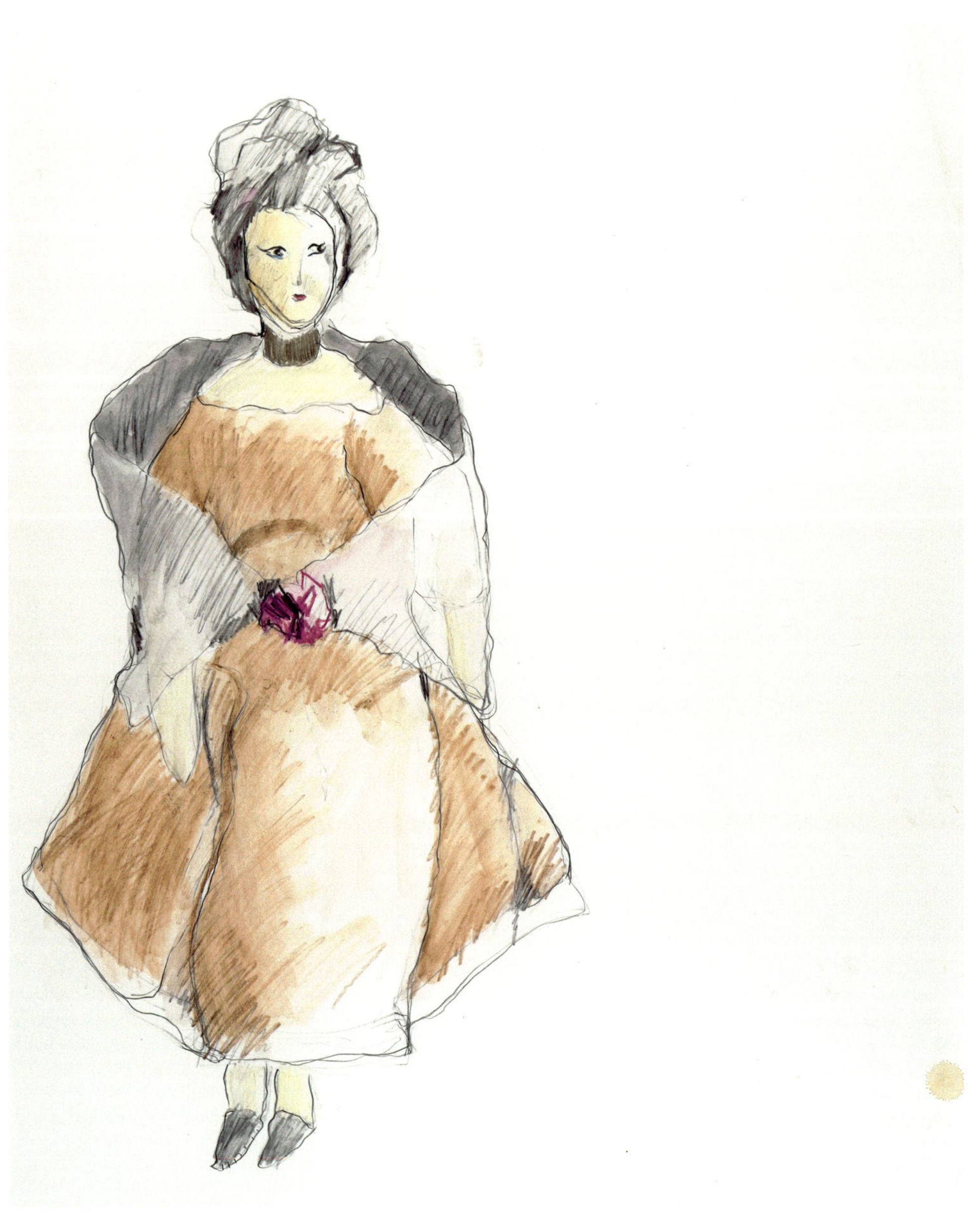

Joey Kirkpatrick, **French Doll**, 1982
Graphite and gouache on paper, 26¼ × 20 inches

French Doll, 1982
Glass and wire, 11½ × 6 × 6 inches

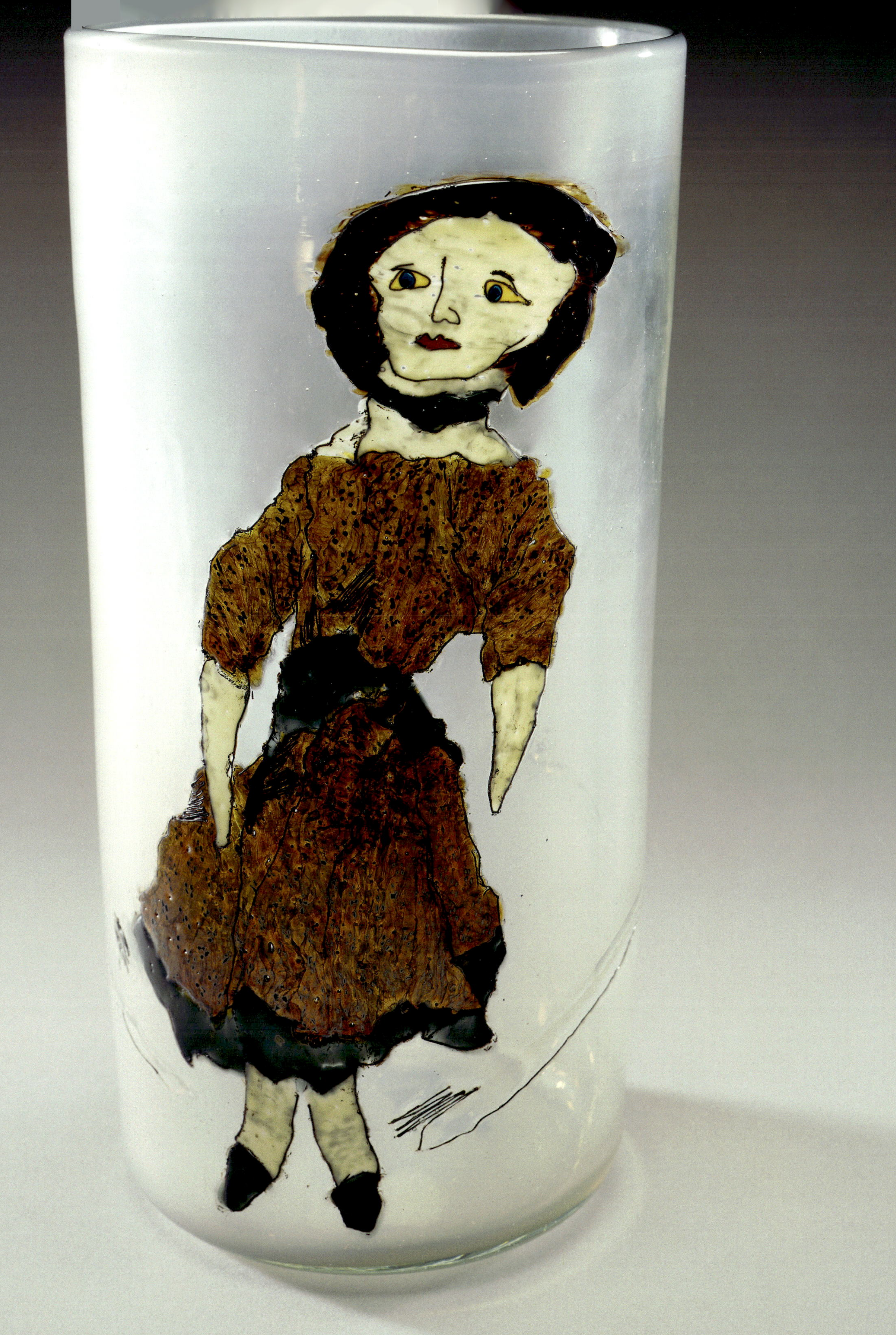

costume specific to the doll's origin. Kirkpatrick began to name each doll, further imbuing personality to each character. A male doll was called François; others were christened Rebecca and Kally. A particularly beloved figure was an elderly Chinese gentleman doll, another was "the French doll," who wore an elegant dress and choker. In addition, as Kirkpatrick made larger and more complex drawings, Mace further developed her ability to color in the figures. The later and most complicated wire drawing cylinders include more than one doll on their surfaces, creating relationships between the two figures, and always the facial features are expressive. Even the "fabric" of some of the costumes was patterned by Mace in glass.

Mace has often been quoted as saying that "glass is the third collaborator," a sentiment particularly true to the making of the wire drawings on glass cylinders. As the artists placed the image onto the cylinder fairly early in the process of making a piece, there was no way they could ascertain with complete accuracy how that image would shift or distort. In this way, the medium itself, as well as the act of blowing glass into a vessel shape, contributed an element of chance or, more accurately, another layer of spontaneity to the finished image.

The composition of the drawings on the vessels was finally determined in the hot shop. In order to get the paper-thin wire and glass drawings onto the molten glass, Mace held the pipe with a partially blown vessel while Kirkpatrick carefully positioned the pre-heated image, lifted with tweezers, over the cylindrical surface before releasing it onto the hot glass. The artists' lively dialogue during the process guided the placement of the separate pieces—the posts that anchor the *koinobori*, for example. Once a drawing component was placed onto the hot vessel, it could not be moved. The final step was the blowing of the cylinder to its final dimensions—again, a process that was ultimately vulnerable to chance.

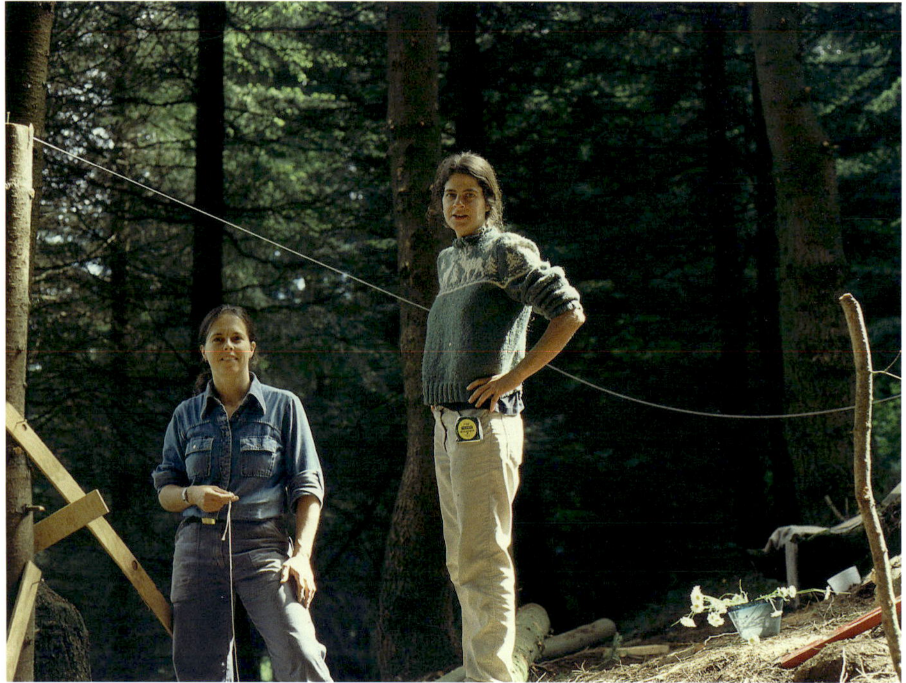

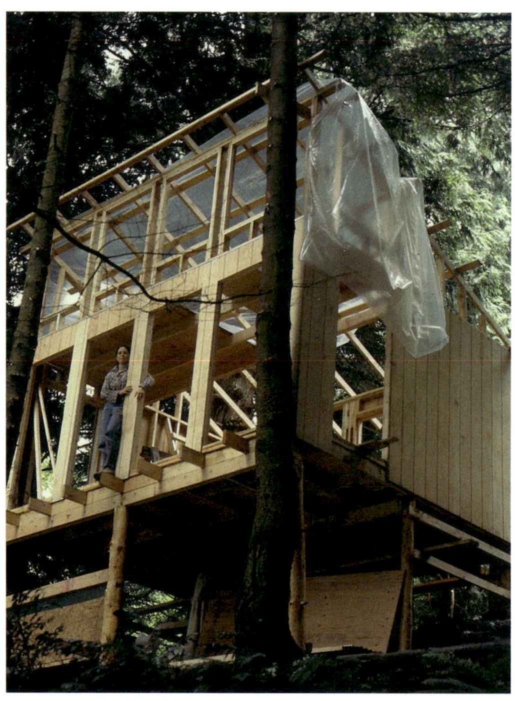

   Joey Kirkpatrick and Flora C. Mace

Removing the Figure from the Vessel, 1983–1990

By 1984, Kirkpatrick and Mace had made their last wire drawing cylinders. After five years of exploring the possibilities of drawing in glass, the artists found that hot shop work was both too physically limiting and restrictive. They were interested in making larger sculpture than was then possible in the hot shop, and they resisted the seductiveness of the glass material alone. They decided to consciously allow their ideas to drive the work instead of vice versa and to engage concept as the central and determining factor in dictating which medium should be employed in the expression of those ideas. A prevailing theme, the human figure, emerged as a core motif. Quickly, the artists determined not to altogether eliminate glass blown in the hot shop but to use glass as an element in combination with other mediums.

Kirkpatrick remarked:

> Once we decided to bring the figure off the cylinder, a reaction to the restrictions of working with the traditional vessel form, our entire creative process changed. The nice thing about fabricating our pieces, that is, blowing glass parts and bringing them together sculpturally in a private studio, is the enormous difference in decision making. It opens new doors, allows more time. It offers our collaboration more freedom, not only to be technical partners but to really create collaboratively.

Their work evolved into various series that called upon the drawings of the earlier cylinders, but moved firmly into the realm of traditional sculpture by removing the figure from the vessel and bringing it into three dimensions. Transitional works include sculptures the artists called *Cloaked Dolls* (right), in which slight blown-glass heads sit atop cylindrical bodies of wood. The wood bodies are carved, detailed with graphite, and, in some cases, adorned with wire and glass beads—an ironic recombining of elements from the wire drawing cylinders (glass, wire, "drawing," "cylinder"). The *Cloaked Dolls* were also an obvious reference to the doll subjects of the latest wire drawing cylinders, while remaining resolutely anonymous and androgynous, so contrary to the real dolls' expressive and specific characteristics.

Kirkpatrick credits a 1984 visit to the exhibition *Praise Poems: The Katherine White Collection* at the Seattle Art Museum[7] as an experience that allowed the artists to think more liberally about the human body, as both a metaphoric *vessel* and as a *canvas* to be adorned. The African sculpture on view in the exhibition introduced them to concepts of Primitivism and raised the possibility of abstracting the figure more than the figurative wire imagery of the early cylinders.

The common attributes of the artists' subsequent sculptures include the small, minimal, milky-white human head of the *Cloaked Dolls*, but now attached to a slim, hollow, glass column. The figure thus becomes non-narrative, rejecting any ethnic, historical, or even gender specificity and becoming instead more conceptual and depersonalized—the carrier of collective personae. The heads are joined to the coolly tusklike bodies;[8] both head and body act as vessels conjuring invisible contents: thoughts, feelings, knowledge, impulses.

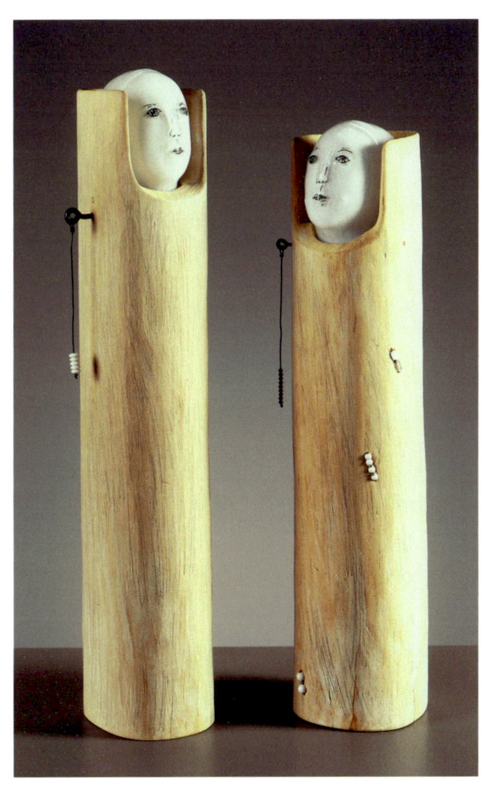

Cloaked Dolls, 1983
Wood, glass, graphite, and wire, 16 × 2½ × 3 inches;
15½ × 3 × 3½ inches

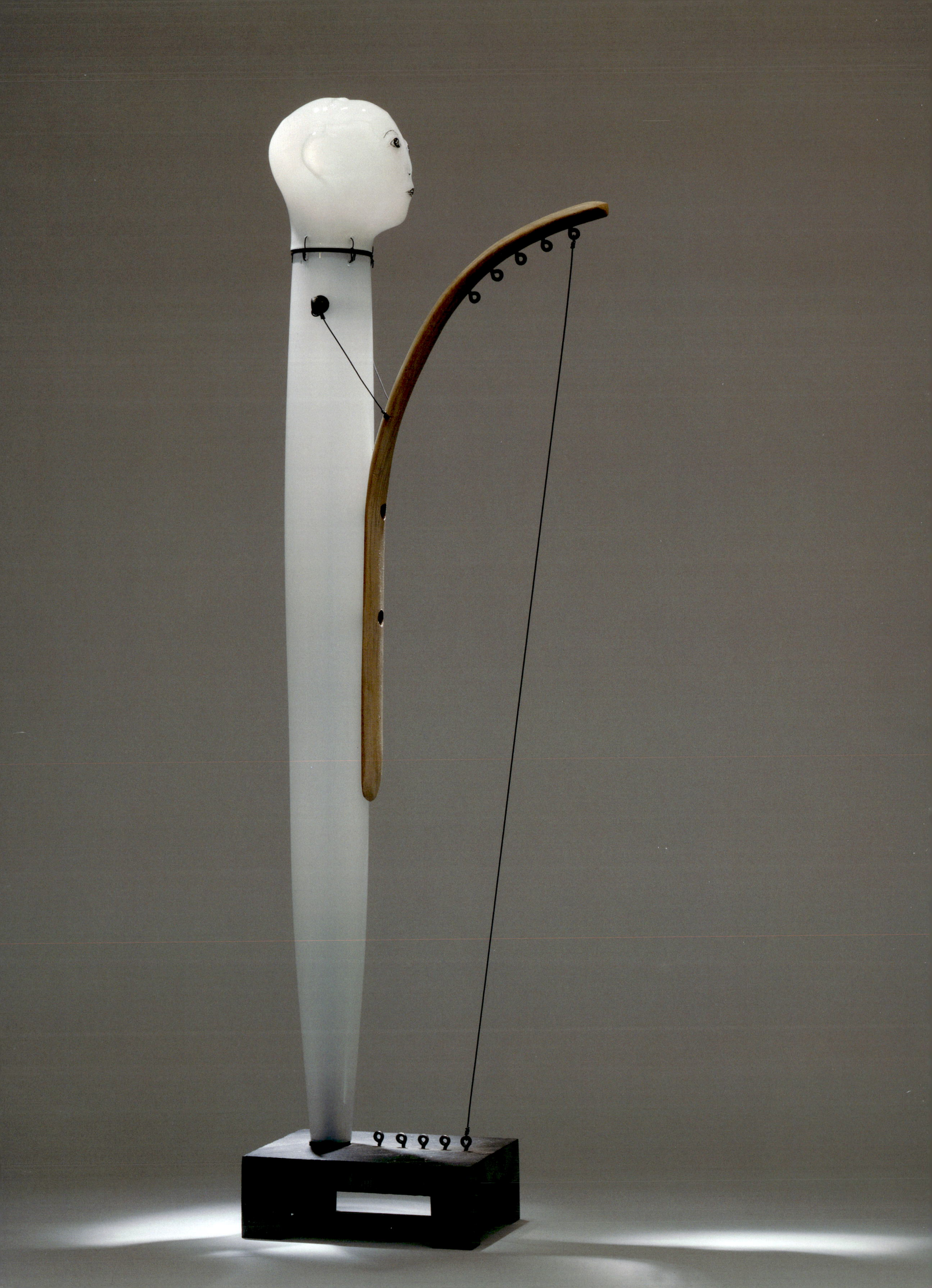

Harp (1983, opposite) is one of the earliest examples from this body of work, often referred to as the white-tube figures. It is also among those works that make the strongest reference to the anthropomorphic male and female harps from Zaire seen in the Katherine White Collection. The sculpture consists of a very spare composition comprising head and body attached to a simple, bentwood arc and wire "string." The body and harp-form join together as a metaphor for the human voice and also, perhaps, as a visual synonym for the artists finding their own voice.

Like *Harp*, other early sculptures typically combine head and body with a vocabulary of spare but elegantly evocative, iconic symbols. Oars are combined with the figure in *Foretold Journey* (1984, p. 113), a visual metonym for physical and metaphysical transference. *Garden of Ladders* (1985, p. 116) includes zigzagged, notched poles—ladders—which reference African art and suggest implements that aid in the toil of daily life.

In other works, a boat form becomes the prevalent leitmotif, and, at times, the boat shape is filled with multiple white-glass heads, the passage and evolution, perhaps, of the collective unconscious, as in *Cargo* (1984, p. 119). In other works, such as *Voyage Carrier* (1985, p. 118), the boat is filled with blown-glass bowls. Like the head, this bowl form—similar to a Tibetan singing bowl—suggests a container for spirituality, as well as a rudimentary instrument for making music. In *Foregather* (1985, p. 212) and other examples, the glass cups are tethered directly to the figures, which are, in turn, conjoined. In this poetic composition, the sacred burden of the individual and the interrelatedness of humankind are expressed.

Sometimes the spare, glass sentinels relate to one another without accoutrements. In *Figure Shoring* (1986, right), for example, two figures evoke a parent-child relationship by the scale of a larger figure paired with a smaller one. Here, the larger figure bows slightly and protectively toward the more diminutive figure, and the two are physically harnessed with a wire connecting the forms.

How did Kirkpatrick and Mace determine the composition of these works and address other germane formal considerations? The artists made a tremendous number of drawings—on napkins over dinner, on a huge blackboard, in an ongoing sketchbook. Most of the drawings were quick sketches that flew back and forth, from one artist's hand to the other's, like a conversation in the language of line on paper. Further-resolved drawings followed until a consonance of forms was achieved.

The making of these glass figurative works, like the wire drawing cylinders, involved new technology in the hot shop. A head was crafted first in clay by Kirkpatrick, and then a plaster mold was made of the clay form. The perforated mold was thoroughly soaked in water before molten glass was blown into it; the steam from the hot glass hitting the wet plaster created a resist, which prevented the glass from sticking to the mold. Once the glass was annealed, Kirkpatrick used a diamond-tipped stylus to scratch the slightest, expressionless features—eyes, brows, nose, and lips—onto the face. Glass enamel was rubbed into the incisions, and the head returned to the kiln. These inscribed features are evocative of a pencil line on paper, with a nod to the graphite-like line qualities so painstakingly wrought in the wire

Harp, 1983
Glass, wood, slate, and steel, 28½ × 7 × 4½ inches

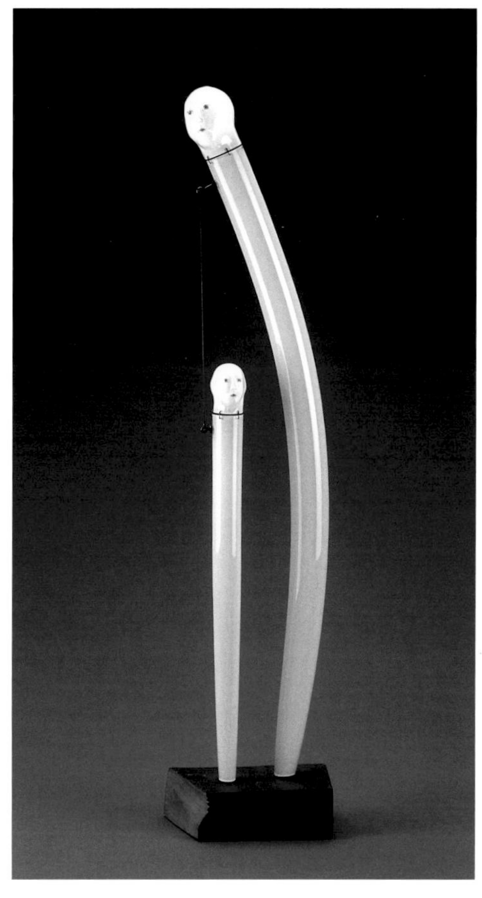

Figure Shoring, 1986
Glass, slate, and steel, 38½ × 8½ × 5 inches

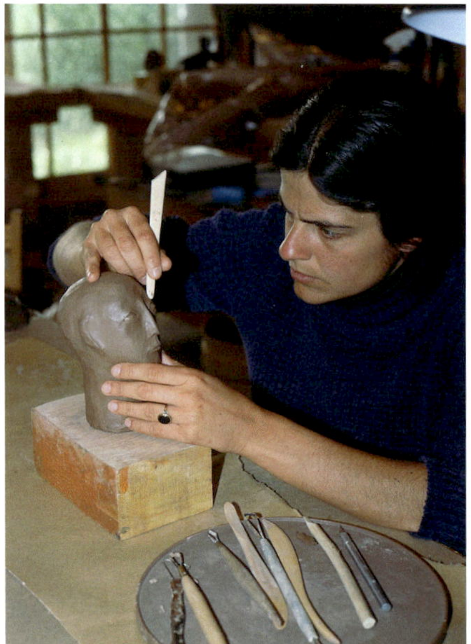

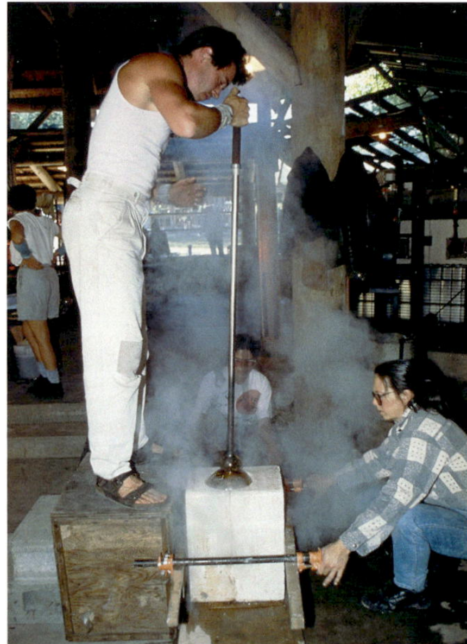

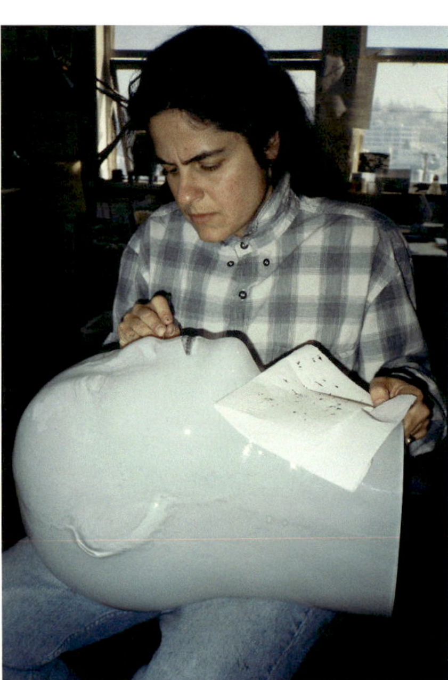

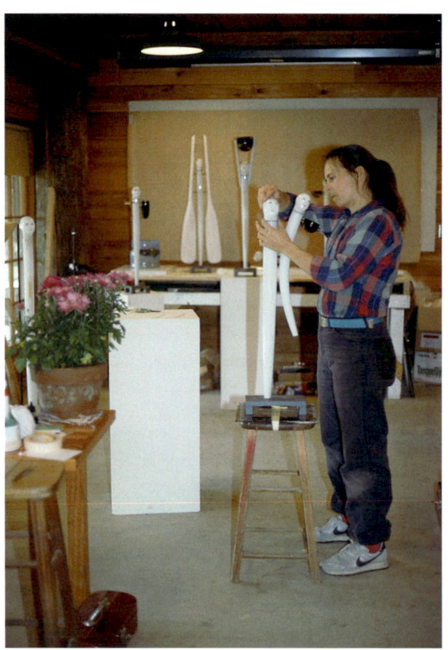

drawing cylinders. The tubular white bodies were made by William Morris, who traded the labor to make the white columns (the size of which demanded physical strength and technical skill in the hot shop) in exchange for Mace creating cane drawings for Morris's work.

To attach the head to the body, Mace developed a tool to cleanly slice the base of the neck and the top of the "tusk" to create joinable surfaces. At the time, implements such as glass cutting tools were not readily available to glass artists. She made an electrical hot-wire loop that could be noosed around the glass and charged to create a smooth break around and through the circumference. This allowed for the head and body apertures to be matched in size. Mace would then hold the head or body, while Kirkpatrick drilled five or six holes around the rim. The head was then sutured to the

Joey Kirkpatrick and Flora C. Mace

body with wires, a witty reference to the earlier wire drawings. The figure was then mounted onto an inner armature and base for stability.

The paleness of these works, the whiteness of the figures in particular, stands in stark contrast to the colorful drawings one finds on Kirkpatrick's and Mace's latest wire drawing cylinders. Why the absence of color, especially at a time when the studio glass movement was virtually exploding with mesmeric color? It was partially in response to the wire drawing cylinders and their decorative surfaces, as well as the artists' attempt to refocus their attention to issues of sculptural form and the conveyance of ideas. Nonetheless, the palette of these works recalls the earliest wire drawing cylinders, the grisaille-like line drawings of women on ladders and chairs in black line on creamy, smoky, or clear glass vessels.

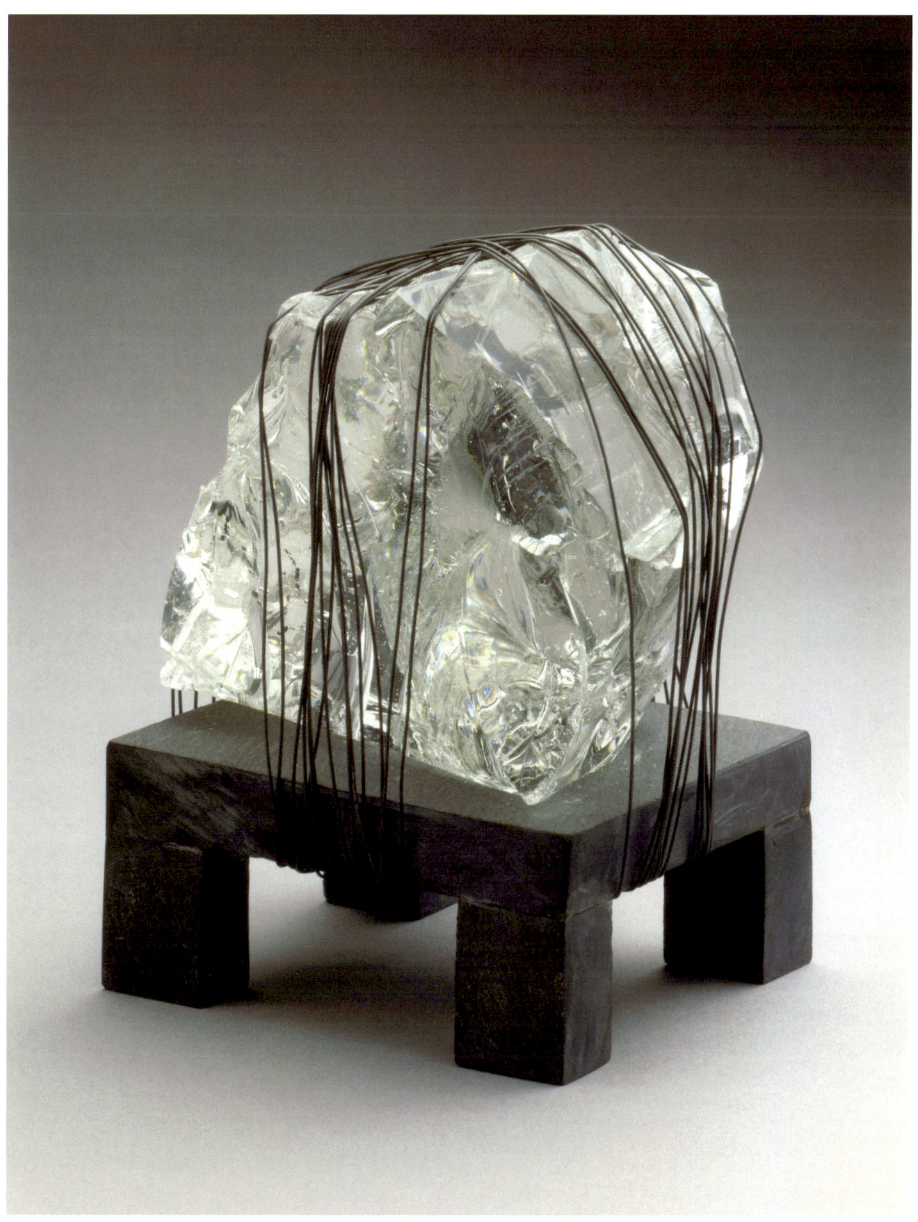

Around the time that Kirkpatrick and Mace withdrew from the wire drawing cylinder series and began to concentrate on figurative sculpture, they crafted a humorous sculpture to visually convey their new direction. *Wire Drawing on Glass* (1983, 6 × 5 × 5 inches) is a chunk of clear glass, wrapped in wire and mounted on a pedestal—an abstract "drawing" in wire in sculptural form.

Elements of Nature, 1986–2000

Seeing and feeling are not contradictory things; it's through the surface that we get to the core. Looking outward and looking inward can happen at once. A painting, like a poem, is a meeting ground between the interiority of the artist and the surface of the world; the power of the artist is to make such an encounter available to the viewer or reader, so that it becomes *our* encounter as well.

—Mark Doty[9]

Kirkpatrick and Mace continued to explore the concept of the human form, but gradually moved away from the milky-glass tube sculptures and began to isolate the human head, sometimes in white glass, sometimes in clear, as an element in now life-size sculptural assemblages. Works such as *Celestial Eclipse* (1986, p. 75) and *Tidal Eclipse* (1986, p. 120) indicate the artists' experimentation with more constructivist compositions. In these works, the eyes are dreamily closed and the human heads are again true containers, while hoops, balls, half circles, and poles suggest rational thoughts or memories tottering and swirling at the heads' periphery.

As always, whatever Kirkpatrick and Mace were observing in their day-to-day life would likely find its way into visual expression in their art. At the time that these sculptures were made, the pair had moved from Pilchuck to Seattle and had a studio on Lake Union, surrounded by nautical contrivances. One day Kirkpatrick looked out the window, spied buoys piled up on each other, and thought, "Oh, that's where the colored ball came from." Other sculptures, such as *Waterborne* (1986, left) contain an oar form interwoven between hoops, an image inspired by a moment when the artists were outside rowing on the water. Mace noticed how, when the oar was lifted, the water dripped off it and created concentric circles on the lake's surface.

Out of this experimentation came a revelatory moment in which Kirkpatrick and Mace paired the human head with natural elements, generating *In Nature* (1987), *Round of Years* (1987), and *To Bear Fruit* (1987, opposite). In these works, the human element confronts not only abstruse formal elements (like balls or rings) but the presence of nature in the form of small, blown apples, pears, and peaches. The formal elements of earlier compositions become smooth branches with attached green-glass leaves or are transformed completely into barkless trees bearing attached fruit. *Century's Rounding* (1989, p. 125) implies the interaction of the human presence with nature, as the tree form contains, instead of fruit on the vine, a bowl in which a still life of fruit is carefully arranged. The artists encountered in their own work "an expression of that moment of tension when human intervention in, or collaboration with, nature is recognized."[10]

Curiously, out of these sculptural encounters with nature came Kirkpatrick's and Mace's first "bird drawing" in glass, an early

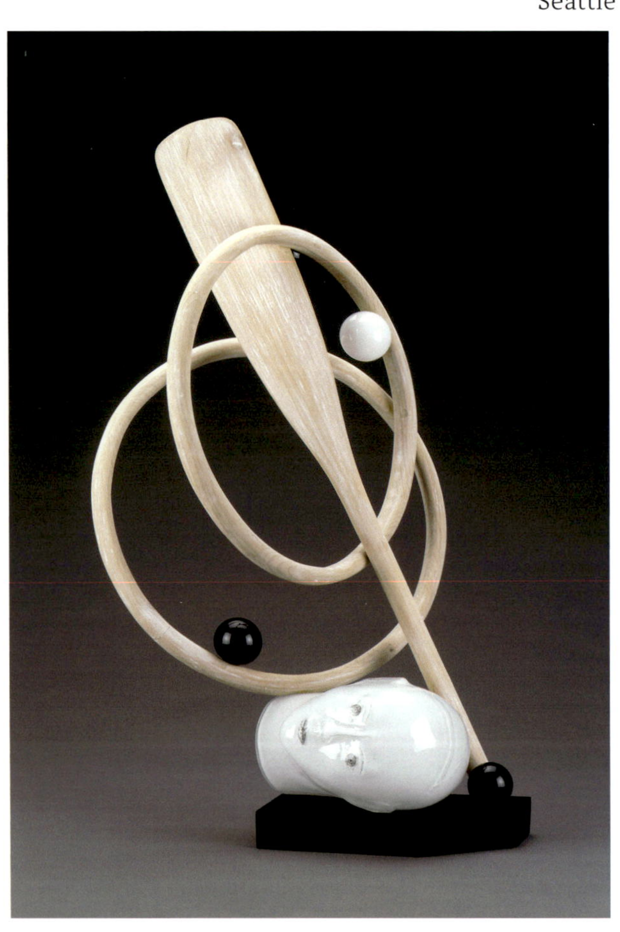

Waterborne, 1986
Wood, glass, paint, and steel, 38 × 21 × 18 inches

Joey Kirkpatrick and Flora C. Mace

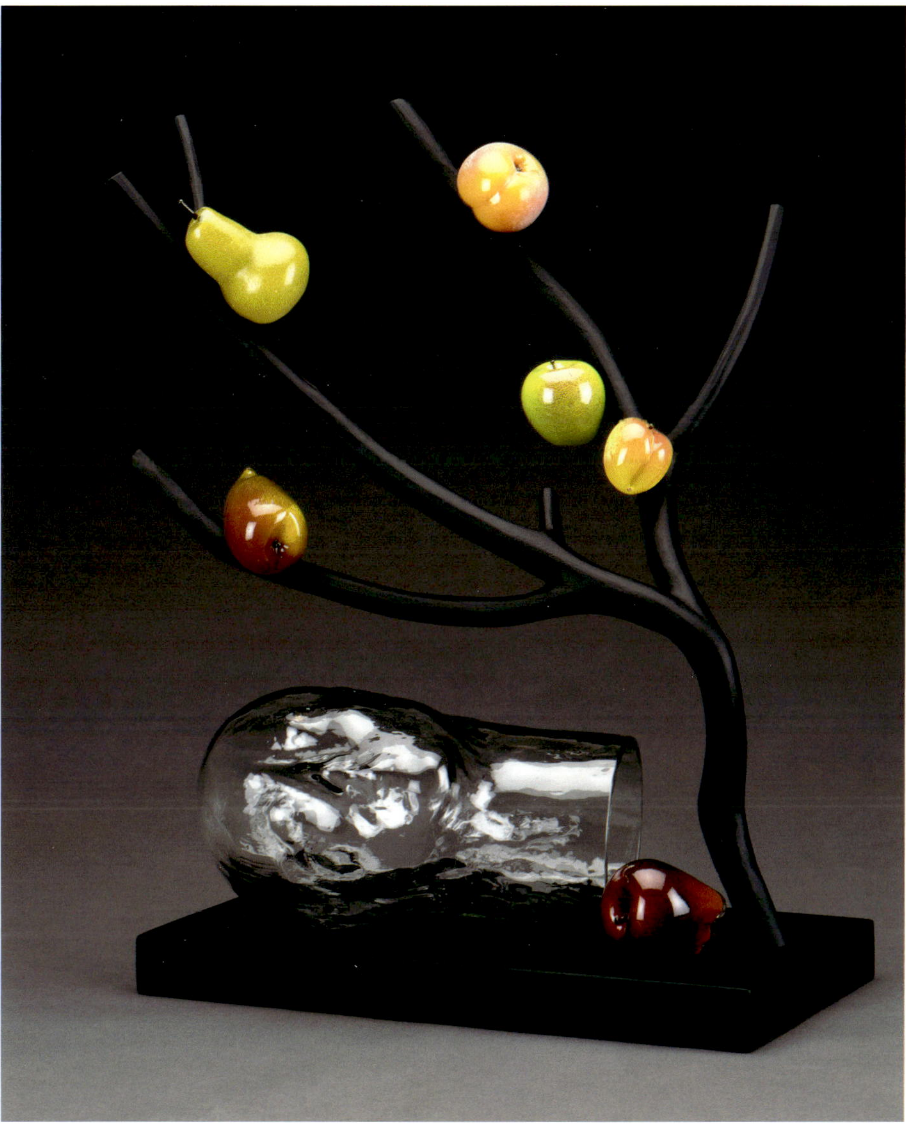

predecessor to their *Bird Pages: First Facts* (2003–2006). The sculpture *Change of Place* (1987, p. 124) replaces fruit with the silhouette of a small, black sparrow, cut from plate glass and infilled with black enamel. The artists retained the human head as an alternative vessel form, for it "holds something" in spirit rather than literally.

Nature's Palette (1990, p. 34) is a milestone in Kirkpatrick's and Mace's oeuvre, because it is their earliest sculpture to address the human form in approximate life-size and so harmoniously conflates humanness and nature. The sculpture is notably anthropomorphic in that its overall shape is that of a tree branch—removed of its bark and natural leaves—turned upside down, so that the limbs of the tree are the limbs of a human figure, arms and legs outstretched and engaged with the world. The surface of the bough/body is carved, whitewashed, and sanded to create a slightly ghostly appearance, while the milky-glass head assures a human allusion. The body sprouts green-glass leaves and cradles a wood platter with a still life of glass fruit, which could also be read as colors on an artist's palette. The sculpture visually answers the question: Are we humans part of nature, or are we apart from it?

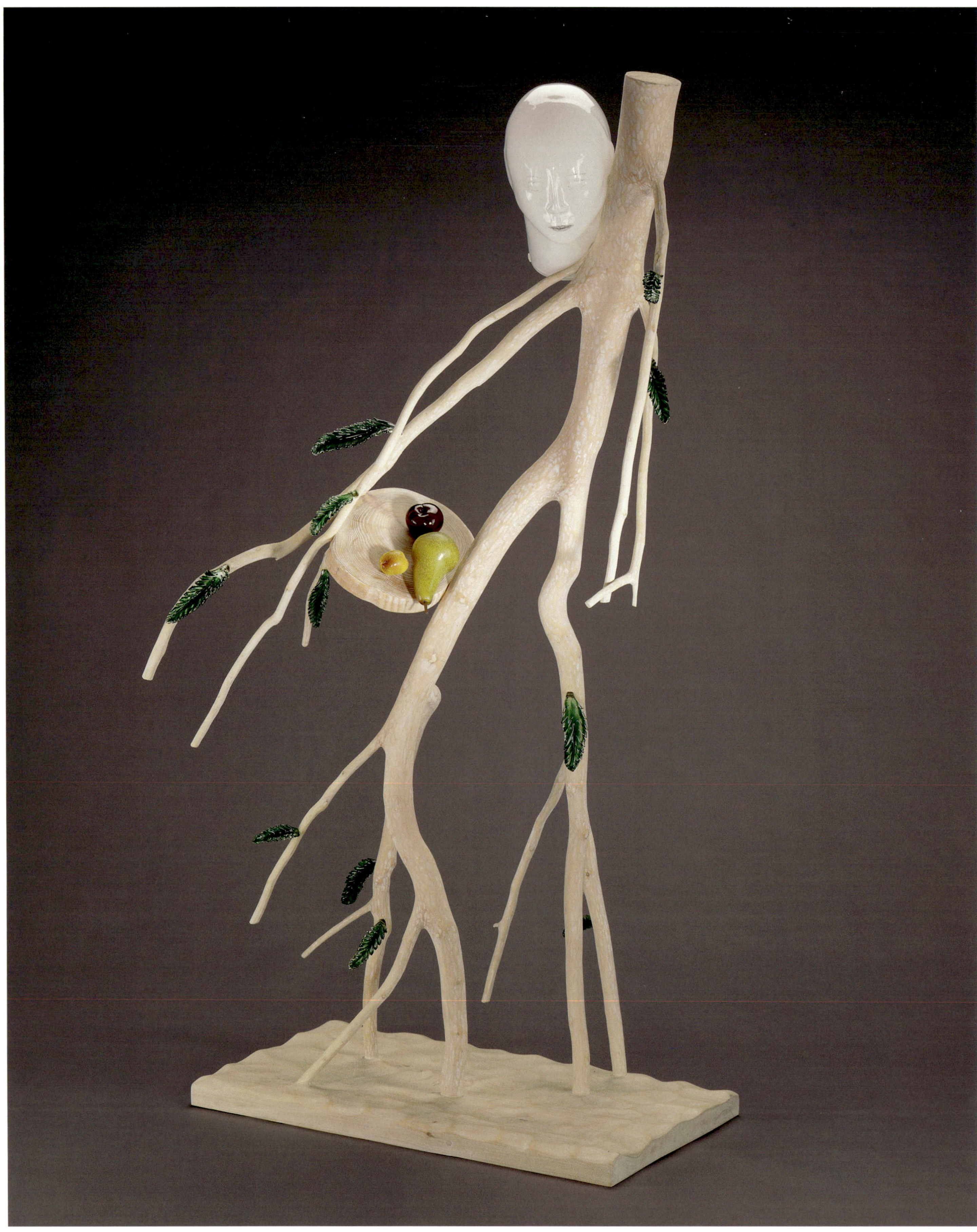

Since the making of *Nature's Palette*, Kirkpatrick and Mace have amassed a significant body of sculpture that continues to explore the human figure in relationship to the world as a metaphor for how we make do in that world. They continued to include the white-glass head in works such as *Limbed Tumbrel* (1992, p. 128)[11] and *Wooded Hollow* (1993, p. 36); in these, the head is tipped onto one ear, suggesting a head cocked to ask the viewer what he or she thinks in response to a query posed.

The artists began to incorporate other non-glass containers as components of their works, such as deep and narrow forms made from stripped alder and molded into splint baskets. Sometimes a basket/container is made in the shape of human legs, suggesting how we "walk" in nature. Often a basket form contains blue-glass bottles or white-glass fruit, introducing the notion that humans are reliant on nature for water and other sustenance. As always, Kirkpatrick explored the pair's themes in two dimensions as well, including sketches and fully realized monotypes such as *Sylvan Figure* (1995, right).

Wooded Hollow is another large-scale sculpture to mine these motifs and interconnections. The anthropoid component of this work is greater than life-size, at seven feet tall. When Kirkpatrick and Mace search, around the Pilchuck Glass School and Stanwood, for wood to use in their work, they keep their eyes open for materials that are already inclined to express the stature and movement of a human form. In the case of *Wooded Hollow*, the tree limbs that form the trunk and legs of the body artlessly convey the sense of one leg crossed over the other. The attenuated twigs that form the arms are outstretched. The way in which the arms intersect with the basket form, which also has the shape of a figure, suggests, perhaps, that the figure is carrying a harvest basket. But the composition also plays with positive and negative space, establishing a balance, even alluding to an elegant parity between the figure and nature's bounty.

Other sculptures from this period also rely on twig forms in the shape of the figure. Additionally, they imply a sense of human-initiated execution, if not human activity itself. *Water's Edge, Year's Round* (1994, p. 37), *Pale Divine* (1994, p. 132), and *Water Catcher* (1995, p. 134) are examples. In these works, luminous clear-blue vessels are simulacra of precious water, with the literal containers representing something to be contained. The blue bottles are suspended in a tumble from a bucket (a human-made object) as if being poured (a human action). In the case of *Pale Divine*, the blue-glass "water" connects a downward-pointing dowsing device to a collection bucket. *Divine* in the title then is a double entendre: there is a visual play on words between a *divining* rod and the sacredness of fresh water.

Slightly later works, such as *Holding the Williwaw* (1996, p. 135) and *Steering Shallow Waters* (1996, p. 139), continue to investigate these themes. The human-like figure in *Holding the Williwaw* seems braced against the wind. (*Williwaw* is a nautical term for a sudden blast of wind descending from a mountainous coast to the sea.) The boat form, again a container holding watery-blue vessels, seems to have blown ashore in a conceit that represents the constant interchange encountered by human beings in nature. Again, are we pitted against nature or dancing along within it?

Nature's Palette, 1990
Glass, wood, paint, and steel, 69 × 32 × 18 inches

Joey Kirkpatrick, **Sylvan Figure**, 1995
Monotype, 41 × 29 inches

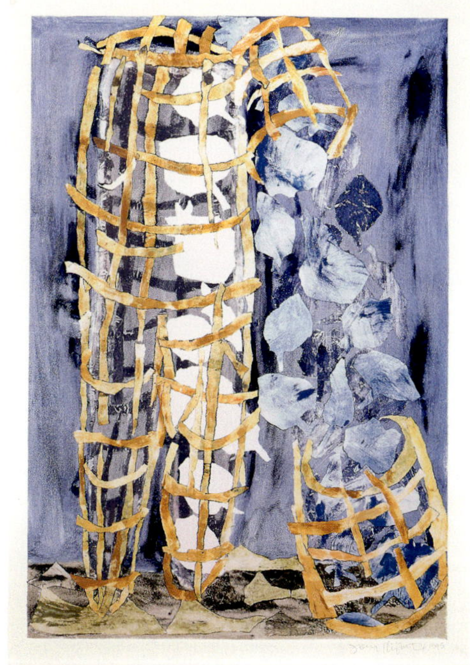

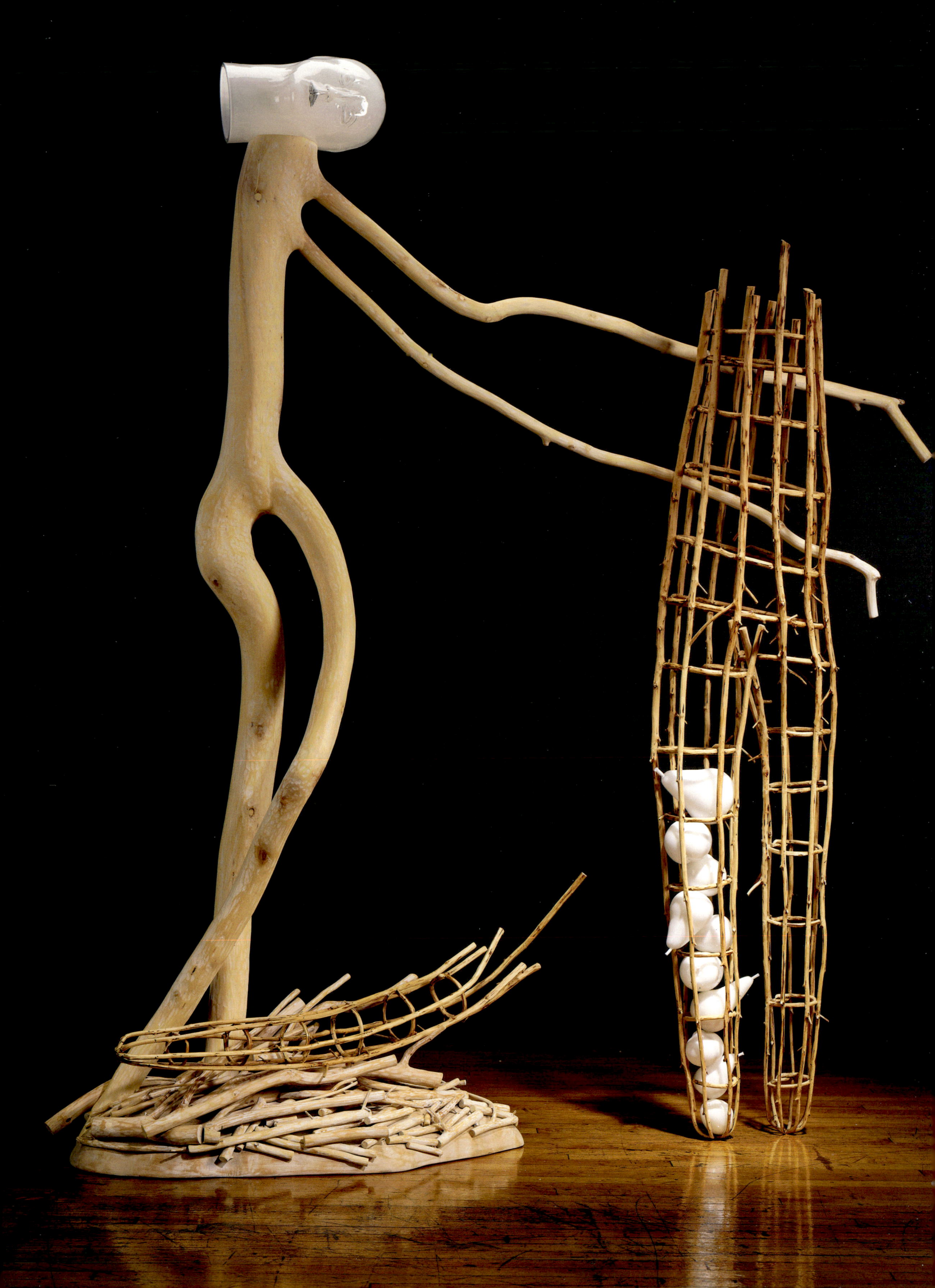

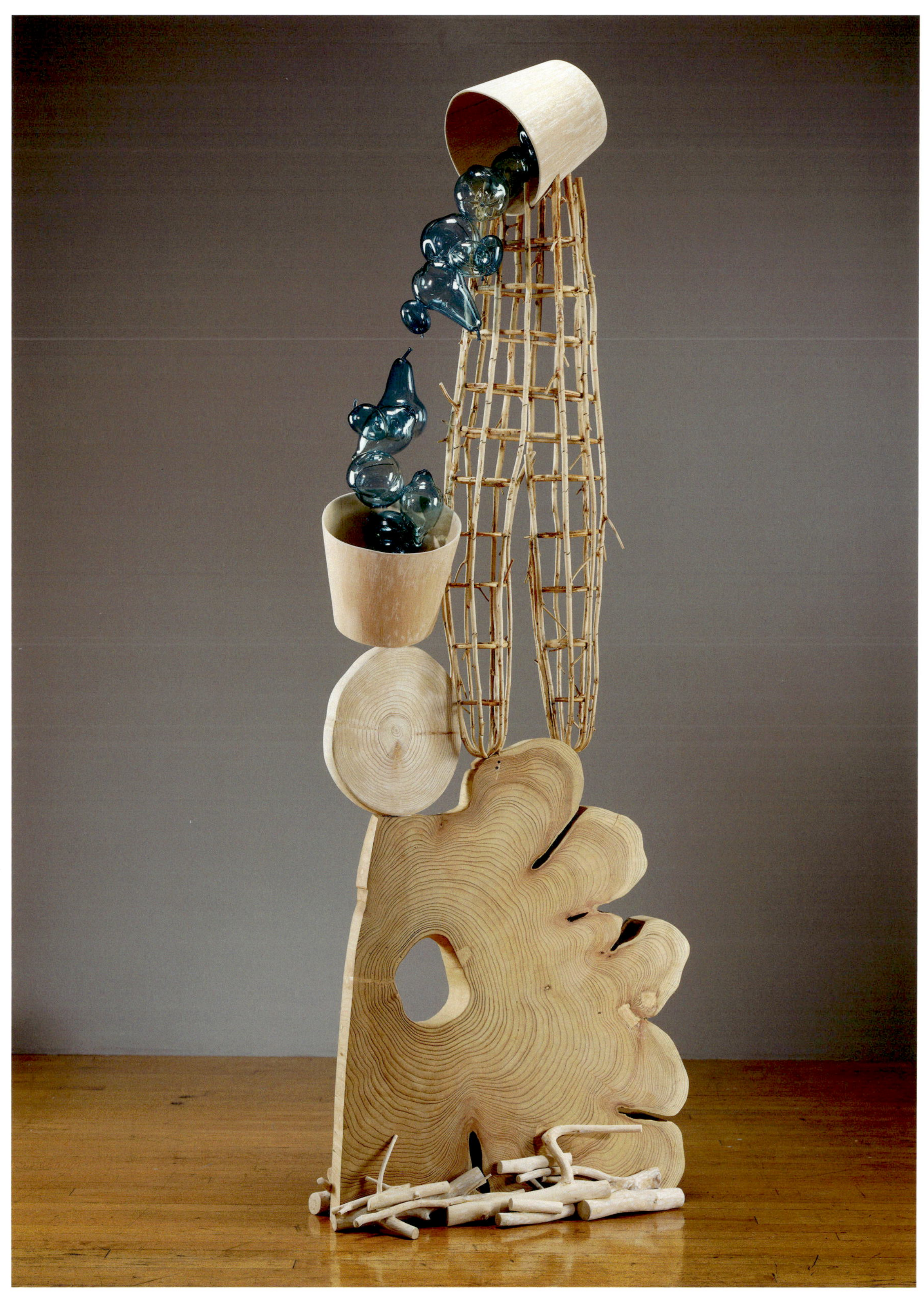

Wooded Hollow, 1993
Glass, wood, paint, and steel, 84 × 75 × 25 inches

Water's Edge, Year's Round, 1994
Glass, wood, paint, and steel, 79 × 30 × 11 inches

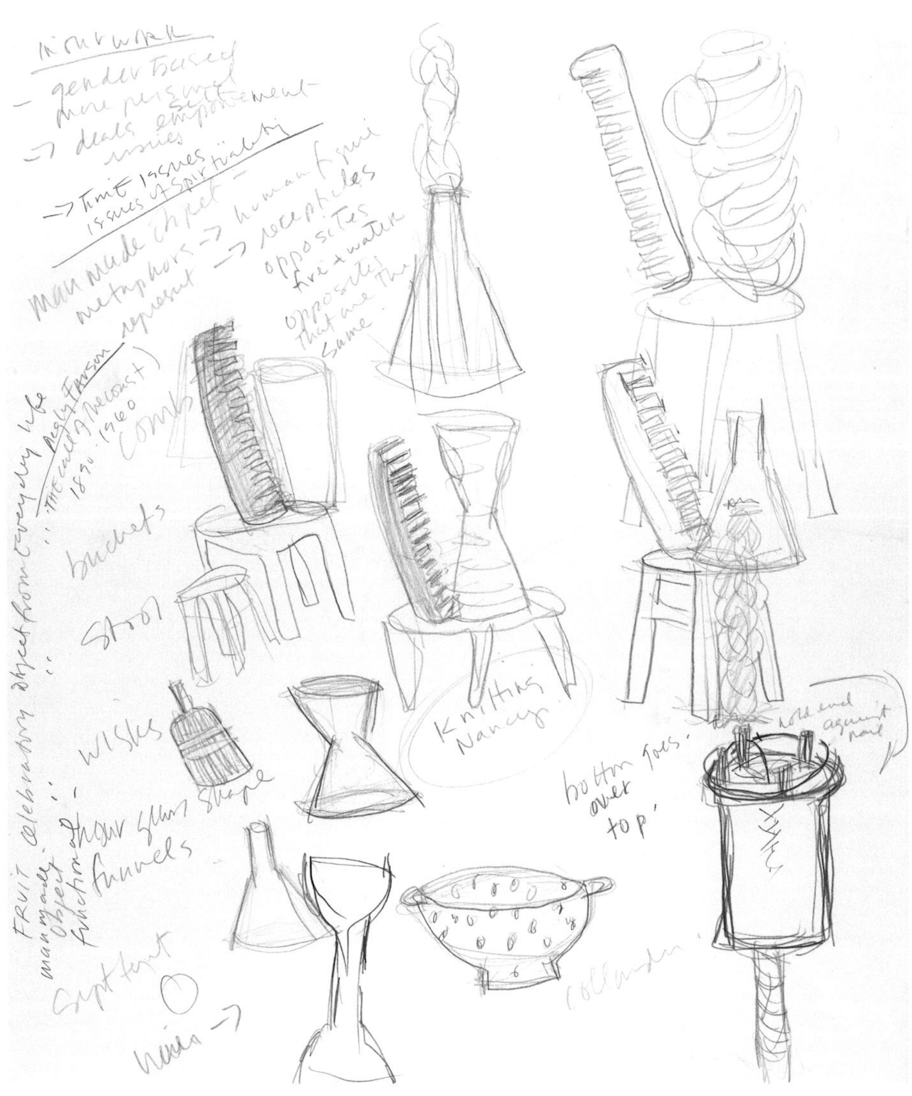

Joey Kirkpatrick, **Untitled I**, 1998
Graphite on paper, 16¾ × 14 inches

The metaphoric content of *Steering Shallow Waters* is yet another recombination of the human mark. In this work, a boat, filled with citrine-colored glass vessels possibly suggesting the supplies for a journey, is balanced atop a glass vessel containing sea-colored bottles, perhaps representing the flotsam and jetsam of the sea. Those bottles are also reminiscent of Japanese floats or the almost translucent, bulbous kelp found at the ocean's edge. Even the breath implied by the hand-blown nature of these vessels conjures a sense of the wind.

Eventually, Kirkpatrick and Mace shifted once again to investigate other aspects of human nature. The artists began to think about domestic labors, daily tasks that are most often attended to by women, and the archetypal symbols that might evoke those chores. As usual, new ideas for sculpture took shape through drawings made by Kirkpatrick and dialogue between the two artists.

John Berger says that there are "three distinct ways in which drawings can function. There are those that study and question the visible; those that record and communicate ideas; and those done from memory."[12] Kirkpatrick's drawing practice engages all these objectives at different times. However, her sketches that come out of the discourse between the two

　　Joey Kirkpatrick and Flora C. Mace

artists and eventually yield sculpture are of Berger's second type. A sheet of rough diagrams from 1998 (opposite) chronicles their thought processes. Here there are perhaps a dozen rapidly jotted schemes for sculptures or components of potential works: several versions of a comb, funnels, a colander, a whisk, stools, a bucket, together with a human torso. Marginal notations list conceptual concerns—"time issues," "issues of spirituality," "self-empowerment issues"—along with the name of the American author and adventurer Negley Farson. This is how Kirkpatrick and Mace flesh out their ideas.

Their ongoing duologue resulted in works such as *Braided to Great Effects* (1998, right) and *From the Reach of Memory* (1998, p. 140), in which rudimentary tools—a stool, a knitting nancy, a comb—stand in for the suggestion of women's work. Each component of Kirkpatrick's and Mace's sculptures is meticulously made by hand in their studio. The recurrent knitting nancy is a primitive "machine," remembered from childhood, made of a spool and four finishing nails, which allows the user to craft a knitted rope that emerges from the bottom of the spool. The "tail" that is wrought by the artists' knitting nancy is typically braided fiber (not knitted), another allusion to a girl's childhood memories. But the symbolism associated with the plaits is more potent than simply evoking youth: hair is often considered a source of one's strength and, in many cultures, is an eternal image of beauty, fertility, and even creativity. The idea of cutting off one's hair is often associated with repentance, and, for some groups, the covering of a woman's hair is a rite of passage.

Spooled Torso, So Made (1998, p. 40) and *The Edge of Certainty* (2002, p. 145) introduce another iconic form in these sculptors' oeuvre: the human torso. Their human embodiments are essentially drawings in three dimensions that look as if the artists "drew" the contours of the human frame by tracing a cyclonic line around its form. While the figures evoke the sense of cursory sketches, they are actually made of steel armatures, faced with alderwood that Kirkpatrick and Mace harvested, peeled, and steam-bent. The torsos are nest-like and basket-like, suggesting both *home* and *spirit container*; they are headless to deny individuality and to convey a collective concept of human being. Within the torsos are glass bottle forms, blown by the artists in the hot shop, containers that serve to keep something in while simultaneously keeping something out. What might those things be? According to the artists, they are memories, experiences, belief systems, knowledge, thoughts, hopes, desires—the consciousness implied by being human.

A small sculpture made during this period expresses Kirkpatrick's and Mace's deep interest in the work of art as a potent metaphor for a specific concept. *Island* (1998, p. 143) is a visual abstraction of its title. The work consists of a clear-glass vessel, with a deep-blue line around the container's circumference. Within the vessel is an assemblage of twigs and sticks. This paradoxically simple work is like a visual mnemonic for the term *island*: terrain, isolated, and surrounded by water.

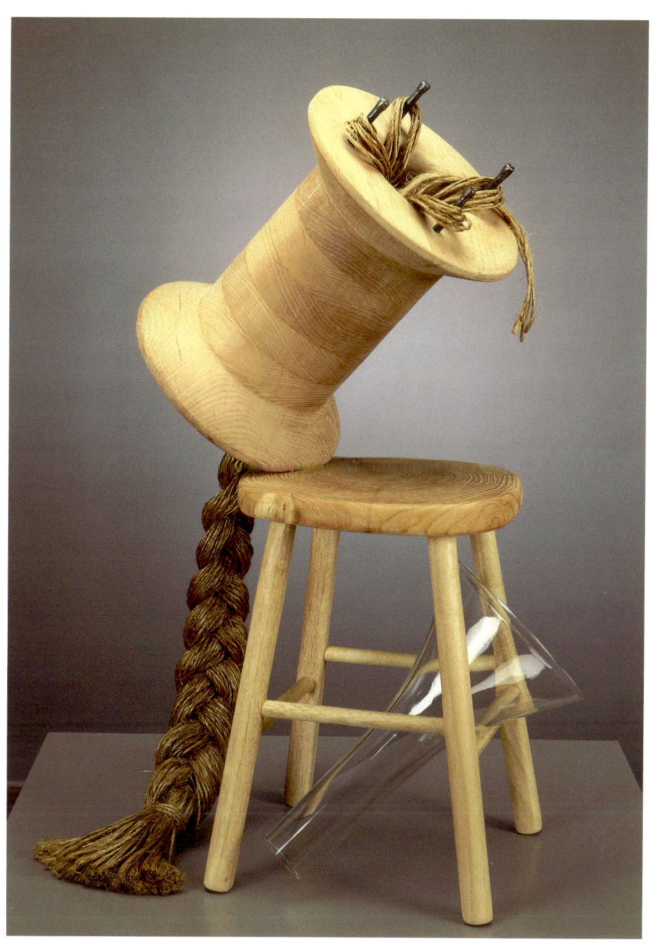

Braided to Great Effects, 1998
Wood, glass, sisal, and steel, 37 × 24 × 8 inches

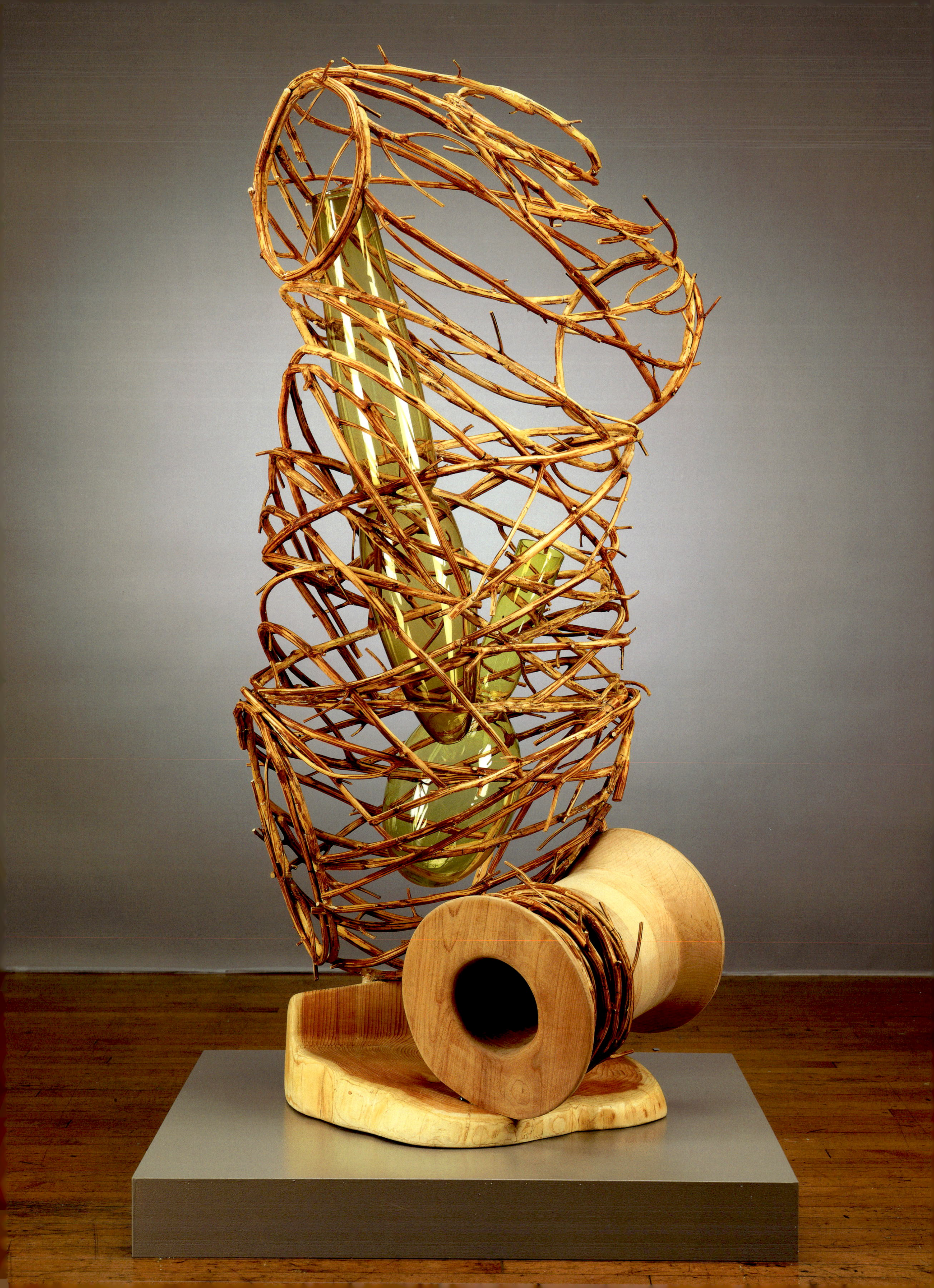

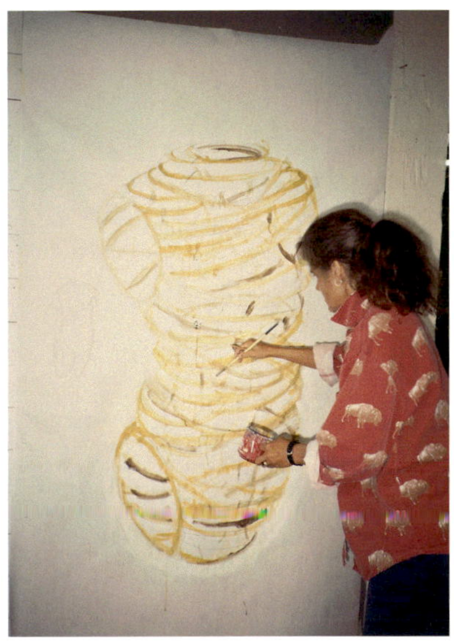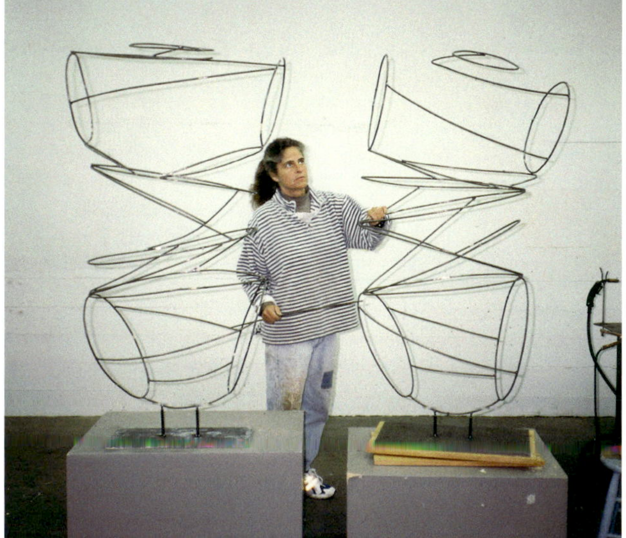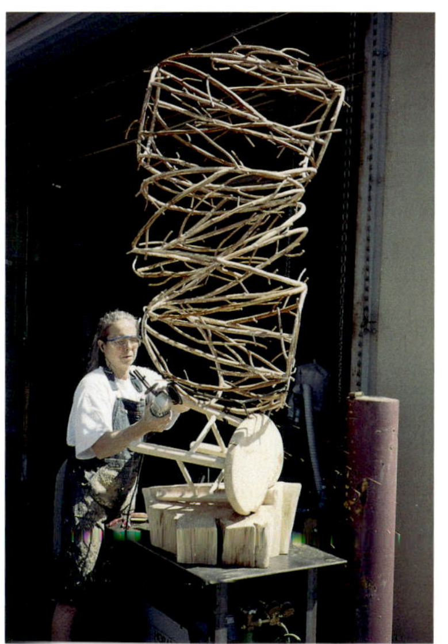

Kirkpatrick's and Mace's interest in language and metaphor drove them, in 1998, to investigate both in another body of work. Their considerations of women's work and the tasks of daily life led them to think about how many colloquial proverbs evolved out of simple labors. They decided to make sculptures to illustrate each of these aphorisms:

As little alike at bottom as fire and water.
Look upon the vessel for what it holds.
By the thread the ball is brought to light.
Every soil bears not everything.
As welcome to it as the water that runs.

The common component of each of these works is that the proverb is spelled out by individual, clear hand-blown cups, onto each of which is melded Mace's signature black-glass-cane text, with one word incorporated on each cup's surface. Thus *Every Soil Bears Not Everything* (2008, p. 148) includes a shelf with five vessels displaying the five words of the title. Four cups contain something: *every* contains sticks that recall Kirkpatrick's and Mace's sculpture; *soil*, *bears*, and *everything* contain glass frit, another reference to a consistent material in their work. The cup marked *not* contains nothing. Each word contributes equally to the sentence; if one vessel/word were missing, the truth of the saying would be lost.

The adage is surrounded and contained by a drawing-like outline of a log, while atop the log are a basket-formed abstraction of a figure as well as a cluster of sticks. Perhaps more than any other work in Kirkpatrick's and Mace's oeuvre, this sculpture is a rebus for the life of the artist. The placement of the human element opposite the pile of raw materials conveys that point in the creative process when an artist must address his or her medium. But, as Kirkpatrick and Mace are fond of saying, not every idea can be expressed by the same medium. In their instance, although glass is often the means to convey their concepts, it is not the only tool in their visual vocabulary.

Spooled Torso, So Made, 1998
Wood, glass, paint, and steel, 75 × 31 × 23 inches

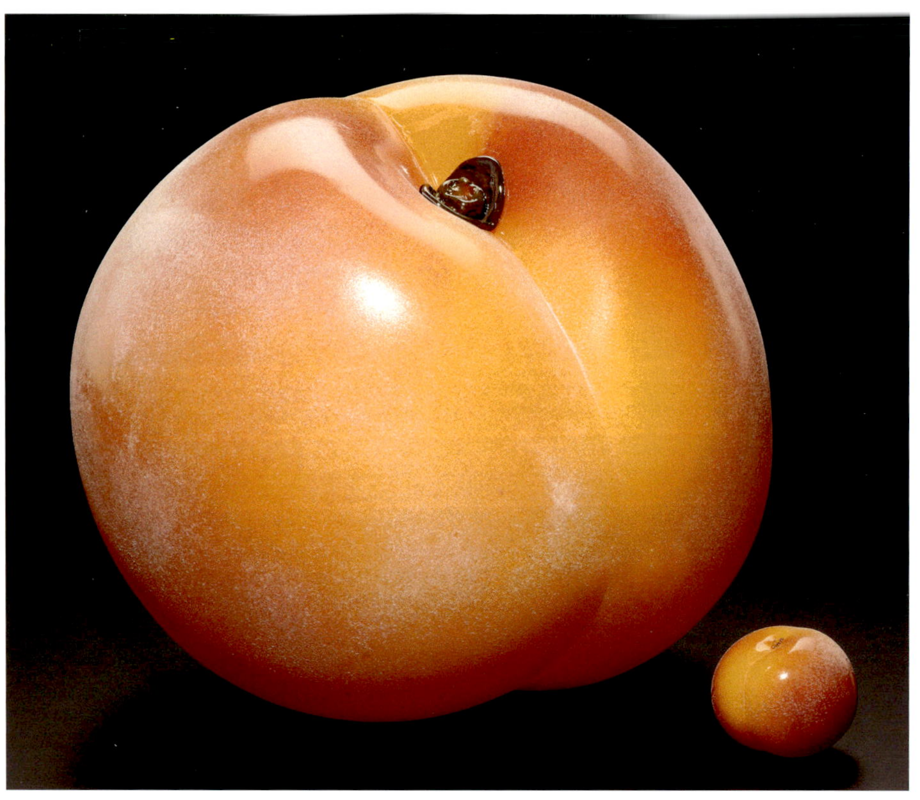

Issues of Scale: The Fruit, Vegetables, and Paintbrushes, 1990–2007

. . . fruits are more reliable. They like having their portraits done. They are there as though they were asking forgiveness for changing color. Their essence is exhaled along with their perfume. They come to you with all of their odors, speaking to you of the fields they have left, of the rain that has nourished them, the sunrises that they have seen.

—Paul Cézanne[13]

By 1990, Kirkpatrick's and Mace's work had shifted markedly in scale. At this time, the artists were still interested in applying glass drawings to the cylinder. They worked with their friend William Morris to blow oversized clear-glass vessels onto which the artists introduced simple but monumental black line still lifes of pears, apples, lemons, and berries. Unlike the earlier cylinders with wire drawings, these drawings were not created prior to or separately from the blow. The glass-cane drawings were drawn directly onto the vessel during the blowing process. Kirkpatrick would "direct" the drawing by making pencil sketches on paper, or drawing on the hot shop floor with chalk, to indicate composition and placement. Once the vessel was about three-quarters blown, Mace would methodically transfer Kirkpatrick's drawing in black-glass cane directly onto the hot glass vessel. This was an extremely challenging process, as the size of the vessel required multiple reheats to maintain its shape. One overheat and the vessel would slump, or if the glass was not heated enough the vessel would crack or the drawing

Joey Kirkpatrick and Flora C. Mace

would not adhere. The making of these complex cylinders was something of a rare event, as the artists made them over only four or five blows during the course of their career.

These fruit cylinders were made in the hot shop at roughly the same time that Kirkpatrick and Mace were incorporating true-to-scale glass fruit elements in sculptures such as *Nature's Palette*. To these artists, the use of fruit forms was quite literally a reference to nature's bounty and the pleasure humans take from the earth's largesse.

Kirkpatrick and Mace are perhaps best known for their virtually trompe l'oeil sculptures of fruit and vegetables. These works, along with their enormous paintbrush sculptures, known as the series *Making Before Meaning* (1999–2007, p. 45), are often mistakenly referred to as Pop art or some hybrid version of Claes Oldenburg's and Coosje van Bruggen's very large replicas of everyday objects. In fact, one could posit that Kirkpatrick's and Mace's fruit sculptures are antithetical to Pop. For one thing, there is no sense of irony or cheekiness intended by the artists. For them, the abundance of nature is to be revered and celebrated.

Instead, other concepts inform the fruit sculptures. The women were always intrigued by new technologies they were learning in the hot shop. In the early 1990s, the ability to make glass sculpture in a very large scale had been only recently acquired. Morris, who got his start as Dale Chihuly's

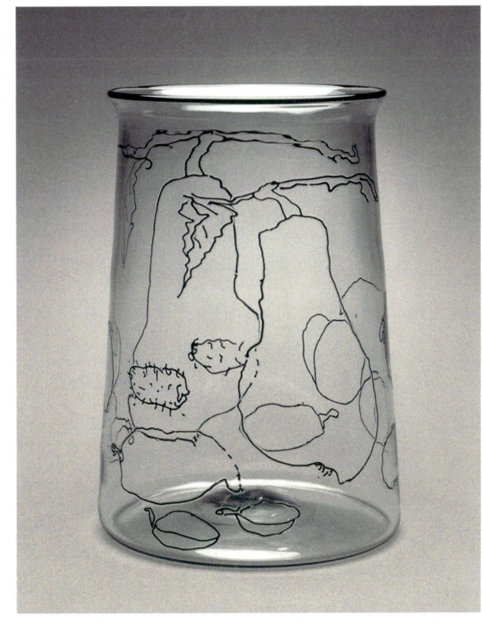

Cylinder with Fruit Drawing, 1990
Glass, 18 × 11 × 11 inches

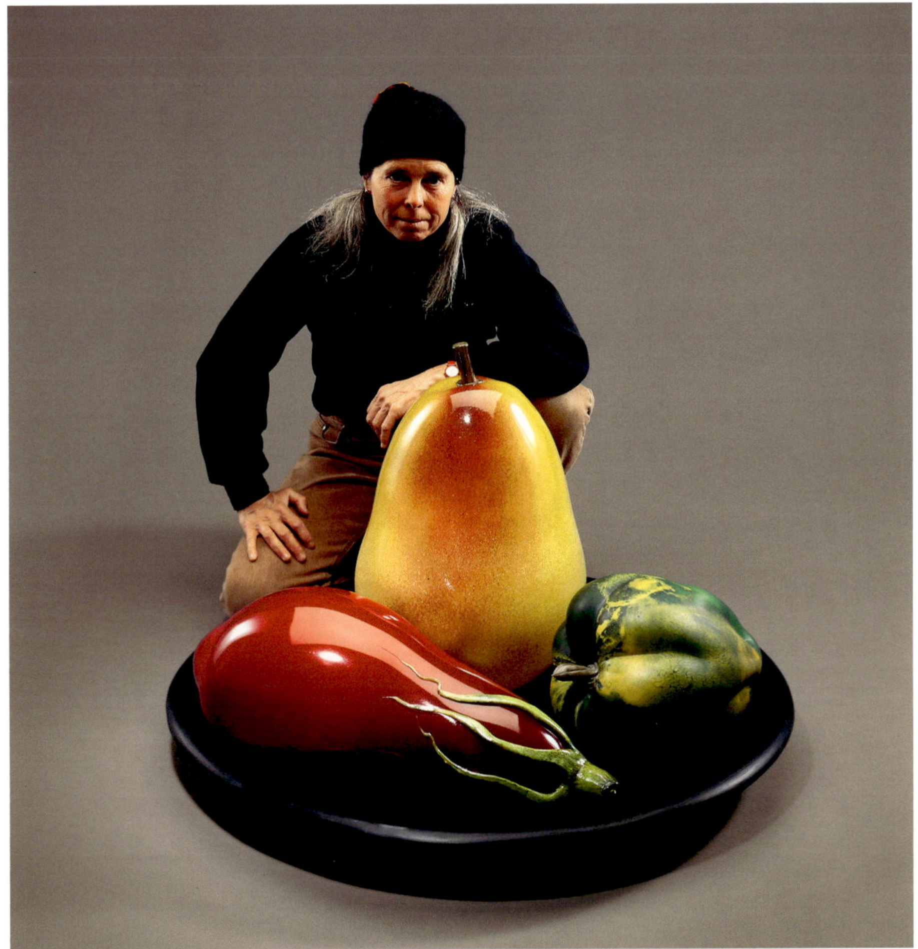

Mace with **Still Life with Pear,** 1994
Glass, wood, and paint, 28 × 34 × 34 inches

gaffer and was responsible for the ever increasing girth of Chihuly's famed *Macchias* from the 1980s, was again trading his skills as a gaffer for glass-cane drawings that Mace made for his vessels and sculpture.[14]

Furthermore, the size and shape of the fruit were virtually another "ground" on which Kirkpatrick could exercise her deep interest in two-dimensional painting traditions. This sounds contradictory, but, in fact, the fruit sculptures are in a real sense color studies. Just as a painter would layer pigments to achieve depth and complexity, so too did Kirkpatrick and Mace build up layers of color—shading—on the hot glass by sifting crushed-glass powder onto the fruit and vegetable forms. The blush of a ripe peach, the russeting of a pear, the dissolution of green into red on an apple's skin, or the slightly glaucous surface of an acorn squash were opportunities for the artists to use glass in a paradoxically painterly fashion. In the most complex of these sculptural works, Kirkpatrick and Mace combined a variety of fruits or vegetables in large wood "bowls" handcrafted by Mace.

This was a period of intense interchange between American pioneers of the studio glass movement and visiting Muranese maestros at the Pilchuck Glass School, where Kirkpatrick and Mace taught from 1981 through 1983 and again from 1986 through 1990.[15] At that time, American glass artists were focused on an experimentation based on traditional methods. Occasionally, Kirkpatrick and Mace had the impulse to make overscale fruit and vegetable sculptures *à la façon de Venise* in *zanfirico* cane.[16] Also referred to as *filigrana a retorti* (twisted filigree), the delicate and colorful cane was pulled in the hot shop by Kirkpatrick and Mace, then laid out in individual pieces like sentinels, and rolled up onto the blowpipe. When assimilated into the clear gather and blown out, the canework became the peel of the apple, pear, or chili pepper.

The success of the fruit sculptures, and Kirkpatrick's and Mace's interest in the history of glass, encouraged their series of *Fruit Goblets* (1992–2013, p. 157) that took the artists in the opposite direction of scale. Goblet making

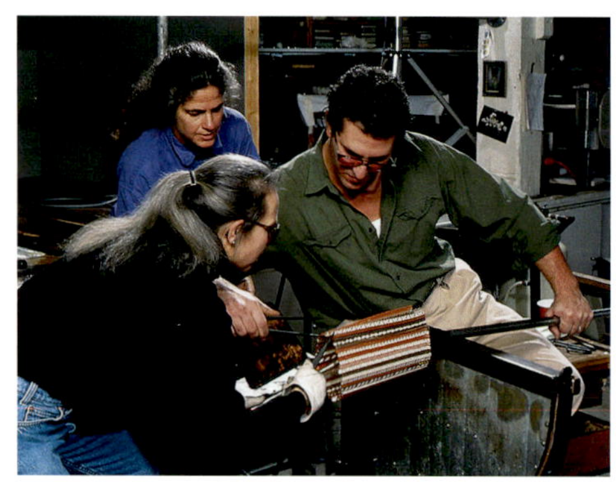

Mace and Kirkpatrick, working with gaffer Paul DeSomma to make *zanfirico* fruit, 1997.

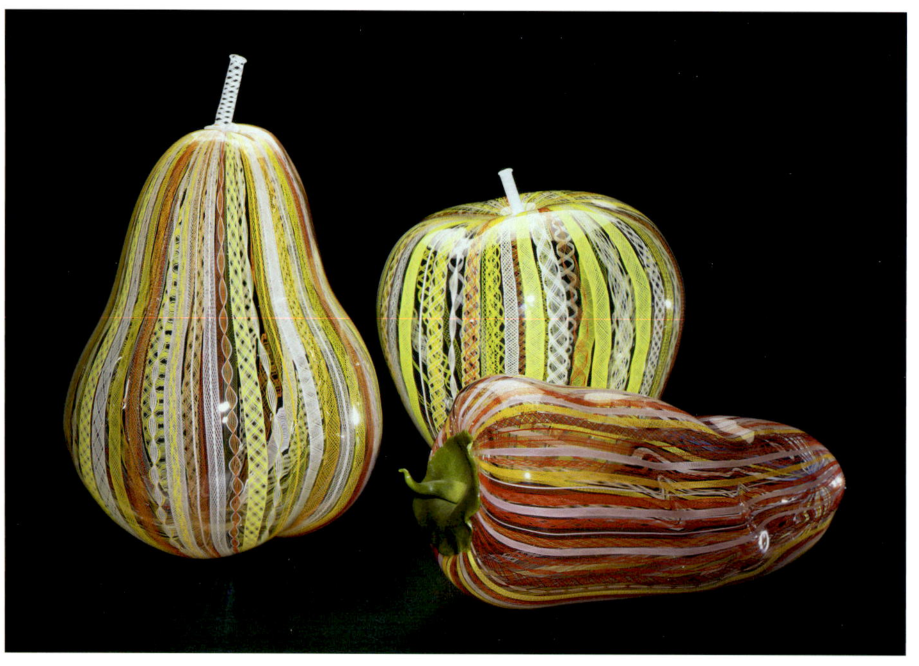

Zanfirico Still Life, 1996
Glass; pear: 25 × 15 × 16 inches

Joey Kirkpatrick and Flora C. Mace

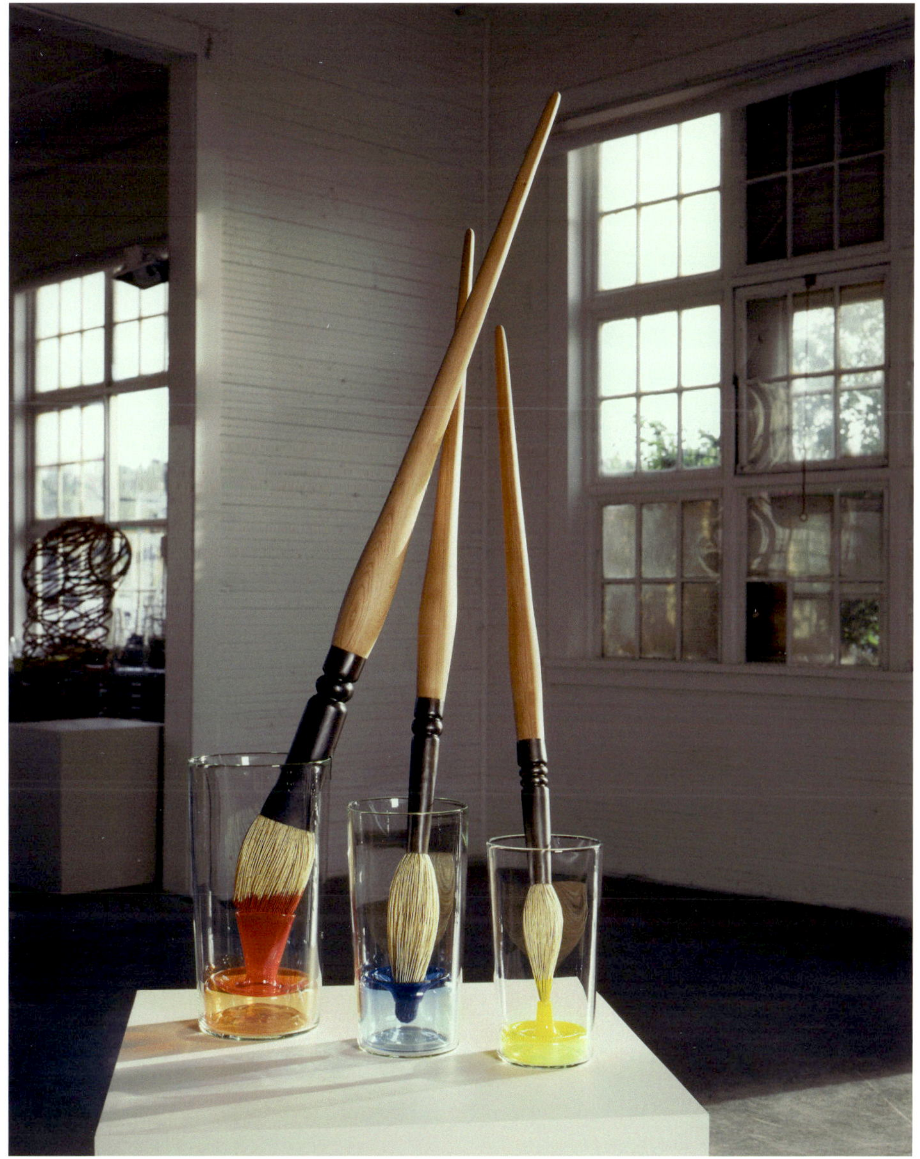

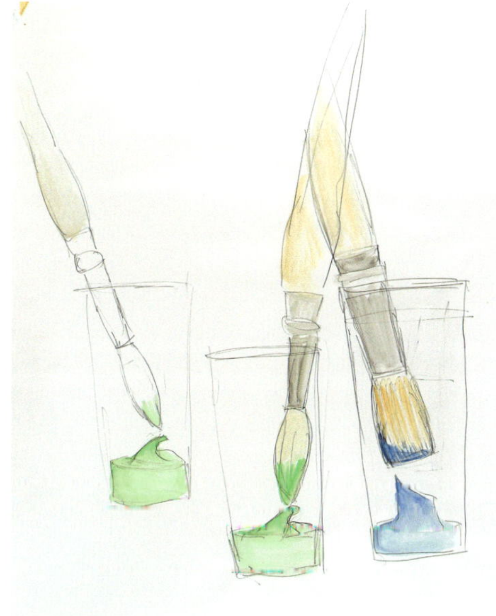

Joey Kirkpatrick, **Untitled**, 2001
Graphite and gouache on paper, 23½ × 18 inches

Making Before Meaning: Primary Colors, 2001
Glass, wood, sisal, dye, and steel;
red brush: 74 × 28 × 11 inches

is considered a serious challenge in the hot shop, and the artists wanted to create cups in their own signature style. The goblets, most often shown in wall installations that almost resemble a form of field guide, represent all manner of fruits and vegetables—eventually Kirkpatrick and Mace formed forty-eight different varieties of produce. The fruit or vegetables were contracted into a consistent size and mounted as the stem of conical flutes. The cups were blown into an optic mold that, when blown and twisted, assumed a spiral design.

Also in monumental scale are Kirkpatrick's and Mace's numerous paintbrush sculptures, *Making Before Meaning*, which again exemplify these artists' facility with varied materials. These works had their nascence in earlier sculptures exploring images associated with women's work. Sculptures such as *Braided to Great Effects* and *Assembling Memory* (2000, p. 144) introduced fiber as a medium, first as the braided "tail" produced by a wood spool-and-nails knitting nancy and as a sculpture assembled with a wood stool and bobbin, a bentwood torso, and cool-blue bottle forms.

The first paintbrushes also coincided with the artists' move into a new studio, where there was a lot of renovation to be done. Kirkpatrick recalls being frustrated at how much time it took to settle into their new space, time that they might have otherwise been working on their art. Kirkpatrick started making pencil drawings in her sketchbook of paintbrushes and soon began to think of them as sketches for large sculptures. Both Kirkpatrick and Mace realized that the paintbrush is an apt metaphor for the creative act, that the very moment when the brush hits the paint and someone starts to use it is a potent symbol for the intention of being creative.

The paintbrushes, like the fruit, have posed a challenge to the artists to create an effective trompe l'oeil impression. Each component of a sculpture is laboriously crafted. The clear paint pot is blown, as is the "paint," which insouciantly crests upward, as if the sculpture arrests the very moment when a human hand draws the tip of the brush up from the pigment. The paintbrush bristles are fiber, molded in the likeness of a pointed-round brush used in an artist's studio, or a sash brush employed, perhaps, for painting a fence. Each brush has clearly been "dipped" into the paint, as the paint color has already been wicked into the bristles. The handle of the brush is wood, carved into an elongated, sinuous mount. Even the ferrule and crimp are resolutely fabricated and burnished from sheet metal. Often Kirkpatrick and Mace exhibit the paintbrushes in groups that might simulate the receptacles resting near an artist's easel in the studio.

Field Notes, 2003–2012

In 2003, Kirkpatrick and Mace began a new series of work: the *Bird Pages: First Facts* (pp. 48, 52). Harking back to the wire drawing cylinders in that the *Bird Pages* are literally drawings in glass, the *Bird Pages* are further evidence of how these artists explore the natural world.

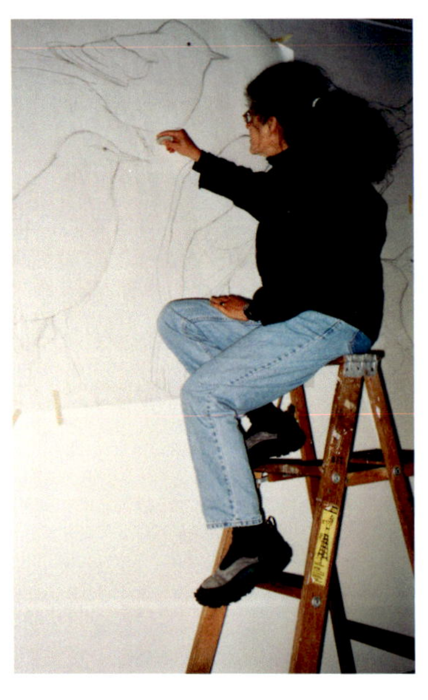

The studio where Kirkpatrick and Mace work is on the canal that connects Puget Sound with Lake Union. There Kirkpatrick is often found in her daily practice drawing that which she sees; from the second-floor windows, Kirkpatrick is known to sketch native birds that perch nearby. Both Kirkpatrick and Mace are serious birders. As Kirkpatrick sought to teach Mace more about classifying birds, she began sketching field guides—flashcards almost, but with the fundamental markings to aid in an accurate identification. Mace literally used Kirkpatrick's hand-drawn keys on their excursions by foot or by boat.

Their investigation into bird watching diverged into other inquiries. Kirkpatrick began to study the history of ornithological painting and was deeply inspired by the work of John James Audubon, Thomas Bewick, Louis Agassiz Fuertes, and Alexander Wilson, among many others, including Iowan self-taught bird painter William Savage. She collected books about birds and rendered their images on paper.

Kirkpatrick's drawings led the artists to think about how and why birds are named as they are. When Carolus Linnaeus developed a classification system for animals in 1758, a taxonomy evolved to inform us that, say, *Turdus*

Kirkpatrick sketching for Woodland Drawings, 2003.

Joey Kirkpatrick and Flora C. Mace

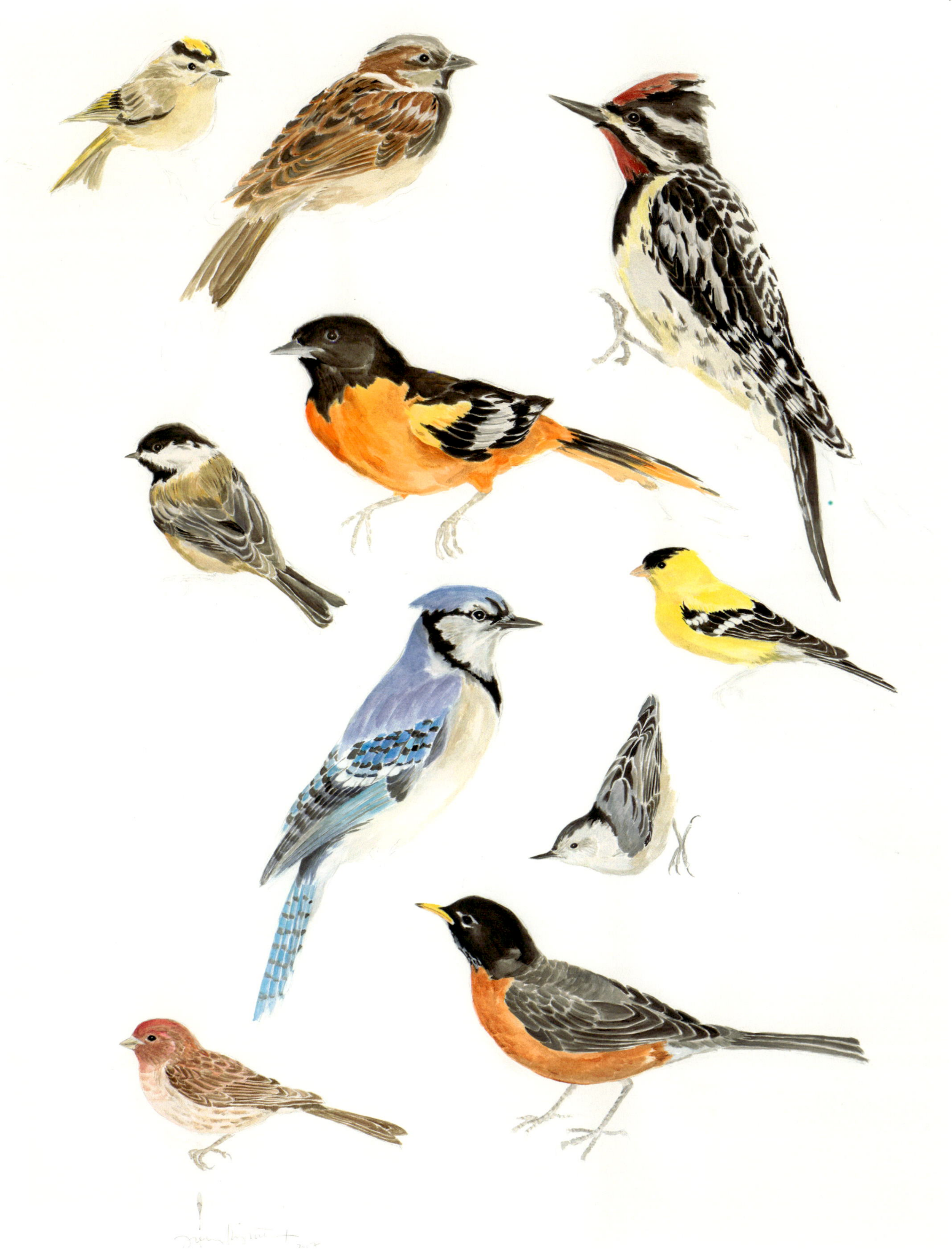

migratorius is an American robin and *Bubo scandiacus* is a snowy owl. The impulse to name things is a uniquely human endeavor. Paul Gruchow writes, "It is perhaps the quintessentially human characteristic that we cannot know or love what we have not named. Names are passwords to our hearts, and it is there, in the end, that we will find the room for a whole world."[17] In other words, a Cooper's hawk does not refer to itself as a hawk, let alone one named for William Cooper, an American naturalist. Even the serious birder's compulsion to keep track of sightings, in a life list, is a purely human preoccupation.

Kirkpatrick's sketches, with the attendant observations, led her and Mace to once again think about how they could translate Kirkpatrick's drawings into the translucent medium of glass. Mace likes to point out that glass is among the most obdurate of materials. Unlike paper, paint on canvas, metal, and even stone, glass, if unbroken, has the capacity to last millennia. Early explorations of applying a bird drawing onto glass involved a more traditional method of picking up a glass-powder drawing onto a clear-glass pitcher form, but the artists sought to present the bird drawings in a way that would more closely resemble works from the history of ornithological

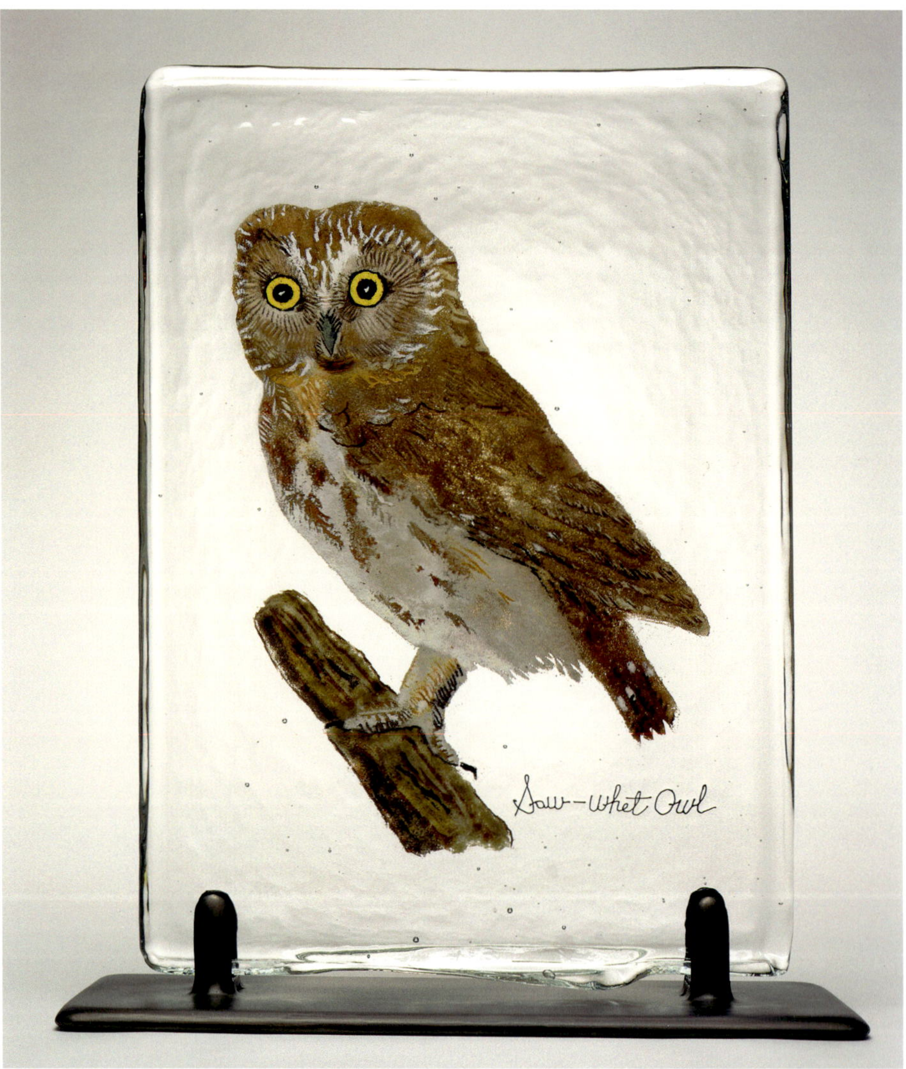

Bird Page: Saw-whet Owl, 2004
Glass and steel, 17½ × 14 × 6 inches

   Joey Kirkpatrick and Flora C. Mace

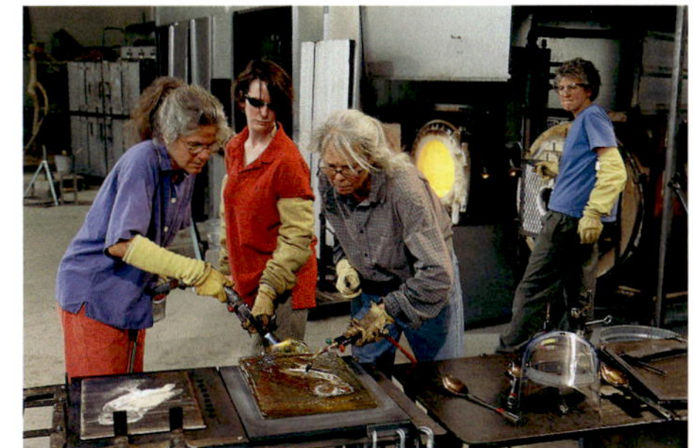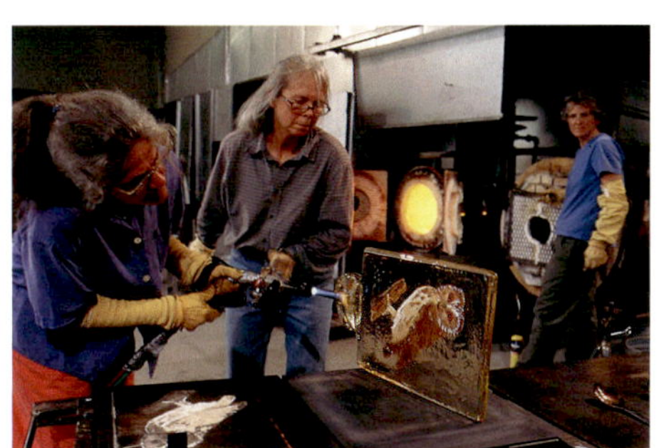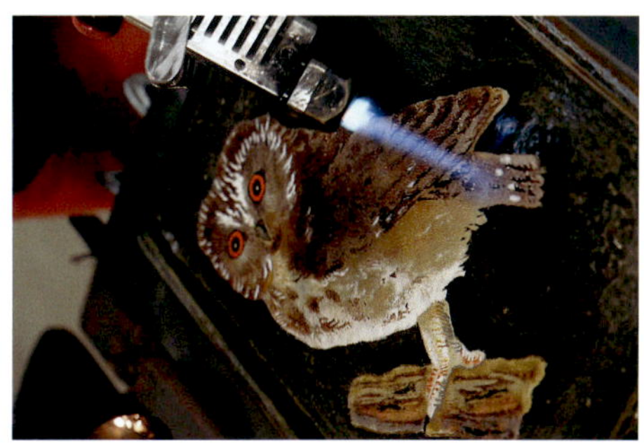

Making a *Bird Page:* Kirkpatrick and Mace working with Tracy Kirkpatrick, Paula Stokes, and Ann Welch, 2004.

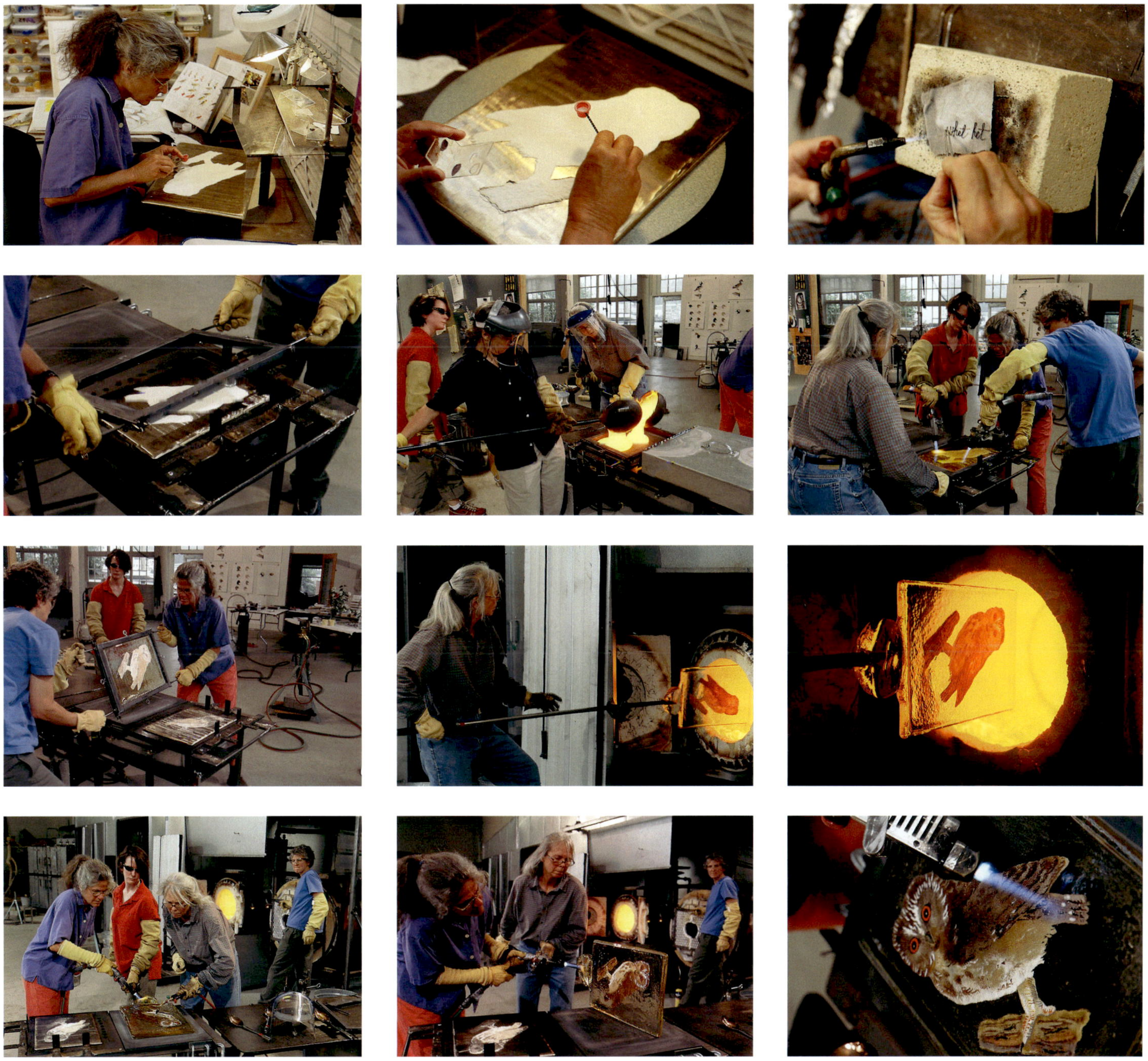

painting. How could Mace devise a method for transferring Kirkpatrick's bird drawings onto a glass "page"?

Each *Bird Page* began as a sketch on paper made by Kirkpatrick. One of the objectives of each *Bird Page* was to record the "first facts" of a species: the color, shape, size, and wing and head markings. A similar, but more subtle, goal was to evoke the *jizz* of the bird.[18] Jizz refers to the inherent but almost indefinable "isness" of a particular bird, the characteristics that allow a seasoned birder to identify a bird from a distance, even if the bird is in flight or perched in a tree, backlit by sunlight. It is "an inward fabric of characteristics which crystallise out in some unique and recognisable identity. . . . this subjective *feel* for the bird."[19]

Using her sketch as a guide, Kirkpatrick then drew a portrait of the bird in colored glass powder on a metal plate. Her method is similar to other forms of painting on glass (such as Eastern Orthodox glass icons) in that she would build her drawing in reverse, setting details and highlights of the drawing onto the plate first and ending with the larger shapes of color that would become the bird's body. Kirkpatrick used a tiny strainer the size of a thimble to sift glass powder onto the plate. Mace made her partner a set of tools that allowed Kirkpatrick to push the powder into lines and furrows to create the eye ring and supercilium, the scapulars, wing coverts, breast, belly, crown, and rump. This process was doubly tricky, as glass powders are similar to ceramic glazes in that the true color of the powder is not revealed until firing. To aid herself, Kirkpatrick employed her own sort of artist's field guide, a chart indicating the eventual hue and saturation after firing of each glass powder in her palette.

An important detail of each *Bird Page* is the inclusion of the bird's name in black cursive text, in reference to, and in continuation of, the tradition of the human impulse to designate appellations to the inhabitants of the natural world. To quote Alison Hawthorne Deming, "The process of naming has an evolution as well, inspiring a sense of renewal, of reaching to correct the inaccuracies of the past, of retelling the stories we live by."[20] The text identifiers were made by Mace, who used a hybrid form of lampworking to melt thin black-glass cane with a torch to scribe the bird's common name.

Once they readied several glass-powder drawings, Kirkpatrick and Mace fired up the hot shop. This process required that the partners were joined by other experienced glass artists to assist. After much experimentation, Mace devised a method by which she could form a clear glass "page" by ladling molten glass into a graphite frame of her own invention. The frame contained the hot glass in a rectangle, similar to the deckle that fences in pulp slurry in the making of a sheet of paper. In a single, swift, and deft motion, the frame filled with hot glass was placed on top of the dust drawing.[21] The process is exceedingly similar to printmaking, as the resulting *Bird Page* is essentially a monoprint (a single, unique impression made from pressing paper onto an image in ink). Once the dust drawing was adhered to the glass page, the frame was removed to reveal slightly undulating edges, reminiscent of the feathered edge of deckled paper. Even the way in which the clear glass pooled in the frame created tenuous, almost imperceptible ripples, so similar to the toothy ground of a sheet of paper.

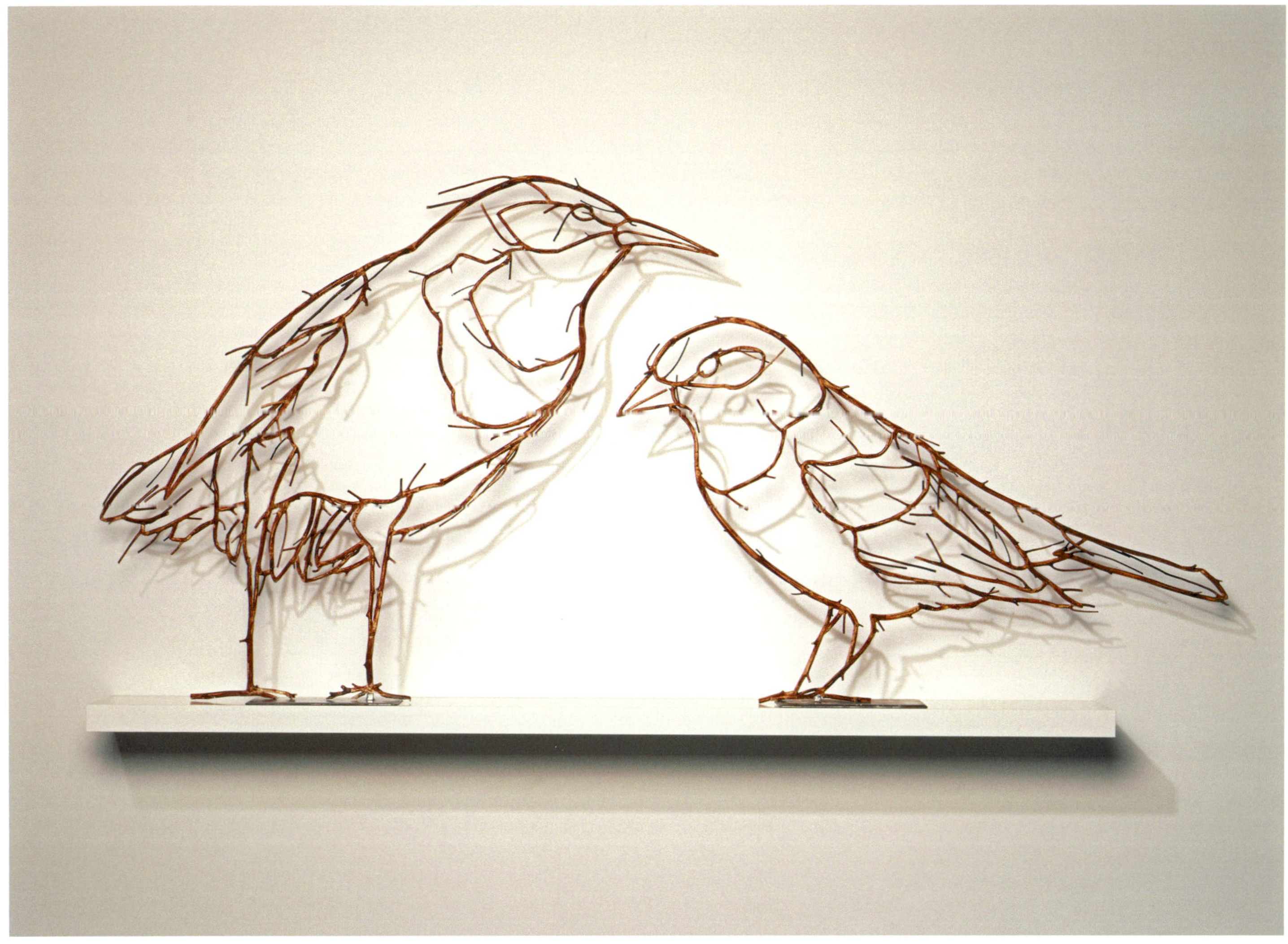

Each *Bird Page* had to be annealed in the kiln until cool. The artists did not really know how successful each *Bird Page* drawing was until it came out of the annealer, when the true colors of the glass powders became evident. For presentation, the finished *Bird Page* was mounted into a metal stand fabricated by Mace.

The artists started out making backyard birds, ones that they might see themselves, but the project grew into a much larger American anthology. Eventually, they created *Bird Pages* in homage to three extinguished birds: the passenger pigeon, the Carolina parakeet, and the ivory-billed woodpecker. In two instances, Mace's cane text included the word *extinct* in the names of the species.

Kirkpatrick and Mace loved the idea of making single *Bird Pages* that could then be grouped into larger bodies of work, suggesting their own interpretation of field guides. In all, they created ninety *Bird Pages*, a "portfolio" of bird likenesses that join the canon of ornithological illustration. Unlike drawings or prints on paper, the glass pages and the glass-dust drawings are translucid, imparting a luminosity that almost seems to originate within the page itself.

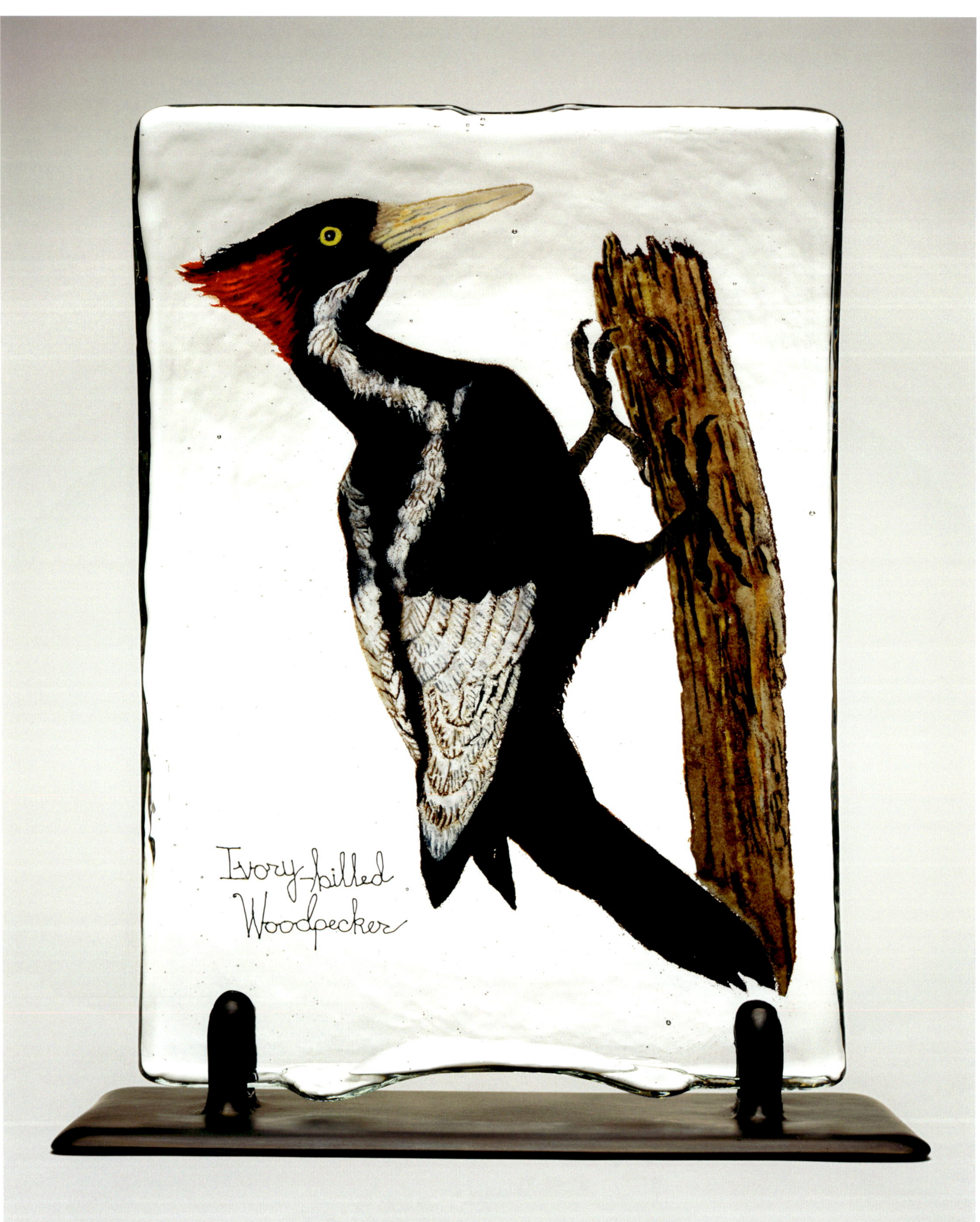

Ivory-billed
Woodpecker

"Drawing is a form of measuring rather than a way of naming."[22]

Concurrent with making the *Bird Pages*, Kirkpatrick and Mace were immersed in creating "drawings" of birds (and other objects) in three dimensions. In a series they came to call the *Woodland Drawings* (2000–2005, p. 51), once again the artists investigated the theme of drawing but in a form quite opposite to the *Bird Pages*.

Kirkpatrick and Mace have often been quoted as saying that glass, as seductive and beautiful a medium as it is, is not the answer to every query they encounter in their studio. Rather, once they commit to a concept, they are more interested in finding the right materials to express their ideas. Drawing remains an abiding interest for these artists, as does sculpture. As Mace has expressed, "Sculpture is just hundreds and hundreds of drawings." How might they further investigate the notion of drawing in a sculptural object?

The *Woodland Drawings* are deceptively simple and lyrical "line drawings" with the evocative immediacy of sketches. They are made using the same methods that Kirkpatrick and Mace employed in making earlier sculptures. The outline of a crow, an owl, or a wren is fabricated into a welded-steel armature. Other shapes in this series include suggestions of a tree stump or the trunk-like forms of human torsos. The artists then meticulously cover the framework in a skin of wood. Harvested from the forests around Pilchuck Glass School in Stanwood, young alder saplings are stripped, steamed, bent, and dried by Kirkpatrick and Mace to create a natural cladding for the steel frames. The alder tree bark is transmuted into the seamless "bark" of the sculpture by laboriously patching the natural material onto the elegant silhouette of the bird, stump, or torso. The magical effect is that of a natural form having been grown in nature of twigs and branches. There is a witty paradox to this arduous method as well: the life form represented is literally enveloped by "nature," a woodland form rendered as a drawing in wood.

> There is another alphabet
> Whispering from every leaf,
> Singing from every river,
> Shimmering from every sky.
>   —*Dejan Stojanović, "Forgotten Home"*[23]

The *Bird Pages: First Facts* and the *Woodland Drawings* influenced consequent series that further explore the theme of how humans intersect with nature. As artists, Kirkpatrick and Mace see their work's mission as a means to re-create or reinterpret the natural world in some way. In the same vein that the *Bird Pages* represent a compendium of field notes, the artists' *Alphabet* series is a visual syllabary prompted by the letters of the English alphabet.

Kirkpatrick and Mace created two series: *Alphabet of Animals* (2012, p. 55) and *Alphabet of Flowers* (2012, p. 54). In both, the organizing taxonomy is simply the twenty-six letters of the alphabet and a corresponding animal or flower whose name begins with each letter. Animal choices are purely visual and idiosyncratic. In the Kirkpatrick-Mace *Alphabet of Animals*, *C* for chicken and *Q* for quail are interspersed with *E* for elephant and *T* for tiger, mixing fowl and mammals. Zoo animals, like *G* for giraffe and *R* for rhinoceros,

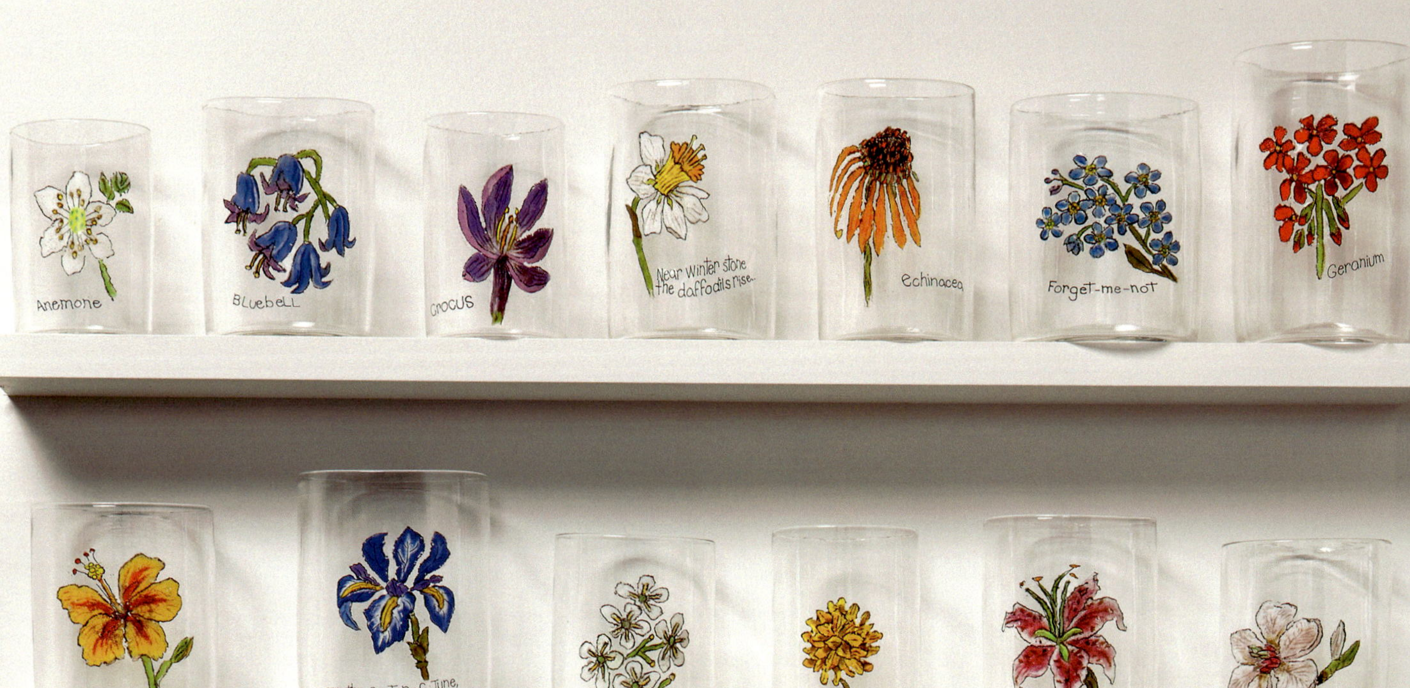

Anemone
Bluebell
Crocus
Near winter stone the daffodils rise...
Echinacea
Forget-me-not
Geranium

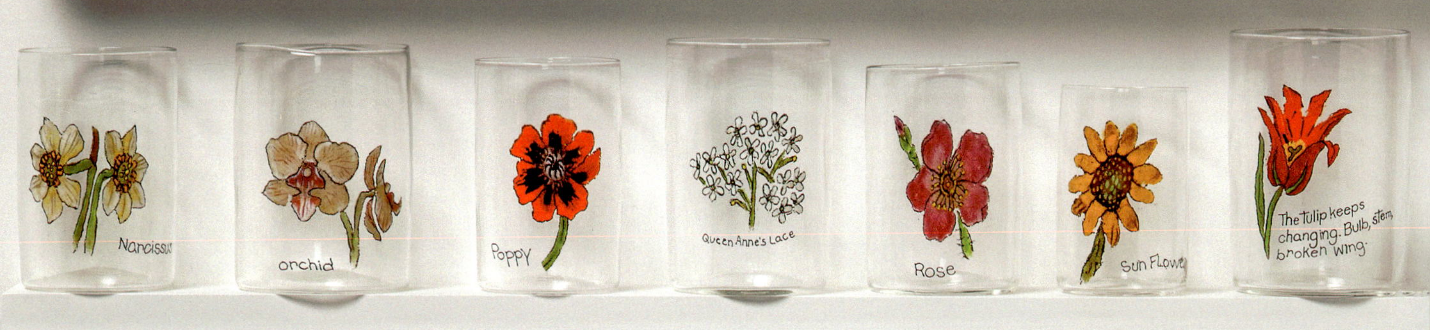

Hibiscus
In the center of June, the Iris quivering...
Jasmine
Kerria
Lily
Magnolia

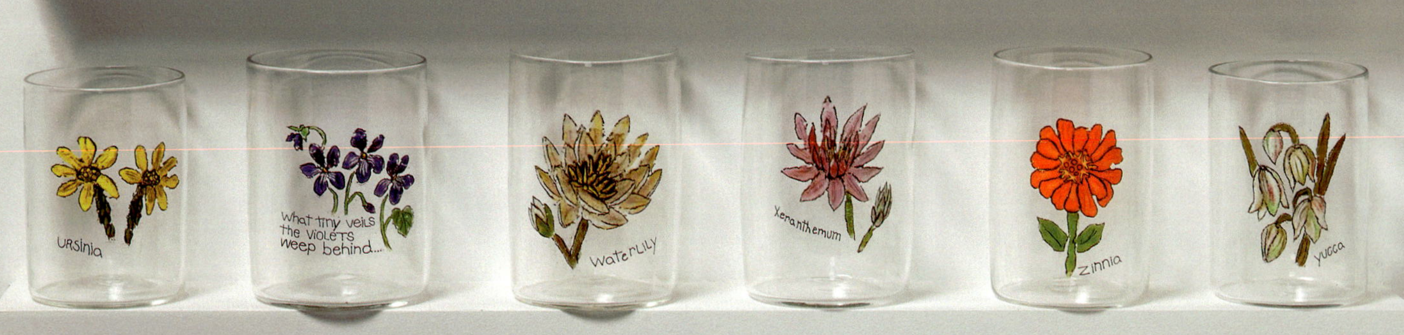

Narcissus
orchid
Poppy
Queen Anne's Lace
Rose
Sun Flower
The Tulip keeps changing. Bulb, stem, broken wing.
Ursinia
What tiny veils the violets weep behind...
Waterlily
Xeranthemum
Zinnia
Yucca

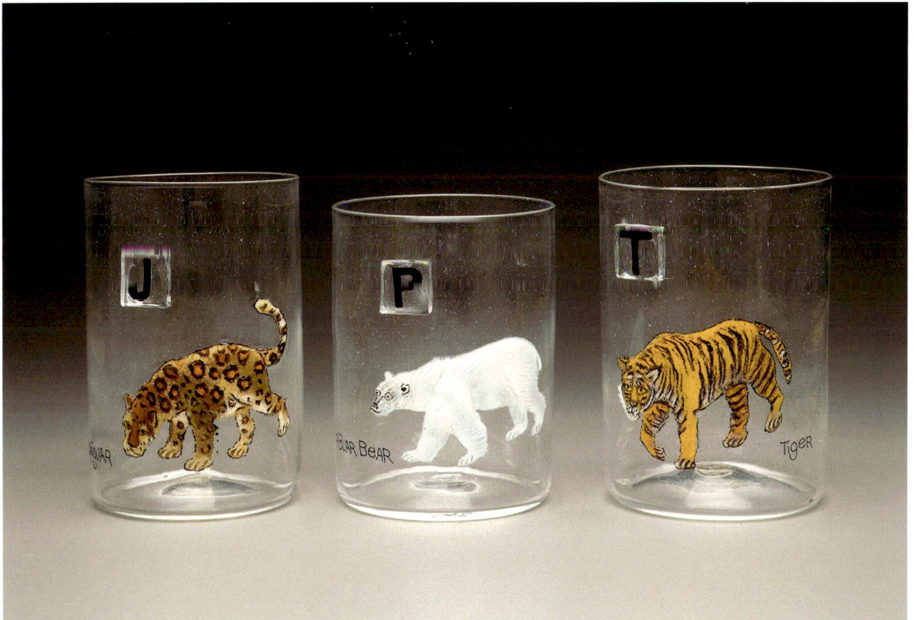

The Alphabet of Animals: Jaguar, Polar Bear, Tiger, 2009
Glass; jaguar: 9 × 5½ × 6 inches

intermingle with farm animals, *P* for pig and *S* for sheep. Even the nomenclature is irregular, as the *U* for uakari uses the common name for a New World monkey, while *X* for *Xerus* is a genus term for an African ground squirrel. The quirkiness of Kirkpatrick's and Mace's classification and the presence of the alphabet letter as a glass block applied to each vessel reference children's word games, flashcards, and lotto pieces.

The *Alphabet of Flowers* pairs letters with the names of flowering plants, anemone through zinnia. Again the illustrations are glass-powder drawings made by Kirkpatrick; pistils and stamens are detailed with thin, black-glass cane. Here Mace wrote the name of each blossom in black cane text, but for some specimens she alternatively scribed a short haiku-like poem written by Kirkpatrick's sister Patricia Kirkpatrick. The tulip is identified by "The tulip keeps/changing. Bulb, stem,/broken wing." Violets are described by "What tiny veils/the violets/weep behind," while the Dutchman's breeches reads "Yes, break my heart/but leave me/the Dutchman's breeches." The ground for the flowers (and the animals) is a clear-glass cylinder, a metaphoric container for the ideas and memories that humans assign to elements of the natural world.

Portraits from Fifty Acres, 2010–Present

At the center,
white pages, scarlet thread,
poet's narcissus.

    —Patricia Kirkpatrick

For most of Kirkpatrick's and Mace's careers, their work has investigated the intersection of human beings with nature. In their most recent bodies

The Alphabet of Flowers, 2012
Glass, 72 × 60 × 7½ inches

of work, the artists have turned their attention to nature itself, specifically flowers and trees.

In 2007, Kirkpatrick and Mace purchased a farm at Chimacum, near Port Townsend on the Olympic Peninsula of Washington. As the women pondered the fifty-acre property and how they intended to live on it, they became fascinated by the abundant botanical life now in their midst. In the process of clearing the land, the artists began to scrutinize the native plants, inspecting the most tender wild flowers to the stands of trees that parenthetically surround the farmstead. Mace, in particular, was entranced by the flowers, which led her to contemplate the history of plant collecting and herbaria as the predominant and traditional methodology for preserving plant life.[24]

The first herbarium is believed to have been established in 1570 in Bologna, Italy, by Luca Ghini.[25] Now there are around four thousand herbaria in the world, all in the pursuit of preserving plant life in some form of perpetuity. But despite more than four centuries of plant collecting, the time-honored method of pressing and drying botanical specimens has remained largely unaltered. The problem, of course, is that in the preparation for mounting a specimen much of the visual allurement of the plant is lost. The pressing completely flattens the cutting, so that the composition of root system, stems, leaves, and flowers is compromised. Moreover, regardless of how riotous the color of a blossom might be in life, nature's palette is vulnerable and fugitive. Herbaria specimens turn varying shades of ecru and brown, and the true hues of the flower and foliage are forever lost.

Mace, who has the heart of a sculptor, was curious about whether there could be another means to preserve botanical life, a method that would both preserve the physical structure of the plant in three dimensions as well as arrest the colors of the plant in full flower. Mace is also a tinkerer. Traditionally, her partnership with Kirkpatrick has involved their collaboration on a work of art. The concept is likely to have been driven by Kirkpatrick, while Mace resolves the technical challenges of manifesting their vision. (Many

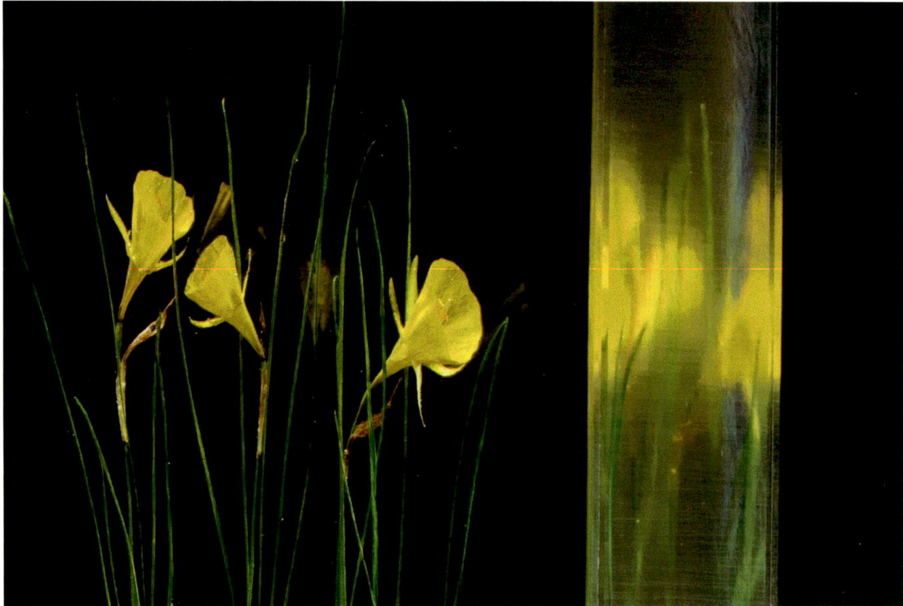

Hoop-petticoat Daffodil (detail), 2015
Flower, composite, glass, and steel, 18½ × 17 × 6 inches

Joey Kirkpatrick and Flora C. Mace

series exemplify this, but the *Bird Pages* series is a good example of Kirkpatrick making drawings that Mace then figured out how to engineer into a joint finished work in the studio, often by innovating tools or mechanisms needed to actualize their concept.)

Mace discovered an alternative method for preserving blossoms by drying them in oolitic sand gathered from Utah's Great Salt Lake. This, remarkably, stabilizes the colors of a plant. In order to re-present the flower as it once grew in nature, Mace must literally deconstruct the specimen, dry its components, and then reassemble the parts. The success of this regeneration has everything to do with Mace's visual acuity as an artist. She has to rely on her own ability to scrupulously inculcate herself in the plant's structure by observing it first in life.

Once the plant is desiccated and reconstructed, Mace devises a complex system for suspending the plant in a frame, while she slowly, arduously, captures the plant within layers and layers of composite and glass. This is a laborious process, as it takes enormous amounts of time and hand workmanship to patiently encapsulate the specimen so that it will appear frozen in time and space. An additional challenge to Mace's process is that she must wait until the specimens that she wishes to use are at their prime. This means that she has a very narrow window each year in which to harvest the specimens that she will work on for the following months.

The experience of viewing one of Mace's *Botanicals* (p. 59) is nothing short of beguiling. The effect is as if Mace has simultaneously slowed down time and placed the specimen under a microscope for the sheer pleasure of viewing it, so wholly focused is one's view of the organism. It also seems as if the specimen is housed within its own microcosm, not so much because the plant is encased in composite and glass but more because it is presented to the viewer in a way in which one rarely ever experiences a plant in toto, removed from the soil that once stabilized it and separated from the rest of its plant community. The interplay between the root system, occasional bulb, stem, leaves, peduncles and pedicels, and blossoms is somehow both lyrically calligraphic and statuesque.

To date, Mace has accumulated an extraordinary herbarium of her own, having collected and "mounted" more than twenty different specimens. Included in her botanical collection are the *Narcissus poeticus* (poet's daffodil) and *Narcissus bulbocodium* (hoop-petticoat daffodil), twinflower, gloxinia, violets, pansies, tiger lilies, iris, fritillaria, ferns, lily of the valley, carnivorous pitcher plants, shooting star, and trillium. Not every species has cooperated successfully with Mace's methods: tulips and magnolias have remained intractable.[26] But Mace is also headstrong. Part of her joy in making has to do with solving seemingly insurmountable challenges.

The *Botanicals* are each mounted in a steel stand devised by Mace. The resulting works in the *Botanicals* series are signed jointly by Mace and Kirkpatrick, as Kirkpatrick is also involved in the strenuous processes to rebirth a fragile plant as a lasting sculpture.[27]

The haiku and the object poem are usually written away from the writer's desk, and in the presence of the object. Basho said, "If you want to know

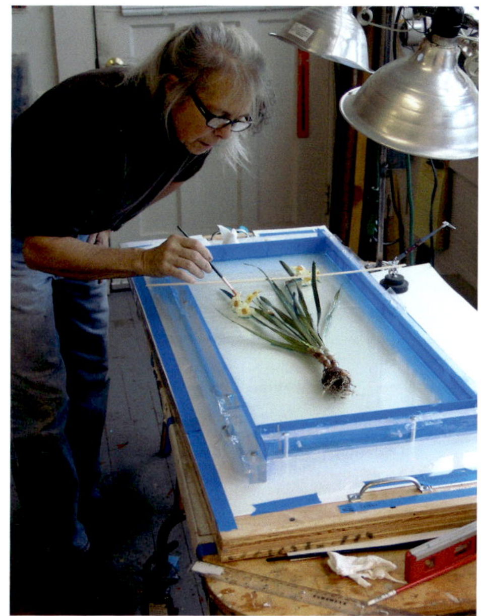

Mace preparing a botanical specimen prior to encasement in composite and glass, 2014.

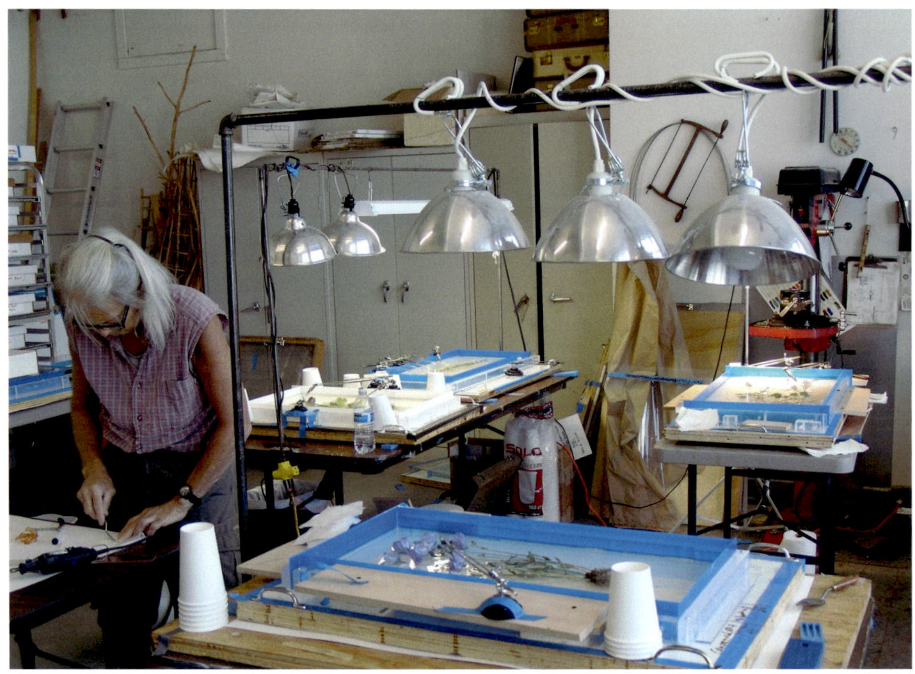

about the bamboo go to the bamboo; if you want to know about the pine, go to the pine." Emerson drew from Coleridge the idea that "every object rightly seen unlocks a new faculty of the Soul." The Buddhists would like Emerson's "rightly." When a human mind honors a stump, for example, by giving it human attention in the right way, something in the soul is released; and often through the stump we receive information we wouldn't have received by thinking or by fantasy.

—*Robert Bly*[28]

While Mace's attention focused on blossoms, first those around their Chimacum home and then later broadening to include all sorts of flora, Kirkpatrick's creative process took her in a different direction. Again in the process of clearing their land, the couple had to fell a number of ancient trees. A lone incense-cedar stump found its way into Kirkpatrick's drawing studio, a respectful memento of sorts in honor of the tree that once stood sentinel on their property. Kirkpatrick loves nothing more than drawing *sur le motif*. She began to draw the incense cedar in the almost automatic way that an artist given to drawing is compelled to do. She became fascinated with the depth of color and textures within the wood, the furrowed and fibrous cinnamon-colored bark, and the fine-grained heartwood.

Kirkpatrick soon assembled other cords of wood and arranged them, most often in quaternary still lifes, in which she could juxtapose the infinite variety. In her *Cordwood Paintings* (p. 61), papery white birch might oppose the lenticular bark of cherry or the scales and plates of brawnier trunks of oak, ash, and maple. Dapples of silvery lichen or patches of fading green moss cling to some logs but not others. Kirkpatrick's eye delights in the gnarly cuffs left by branches long lopped off and the dendrochronology evidenced by tree rings, nature's own line drawings.

As much as Kirkpatrick painted the cordwood arrangements as still lifes, she also perceived that her paintings on paper shared something with

Joey Kirkpatrick and Flora C. Mace

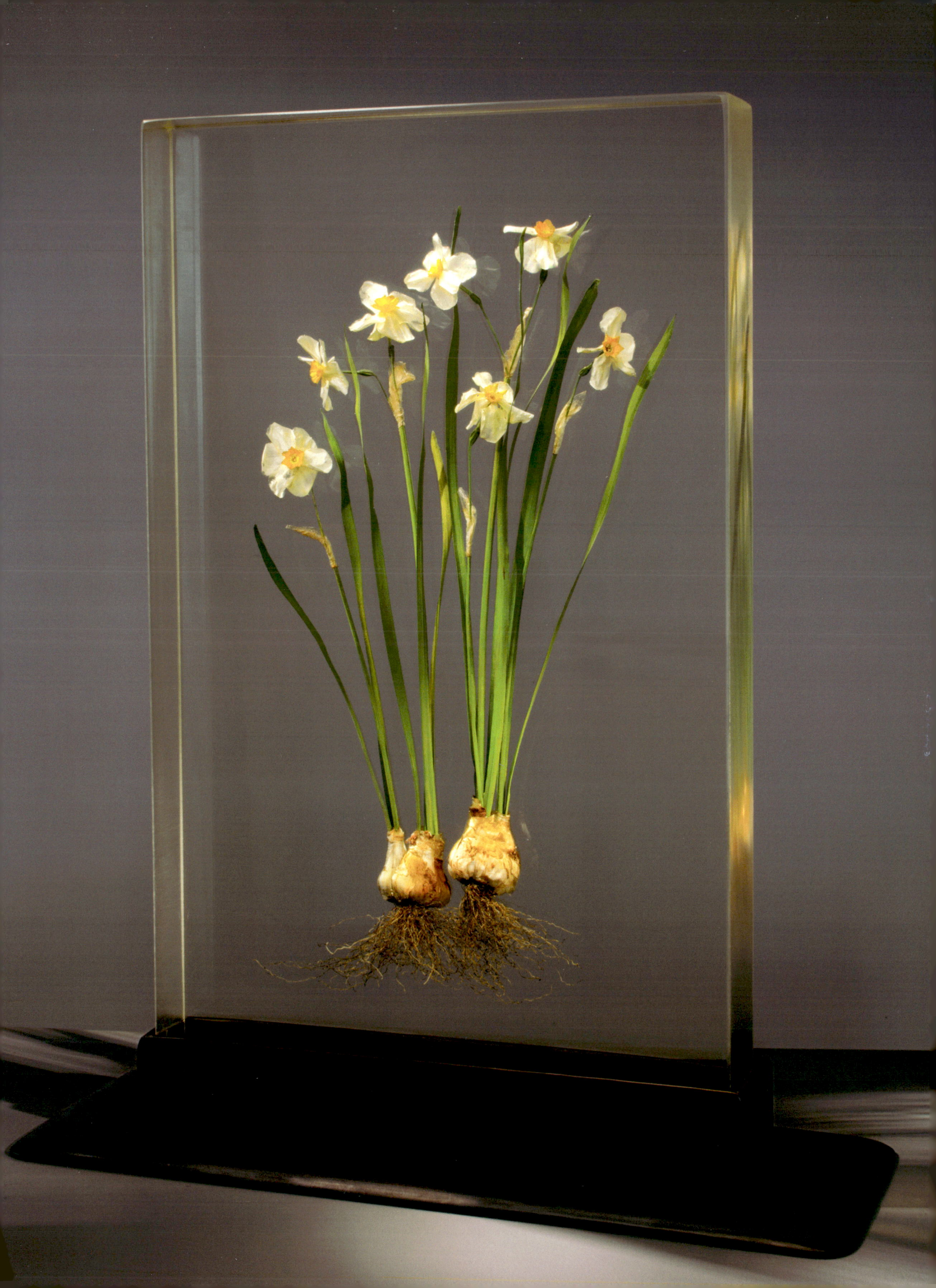

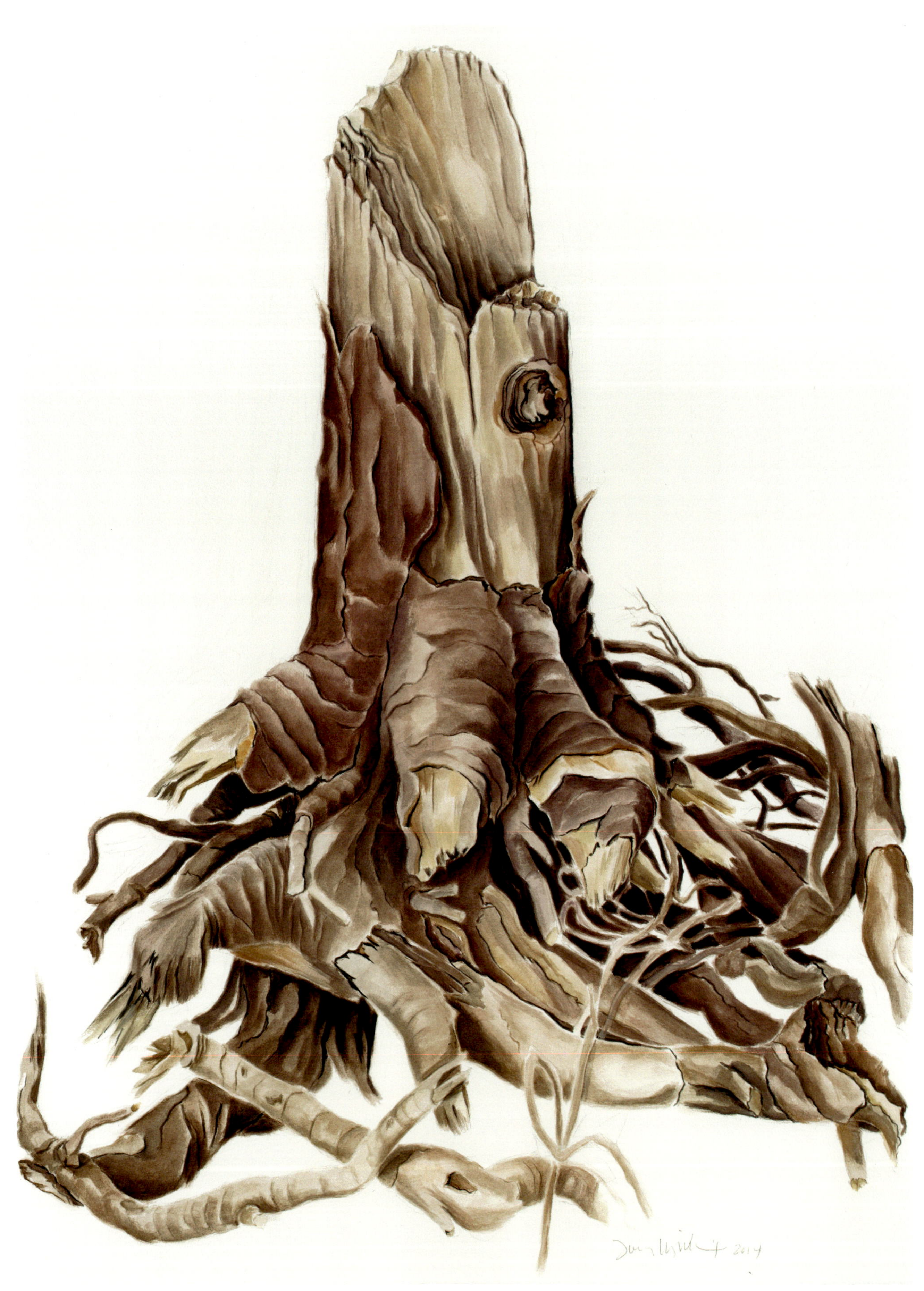

portraiture. The activity of painting the wood allowed her to look intensely at her subject, while capturing the essence of the wood's character and personality in her experience of painting it. In this practice, she shares her approach with the "portraits" Giorgio Morandi painted of bottles and jars. Of Morandi, Gottfried Boehm said: "Nature did not prescribe an order but art was to create or fathom one through its possibilities and visual approaches. Order is neither invented or imagined, it results from the act of contemplation."[29] This is a maxim embraced by Kirkpatrick in her ongoing investigations of wood.

Perhaps in response to Mace's *Botanicals*, in which bulbs and roots are considered to be as intrinsically beautiful in their frazzled bundles as the blossoms themselves, Kirkpatrick has most recently begun to paint tree-root systems. It is characteristic of Kirkpatrick to discover the allure of an aspect of nature that is typically hidden or unobserved. In the tree-root paintings, Kirkpatrick arrests the maniacal tangle of a tree's massive root colony, ruptured from its security in the earth. She also respects the almost animistic spirit of the once-living specimen.

Embracing the Natural World

I took it [an etching of apple trees] into the orchard and compared it with the trees. Then I saw that the artist had simplified and made more evident certain characteristics of the trees themselves—once more a matter of composition—and I improvised a definition of art: that it is nature seen in the light of its significance. Then, recognizing that this significance was one of forms . . .

    —*Leo Stein*[30]

There are many threads that weave through the work of Kirkpatrick and Mace. In academic terms, there are the leitmotifs of drawing and how drawing might be expressed in traditional and nontraditional ways—in two dimensions but also, with tremendous fluidity, in three dimensions. From the earliest wire drawing cylinders through over-life-size figurative sculpture to *Bird Pages*, *Botanicals*, and *Cordwood Paintings*, and virtually every work in their oeuvre in between, the mark of the artists has remained preeminent and singular.

A second motive—and motif—has been the plenitude of nature. These artists, assiduous and indefatigable observers of the world, have embraced the natural world, and how humans move through that world, as the wellspring for inspiration. What they see and contemplate transmutes into what they create. Just as Jasper Johns spoke of "things the mind already knows,"[31] enabling the viewer to ask *why* instead of *what*, Kirkpatrick and Mace offer the viewer insights into the realm of human experience by focusing on flora, fauna, vessels, the figure, and language. The quotidian, in their hands, becomes sublime.

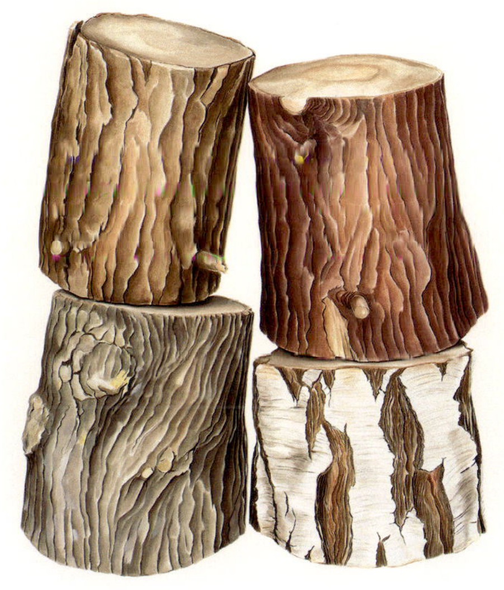

Joey Kirkpatrick, **Cordwood 4: Cherry I**, 2012
Graphite and casein on paper, 51½ × 40 inches

Joey Kirkpatrick, **Root I**, 2014
Graphite and casein on paper, 40 × 28 inches

Notes

1   For a discussion of Dale Chihuly's *Irish Cylinders*, see Donald Kuspit and Kathryn Kanjo, *Chihuly: The George R. Stroemple Collection* (Portland, Oregon: Portland Art Museum, 1997). Both Kirkpatrick and Mace have continued to work with Chihuly on special projects incorporating cane drawings.

2   Lenore Tawney (1907–2007) and Claire Zeisler (1903–1991) were both former students at the Institute of Design (previously the New Bauhaus), Chicago, studying under Alexander Archipenko and László Moholy-Nagy. Interestingly, both Tawney and Zeisler explored a traditional craft medium—in this case fiber arts—and transcended tradition by eventually working in freestanding sculpture. In this regard, Tawney's and Zeisler's careers have a certain parallel to Kirkpatrick's and Mace's.

3   John Kobler, "The Torment of Alberto Giacometti," *The Saturday Evening Post* 238, no. 15 (July 31, 1965), pp. 68–71.

4   In preparation for writing this essay, I spoke with the artists on several occasions from 2004 through 2015. In this essay, if one of the artists is mentioned as having provided specific information but no note appears, these conversations were my source.

5   Japan now celebrates May 5 as Children's Day.

6   Plique-à-jour translates loosely as "light of day." Often called *backless cloisonné*, the technique refers to the art of placing enamel within cells of metal wire that do not have any metal backing, so that light can shine through the artwork and create a translucent stained-glass effect.

7   1984.

8   Patterson Sims has written that the facial features of the glass head sculptures are a portrait of Mace. This is true only in the sense that Kirkpatrick observed Mace as a reference in drawing the human face. There was no intent to create a face with any specificity; in fact, Kirkpatrick says that the opposite was the goal. Sims also suggested that the human-headed hollow-glass tube sculptures derive from the shape of the long globular-headed kelp found along the Northwest coast. This understandably convincing reference likewise was not an intention of the artists. *Figures of Translucence*, Documents Northwest: The PONCHO Series brochure (Seattle: Seattle Art Museum, 1989).

9   Mark Doty, "An Easel beside the Marsh: Poetry and the Landscape Painter's Art," in *Lyrical Landscapes*, by Doty and Ann Finholt (Hartford, Conn.: Widener Gallery, Trinity College, 2003), p. 6.

When Kirkpatrick returned to Des Moines following graduation, she met poet Mark Doty when they both worked at a local daycare center. Years later, in 2005, Kirkpatrick and Doty were reconnected through Kirkpatrick's sister, poet Patricia Kirkpatrick.

10   Lucy R. Lippard, *Overlay: Contemporary Art and the Art of Prehistory* (New York: New Press, 1983), p. 4.

11   In the case of *Limbed Tumbrel*, the human-like form is crafted from the limbs of a tree. The word *tumbrel* is an archaic term for a handcart, suggesting that the entire sculpture "carries" content, demonstrating how carefully these artists ponder language and how a title might enforce the conceptual bearings of a piece.

12   John Berger, "To Take Paper, to Draw: A World through Lines," in *Drawing Us In: How We Experience Visual Art*, ed. Deborah Chasman and Edna Chiang (Boston: Beacon Press, 2000), p. 120.

13   Translated from a letter quoted by Joachim Gasquet, *Cézanne* (Paris: Éditions Bernheim-Jeune, 1926, p. 202) in *Corot to Braque: French Paintings from the Museum of Fine Arts, Boston* (Boston: Museum of Fine Arts, 1979), p. 84.

14   In 1993, William Morris completed his masterpiece installation *Cache*, which required that he blow replicas of elephant tusks that measure up to six feet across. This scale represents a remarkable achievement in blowing and sculpting glass.

15   Kirkpatrick and Mace were also artists-in-residence at Pilchuck in 1980, 1987, and 2001, and they were artist-in-residence assistants in 1984. During their years at Pilchuck, they worked with other contemporary artists such as Lynda Benglis, Judy Pfaff, Italo Scanga, John Torreano, and Christopher Wilmarth.

16   The term *zanfirico* is a corruption of the name of a nineteenth-century Venetian antiquarian, Antonio Sanquirico, who commissioned copies of eighteenth-century filigree vessels, which he nefariously passed off as authentic antiques.

Joey Kirkpatrick and Flora C. Mace

17 Paul Gruchow, *Grass Roots: The Universe of Home* (Minneapolis: Milkweed Editions, 1995), p. 130.

18 The etymology of the word *jizz* is likely a corruption of GISS (general impression of size and shape), a concept created by British plane spotters during World War II to distinguish enemy from friendly aircraft.

19 Mark Cocker, *Birders: Tales of a Tribe* (New York: Grove Press, 2001), p. 86.

20 Alison Hawthorne Deming, *Temporary Homelands: Essays on Nature, Spirit, and Place* (New York: Picador USA, 1994), p. 115.

21 To view a video of a *Bird Page* being made, see http://www.kirkpatrick-mace.com.

22 John Yau, *James Castle: The Common Place* (New York: Knoedler & Company, 2001), p. 22, paraphrasing Betty Andrews, *Drawing on the Right Side of the Brain* (New York, Penguin Putnam, 1979, 1989, 1999).

23 Excerpt from Dejan Stojanović's poem "Forgotten Home," *PoemHunter*, http://www.poemhunter.com/poem/forgottenhome/.

24 Mace was sixty when her obsession with flower preservation began, which is fairly late in the life of an artist to embark on wholly new bodies of work. In this, Mace's fascination is similar to that of Mary Granville Pendarves Delany, who at the age of seventy-two took up mixed media (cut paper) collage to amass an "herbarium" of botanical "portraits."

25 University of Florida Herbarium, Gainesville, "Herbaria and Herbarium Specimens," http://www.flmnh.ufl.edu/herbarium/herbariaandspecimens.

26 Some of the challenges Mace faces are plants with different densities of stems, leaves, and petals, which create variable drying times; "meaty" leaves, such as those found on some orchids, don't dry as well. Size is also a factor: larger specimens are harder to dig up while preserving the entire root system.

27 Kirkpatrick's and Mace's *Botanicals* join the centuries-old tradition of capturing botanical specimens as natural history artifacts. Besides preserving plants in herbaria, with the attendant challenges of stabilizing composition and color, there are hundreds of artists throughout the history of art who have sought to safeguard plant specimens in painting (Franz and Ferdinand Bauer, Pierre-Joseph Redouté, Maria Sibylla Merian, among many, many others) and photography (Karl Blossfeldt, Robert Mapplethorpe, and Ron van Dongen, among many, many others). Even today Kew Gardens (Royal Botanic Gardens), outside London, commissions about one hundred botanical illustrations annually.

It is obviously much more challenging to present a plant likeness in sculpture. Best known are the Leopold and Rudolf Blaschka "Glass Flowers" in the Ware Collection of Blaschka Glass Models of Plants at the Harvard Museum of Natural History, Cambridge. But contemporary efforts exist as well. Pacific Northwest artist Dan Webb's oeuvre includes three-dimensional representations of dandelions in bronze, cast rubber, and wood (*Night Dandy*, *Rubber Dandy*, and *Woodylion*), although preservation is not the aim of these works. Japanese filmmaker Takao Inoue has also arrested the fragile dandelion in his whimsical *Tampopo* OLED lamps and objets d'art in which real seed heads are encapsulated in acrylic. Korean contemporary photographer Sung Soo Koo has developed a series of botanical photographs he calls *Photogenic Drawings*, some of which are photographs of specimens, dug up to include the root system, as Mace does, but Koo's plants are then sandwiched and flattened between sheets of glass before he photographs them. Koo's work mines issues of artifice as well. Some of his *Photogenic Drawings* are actually photographs of artificial plants that he and his studio assistants crafted in ceramic and painted to look like real specimens. I do not know of any contemporary artist other than Kirkpatrick and Mace who seek to preserve actual botanical specimens as a sculptural lexicon of plant forms.

28 Robert Bly, "The Prose Poem As an Evolving Form," *Selected Poems* (New York: Harper & Row, 1986), p. 201.

29 Gottfried Boehm, "Giorgio Morandi's Artistic Concept," in *Giorgio Morandi: Painting, Watercolours, Drawings, Etchings*, ed. Ernst-Gerhard Güse and Franz Armin Morat, trans. Almuth Seebohm (Munich: Prestel, 1999), p. 14.

30 Leo Stein, "On Reading Poetry and Seeing Pictures," *Appreciation: Painting, Poetry, and Prose* (New York: Crown Publishers, 1947), p. 102.

31 Leo Steinberg, "Jasper Johns: The First Seven Years of His Art," in *Other Criteria: Confrontations with Twentieth-Century Art* (New York: Oxford University Press, 1972), p. 31.

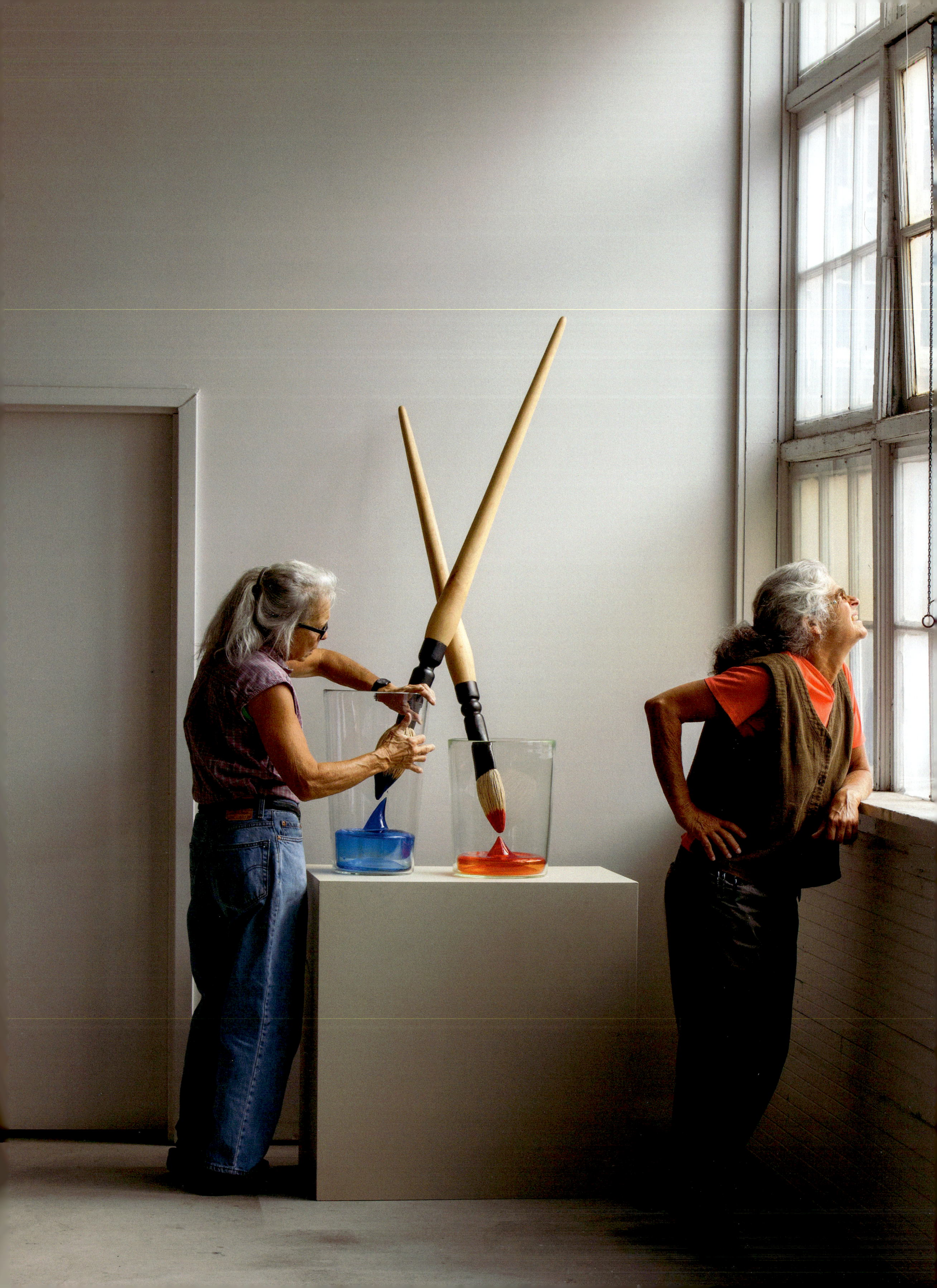

Patricia Kirkpatrick

A Way Is Found

*An Interview with Artists Joey Kirkpatrick
and Flora C. Mace*

The first four of the six text sections that follow were compiled and edited
from a series of conversations I recorded with Flora C. Mace and Joey Kirkpatrick, my sister, between 2008 and 2010. Some conversations took place
with both artists; some took place with Flora alone, and others with Joey
alone. For the first section, "Introduction: A Conversation," the artist Paula
Stokes, who came to work with Joey and Flora in 1993 and assisted them
occasionally over sixteen years, joined the three of us. All conversations took
place at the Kirkpatrick and Mace Canal Street Studio in Seattle, where Joey
and Flora have worked since 2000. At the studio, we sat upstairs in the space
Joey describes as "part library, painting studio, and contemplation room,"
which overlooks the canal between Lake Union and Puget Sound. All kinds of
pleasure and working boats passed on the canal outside, where mergansers
and cormorants swam and poked in and out of the water. The final section
of the interview, "First Facts: Birds and Flowers," comes from discussions we
had in 2015 at the artists' home in Chimacum on Washington's Olympic Peninsula, as well as in email and written correspondence.

1 *Introduction: A Conversation*

PK   Joey, the story goes that when you decided to move from Iowa, you saw an
ad for Pilchuck Glass School in an art magazine and decided to go there. When you
arrived at Pilchuck, you showed your drawings to Dale Chihuly, and he said, "Go
see Flora." Flora looked at your drawings and said to herself, "It will take her ten
years to figure this out." Luckily, when the two of you got together, it didn't take
ten years to figure out how to put drawings on glass.

FM   Joey had to learn to reinvent her drawing technique using wire on glass
instead of pencil on paper.

PK   So the two of you began to collaborate. You came from very different back-
grounds. Joey, you saw yourself as an artist, studied drawing and painting, and
only recently had begun to work with glass. Flora, you were a sculptor, blew glass,
and already had made significant aesthetic and technical achievements in contemporary studio glass.

JK   Flora was a great glassblower when we met. I was attracted to glass, had done some glassblowing, but also had reservations about it. When we started working together, and especially when we taught together, I sometimes introduced myself as somebody who didn't particularly like glass because it's beautiful no matter what you do to it. It's easy to get caught up in the beauty. Gather it up and drop it on the ground, it's still beautiful. It's too facile, too seductive as a material.

In the '80s, a lot of people didn't have the vocabulary to talk about glass as art. People who did wouldn't look our way because our work was glass. Sometimes the people who wrote about glass in the newspaper were borrowed from the food section. That just perpetuated a separation between *art* and *craft*, with glass placed somewhere in between.

FM   Sometimes the less you know about something, the less you know the rules, the less you worry about breaking them. And you don't know what's been done before. That's probably why working in glass was so much fun for us.

JK   Our first pieces together broke the rules that metal and glass are completely incompatible, for example. But we didn't know that that was against the rules.

FM   And we didn't care.

PK   So material, craft, art. How do they all fit together?

JK   One time I was in the Matisse room at the Museum of Modern Art in New York. Of course things have changed now, and you can't look from the Modern to the American Craft Museum. But at the time, Flora and I were standing at the window, and we could look across the street and see one of our pieces in the window of the Craft Museum. As I'm telling the story now, I'm not sure why it was so thrilling, but it was a thrill. Remember that, Flo?

FM   Yes, the way the windows were placed made it seem that both museums were in the same building, and our work was already there in MoMA.

PK   I can picture you both standing there. And it makes me turn to you, Paula Stokes, sitting here with us. You grew up in Ireland, have lived now in the United States for many years, and over the years have worked with Joey and Flora in the hot shop. What's American about Joey and Flora?

PS   I'd say their pioneering spirit.

PK   What have they pioneered? How is that spirit reflected in their work?

PS   It shows up in their subject matter, their forms. Glass, in terms of how contemporary artists are using it, is a relatively new phenomenon and has been perpetuated by this orgy of virtuosity and making fabulously crafted work. But Joey and Flora don't just make beautiful objects. They are devoted to the process of making art. They're masters of the technical aspects of their materials. If you're a master inside the lines, it takes a leap of faith to push outside the lines. Joey and Flora take that leap of faith.

They have also been great mentors. They have a sense of professionalism and integrity. They're honest. They're generous. But when you work for them, you have to work incredibly hard.

   Joey Kirkpatrick and Flora C. Mace

FM   Paula's right about how people want to make beautiful things. Well, Venetians did beautiful glass, Swedes did beautiful glass, but there's already a history of beautiful glass. It's how you take your personal vocabulary, and integrate that with your skill, that matters.

2 *Canal Street Studio*

PK   How often are you in the studio? Nine to five, five days a week?

FM   Well, it's probably closer to ten hours a day, seven days a week.

JK   If we're in Seattle, we come to the studio. It isn't even something we make a decision about.

PK   Do you have other people around when you're in the studio here in Seattle? Do you have companions, literally or figuratively?

FM   No, no one. Most of the time I'd like to keep the front door closed. I don't want to be disturbed here.

PK   What would you say, Joey?

JK   If you mean literally, on occasion we have people who work with us: our sister Tracy and Paula Stokes, or our friend Ann Welch. We found this studio space that happened to be next door to these yellow tugboats of the Western Tugboat Company. During the ten previous years when we had the Yale Street studio, I often came over here to sit outside and paint those tugboats. So we're also surrounded by men and women who are making boats and manipulating materials the way we do. But, generally, we're in the studio by ourselves. Flora and I can both work alone here. Our creativity isn't connected to each other every minute.

PK   What about influences here? I've heard you both refer to Italo. Who's Italo?

JK   Italo Scanga was a sculptor, born in Italy, who lived most of his life in the U.S. We met him through Dale Chihuly: they were dear friends. We worked with Italo for many years. With everything he did—cooking, painting, socializing—there was art involved somehow. He took imagery from all parts of life—music, history, religion—and made it his own. He gave me the permission to use imagery from daily life as my palette.

FM   He would say, "You don't think art into existence: you make it." In the time you spend thinking, you could have already completed a piece. Italo's with us every day, teasing us, inspiring us. He's definitely our muse.

PK   Joey, what is your creative process?

JK   The components, for me, are drawing, thinking, reading. I can't get anywhere without using a pencil and making a drawing. A lot of my work is informed by what I read. Also listening to music: Abbey Lincoln, Betty Carter, Laura Nyro. And the natural world. I'd probably include being on the water in that list. So much of our work is about how people are in relationship to nature.

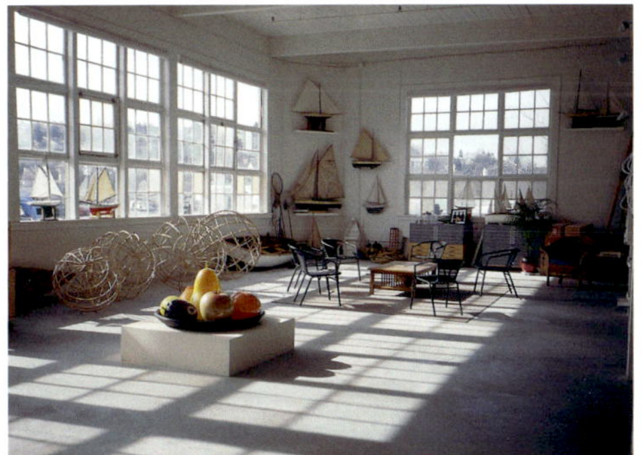

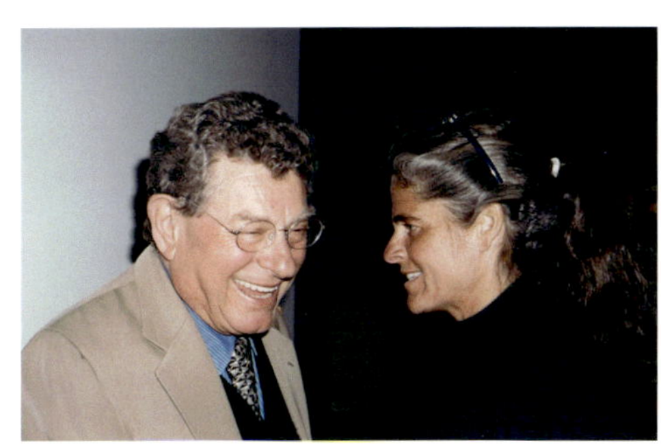

Kirkpatrick and Mace studio, Seattle, 2014.

Italo Scanga with Kirkpatrick, 2002.

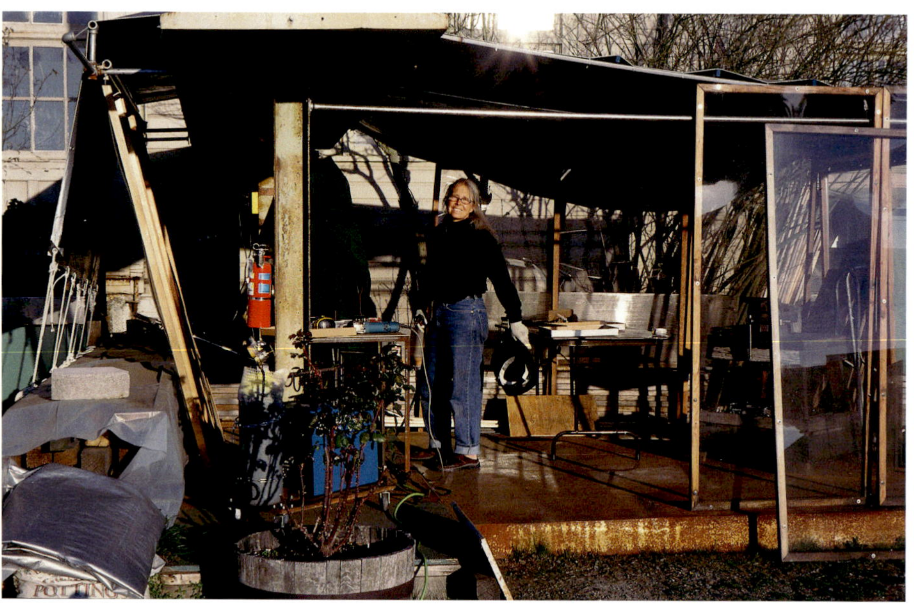

Also, writing in notebooks. For the most part they aren't journals but a sort of ongoing register of my reading. Usually, I read a book, mark it, then go back through it and take notes to organize my thinking. I like to write words down, because I'm usually the one who titles our work. A lot of it is taking words out of books and then almost recomposing and building words on a page until I get a title together.

PK   Flora, most of today you've been standing outside in a little canvas shed you built, facing the canal, grinding metal, sometimes looking up to migrating birds. What do you think about when you're out there with sparks flying?

FM   It depends. So many times when I'm making something, designing something—if I can let my mind run, it's a little bit like daydreaming. All of a sudden something will come to me, and I'll wonder where that came from. It's kind of a vision that hangs in space. It's that one note that does it. Or that little tool I pick up or that little line I draw. Whether it's falling in love or fishing or . . . it's all about patience. All of a sudden it's there, and, if you're ready to see it or hear it, it creates the whole composition. It's the very small part that makes the very big thing.

PK   So walking on the beach or reading a book doesn't help you figure it out?

FM   No. I can get inspired going someplace else. But the reality for me is that the work happens when I'm in the studio. If I go on vacation, I almost have to tune out. Because I get really frustrated if I want to make something and I don't have my tools. Joey can pick up a pencil and draw. I need to pick up cardboard, wire, steel and make something.

JK   Darn. I was hoping the answer would be that she could figure it out while walking on the beach!

FM   I need my tools. When I first met Joey, I was afraid that if we bought tools together I'd have the problem of knowing which were hers and which were mine. Now I've solved that. I get two of everything. I've learned how to fix tools, but if I'm working on something and a tool does not work, I am beside myself.

                                                                                       Joey Kirkpatrick and Flora C. Mace

PK   So with tools, having two hammers doesn't mean one for you and one for Joey. It really means two for Flora!

FM   If I have two tools, I've got twice as good a chance that I can keep working.

3 *We Only Had the Fire*

PK   Flora, I'm interested in the way of life you experienced as a child.

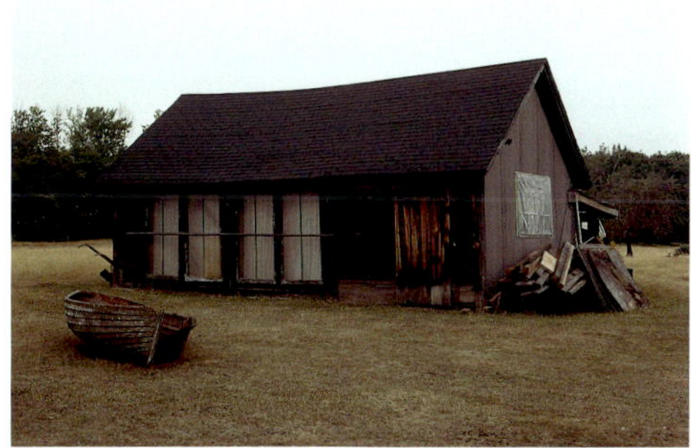

Mace's first studio, Hampton, New Hampshire, 1968.

FM   Well, first, may I say that my ancestors came from Europe, with my dad's family settling the town of Hampton, New Hampshire. New Hampshire has eighteen miles of coast, and I grew up on a farm a mile from the ocean where my family had their homestead. We grew almost everything to eat. Instead of going to the store, we went fishing or hunting or berry picking. We had a fish house at the beach, where we kept our boats, and there's actually a town monument there to my family. Our main house was right on our street, Mace Road. My family lived in that house for 355 years. When I was growing up, my great-grandmother, my paternal grandmother and grandfather, my mother, my dad, my sister, and I lived there.

We only had a wood stove in the kitchen, and there were tons of chores. I always carried wood upstairs from the basement to put in the wood box. The first time I didn't carry wood up was when I had the mumps. I think I was in junior high school. We had the wood stove in the kitchen, a pot-bellied stove in the living room, and soapstones we heated to carry upstairs to our beds. We still had a wood stove when I went to college. That was the first time I saw baseboard heating.

PK   So you have always been around fire, even as a child?

FM   Yes. I was petrified of fire; I still am. And I was told to stay away from the stove. I could bring up the wood and throw a log in when I was told. If you throw a log in at the wrong time, you really burn up whatever food is in the oven. God, how women used to cook—knowing how many logs and what type to make sure everything came out hot and toasty.

Sometimes, after we ate, we would be sitting at the table and there'd be a knock at the door. And my grandma would say, "It's the midnight farmer." He'd come in with his basket full of things to sell that he knew we didn't grow. The midnight farmer would grow his wares, and then, after the sun set, he would go from house to house and knock on the door if he saw your lights on.

PK   How does that life influence your life and work now?

FM   I was aware that my dad and grandfather used certain tools, and that my grandmother and mother used certain tools. I used to get in trouble for borrowing my dad's tools. Tools can enable you to make anything.

PK   What else?

FM   With our being in the same house for all those many years, there were things that got handed down. They weren't of great value; they just didn't get thrown out, because you could use them for something else later. All our boats—

even though we had around ten boats—were working boats. Standing on the porch and looking out to the ocean, you could see the schooners go by. I always wanted a sailboat because I thought they were so beautiful. Now I collect model boats. Those boats I could see as a kid and the ones I have now are the same scale. The real boats were so far out at sea that they looked like toy boats to me. In the studio, I have all these handmade boats on the wall, and they are like the ones in the distant landscape that I grew up with. All the collections Joey and I have, whether they're bird decoys or Inuit dolls, are not mass-produced. They are little things, home pleasures.

My mom taught my sister and me how to sew. My mom's parents were tailors. My father's mother, my grandmother, didn't ever use a sewing machine but she could hand stitch like a sewing machine. I was grumbling one day that all the other kids had store-bought clothes for their dolls, and she said, "Well you could make a dress." She turned around, grabbed a dishtowel, and laid my doll on it. Then she grabbed some scissors and cut out a dress in maybe fifteen minutes for my doll. "You can use anything," she said. "You just have to figure it out." And that's probably the way I started doing my life.

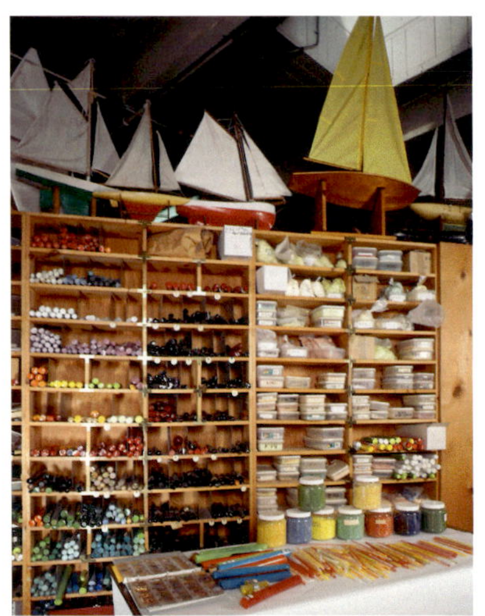

PK   What happened with your doll?

FM   I wasn't so interested in the doll but I liked the concept that you could make clothing. There was a game warden who lived down the street and was a friend of my dad, and they used to trap animals, stretch skins, and tan hides. As a kid I watched them, so when I needed some doll clothes, I'd go out and trap some mice. I would stretch the little hides and use them for trim on my doll's clothes.

When we caught fish, I embroidered the name of the species and how many we'd caught on little cloth tally sheets. It was probably a survival tactic to count how many cords of wood, how many fish, we would need for the winter.

PK   You said the other day that when you're in nature, you want to change or rearrange it.

FM   I spent a lot of time on the beach with my mom, and I loved to rearrange the stones there. I was always building something. Now I almost have to be in a pure, white space not to want to rearrange it. If I am in nature, I want to start cutting weeds and making rows. Which really drives Joey crazy because she wants to sit quietly.

PK   Your mother was French Canadian. Did she speak French when you were a child?

FM   No, she never spoke French. My mom was really sick; she was committed to the state mental institution when I was quite young. She would come home at times, and my dad, on the weekends, would go visit her. Mental illness ebbed and flowed.

PK   Despite that and other losses and challenges in your life, you have a very generous nature. You not only nurture and teach others but you often help people discover their hearts' desire and accomplish their goals.

FM   I realize how lucky I was as a kid that some people showed me some things that made a really big difference.

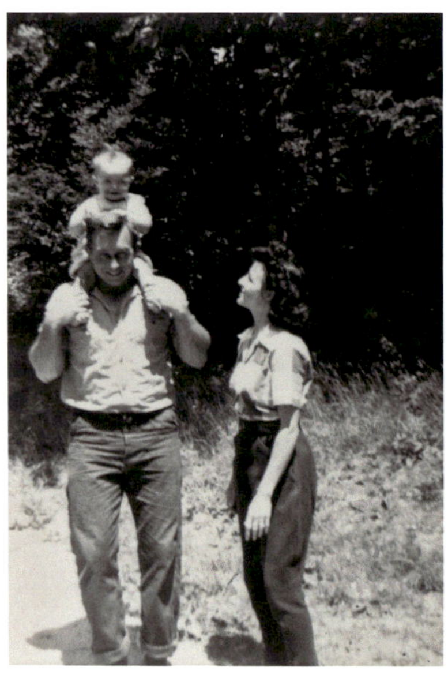

Mace's model boat collection in studio on Yale Street, Seattle, 1998.

Mace with her father and mother, 1950.

    Joey Kirkpatrick and Flora C. Mace

PK   You describe an amazing life, yet, clearly, your family didn't have a lot of money. How did you end up going to college?

FM   Every summer my grandmother took care of a blind woman, Mrs. Young, when she came north to stay at the beach. We used to go over to her house, and Mrs. Young would say to me, "Come over here." Then she would run her hand down my face because she couldn't see.

My mom died when I was in high school. A month later, my grandmother died. Three or four months later, my grandfather died. My sister and I, there was no support system for us. But Mrs. Young's lawyer called my dad and said Mrs. Young would like to talk to you about sending the girls to college. My dad was kind of taken aback. There was no way we could have afforded to go to college: my mom being sick my whole life pretty much drained every bit of possible financial support from our family. If I could get into college, Mrs. Young said, she would give me a four-year scholarship. And my sister. Both of us. I always felt that my sister was the more creative one. She got a degree in education and worked as an art teacher in the public schools for twenty-seven years. I went to college, studied art and, much later, sculpture.

PK   That's an astonishing story both of profound generosity and a tremendous gift of fate that enabled you to study art and especially sculpture. Did you see Mrs. Young again? Did she know what she made possible for you and your sister?

FM   Yes, we would visit her while on school break, speak of our studies, and take her fragrant wildflowers and sprigs of blueberries from the bush. She could find the blueberries with her hands and harvest them. She died before we graduated.

PK   What is sculpture to you?

FM   It's a hundred drawings instead of one. A sculpture is looking at every side. A two-dimensional drawing is only looking at one side, so you have to visualize what's on the back. With a sculpture, you get to look at what's on the back. You know how at school they test you for things? They show you a sheet of paper with something flat on it and ask what would this look like if it were three-dimensional? I used to do so well on those tests. I have an ability, one of my few abilities, to see things in three dimensions. But it didn't make me think I should be a sculptor.

PK   Would it surprise your mother that you became an artist? What would you like your mother—or really any of your family—to know about your life?

FM   That almost makes me tearful. I would tell them that getting involved in the arts has given me a voice and an inner peace. Working with people like Dale Chihuly and Bill Morris, Ben Moore, and, of course, Joey gave me a new family in a way. When we were at Pilchuck in the very beginning, we were all sharing the very basics. We each had to build our own little house. Some of the most beautiful sculptures were those original shelters. Then we had to build a hot shop. There was an incredible community feeling.

I've been in glass for a little over thirty years. For probably the first ten years, I tried to manipulate glass the way I had manipulated materials when I was a welder. I started taking the glass threads that came out of the furnace and sticking them together with a hand torch, as if I were welding. This led to my

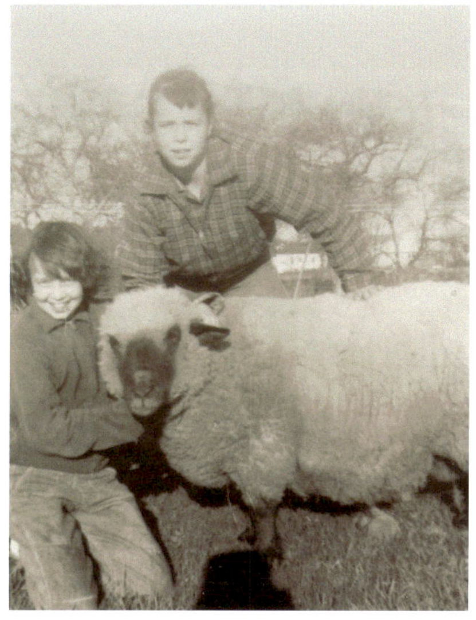

Mace with her sister, Nancy (left), with pet sheep, 1960.

glass-thread drawing technique that I have used ever since. Because the studio glass movement was so new in the late '70s, the other artists and I brought our techniques and aesthetics from painting, sculpture, and printmaking to glass, not knowing what we could and couldn't do in this new medium. That's why so many really interesting things happened for the next twenty years. There was no history for us, even though there were three thousand years of glass already. We didn't have the books. We only had the fire.

4 *Drawings in Air*

PK   Joey, what does it mean to you to be an artist?

JK   I think an artist is a translator. I go out in the world and look at what interests me, and then I translate what I see—what it looks like or the meaning of it—in my work. I don't think anybody ever thought I was going to be an artist. But I can't remember a time when I didn't think I was going to be an artist.

PK   I don't remember you drawing when we were little any more than any of us drew; our mother always had us drawing! You played sports when I was off reading, and later you became a fine athlete. I remember your drawings when you took art classes in high school and your ceramics when you studied art in college. You were always focused and strong willed about whatever you were doing. And, of course, there was the influence of our aunt Elayne in Chicago, who took us to the Art Institute and sent us books.

JK   Elayne was a wonderful artist, and once she took me to a huge construction site in Chicago to photograph the building process. I remember thinking if this is what it is to be an artist, getting to do what interests you no matter how strange it seems, well, I want to be that!

PK   What about drawing now? You make drawings that are finished works themselves and also explorations leading to other works, similar to how writers keep notebooks.

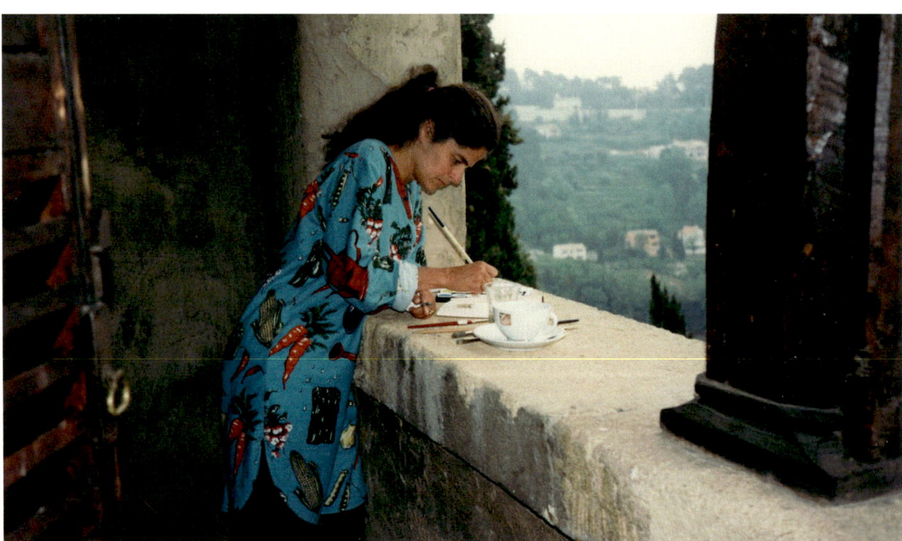

Kirkpatrick drawing at Colombe d'Or, Saint-Paul-de-Vence, France, 1992.

    Joey Kirkpatrick and Flora C. Mace

JK   I think direct drawing—taking a pencil to paper—is the most spontaneous impression of thinking, because your hand is holding the pencil. With a lot of the mediums we use, the ideas may be spontaneous but the actual work is very laborious. Often I joke that once the sculptural concept is decided, I just kind of do what I'm told: I need to sand this; I need to paint that. Drawing allows me to leave a direct impression on the paper not only of the actual pencil lead but of an idea. And if I don't continue to draw during the six months it takes us to learn how to steam-bend wood to complete a piece, for example, then in six months we're asking, "Where do we go from here?" Also some of it is just my pure love for the pencil line.

PK   Your thinking has a physical manifestation.

JK   It's true. I always draw standing up, so that I can use the energy of my whole body. I want that kinesthetic quality in the drawing. It's like when an athlete is off-balance but still makes a great play, or, as Anne Truitt said, it's "at once being totally in jeopardy and totally at home." That's me when I'm drawing.

PK   Mark Doty described your drawings as "loopy, offhand, and vigorous." To me they're lyrical, charged, and questing. How would you describe your drawings?

JK   The loopy drawing style for me is a continuing, single, descriptive line, yet it holds form.

PK   What artists have influenced you?

JK   In terms of drawing, I am taken by the multidimensionality of Egon Schiele's line. I like it when a drawn line is, well, sculptural: thick, thin, flat, round. It holds and gives dimension to the space within it. Of course, Matisse's line is right up there. It's expressive yet very clean. His uninterrupted line, without any loss of control, is amazing. My lines aren't clean.

   And certainly Calder. His lines on paper and in space—the portraits and the circus sculptures—describe an interior space even when nothing is there. They can give form to that space just from the nature of his drawn or bent lines. I love Alice Neel's line, and I can learn a lot about line even in more abstract works like Joan Mitchell's painting and Judy Pfaff's sculpture.

PK   How do your drawings influence the collaborative sculpture?

JK   Even when it's three-dimensional, our work is described by line. The drawing informs the sculpture, and the sculpture informs the drawing. A lot of our sculptures, especially the flat *Woodland Drawings*, are drawings in air. Even the torso sculptures with the steam-bent wood are made up of lines describing form.

PK   As opposed to a plane describing form?

JK   Exactly. Or a volume. The fruit pieces are more about volume. The white, figurative sculptures, they are drawings in the sense that they have a front and a back. That has to do with being informed by the drawings, I think. Before we made the *Doll Drawing Cylinders*, I had been making drawings of dolls, and then we figured out a process to put those drawings, as bent wire, onto three-dimensional glass objects. That kind of process affects how I draw on paper the next time.

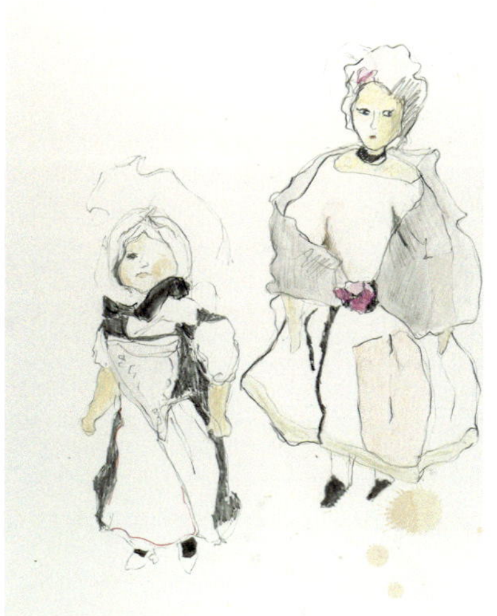

Joey Kirkpatrick, **Rebecca with French Doll**, 1980
Graphite and gouache on paper, 21¾ × 14¼ inches

Untitled, 1979
Glass and wire, 6¼ × 6 × 6 inches

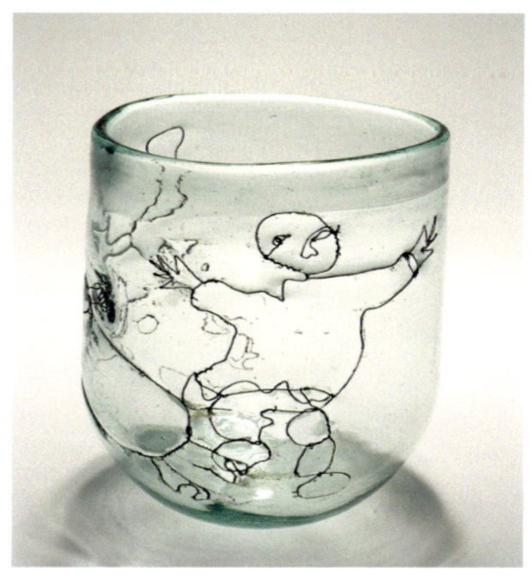

PK   Okay, Joey, here's a big secret. We're sisters. We grew up in Des Moines in a small brick house with a big backyard. We have two other wonderful sisters. Some of us played with dolls; some of us played with cap guns. Some of us wrote poems; some of us played golf. I won't name names. We all took lessons at the Des Moines Art Center. You and our sister Kris worked at the Art Center for years. Tracy sometimes works in the studio now with you and Flora. What do you remember from childhood?

JK   The sense of play and being outdoors is what I think of most, how play and being outside went together. We made things: tree houses, May baskets, baseball diamonds. We bonded as we did projects. Also we had open land behind our house. Climbing trees and running wild back there gave me a sense of adventure.

And having sisters. There's a sense of community and solidarity you feel with your siblings, especially when you're close to them. And we were. We slept three of us in a bedroom, and you made up stories for Kris and me. When Tracy was born, she slept in a crib in our parents' bedroom until we moved to a bigger house. There's a strength from that I feel I have today.

Our mother encouraged our sibling community. Although she was a stay-at-home mother without many resources, she had an artistic temperament and expressed her creativity making our home. She had a sense of wonder when looking at the world and exquisite taste. It showed in how she set a table or arranged a room.

PK   How about the darkness in our lives? I won't be specific, but there were some hard times. Where does that go in your work?

JK   I think it goes into the figurative work and is why the figure is so important for me to keep dealing with. Container making, the figure as a container, the vessel: there's an inside and an outside on so many levels in our work. Sometimes the figure has been an active figure, and sometimes more of a receiver. And sometimes it is more a thoughtful state of mind. The figure itself is illustrative of all the ways people make do in the world: how we cut boats from trees, or hammers from stone. How we use imagination and persevere.

PK   I remember walking into a Pilchuck studio years ago where you and Flora were at work, and seeing bottles of purple tulips and shelves of white-glass tubular pods with heads. You put very uniform facial features on those figures. They looked determined and strong yet also tender and vulnerable.

JK   In the early '80s, the white, figurative, glass pieces were androgynous icons or archetypes. We didn't want them to have personalities. They weren't autobiographical. Think about it: you have an upright figure made of glass. That's an image of strength and fragility at the same time. All of that was intended.

When we moved from living in a tree house at Pilchuck to Seattle, instead of looking out our windows to trees, we looked at Lake Union. Seeing the rings on the water, we started putting life-sized glass heads on their sides, with large, carved, wooden rings on top of them. It wasn't about movement anymore; it was about contemplation. I was reading Emerson at the time. He writes something like, for every visual image in nature, there's a . . .

PK   "Corresponding state of mind."

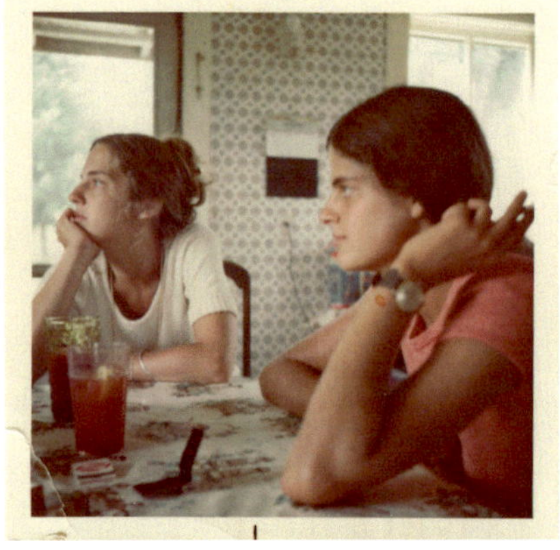

Patricia and Joey Kirkpatrick, 1973.

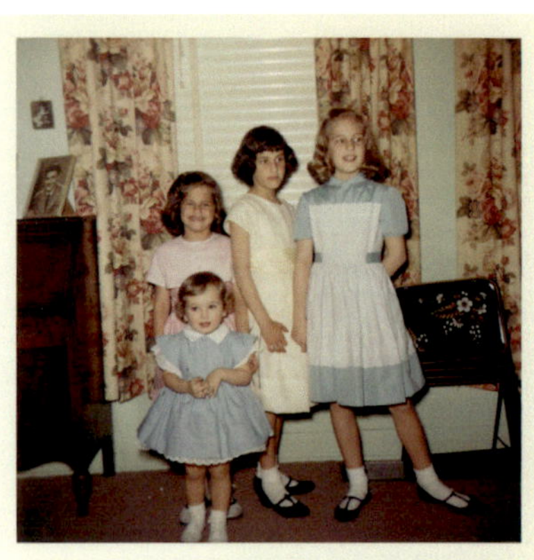

Kirkpatrick sisters, left to right: Tracy (front), Joey, Kris, and Patricia, 1961.

   Joey Kirkpatrick and Flora C. Mace

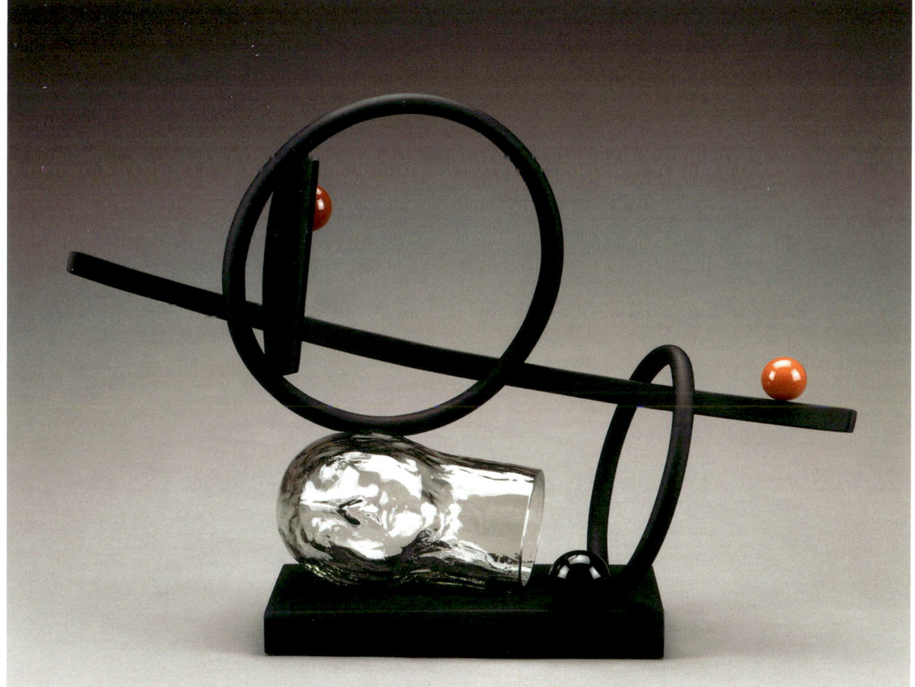

JK   Exactly. And reading that, I thought, *that's it*. How does a person know what it feels like to be eclipsed? Other than as a state of mind, or by seeing the shapes and images from a real eclipse.

PK   Where is the figure now that you're doing the bird powder drawings?

JK   It's in your identification with the bird. There's a literary and scientific history concerning birds, and the bird is identified in our language: *free as a bird*, *a bird in the hand*, that type of thing. The human projection onto the bird is where you find the figure. Our *Bird Pages* are about more than what you see.

PK   So the human figure is an implied presence at the edge of the page?

JK   Yes. That is even truer when you think about the identification of species. Identification doesn't exist unless somebody is seeing something to identify. I don't for a minute think we're teaching people about birds. I want people to look at a piece and see that *that* word matches *that* bird, not just see what a flicker looks like. It's about the brain connecting all those things. It's about naming as well as about culture and language.

PK   Are you working in a different direction compared to many artists associated with modernism? Instead of moving from the representational to the more abstract, you're moving from the more abstract to the more realistic. Instead of shattering the mirror, it seems like you're putting the mirror back together again.

JK   You're right. This *Bird Page* imagery is more representational, a different direction for me. For us. Still, there is interpretation. When I lay down the powder to make a bird for a *Bird Page*, I'm aware that the image now exists in the world and will enter my psyche for the rest of my life. It will never not exist. I can't describe that further, but I find it fascinating.

PK   Earlier Paula referred to your pioneering spirit, saying that the two of you have taken a leap of faith to make art outside the lines. Where do you think you've most taken a leap of faith?

JK   Well, in collaboration. In 1979, when we decided to cosign our work, people— would you say they specifically advised us against it, Flora?

FM   People asked, "Why would you even do that?" I said the work wouldn't have happened if Joey and I weren't both doing it. It felt right to cosign the pieces with Joey. We went into it even-steven. If anything came out of it, OK, and if it didn't, it didn't. I wouldn't have guessed that it would last this long.

PK   Would the collaboration have been possible without a shared personal life?

JK   It's hard to say. I think it could have, but the desire to make things is so pervasive that it would be hard to imagine having a life outside our work. It certainly would have been a different kind of work. We learned early on that we didn't have to duplicate each other's strengths or abilities but we had to have mutual trust that the work comes first, and our decisions are based on what's best for the work. It's not easy.

PK   What if your concepts are in conflict?

FM   Sometimes that piece doesn't get done.

JK   What we gain from working together is bigger than what we lose. There are things that get lost. We are two very different people. We both feel that it is important to have our own working space, which results in us both having our individual obligations to the work. I always say we work together alone, bringing our own individuality to the work.

PK   Are there rivalries within the collaboration?

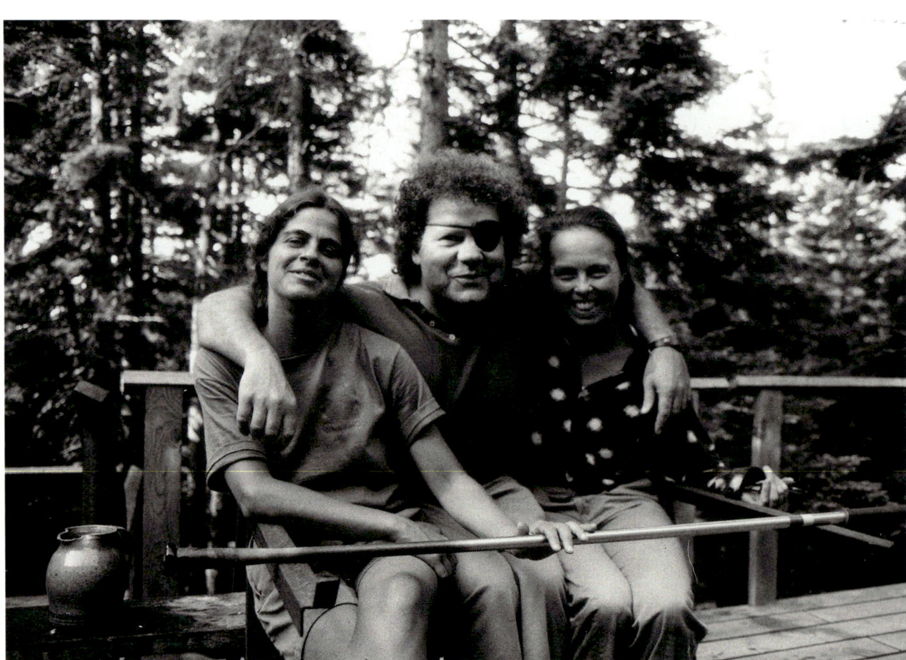

Kirkpatrick, Dale Chihuly, and Mace at Haystack Mountain School of Crafts, Deer Isle, Maine, 1985.

                                                                    Joey Kirkpatrick and Flora C. Mace

FM   I'm down and dirty a lot of the time: I make noise, hammering and building, welding and grinding. When I see Joey sitting in a beautifully clean place, sometimes I envy her.

JK   I think we have avoided rivalry by making our domains so different. Neither of us—because we're so different in our public personae—has much difficulty with how the other is portrayed.

PK   What do you argue about?

JK   We used to have a rule: whoever felt the strongest got her way. If we're looking at a sculpture's composition and I want an element over there, but Flora is pounding the table that it would be much better here, we both sense that we're arguing about the most meaningful part. The pounding helps us get clarity and take away excess. I don't mean our work is simple, but there's a certain simplicity about our work because two of us are investigating it so rigorously. At times, it's difficult to discuss the meaning of a work after it's done, because our views can be very different from each other's.

PK   Dale Chihuly has been not only your matchmaker but a tremendous mentor, colleague, and friend. What have you learned from Dale Chihuly?

JK   The first thing that comes to mind is generosity. Working with him and his team, we got to contribute to the art in a meaningful way. We also learned a way to approach our own work from simply watching him. He's so fearless about trying new things, changing direction. And Dale gave us experiences we wouldn't have had otherwise. I could have never understood, for example, about how different glass colors worked with one another for our large fruit pieces, unless I had the experience of working for hours as a colorist for him.

FM   He mentored us. He respected us. He let us become who we are.

PK   Flora, before Pilchuck, you met Dale at the University of Utah, and he asked you to make drawings for him. What did you think of him then?

FM   He had a lot of advance press that I heard before I got there. Because he was a mile a minute. He flew in his mom, who came with two huge suitcases. There must have been five salmon in each suitcase for a barbecue. He always created an environment. He was always encouraging everyone, very inclusive: "Great job on the furnace." By giving your input, you were part of the in-house survey. "How do you like your fish? Should we cook some in the hot shop?"

JK   Dale Chihuly broke the notion of glass as a craft. He elevated the seriousness of glass as a valid medium to work in. He brought glass to museums. At Pilchuck, he asked Flora and me to help start the artist-in-residence program and bring in New York artists who'd never worked in glass. We had the great opportunity to work with Judy Pfaff, Chris Wilmarth, Lynda Benglis, and John Torreano. And their participation reverberated back to New York and the art world. That in turn helped all of us work without the distinction of whether we were making art or craft.

PK   Is there a feminist dimension to your work?

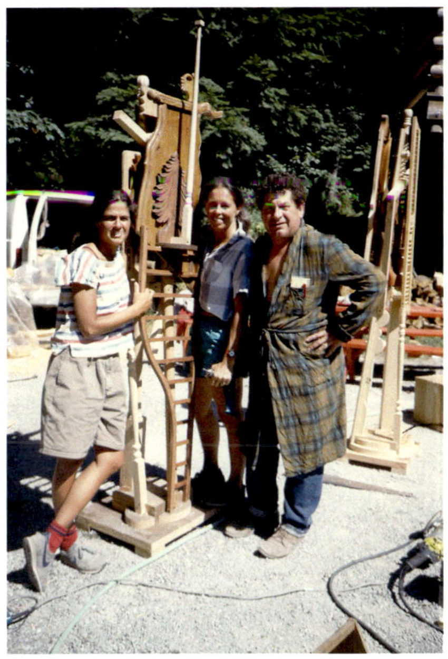

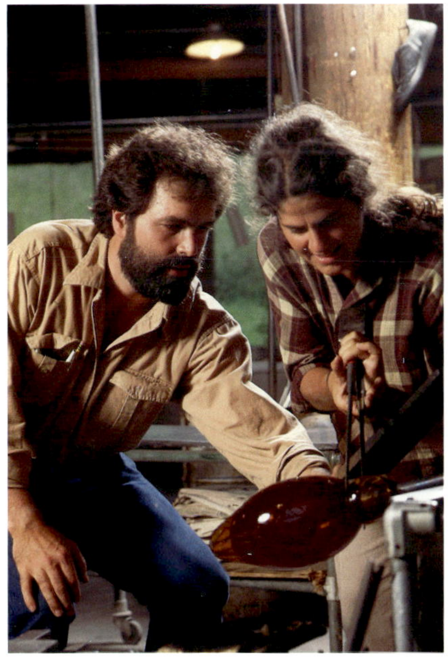

Kirkpatrick, Mace, and Italo Scanga, Pilchuck Glass School, 1985.

Kirkpatrick working with artist-in-residence, Christopher Wilmarth, Pilchuck Glass School, 1983.

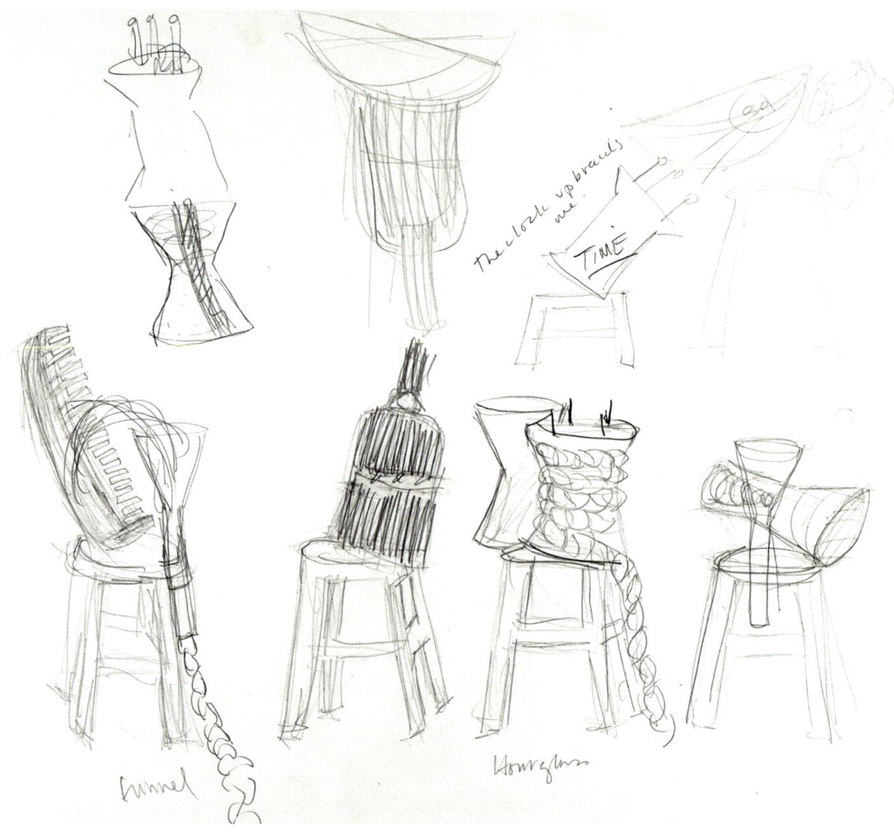

JK   We are women making artwork. We make it differently, and our subject matter is different, because we are women. I think particularly of sculptural pieces that we made in the late '90s, when we were exploring where women find their strength. We'd been making androgynous figurative work for twenty years. Once gender came into it, I became interested in the history of women's work. In a sense, agriculture was invented because women had to stay in one place with children. Traditionally, women's work can be interrupted. It's often tedious, repetitive, and follows a lot of invisible preparation.

Our torso pieces, where the metal is put inside the branches—which Flora does—that labor intensive process is a lot like women's work. We chose imagery like whisk brooms, stools, and bottles. What I love about that series is that, while it's a nod to what's traditionally been women's work, it goes beyond those boundaries in terms of the scale, materials, and how hard it is to make. Also we matured as adults and artists at a time when there was a great deal of upheaval with gender issues in our culture.

PK   What was it like to be women in that early Pilchuck group of artists and glassblowers in the late '70s and early '80s?

JK   Before we met, Flora and I had had similar experiences in settings where we were the only women blowing glass. We both were relegated to blowing glass in the middle of the night. At the university level, early glassblowing was often in the engineering department versus the art department. We were working against the mentality of "Who do they think they are? They don't care how the furnace is built. They care about what they're making."

                                          Joey Kirkpatrick and Flora C. Mace

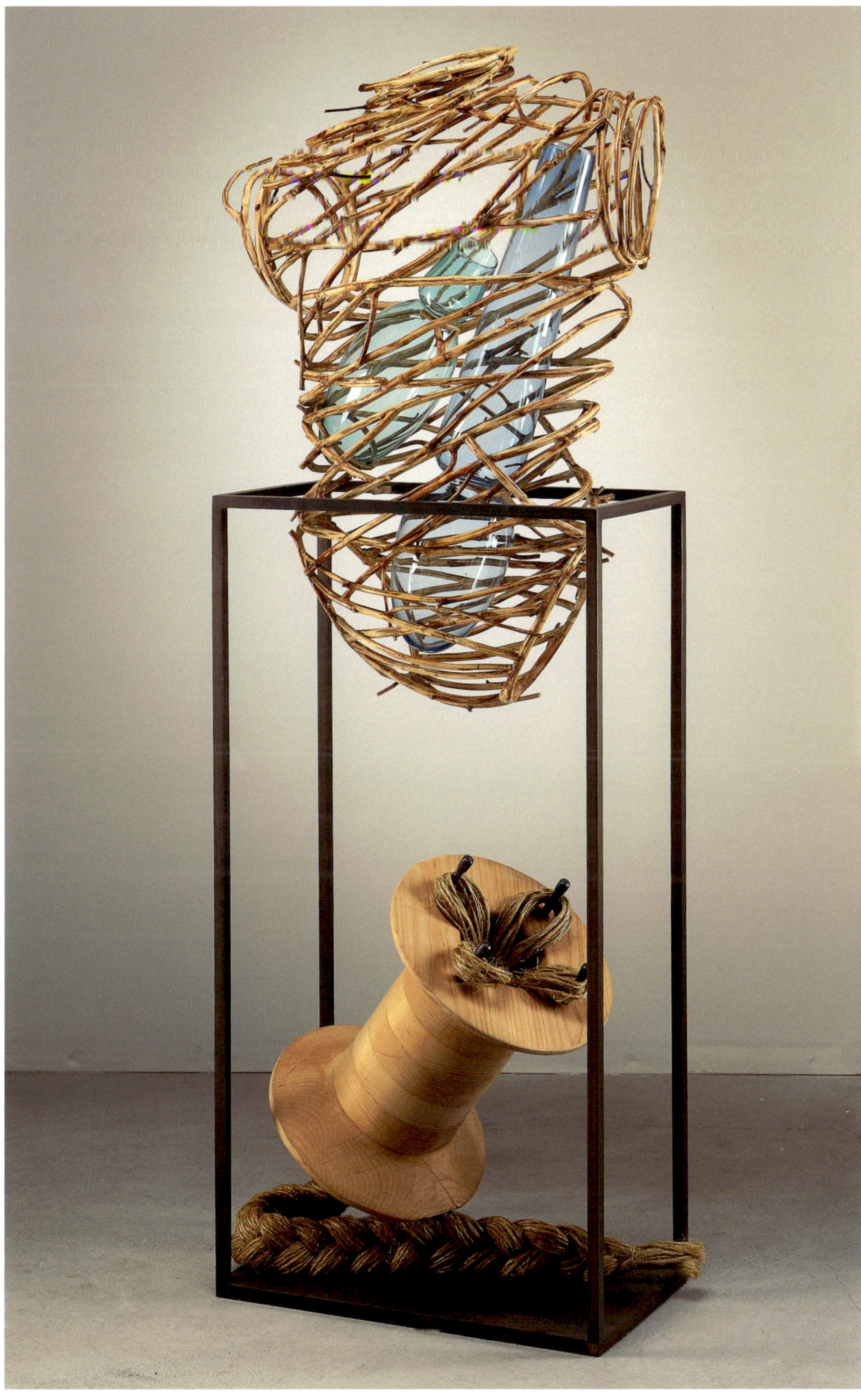

FM   There was the power of the timetable. Women got the last shift with the glass furnace.

PK   How have you avoided being tokens as women?

JK   Number one, we don't know how to cook! And we loved it when Dale and Italo cooked for us. But, seriously, I think part of it was lucky timing. Things were changing for women in many areas. Although slowly. Teaching early at Pilchuck might have helped too. Dale asked us to teach a glassblowing class at Pilchuck,

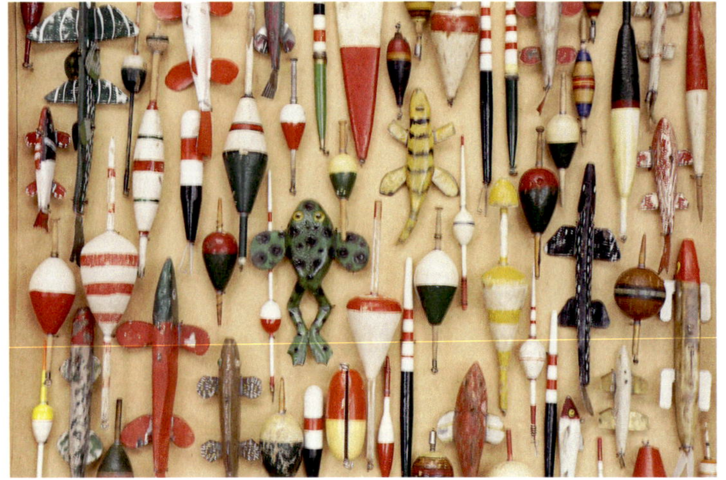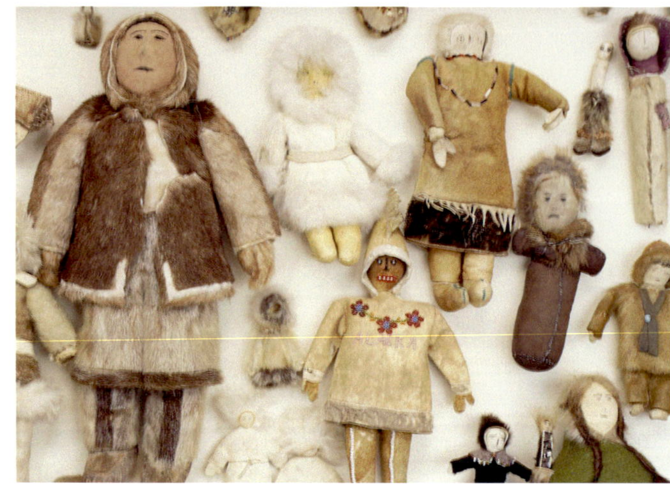

Antique fish bobber collection; Inuit doll collection.

and we were the first women to do so. At first, that didn't translate into more recognition for women artists working in glass but into noting that "women are great teachers." If you look at the announcements for shows at the time—and go down the list of names—there weren't many women, with the exception of us, Ginny Ruffner, and Cappy Thompson. But our classes brought more women students to the school, and, obviously, with more women, there came more opportunities for them. Now the challenge comes when a show announcement lists all women: that shouldn't mean it's a "women's show."

PK   It seems that you were both able to avoid the ways many women have entered traditionally male communities, including by being personally involved with their mentors . . .

FM   Maybe that's because we were a couple and collaborated on our work at the same time. We were dependent on each other and able to avoid the politics of gender roles.

PK   How has your work changed in the last thirty years?

FM   I think our subject matter has become more magnified, especially over the last few years. Where once we were placing the figure, for example, in a larger setting, we now often reduce our subject to something more like portraiture— the bird, the flower, the tree. I don't believe a day goes by that I feel secure in what I'm doing. But if I look at the big picture, I say to myself, it's always like this. Something will come. The doubt is still there, but I recognize it now and try to stay patient until something comes.

JK   When Flora and I started working together, we met success through glass. I'm thrilled with that. But more important, we have always relied on using the material that best answers the question we're exploring. After initially working primarily in glass, we have allowed ourselves to work outside that medium with wood, metal, or bronze, sometimes fabricated with glass parts, sometimes not. Over the years, maybe only half of our work has included glass. A lot of the pieces are more wood and steel. Also prints or drawings. We've now arrived at a place where we are fully using our repertoire; our drawing and technical abilities are all coming together. It's a luxury that we get to make exactly what we want

Joey Kirkpatrick and Flora C. Mace

to. It might not always be the case. It is for right now, and that's a huge thing for an artist.

PK   Much of the imagery in your work, and the collections in your studio—the baskets, fishing decoys, creels, toys—is the stuff of daily life, and in many cases a daily life that no longer exists. Is there an elegy there?

JK   Absolutely. That makes me think of our series the *Proverb Cylinders*, in which we applied mottos and proverbs to the work: "By the thread the ball is brought to light," or "Every soil bears not everything." To me it's the same kind of collecting. It's the things that gave people the power to do their living.

FM   On the top shelf, there are three silhouette duck heads my grandfather made. He was a decoy maker, and he liked to hunt. He made those to use and also created beautiful objects. Those three, depending on the context and presentation, are incredible art pieces. Some of the things that I grew up with on a farm—I didn't know they were art, but I thought they were beautiful. We used to shuck clams and have piles of white shells in the backyard. We would take the clamshells and make white paths through the woods.

JK   We're attracted to an object's materials and surfaces. Those decoys aren't as highly engineered as things we make. But I don't want the complexity and high engineering of Flora's hand, or any nuts and bolts, to show. It's wrong to think that spontaneity is quick. The spontaneity in our work is the idea. Bringing the different materials together takes time. I don't think the work can be judged by how hard it is to make.

PK   Is there a contradiction between your admiration for what might be called *outsider* or *folk* art and craft and the success you've achieved as artists whose work has been exhibited in prominent museums and sold in prestigious galleries?

JK   I don't think so. The art forms and traditions you've mentioned have their own museums now and have great prominence in the arts. Flora and I turn to objects that have been employed in life and, like a traditional proverb, give a truth to life, which we try to incorporate in our work.

PK   Some of your artworks appear to be still life sculptures that are immediately recognizable, like the pieces of fruit, and some appear as more personal compositions, like the clear-glass heads with wooden spheres above them.

FM   It's our two states of mind: our daily life and our dream life. You can't live in your dream life all the time.

JK   One kind of work includes more metaphor.

PK   Perhaps the metaphor comes into both kinds of work but at different stages?

JK   Yes. With the fruit and maybe even the paintbrush pieces and the birds, the recognizable images come from our daily life. The metaphor comes after the conclusion of the work. In the glass and wooden sphere sculpture, we're making the metaphor as we make the sculpture.

PK   We may be talking about the difference between a work's subject and its subject matter. Fruit is a subject matter, but you're making up the fruit to become something else.

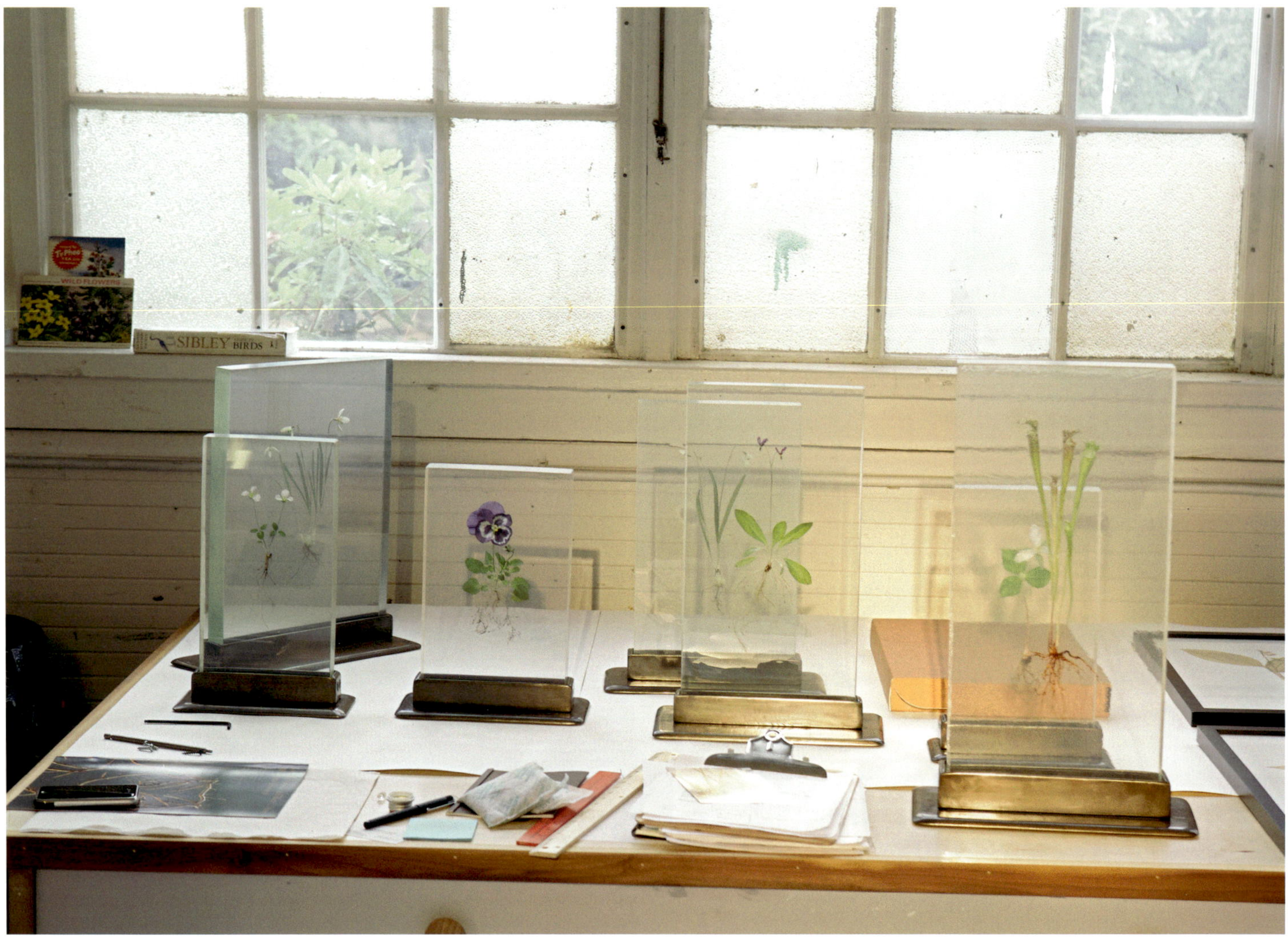

Collection of first *Botanicals,* 2013.

FM   It's hard to live in a world that you're making up all the time.

JK   Not hard for me. That's where I like to be.

FM   Sometimes, for me, doing something that's beautifully simple is relaxing. I can't stand being in the dream world all the time. It's exhausting!

6 *First Facts: Birds and Flowers*

PK   Let's talk about birds. First, Joey, I want to ask you about painting. You've been painting for almost as long as you've been drawing. I've always loved your paintings. You did casein paintings as the illustrations for our picture book, *Plowie: A Story from the Prairie.* You were doing casein paintings of birds before the glass cylinders and *Bird Pages* that you and Flora are making now. Would you say something about what you do differently when you paint than when you draw or make sculpture?

JK   To be honest, I don't really differentiate between drawing and painting when I'm in the midst of it. The paintings always start with a graphite drawing no

                    Joey Kirkpatrick and Flora C. Mace

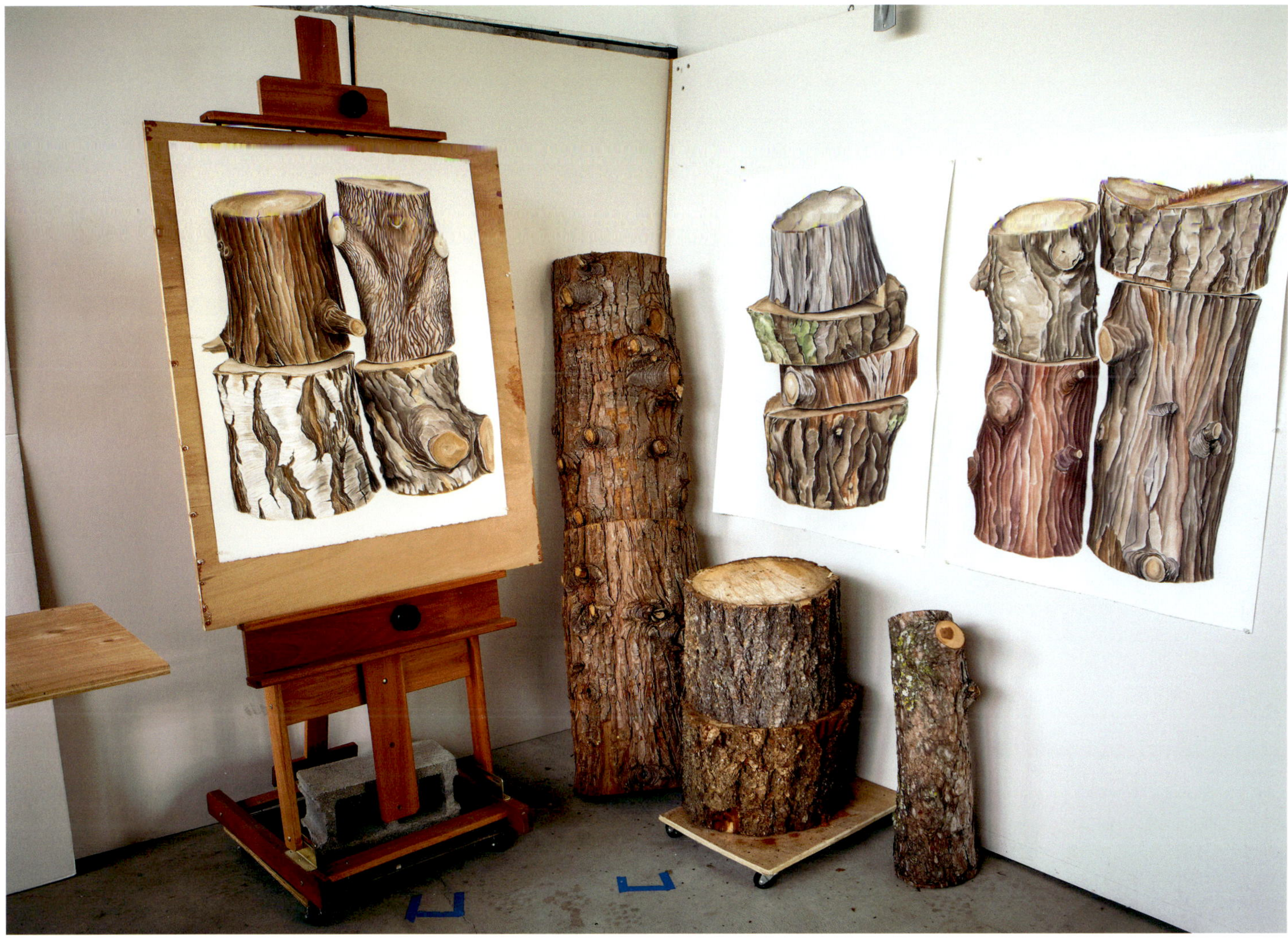

matter what the subject, and often the paintbrush is worked like a pencil. Most of my paintings have strong, descriptive lines made with a brush.

PK   Following your bird paintings on paper, in 2005, you and Flora completed a series of ninety bird drawings on glass that you call *Bird Pages: First Facts*. In your earlier glass pieces with birds, the drawings were more stylized than realistic, like children's drawings or totems. The birds have a watery, an almost otherworldly, quality.

JK   Yes, one series is glass-powder drawing pickups on blown vessels, and the other is glass-powder drawing pickups on solid pieces of cast glass. What is exciting about both ways of working is that the powder drawings represent the personality of my drawing hand in a material I literally can't touch when it is being picked up: it is too hot! It's interesting to have the process be a step away from your hand but still reflect your hand.

FM   With the blown pieces, there was a lot of experimentation. As you blow air into a vessel, the air expands the granules of glass that make up the drawing. We realized we would lose some ornithological aspects of the birds because the body parts moved during the blowing process.

JK   Right. There's a balance. Frankly, sometimes Flora and I feel differently about things we make. Flora was afraid that when you distort the bird on the blown object, the bird can't be identified. I like the look of the blown object that distorts the bird, if you want to call it that. I don't always draw in proportion. I draw from emotion.

But we decided to go to the flat cast object that we refer to as a *page*: it shows all four corners of the finished work. Picking up the bird drawings in this way does not distort them. We wanted to make these pieces about identification, naming the type of bird. At that point, it made sense to follow the tradition of a field guide by isolating the image so it can be seen more clearly. What's exciting to me is to use words on the pages. I think that comes from being a reader. I've always loved putting words in our work.

FM   I think letters are beautiful no matter if they create a word or are just individual entities. When we were doing the original bird powder pickups, the jizz of the bird was what we were after, to capture that on the vessel.

PK   What does the term *jizz* mean?

FM   A jizz would be the quick aspect—I wouldn't even say identification—of a bird.

JK   The personality of that particular kind of bird species.

There is a concept from an American ornithologist, Louis Agassiz Fuertes, about the first facts of bird identification. Birds have what's called concealing coloration. They're colored based on how they can conceal themselves in the landscape. If a bird is yellow, the sun is out, and the blue sky reflects on the bird, it doesn't look yellow anymore. It looks kind of a funny bluey color. The way to teach identification is to isolate the bird from its environment, so you can show its true colors. Then when you go back into the landscape, you can identify the bird. That's called giving people the *first facts*.

PK   This brings us to the *Botanicals* you are making now, in which you suspend an entire—an actual—plant specimen, usually a flower, in composite and glass. For you, Flora, working with flowers seems almost a matter of fate, given your name. How did you get the name Flora?

FM   The name Flora was given to me by my mother, Margaret Saint Marie, who named me after her mother, Flora Saint Marie.

Maybe it was a forgone conclusion that I would eventually put flowers in my work. When I was really small, my sister and I would spend our quarter allowance on geraniums, planting them around our farm in New Hampshire. I drew scientific botanical illustrations in college, and I've always introduced flowers, wherever Joey and I have lived, as part of my nesting routine. Once we acquired the farm in Chimacum, fifty acres, I could put all the parts together, planting and making art with flowers.

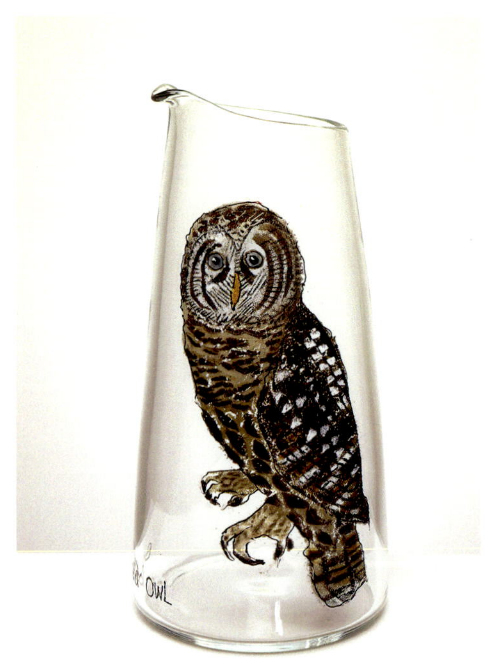

Beaked Vessel: Barred Owl, 2003
Glass, 12¾ × 6¼ × 6¼ inches

                                                                      Joey Kirkpatrick and Flora C. Mace

PK   How did you first come to the idea, and where did you get the patience, for making the *Botanicals*? What motivated you to find a technique to display whole flower specimens in layers of glass?

FM   Out of frustration came a kind of resolve, a challenge to myself. I wanted to see these flowers in three dimensions, not pressed or dried. Their structures are so sculptural that I wanted to build with them. Also, honestly, I was longing to get out of the city at the time—this was before we got the farm—so you might call it a momentary revolt against the studio that would get me outside.

I guess I learned patience early. My dad used to take my sister and me to construction sites on the weekends. We would pick up discarded and bent nails, take them home, and then stand together in the shed and hammer the nails straight, sorting them by size, so we could use them later.

PK   Joey, do flowers have equivalents of the first facts and the jizz you've described for birds?

JK   Absolutely. Flowers have a jizz too with their many leaf configurations and their responses to the environment's wind and heat. It would be hard not to recognize the sorrowful bend of a bleeding heart. As we did with the birds, we have taken the flowers out of their habitat to see them clearly and present the first facts of what makes each species so unique.

PK   Where does the impulse of the *Botanicals* intersect with that of your *Cordwood Paintings*?

JK   Both the *Botanicals* and the *Cordwood Paintings* are like portraiture. They are created out of the impulse to come face-to-face with our subject, without perspective, without consideration of that subject's surroundings. I don't consider either body of work to be realism, because they are deconstructed, in the case of the flowers especially, and put back together again by the artist's hands, as an interpretation.

PK   In science, an *ecotone* is an area of transition where two different kinds of plants meet, such as a grassy field and a woodland. An ecotone is generally a rich plant zone and also a good place to see a variety of bird species. What is the ecotone or zone for art and science in the *Botanicals*?

JK   Where science gives a bird or a flower its name or category, it doesn't make a judgment about beauty. We spend considerable time outside noticing things: in the forest, on the beach, working on the land at the farm. And inside I am constantly reading books about naturalists, ornithologists, first-person outdoor journeys, all nonfiction. This inside and outside work is our ecotone between the real-life parts that lead to our art making.

PK   The *Botanicals* express such joy, such celebration of the natural world, almost a kind of "music of the spheres," if you will. What for you is the joy and mystery of these flowers?

FM   For me, there is a magic in seeing the entire plant out of its ecosystem, suspended at eye level. To include the bulb and root systems references the mystery of the underground, the source of power usually unseen.

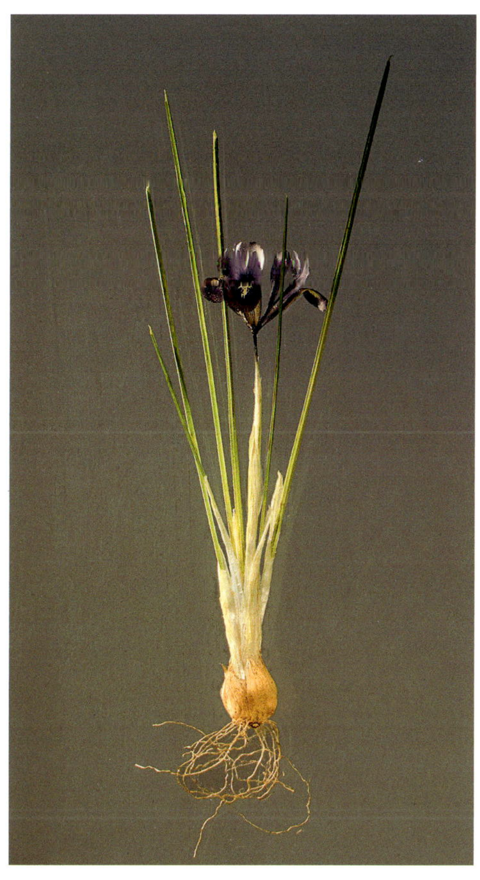

Single Iris (detail), 2013
Flower, composite, glass, and steel, 18½ × 13 × 6 inches

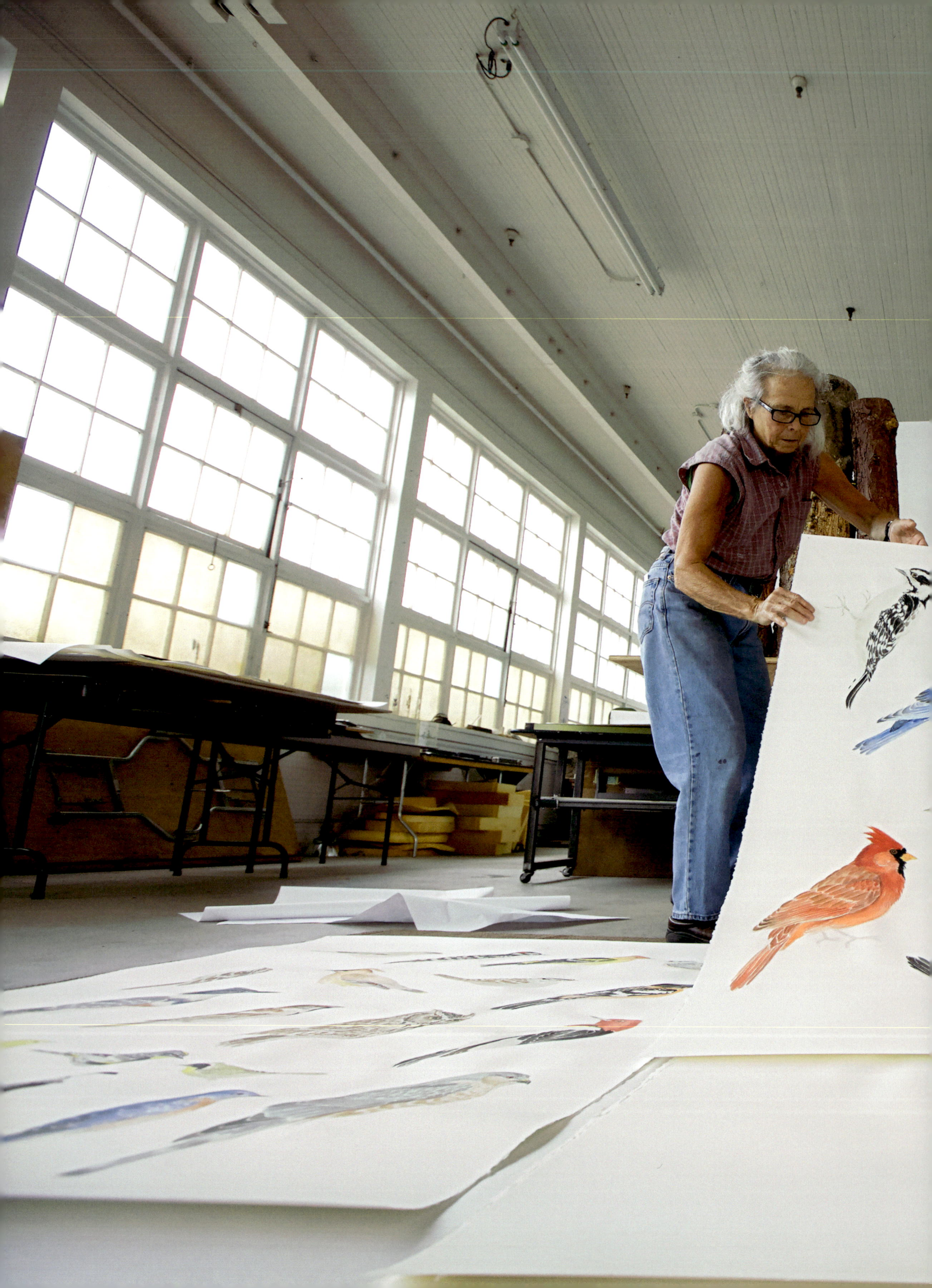

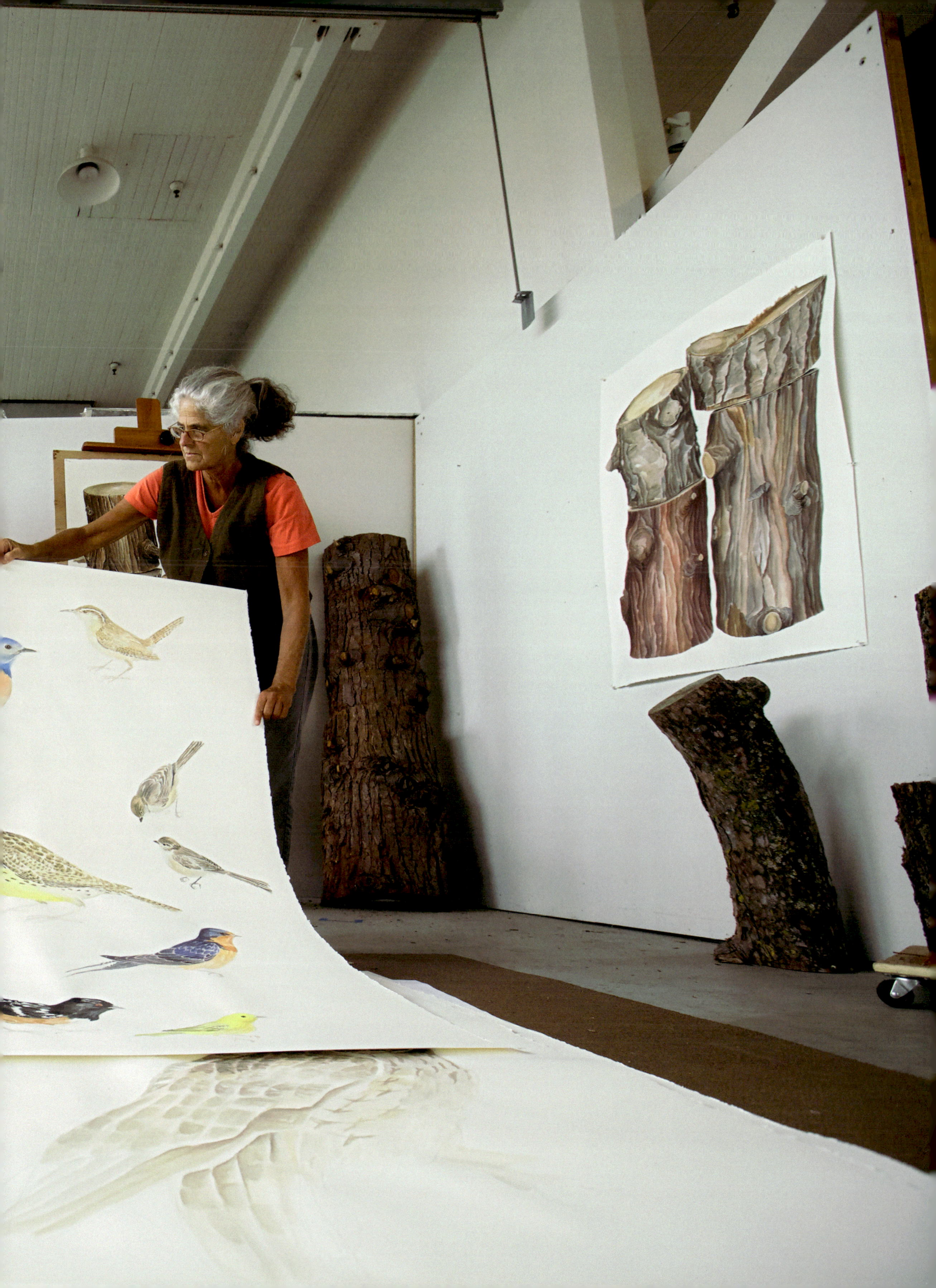

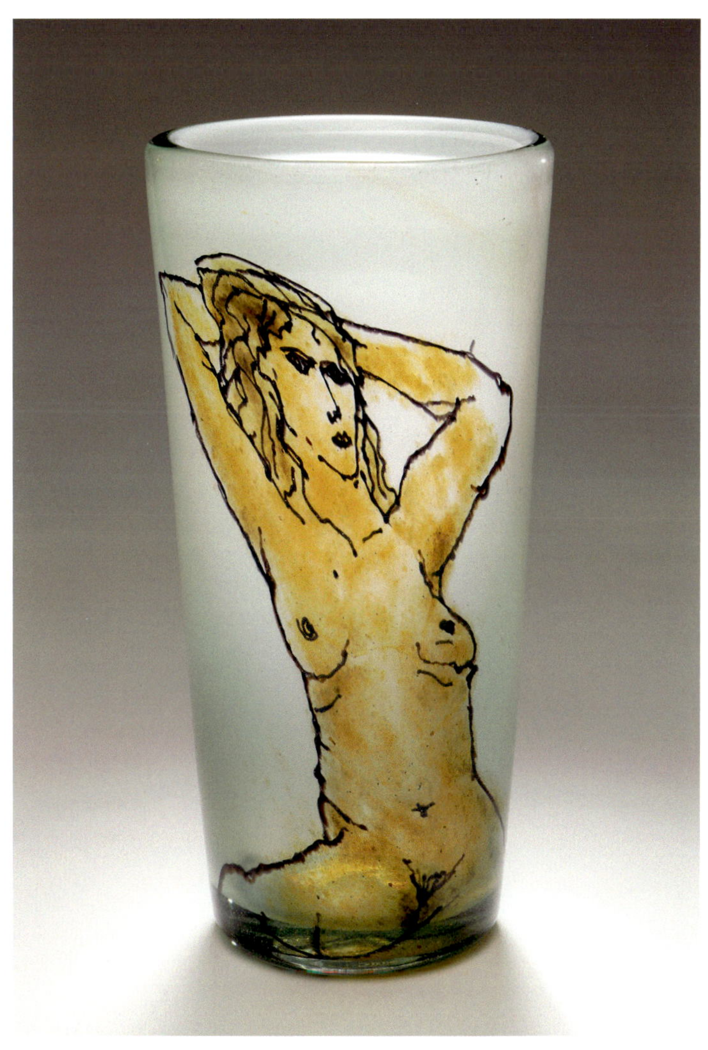

Flora C. Mace, **Figure**, 1977
Glass, 10¼ × 5 × 5 inches

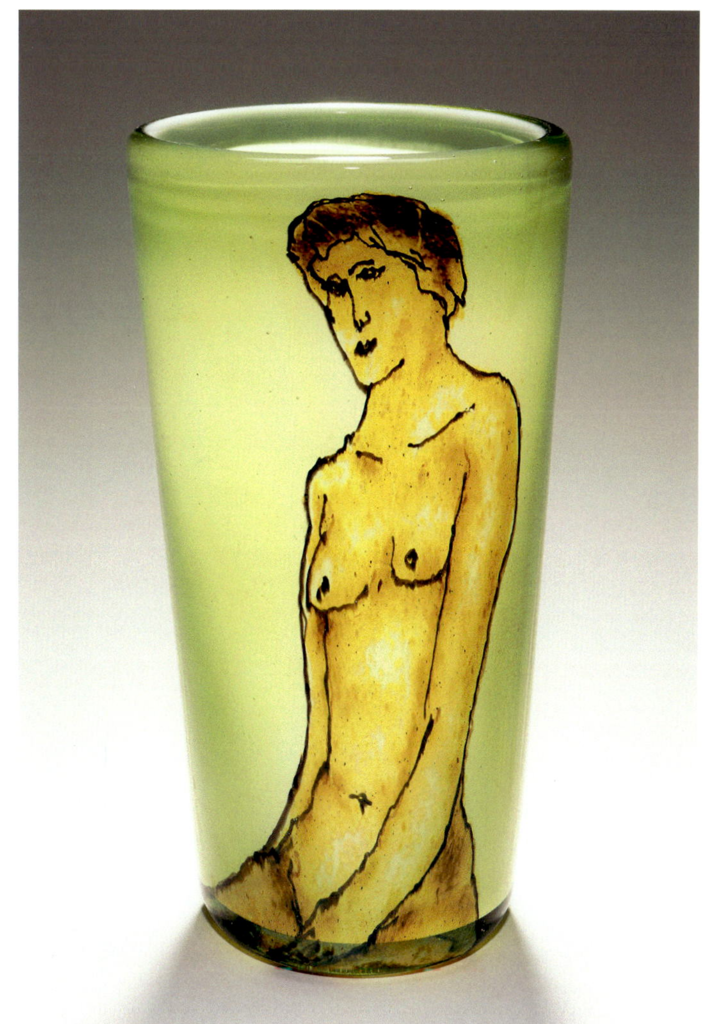

Flora C. Mace, **Figure XI**, 1977
Glass, 11 × 5½ × 5½ inches

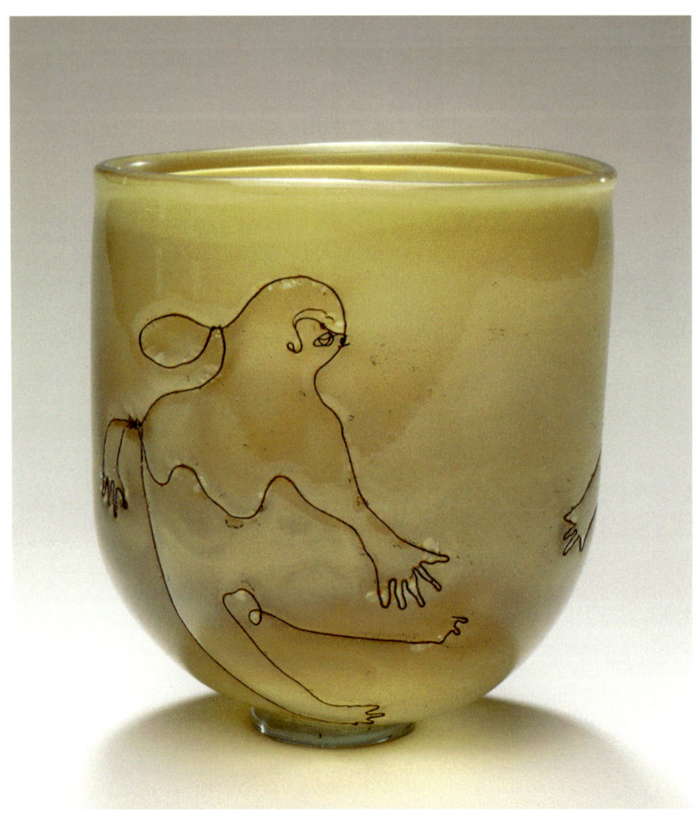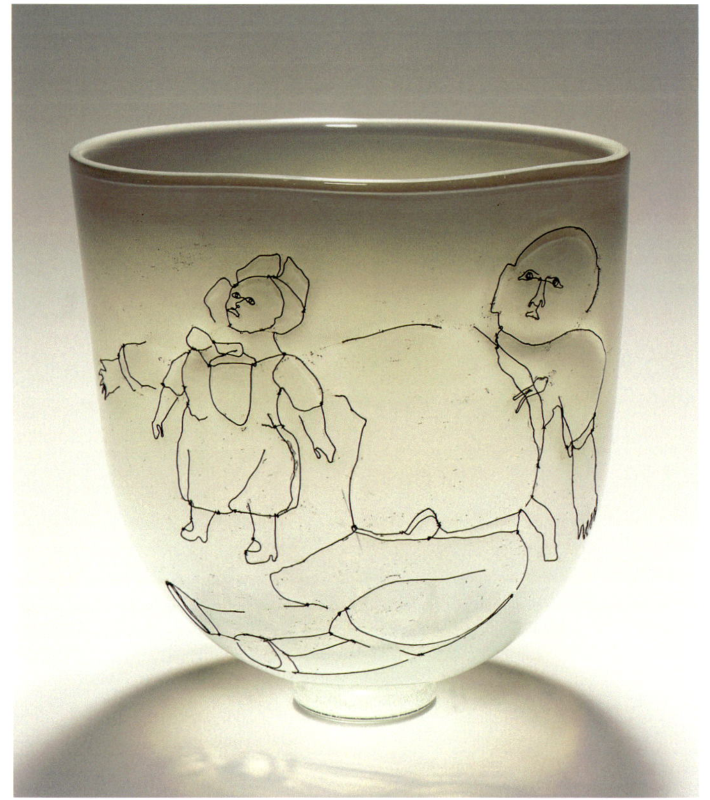

First Wire Cylinder, 1979
Glass and wire, 6 × 5½ × 5½ inches

Rebecca and the Chinese Doll, 1980
Glass and wire, 7½ × 7 × 7 inches

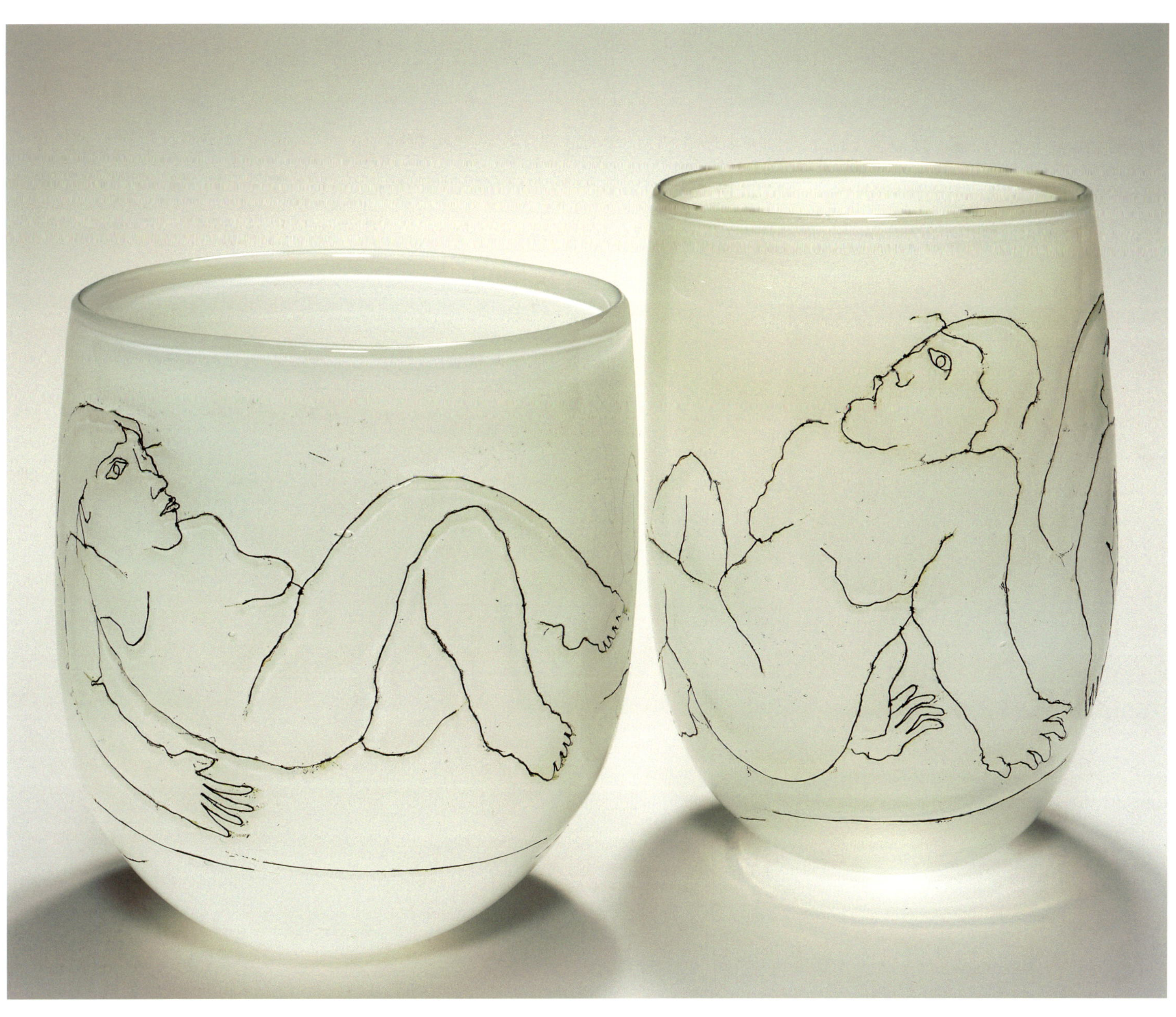

Two Figure Drawing, 1982 (left)
Glass and wire, 9 × 7½ × 7½ inches

Two Figures, 1982 (right)
Glass and wire, 10½ × 6½ × 6½ inches

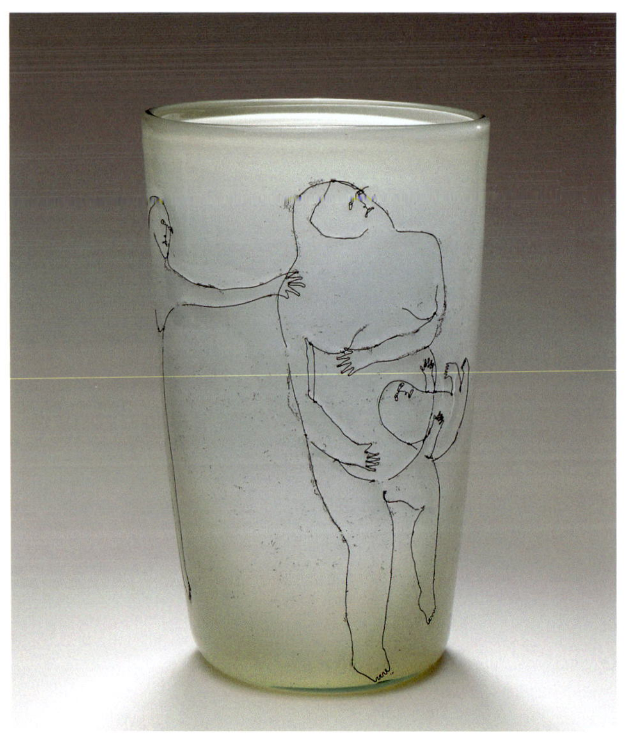

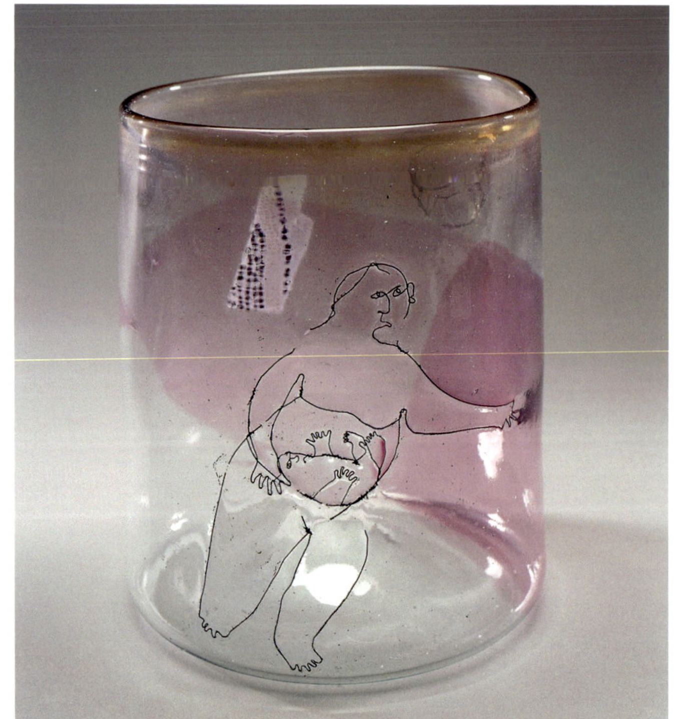

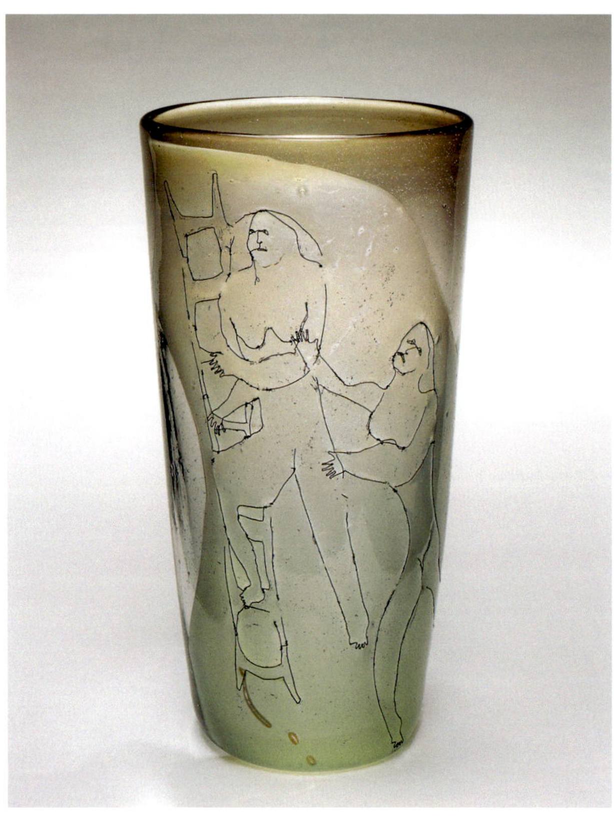

Woman Reaching, 1980
Glass and wire, 10 × 6 × 6 inches

Two Women on a Ladder, 1980
Glass and wire, 12½ × 7¼ × 7¼ inches

Figure with Child, 1980
Glass and wire, 9½ × 6¼ × 6¼ inches

Babies and Baskets Are Not Strangers, 1980 (right)
Glass and wire, 11½ × 6 × 6 inches

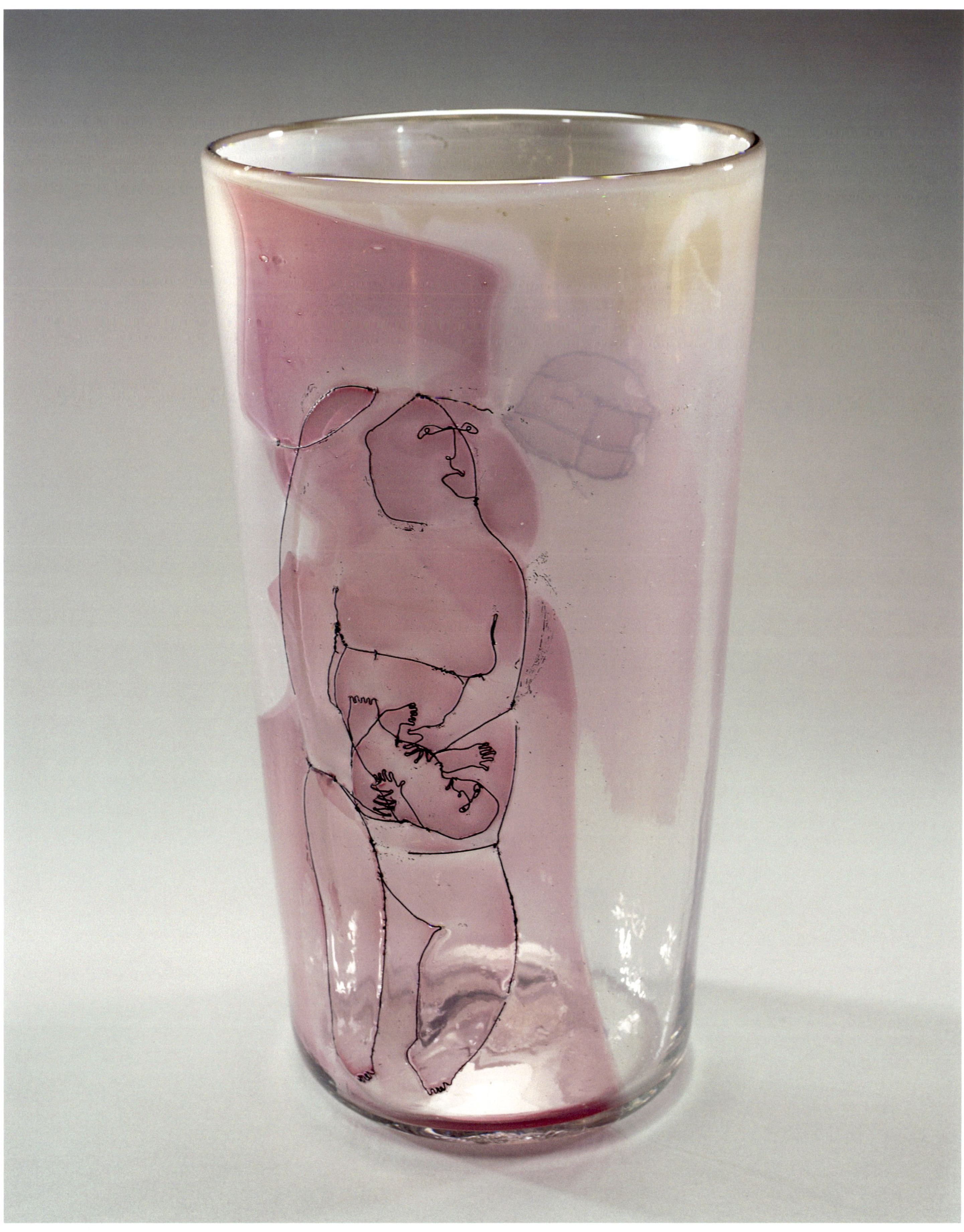

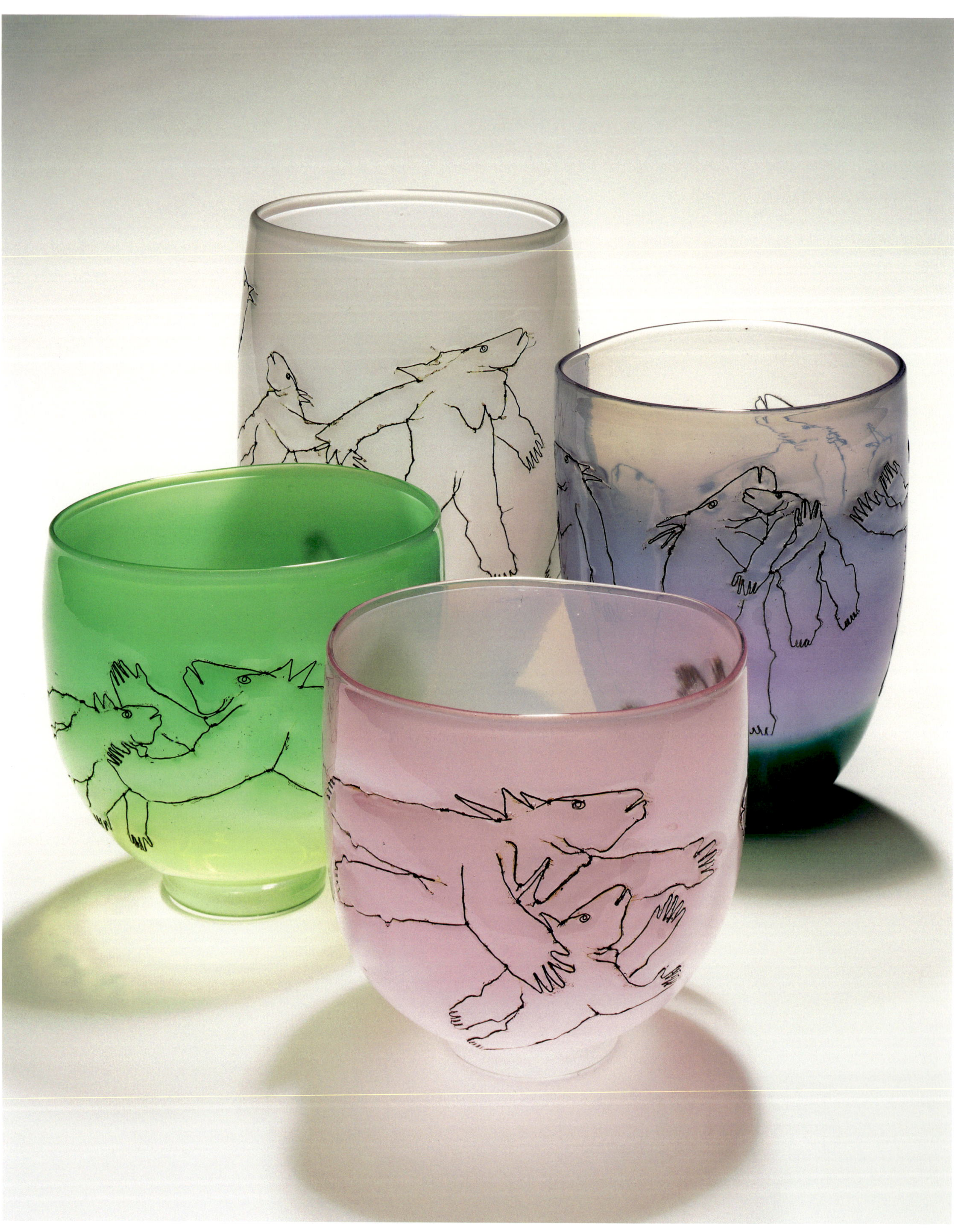

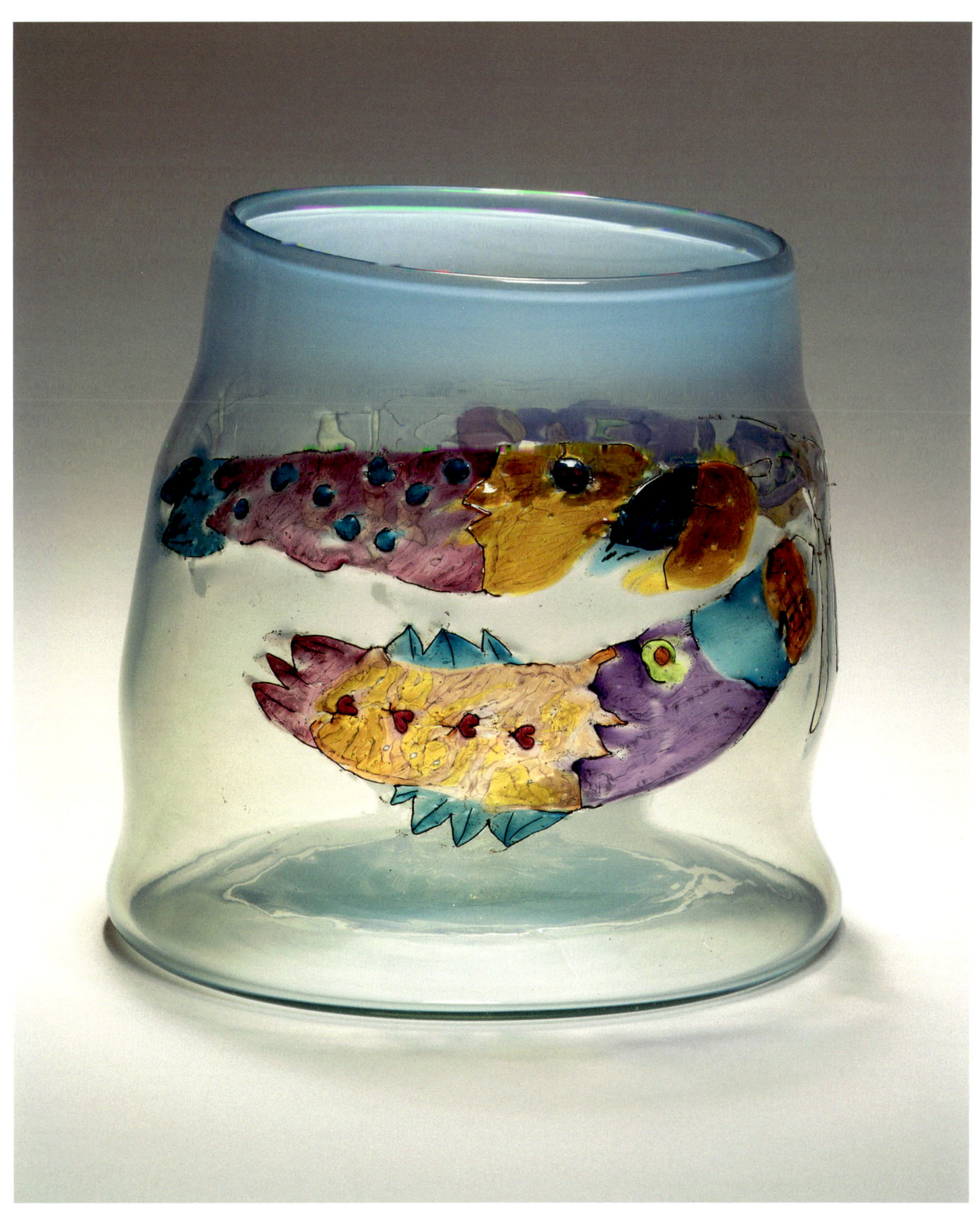

Narwhal Bowls, 1982
Glass and wire, 6 to 10 inches high

Wind Kites, 1984
Glass and wire, 10 × 10½ × 10½ inches

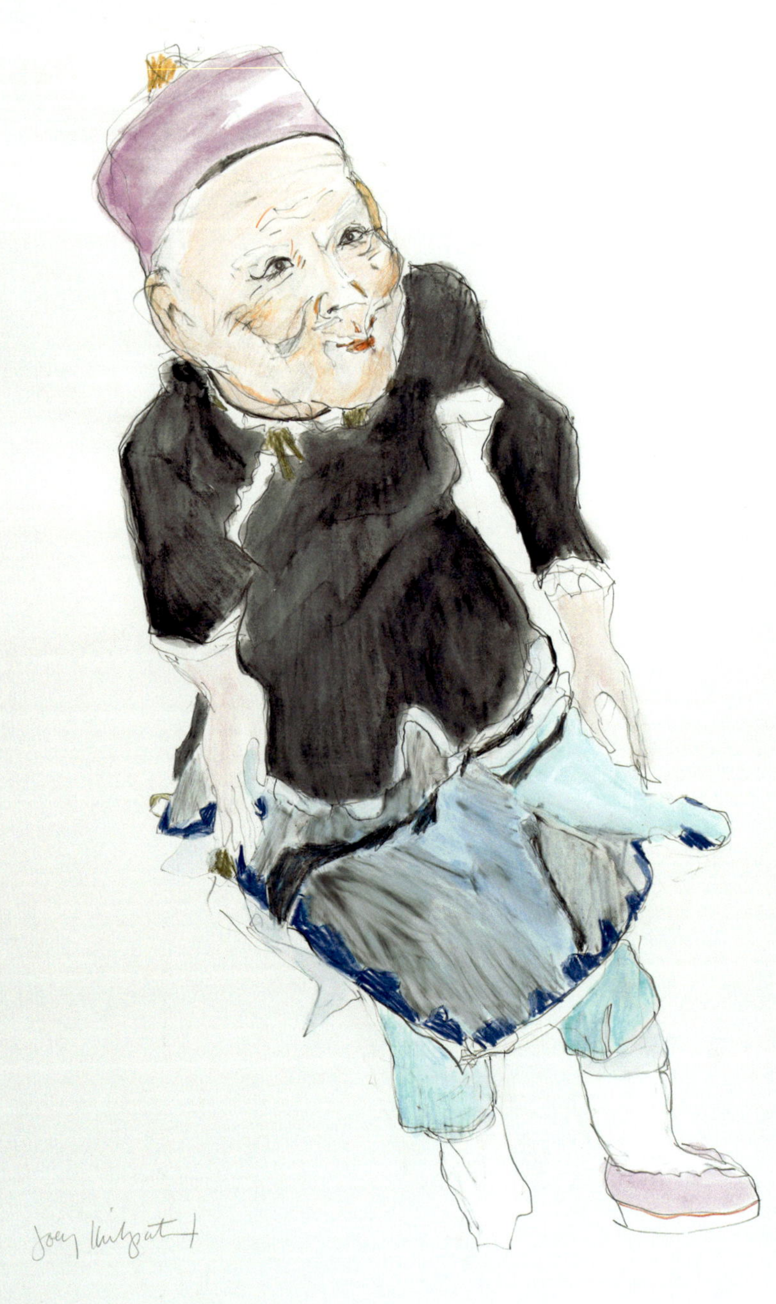

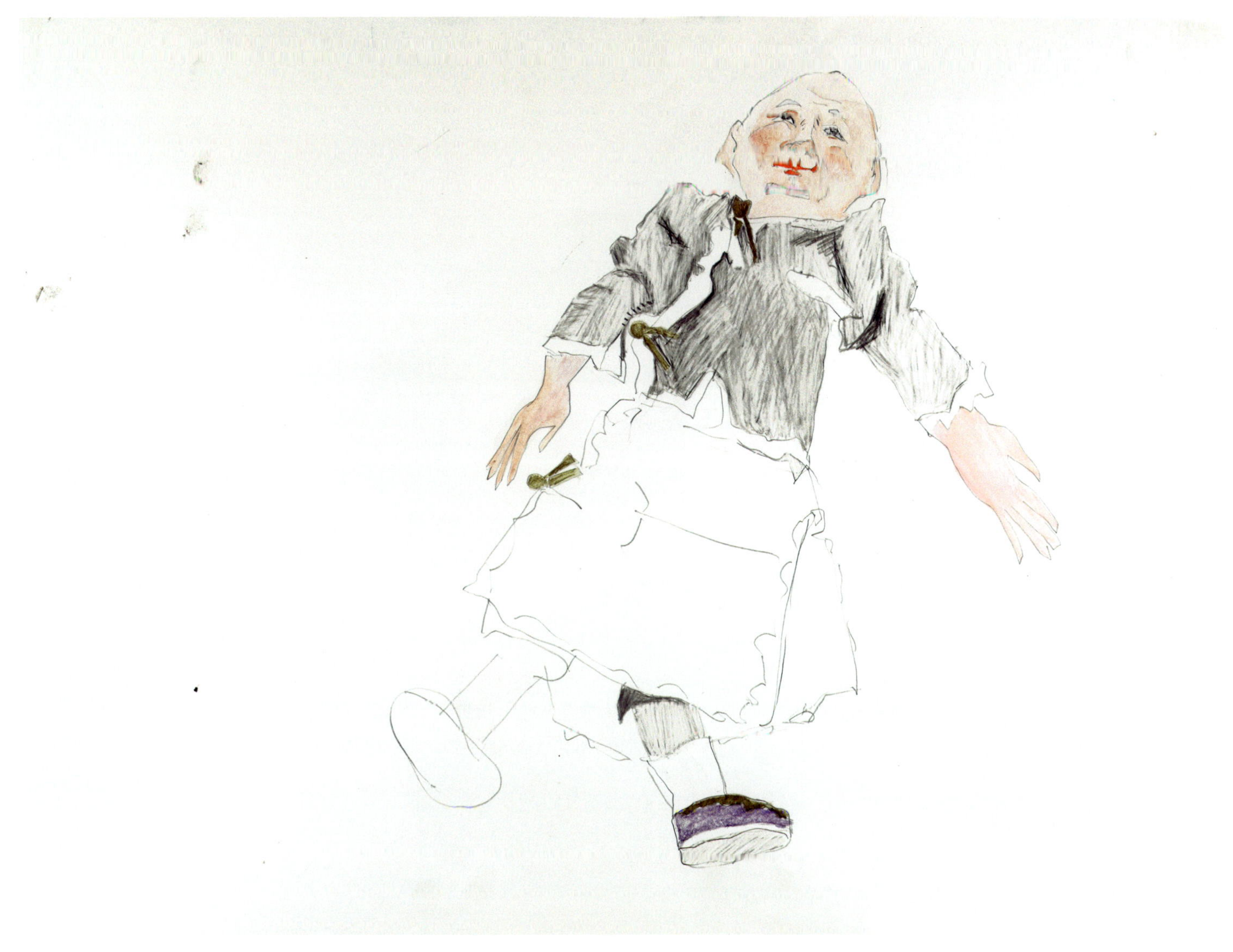

Joey Kirkpatrick, **Doll Drawing II**, 1979
Graphite and gouache on paper, 30 × 23¼ inches

Joey Kirkpatrick, **Doll Drawing I**, 1979
Graphite and gouache on paper, 23 × 30 inches

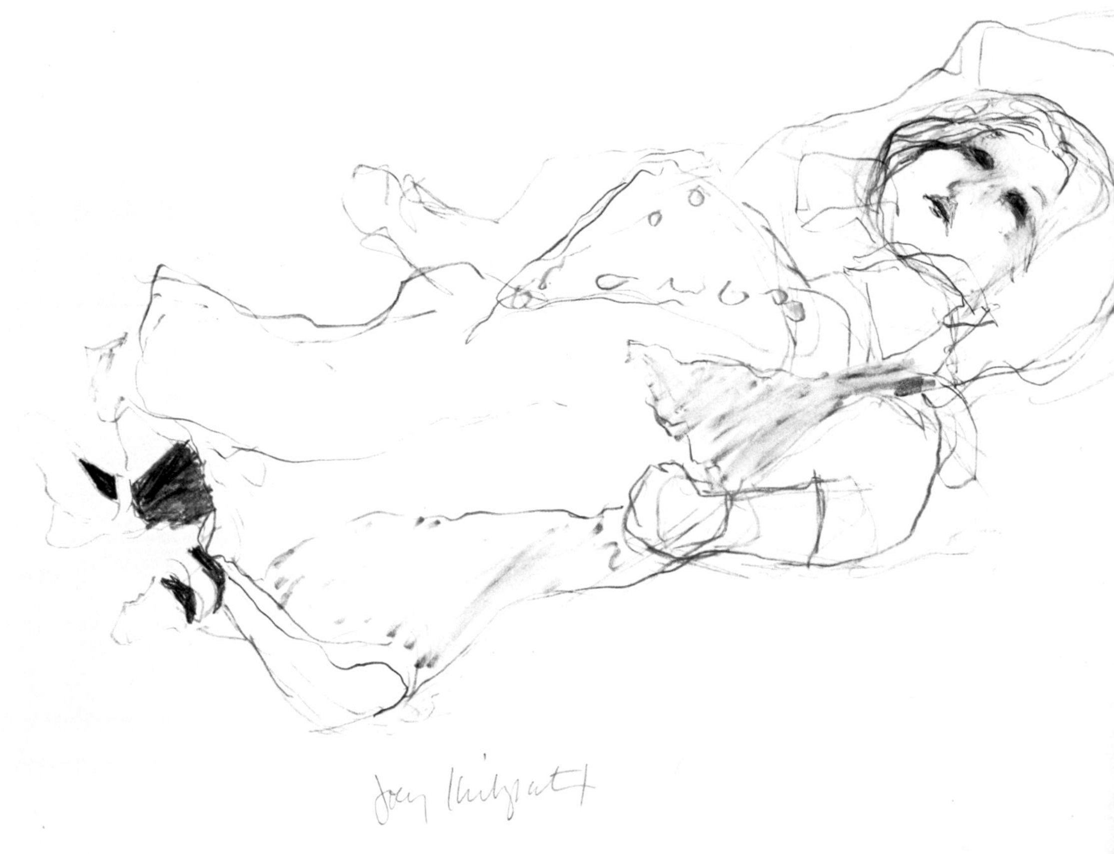

Joey Kirkpatrick, **Rebecca and the French Doll**, 1979
Graphite on paper, 18¾ × 30 inches

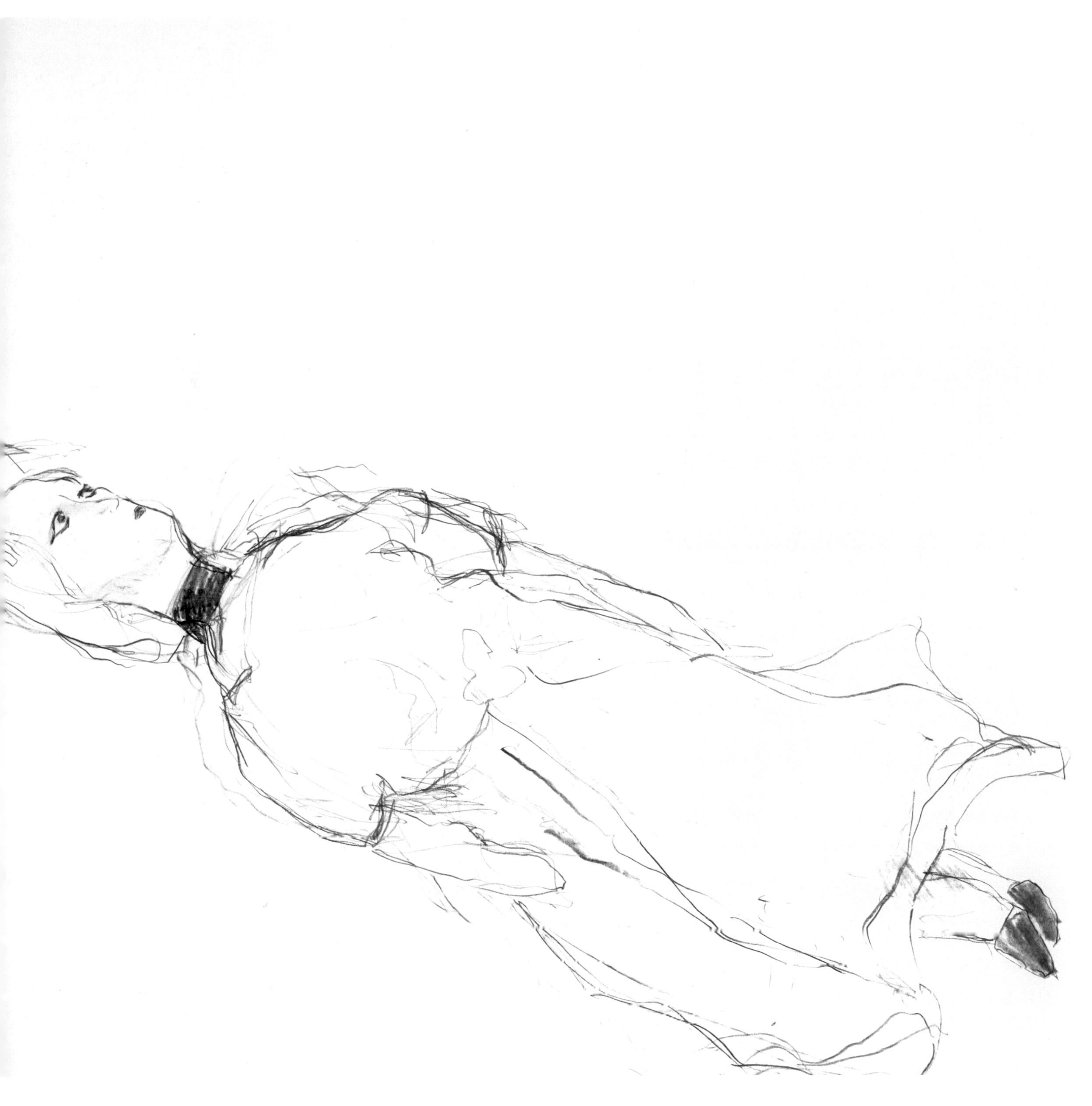

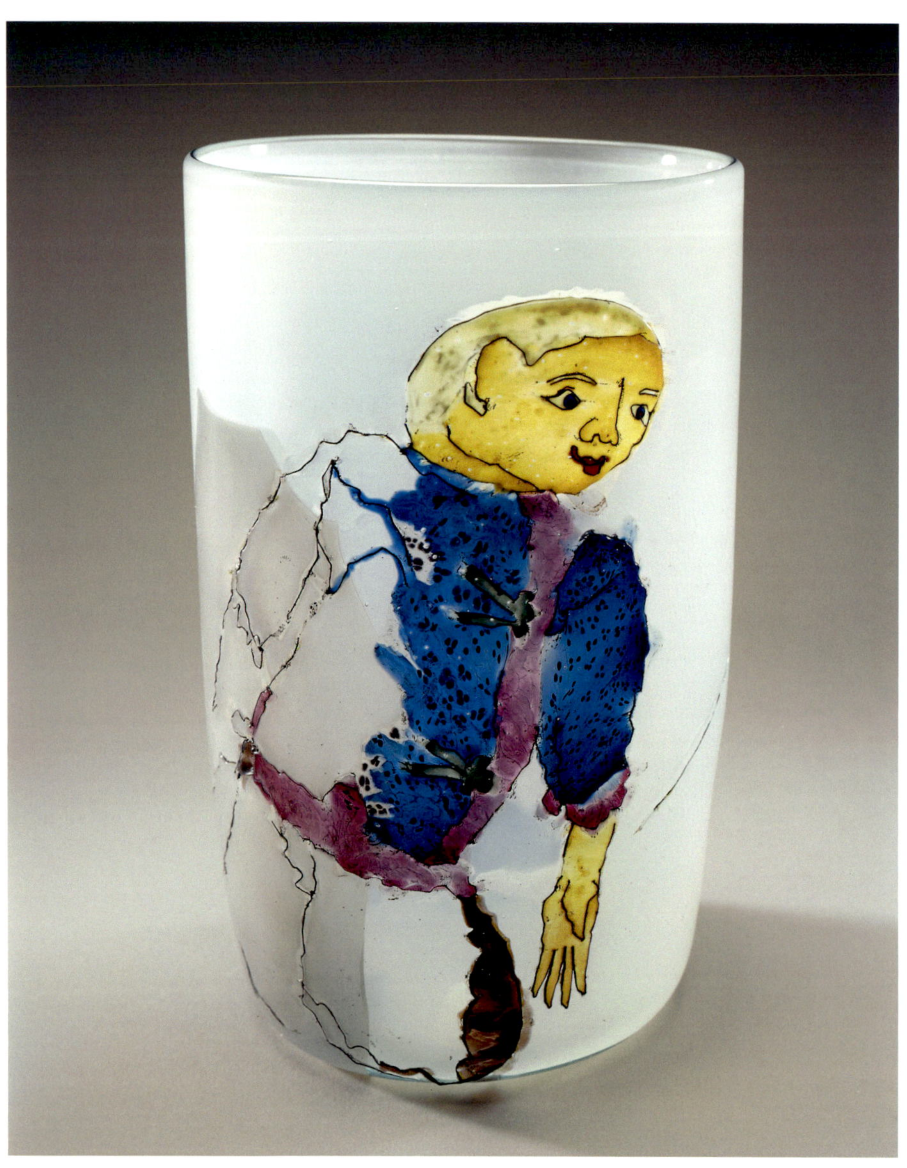

The Chinese Doll (and detail), 1982
Glass and wire, 12 × 7¼ × 7¼ inches

(following spread)
Doll Drawing Cylinders, 1982–1984
Glass and wire, 8 to 14 inches high

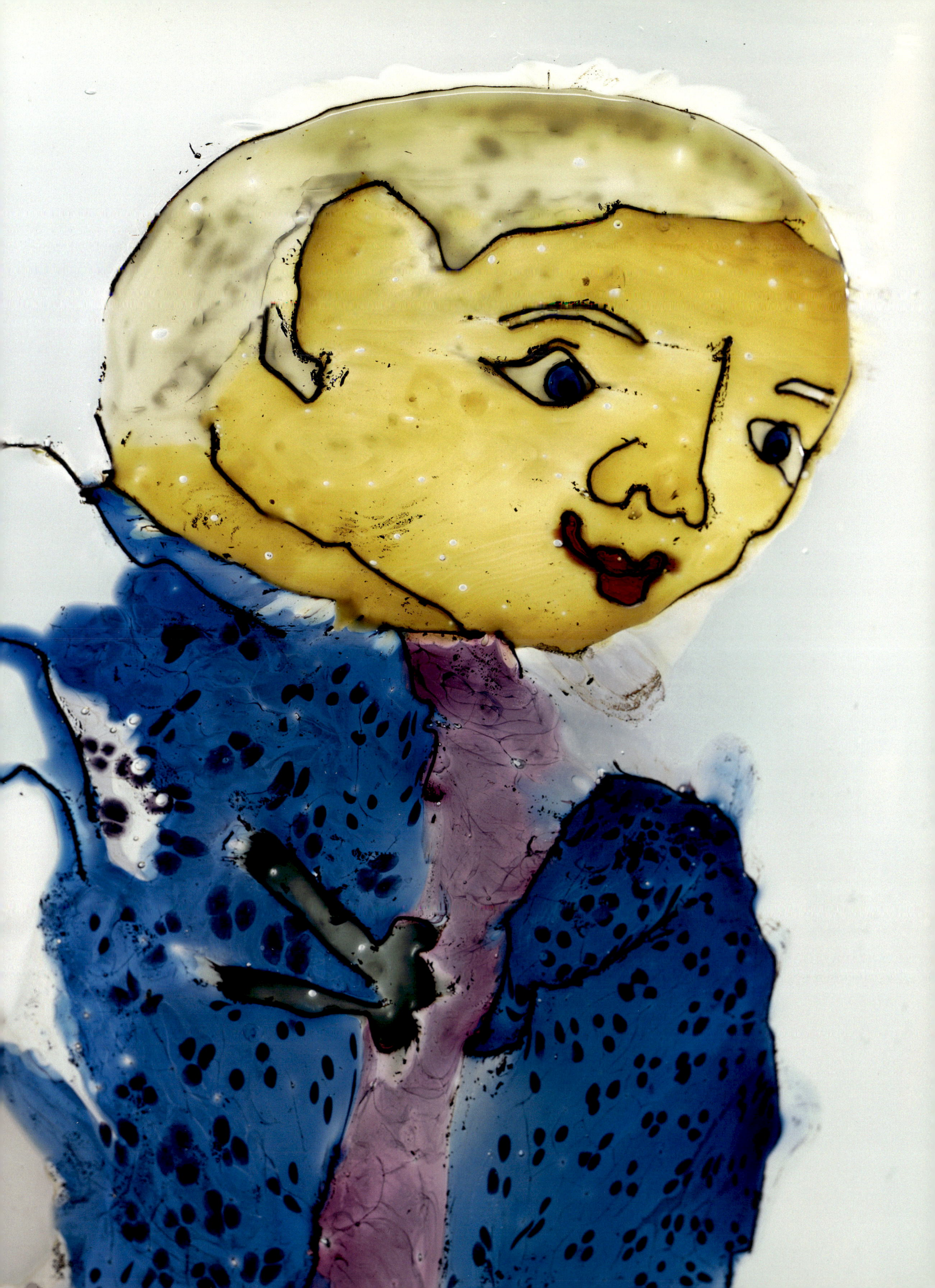

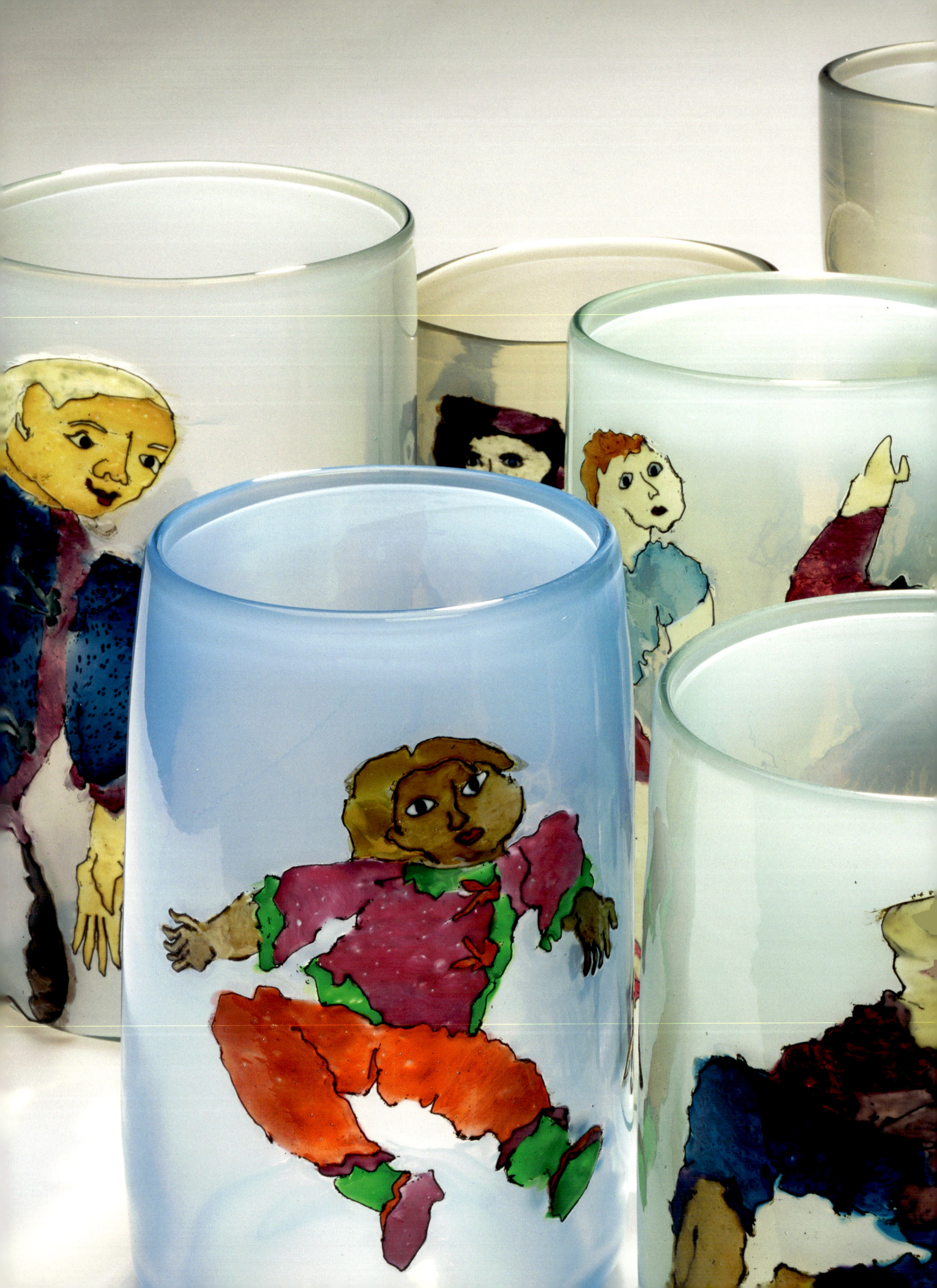

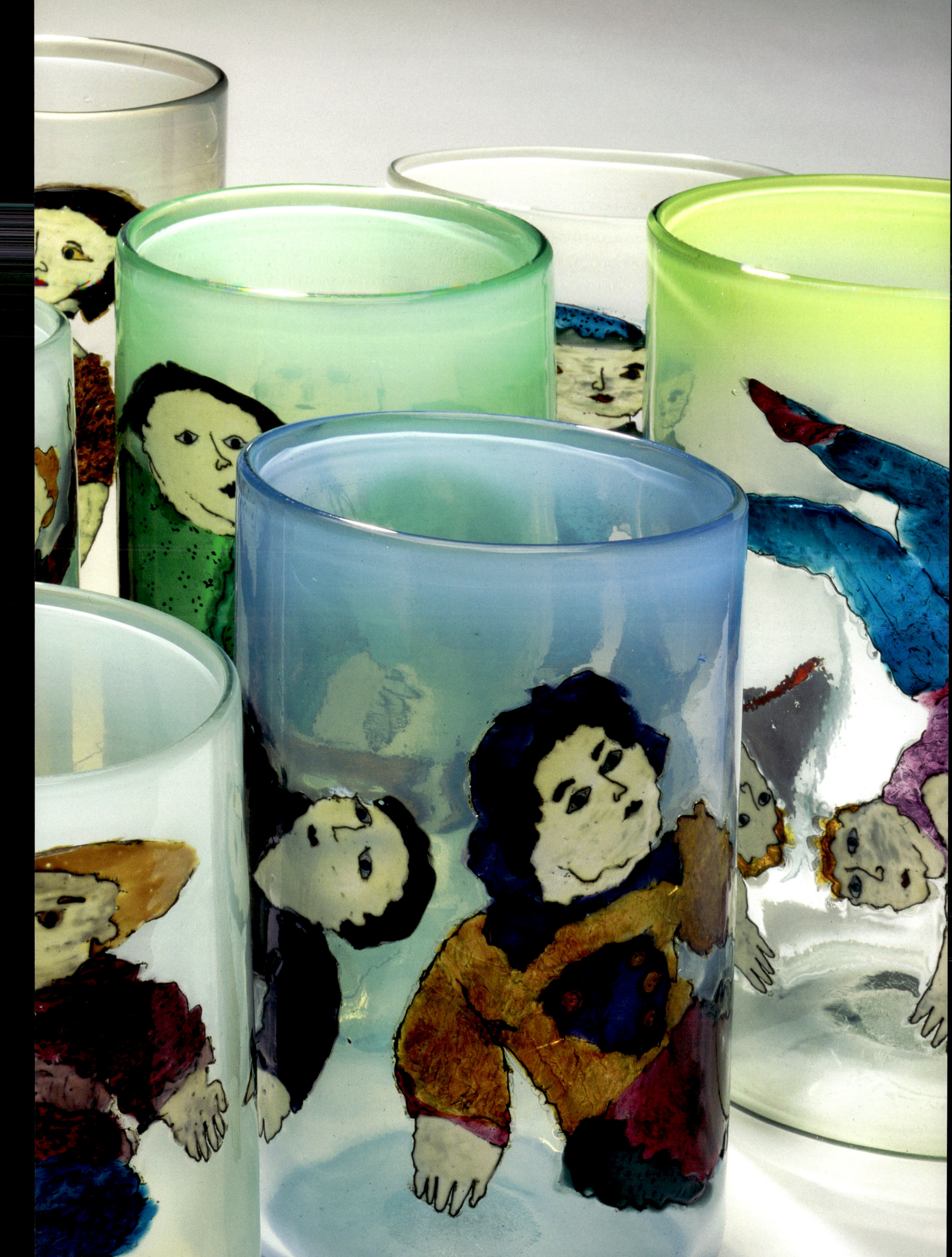

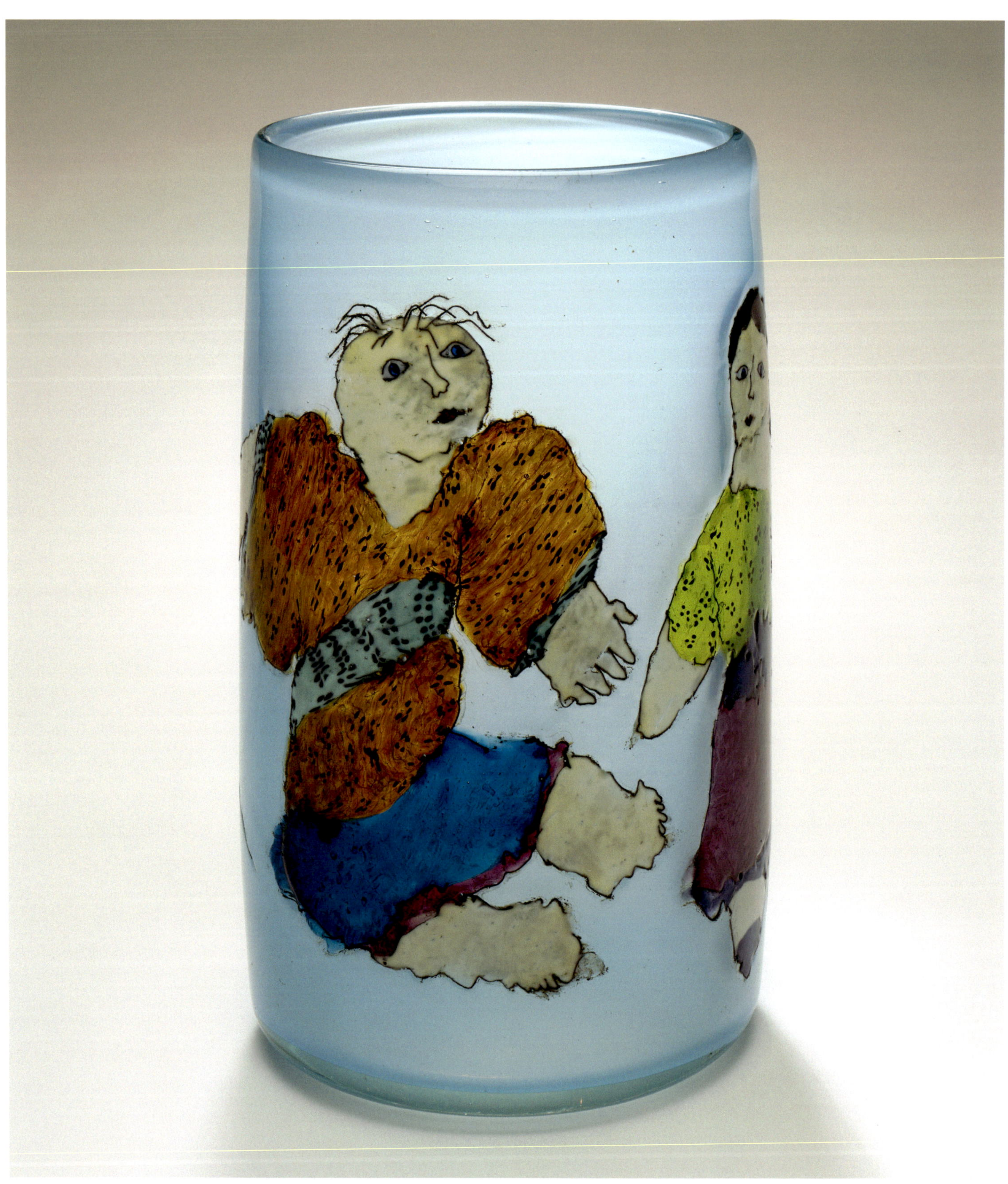

The Conversation, 1984
Glass and wire, 11¾ × 6½ × 6½ inches

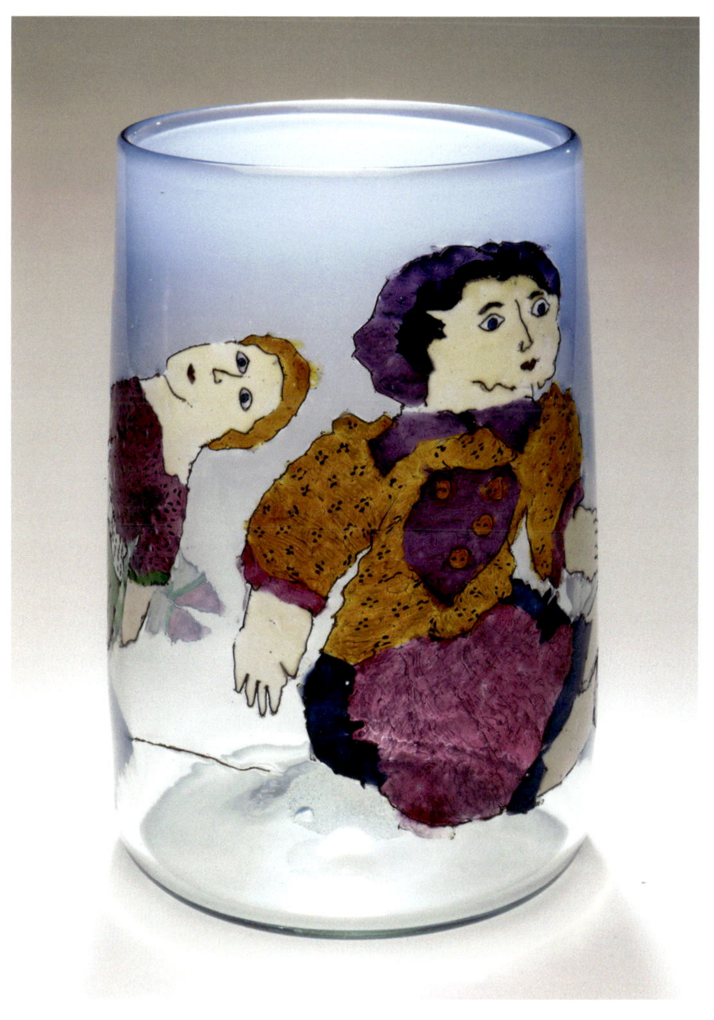

Double Doll on Blue, 1984
Glass and wire, 11 × 5½ × 5½ inches

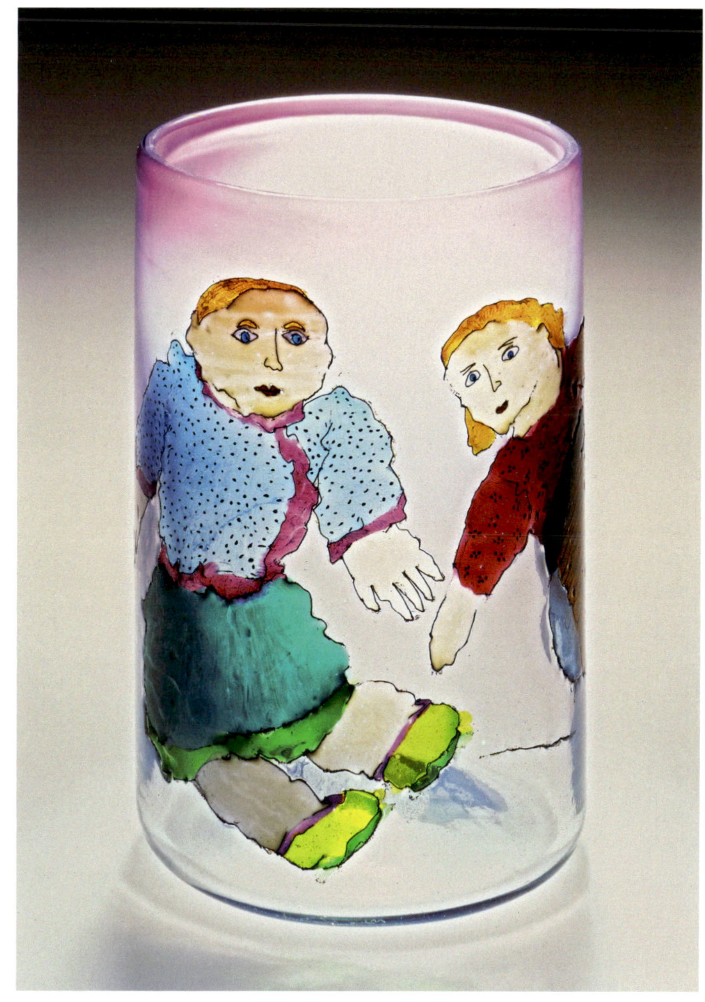

Wishing Will, 1984
Glass and wire, 12 × 6 × 6 inches

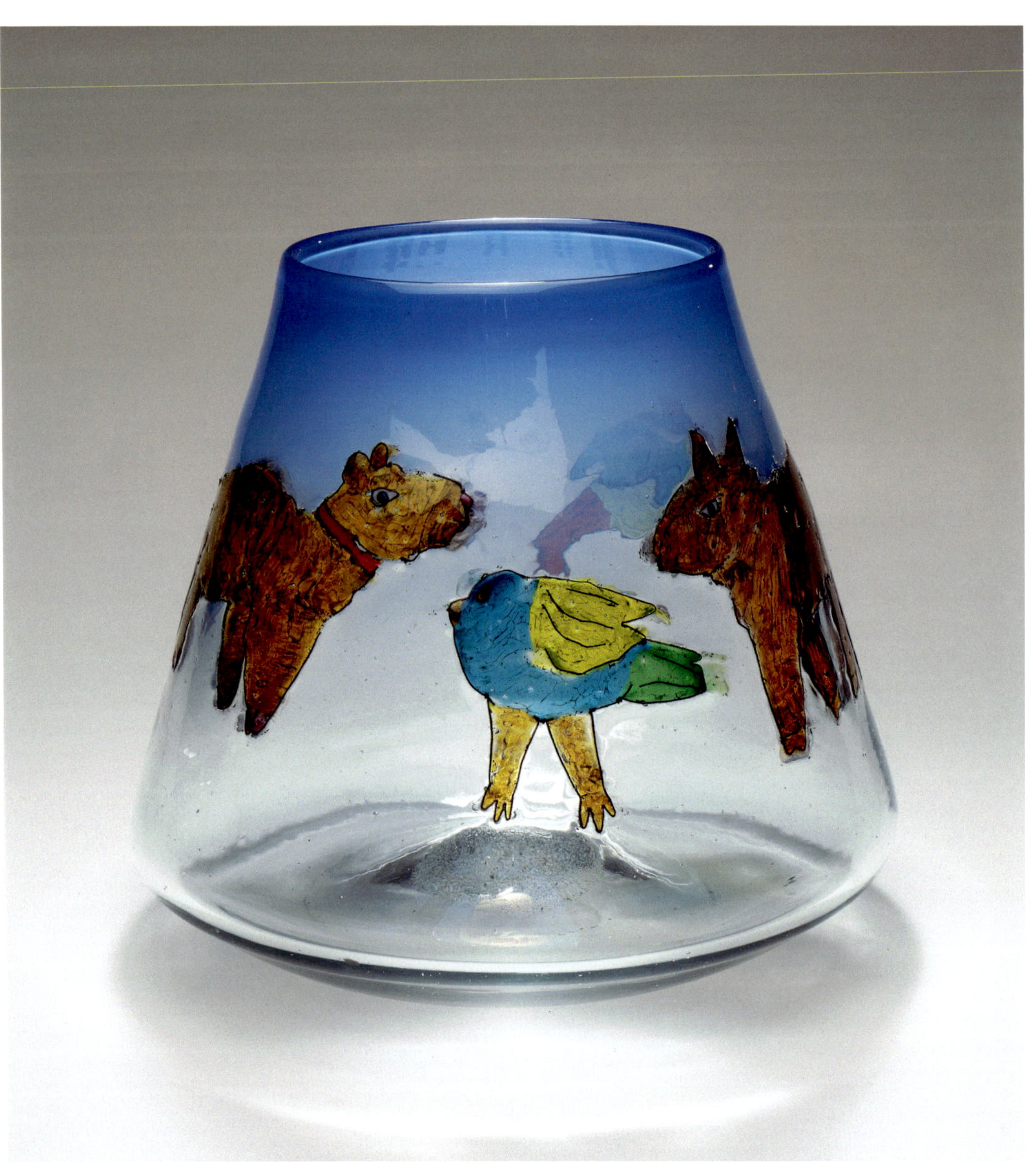

Animal Bowl on Blue, 1984
Glass and wire, 7¼ × 7¾ × 7¾ inches

Lion Tamer, 1983
Glass and wire, 11 × 7 × 7 inches

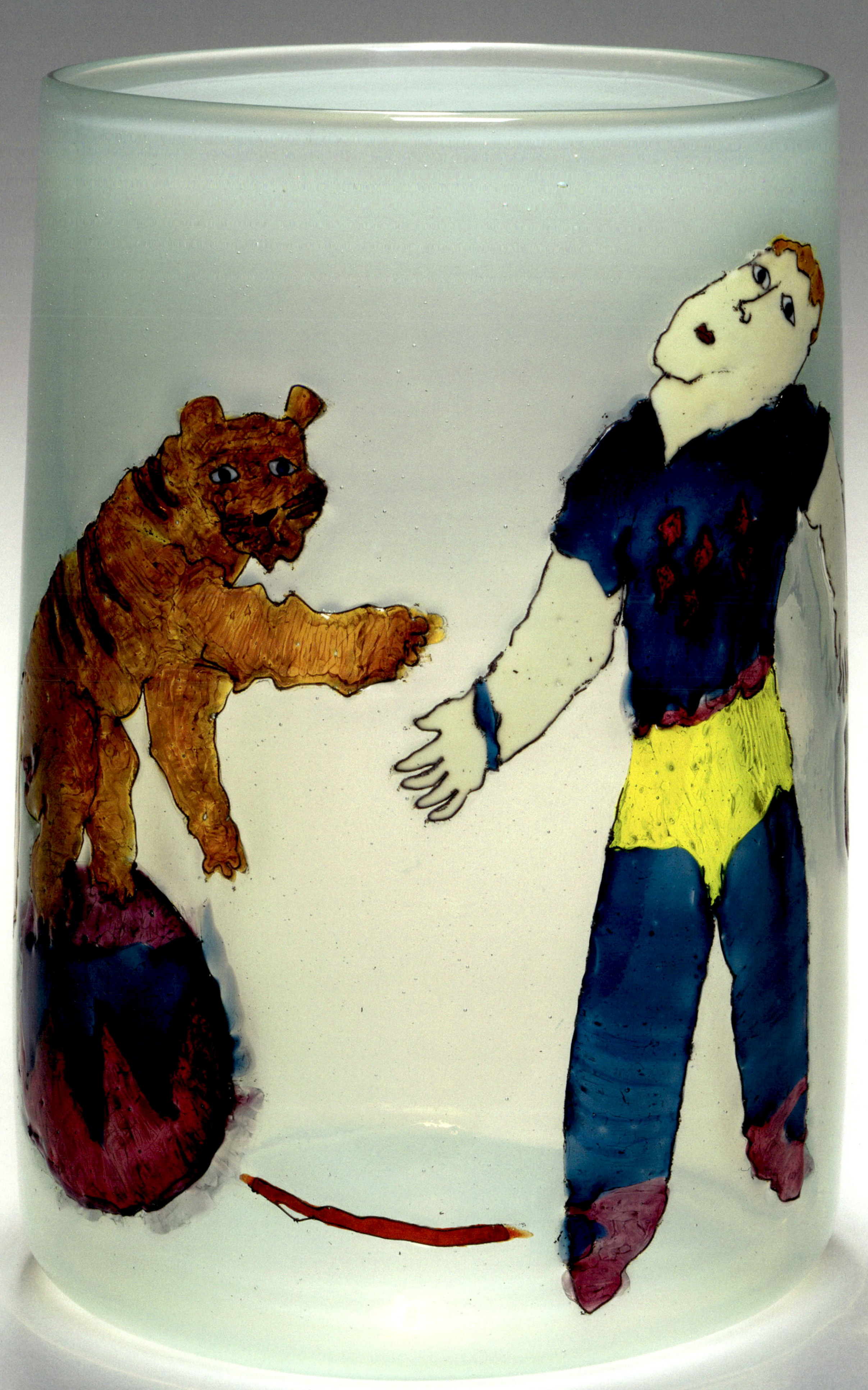

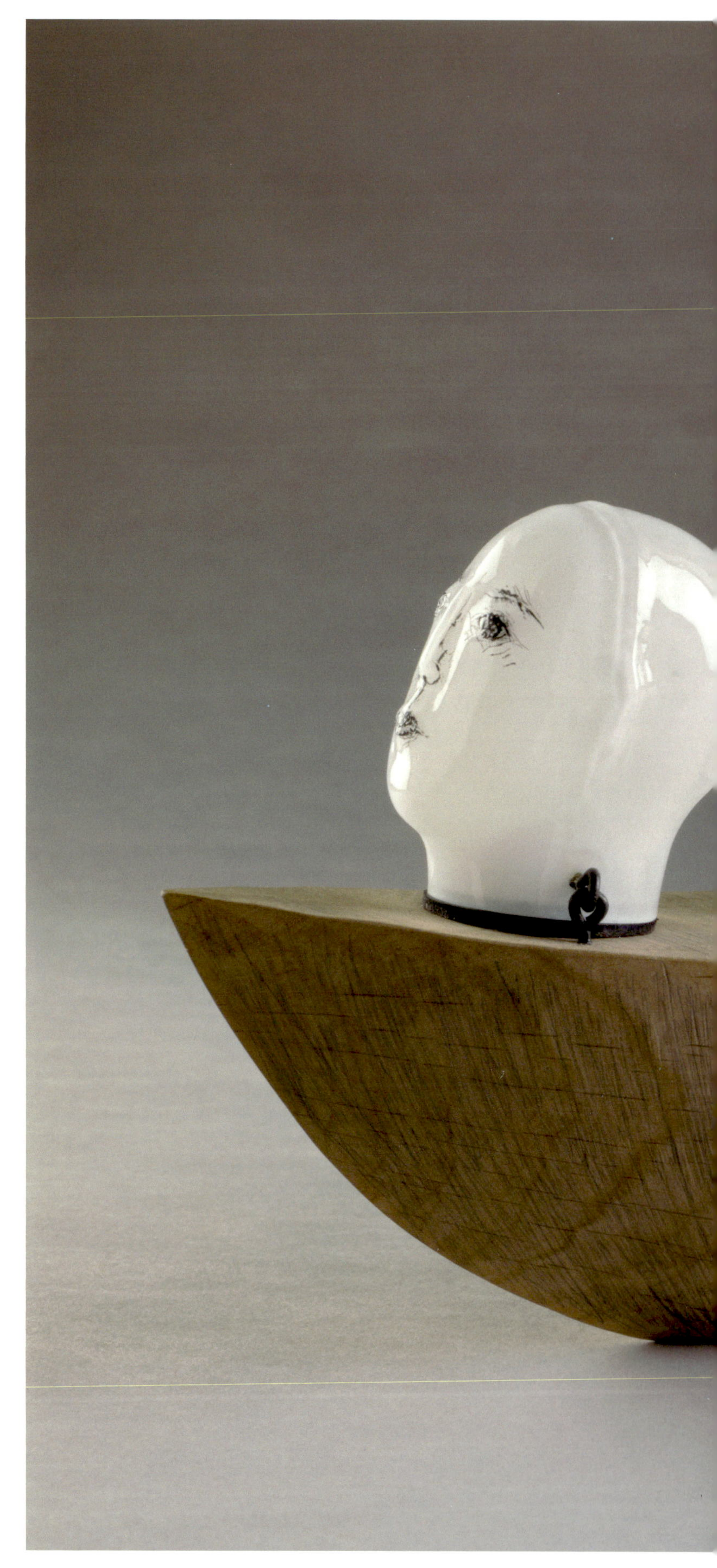

New Moon With Four Riders II, 1983
Glass, wood, graphite, and steel, 6½ × 17 × 3¾ inches

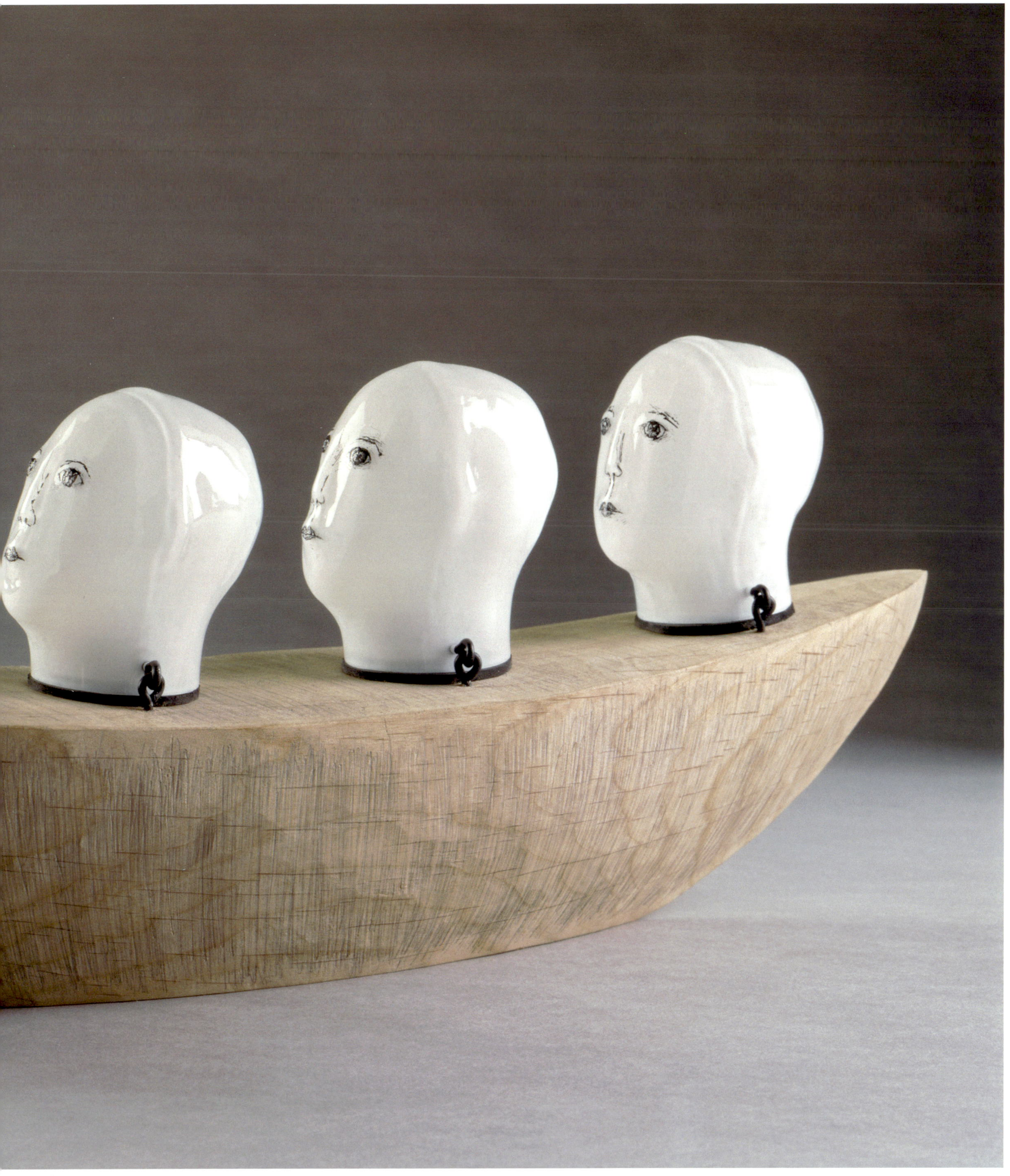

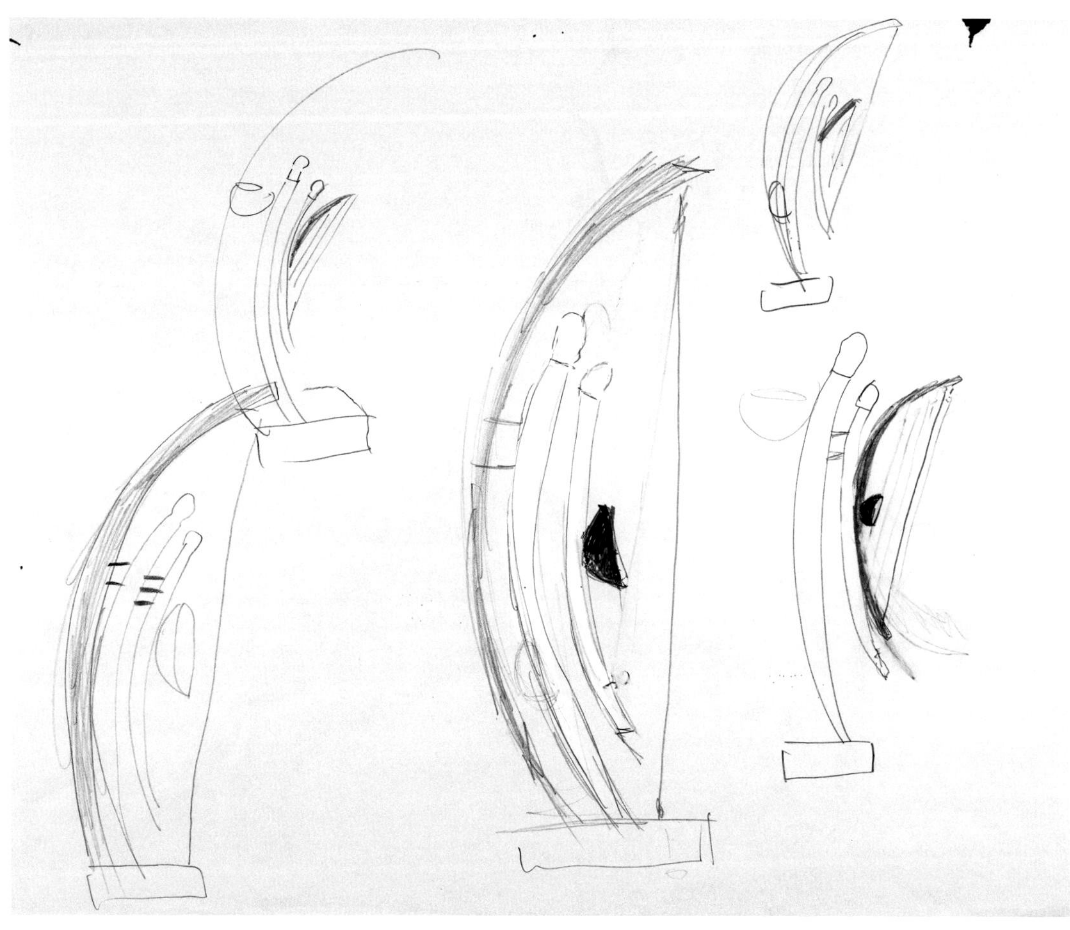

Joey Kirkpatrick, **Untitled**, 1984
Graphite and ink on paper, 14 × 16 inches

Personal Sonata, 1984
Glass, wood, slate, paint, and steel, 34½ × 11 × 8 inches

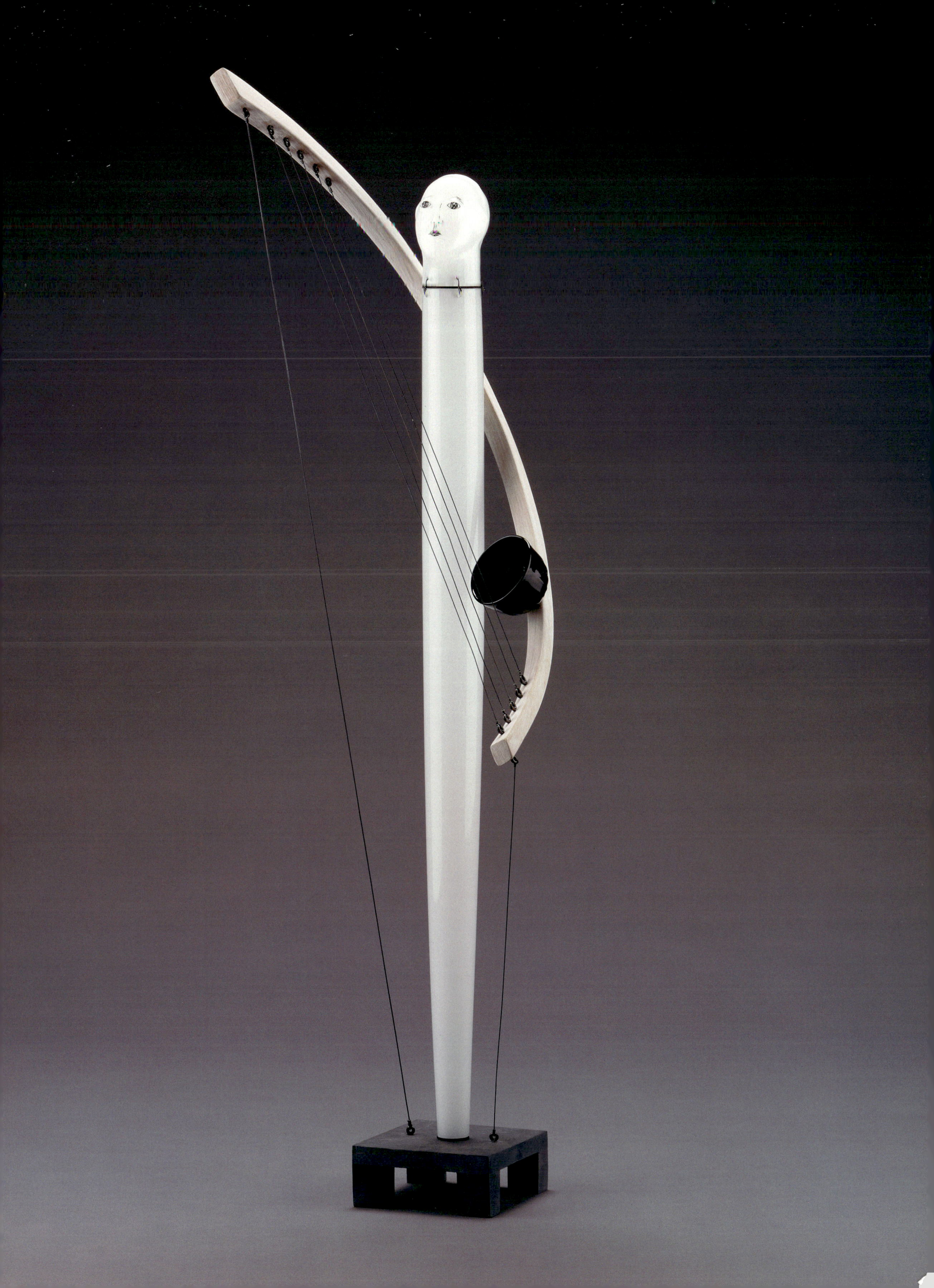

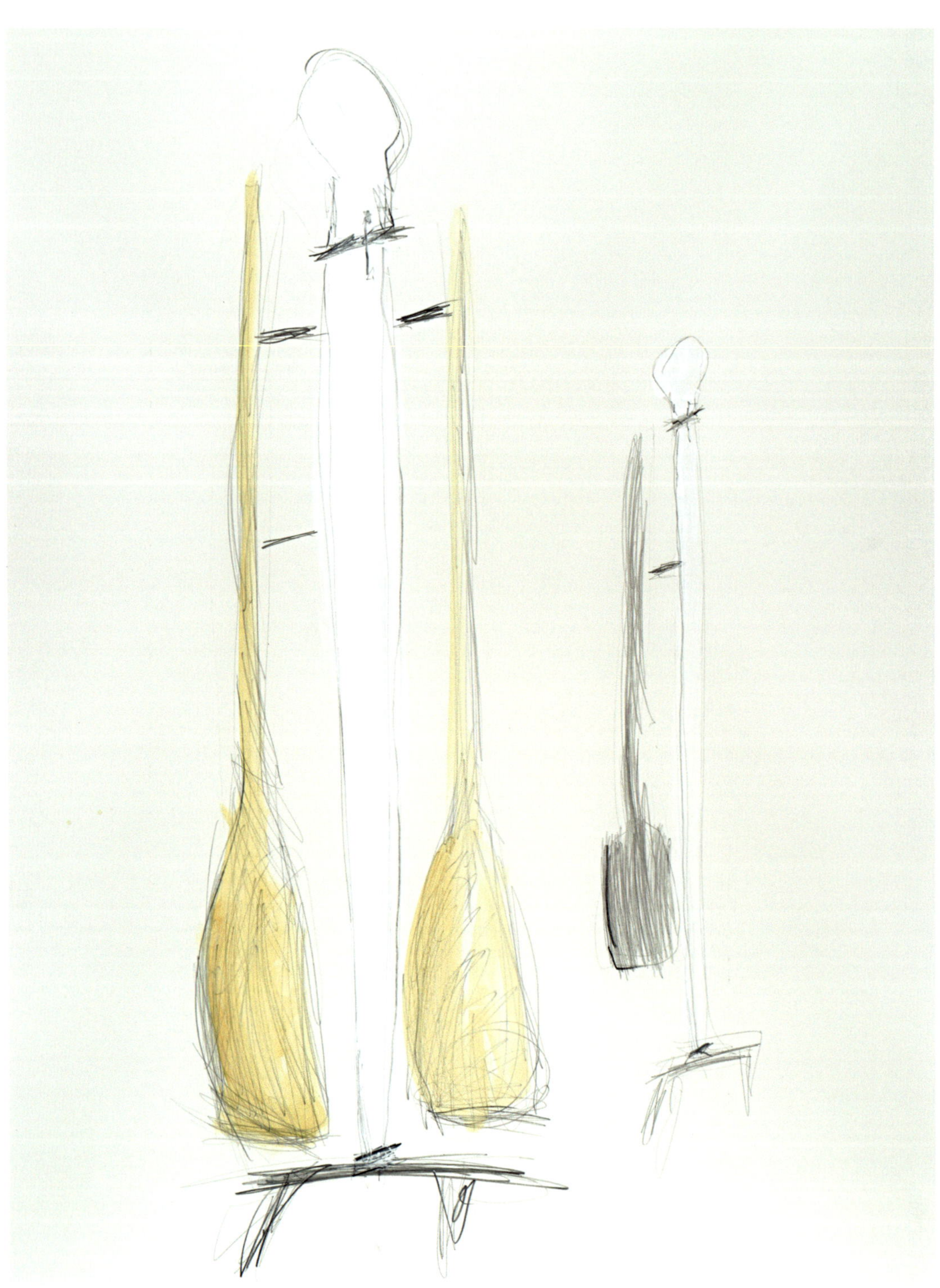

Joey Kirkpatrick, **Untitled**, 1984
Graphite and gouache on paper, 30 × 22½ inches

Foretold Journey, 1984
Glass, wood, slate, paint, and steel, 42½ × 12 × 6 inches

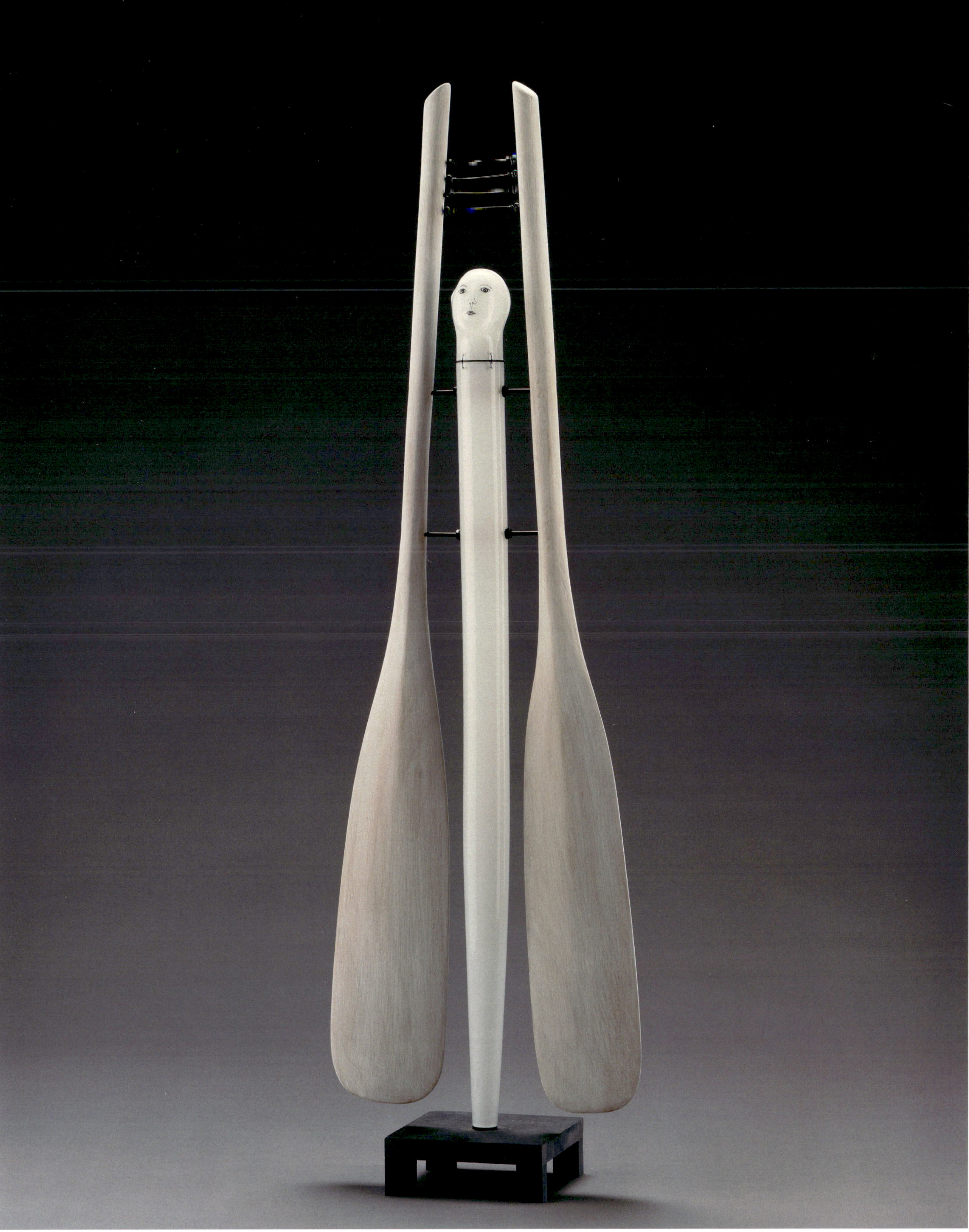

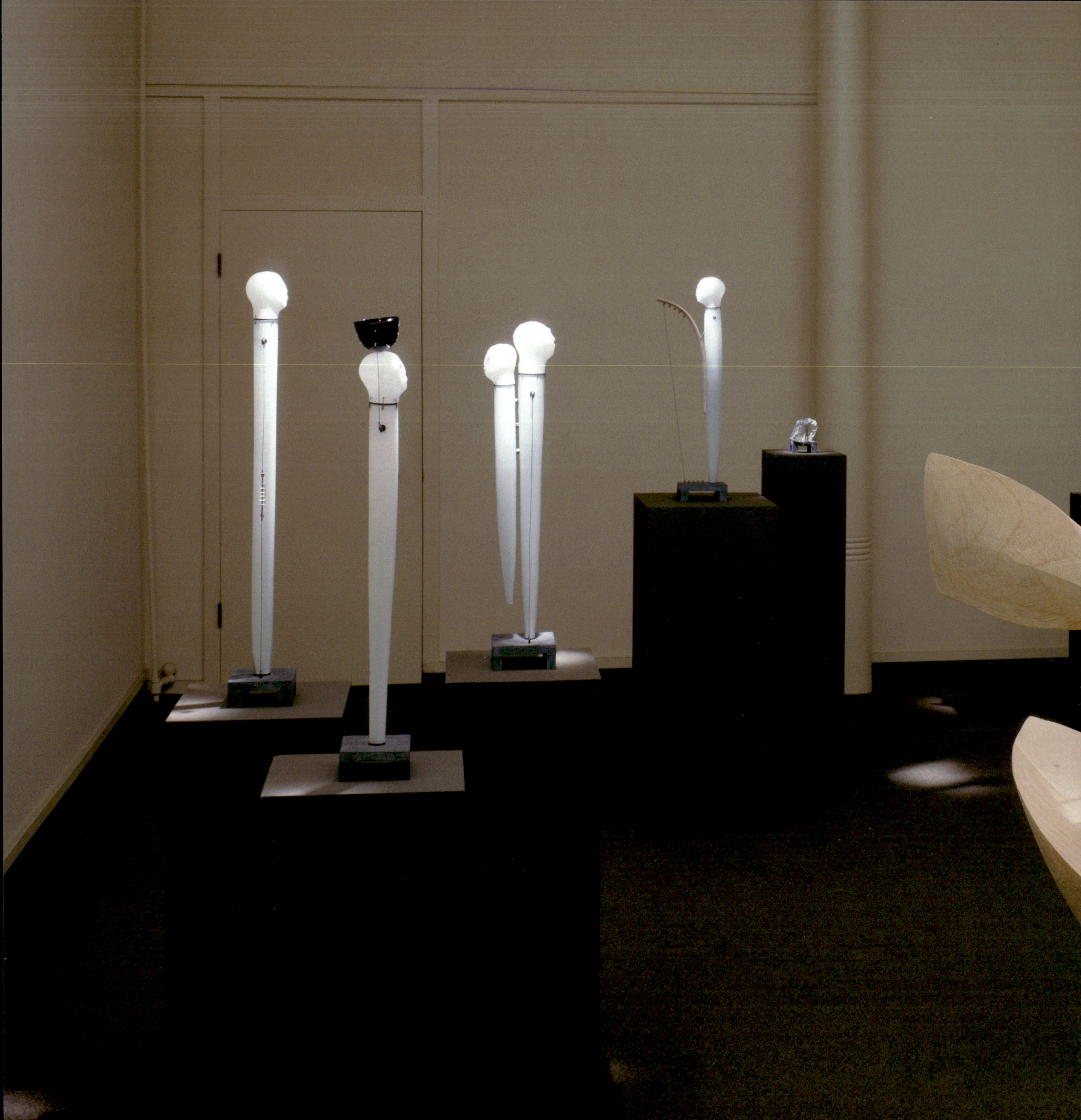

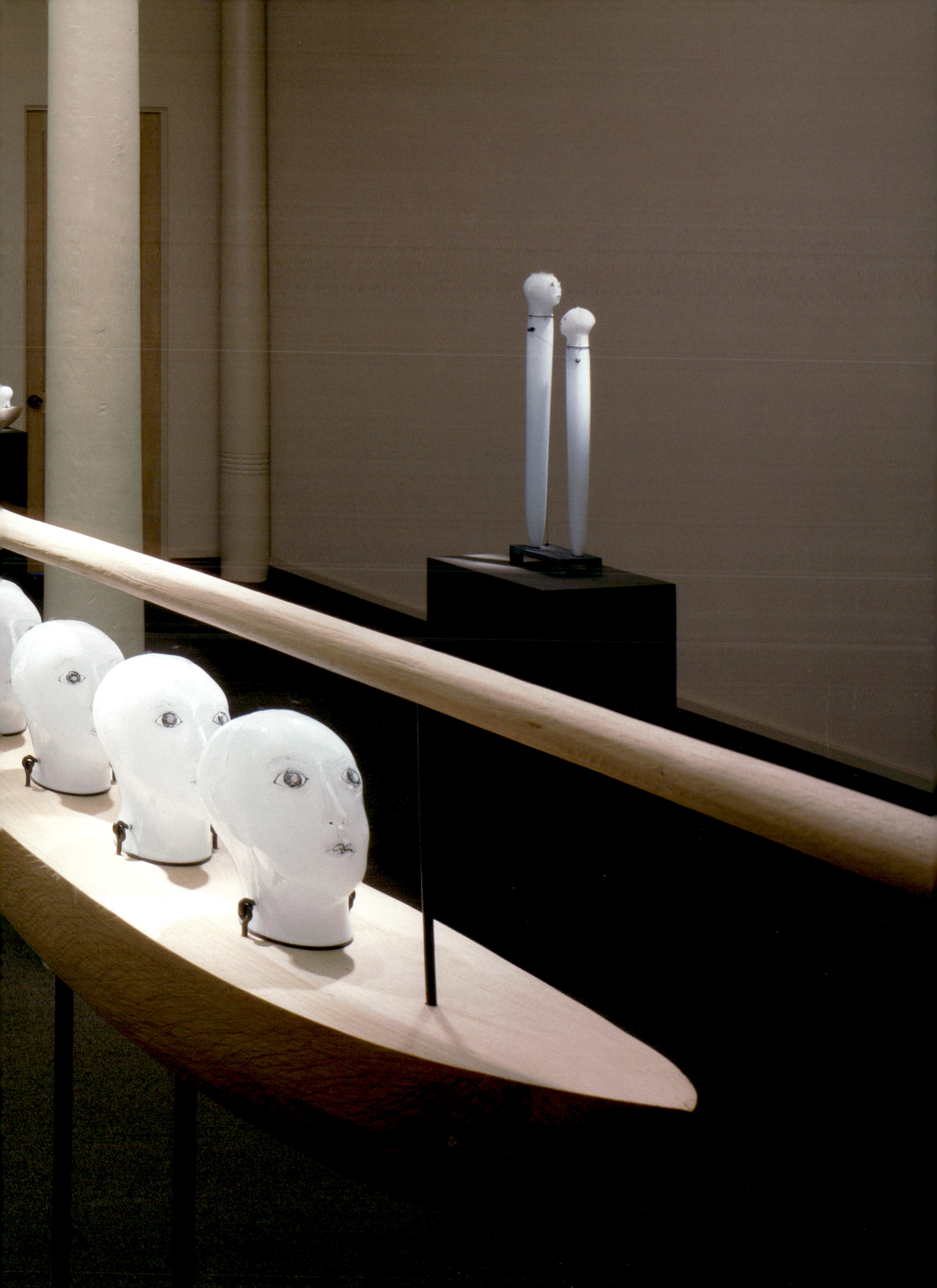

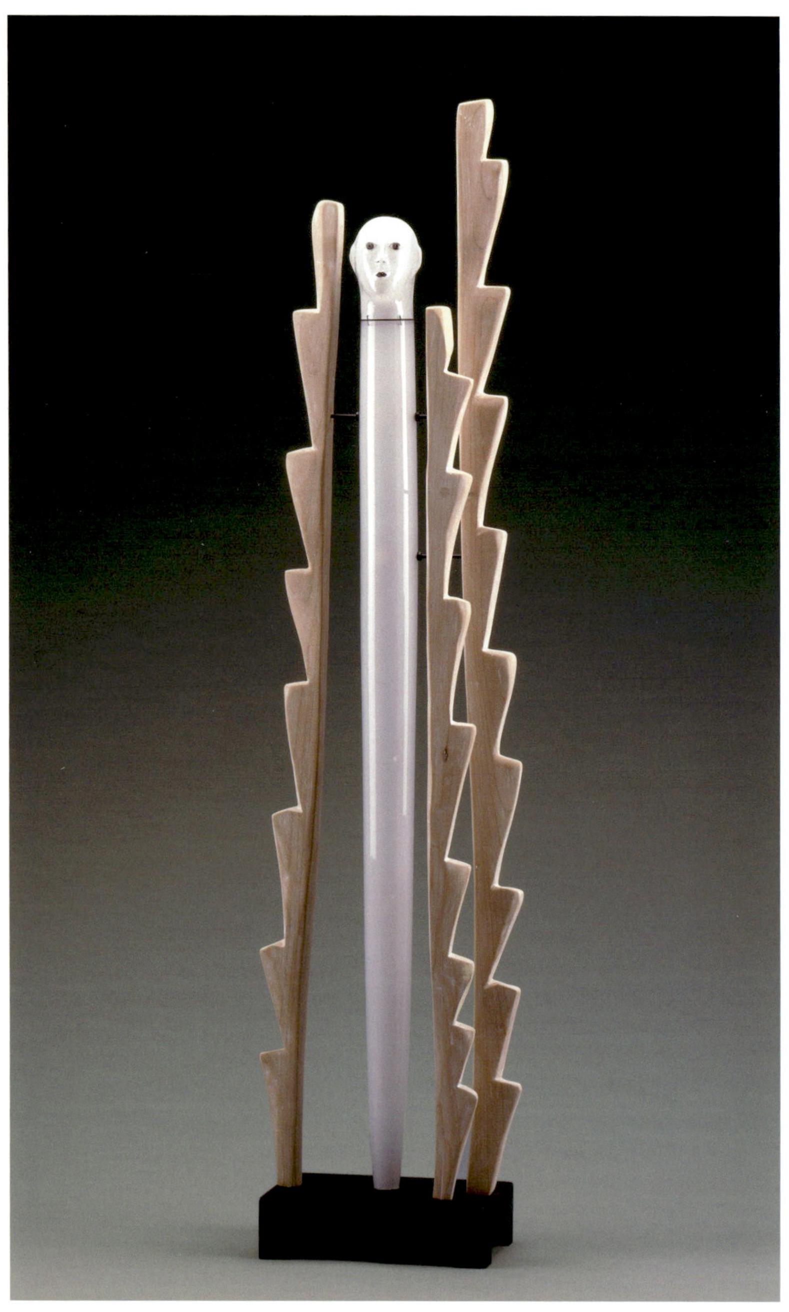

(previous spread)
Exhibition at Foster/White Gallery, Seattle, 1983

Garden of Ladders (and detail), 1985
Glass, wood, paint, and steel, 74 × 16 × 12 inches

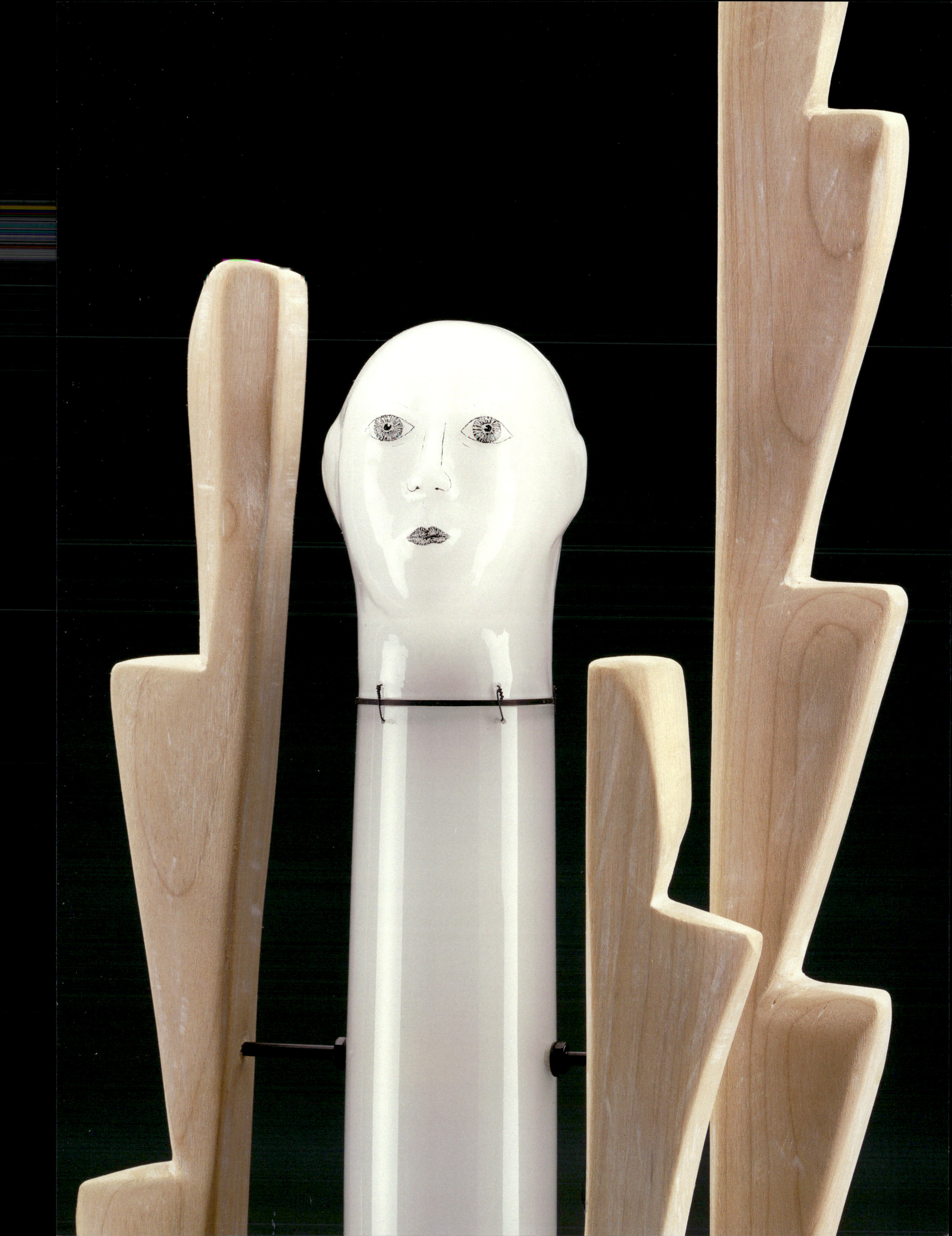

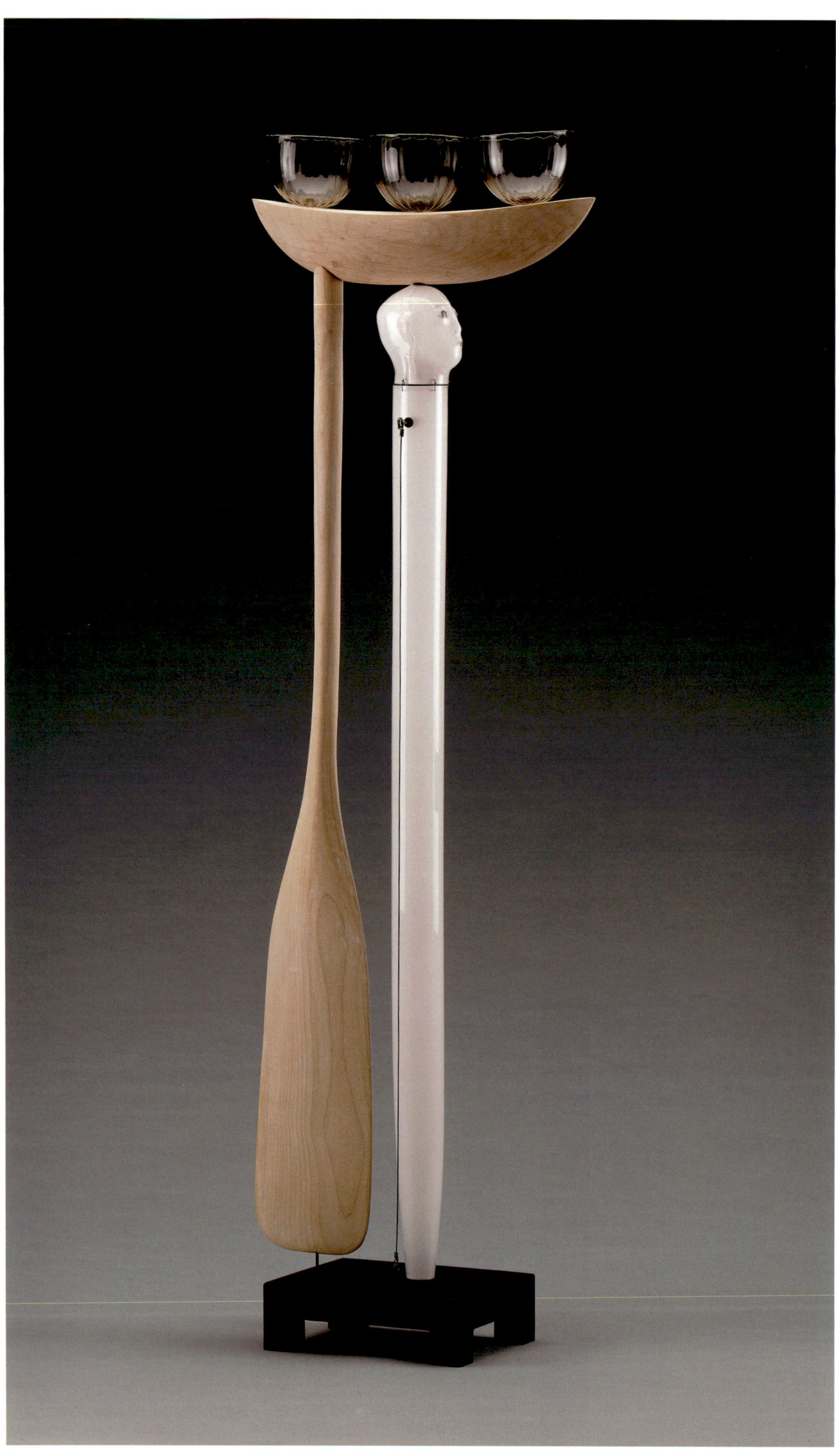

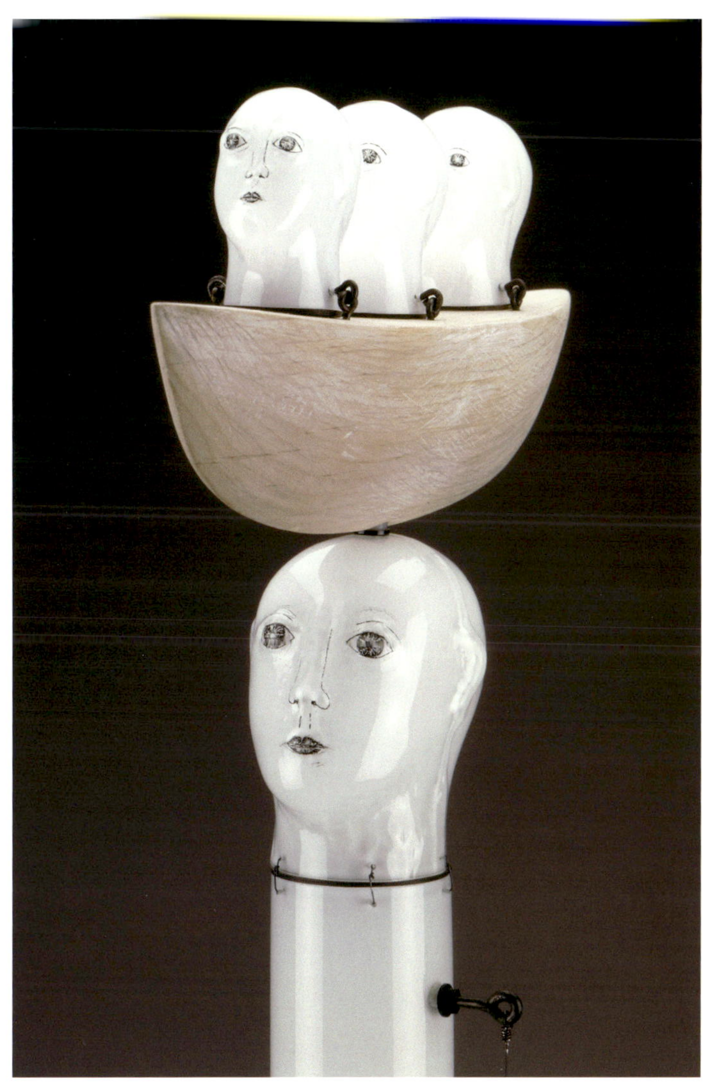 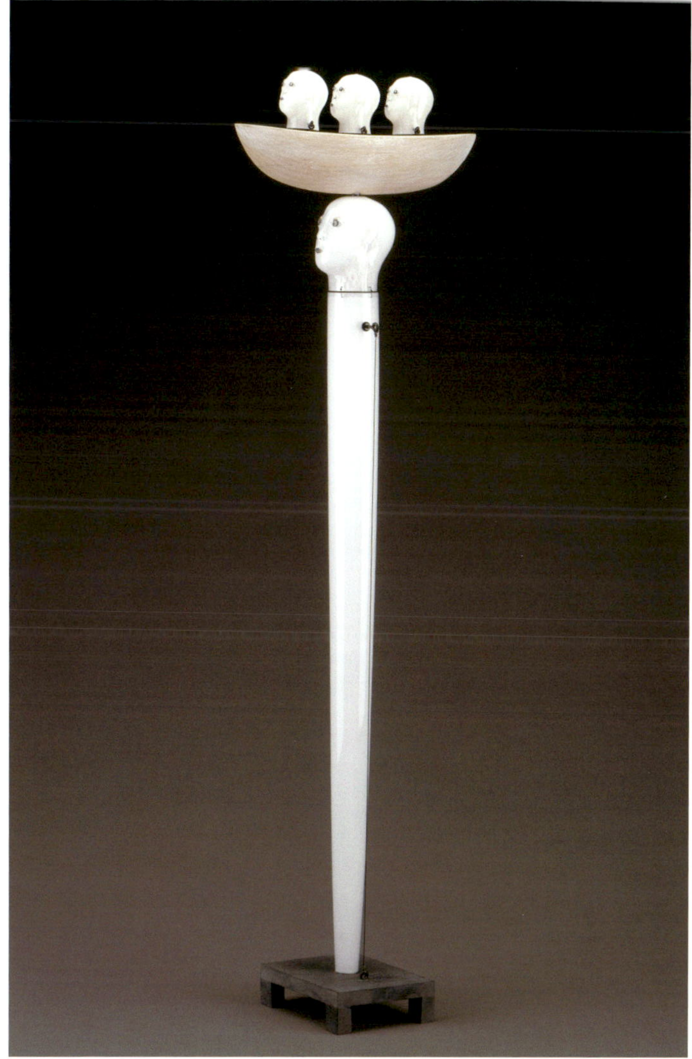

Voyage Carrier, 1985 (left)
Glass, wood, paint, and steel, 55 × 17 × 18 inches

Cargo (and detail), 1984
Glass, wood, paint, slate, and steel, 45½ × 7 × 14 inches

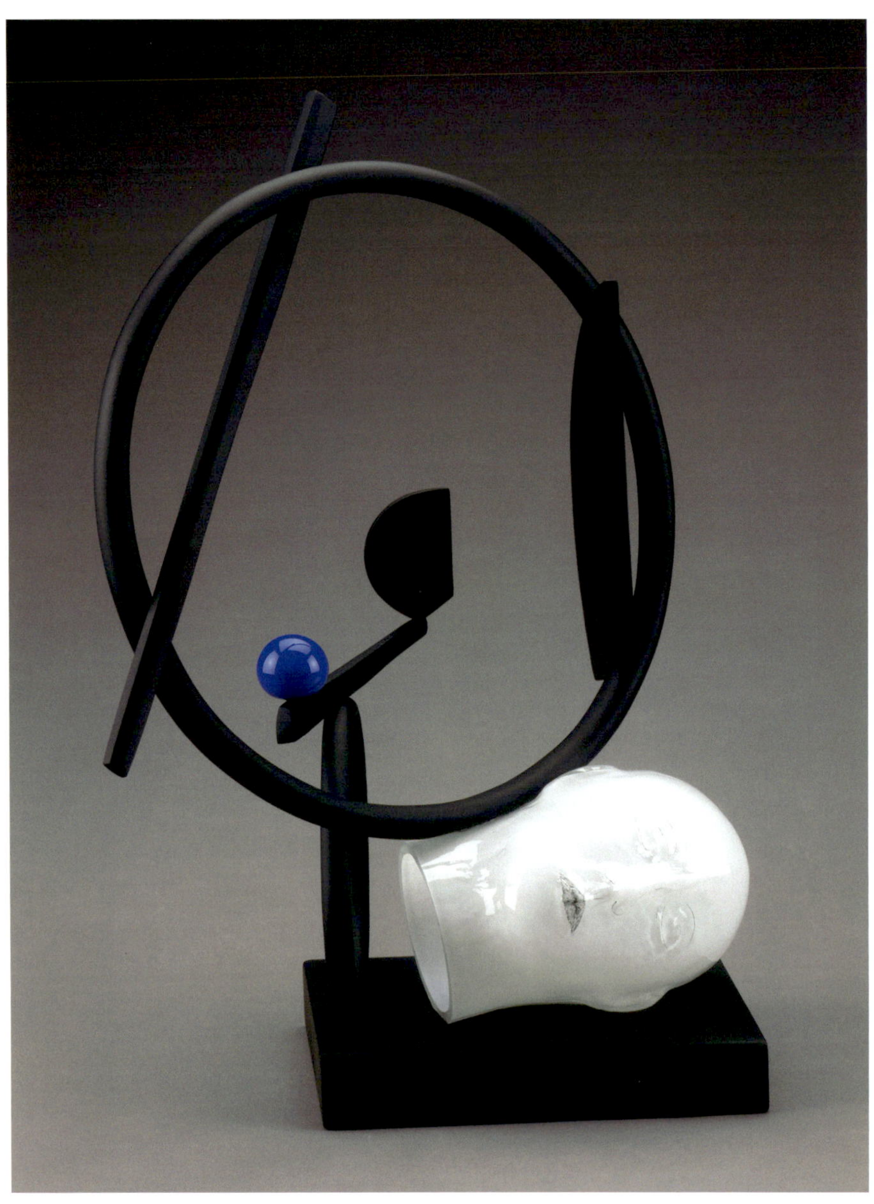

Tidal Eclipse, 1986
Glass, wood, paint, and steel, 27 × 17 × 16 inches

The Juggler, 1986
Glass, wood, paint, slate, and steel, 28 × 12 × 4 inches

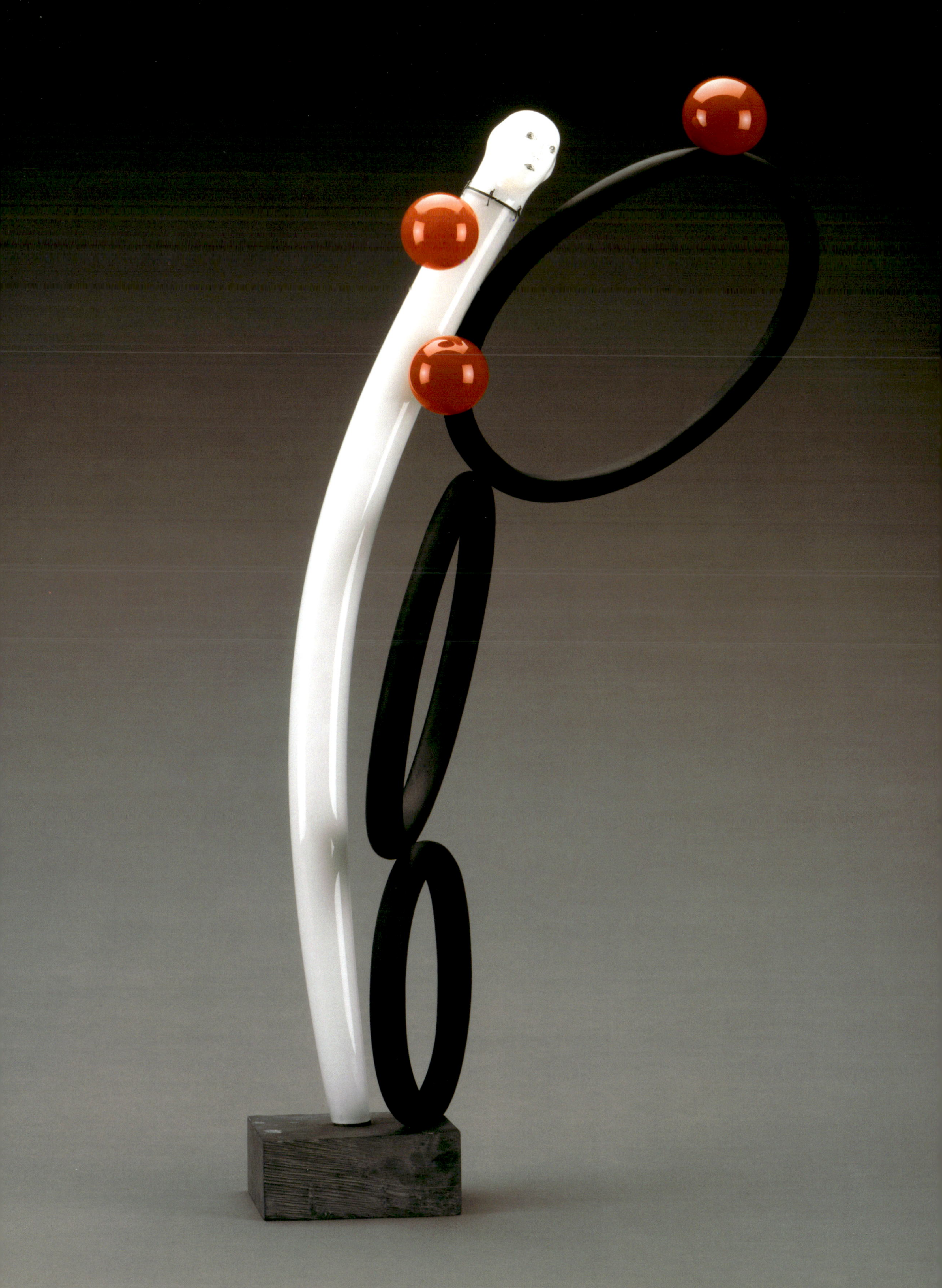

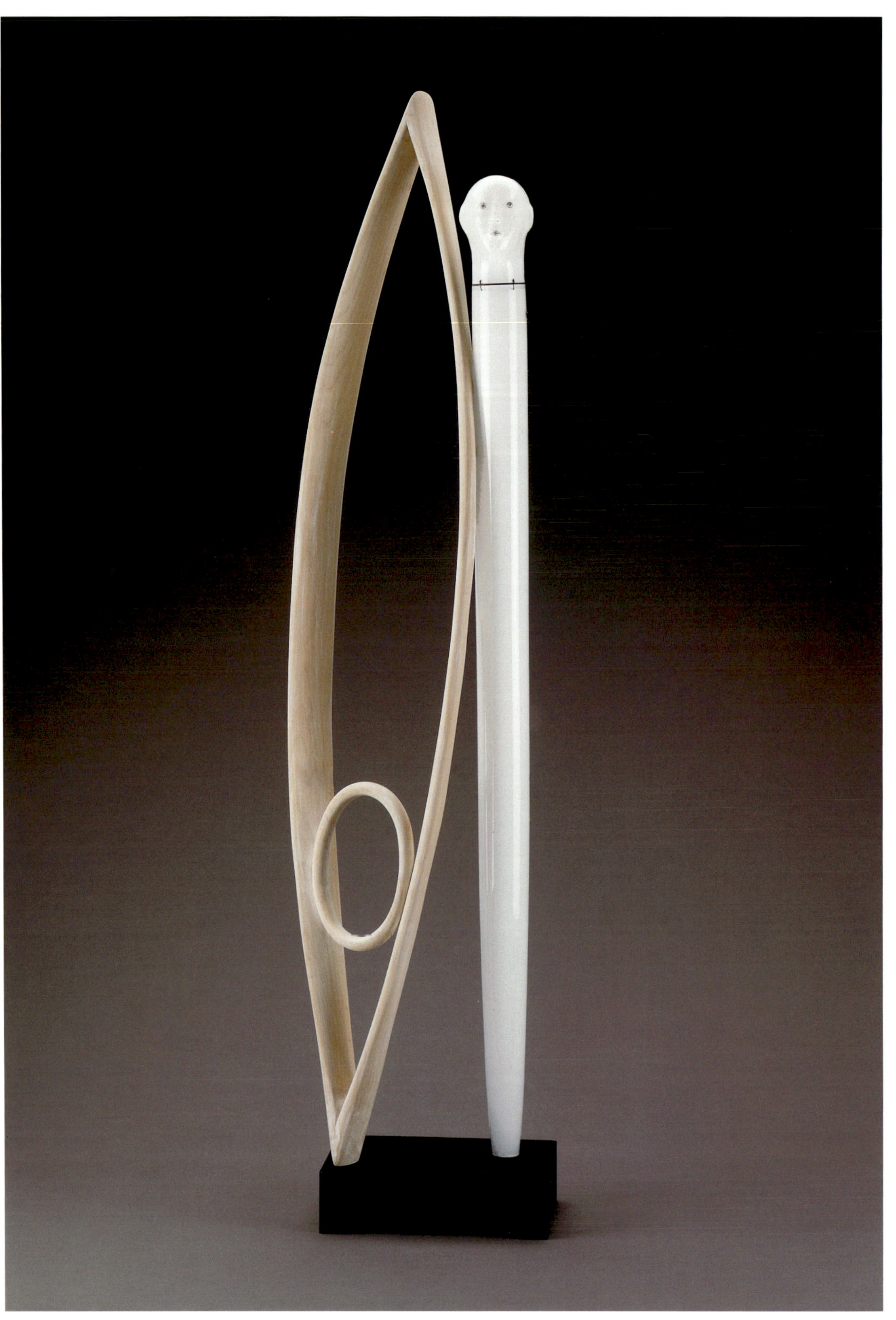

Crossing, 1986
Glass, wood, paint, and steel, 56 × 15 × 8 inches

Passage, 1986
Glass, wood, paint, slate, and steel, 35 × 13 × 11 inches

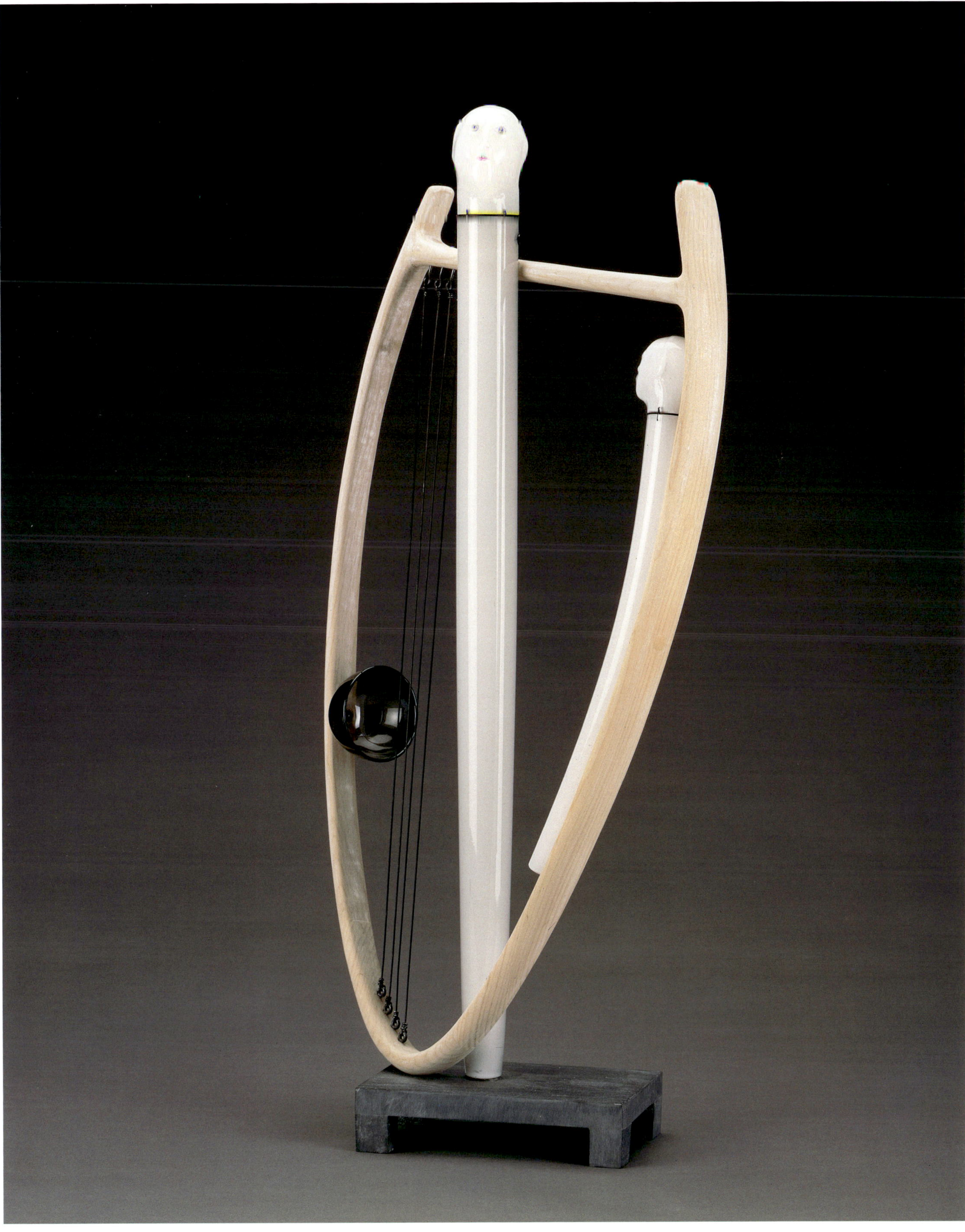

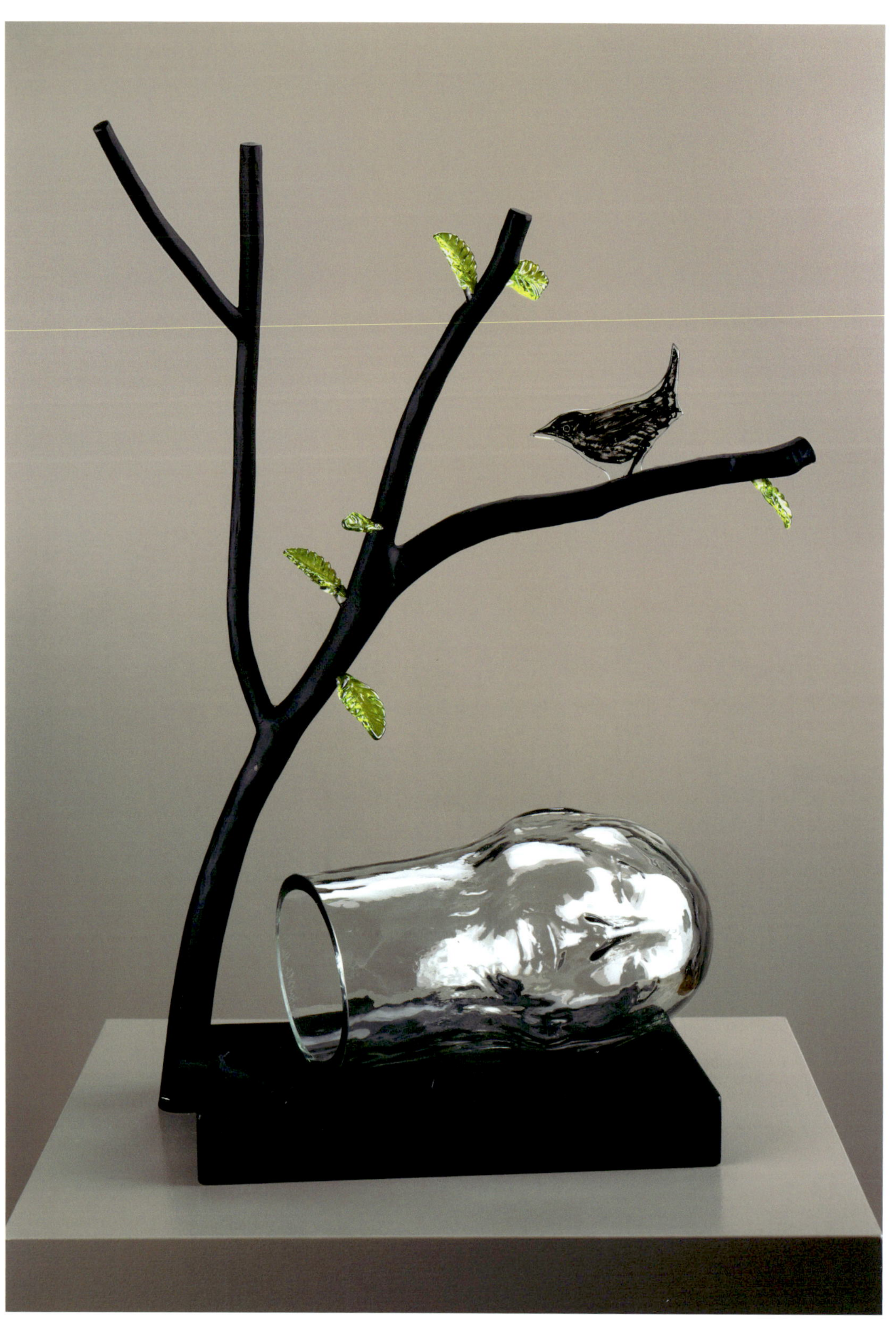

Change of Place, 1987
Glass, wood, paint, and steel, 29 × 22½ × 11 inches

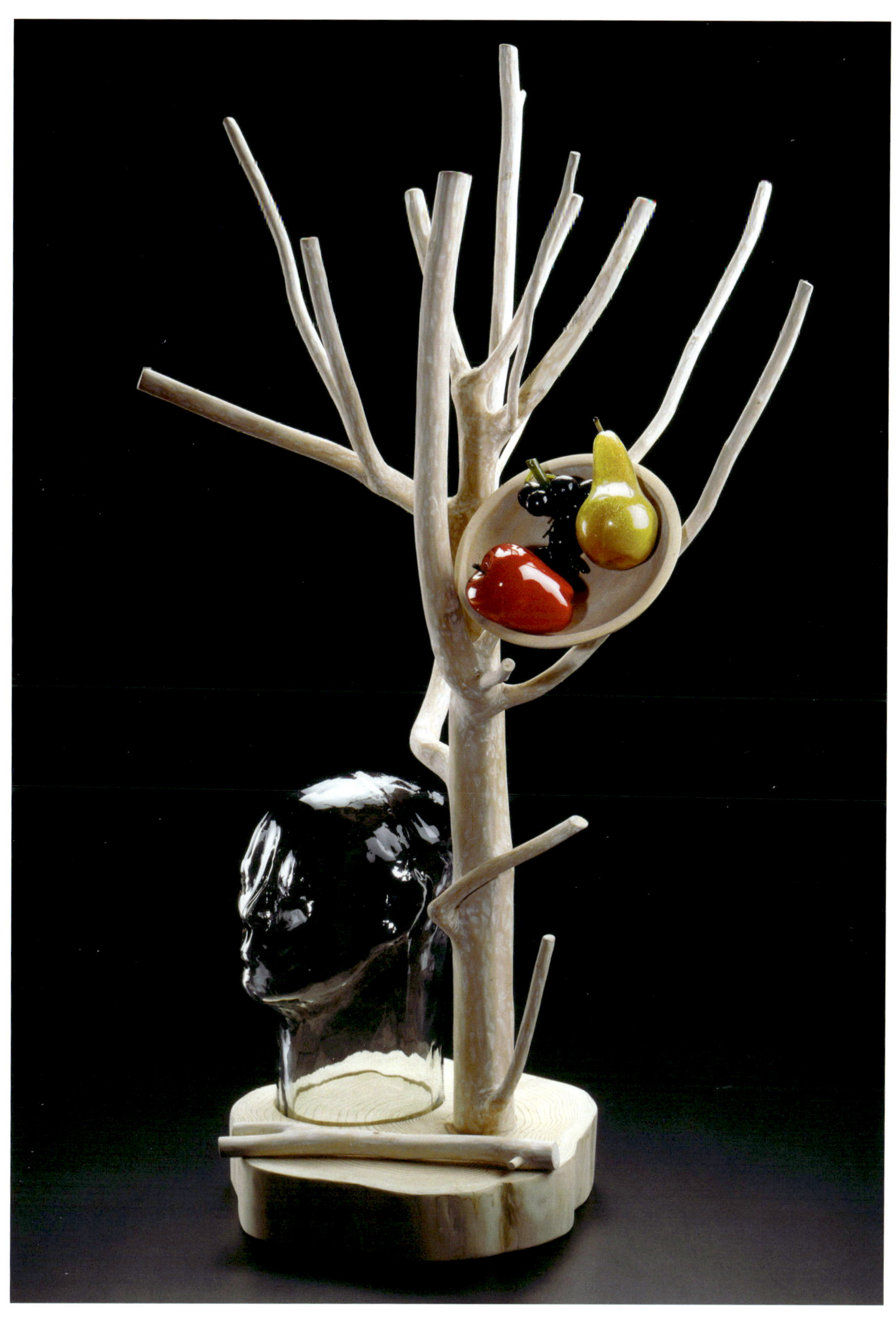

Century's Rounding, 1989
Glass, wood, paint, and steel, 47 × 30 × 23 inches

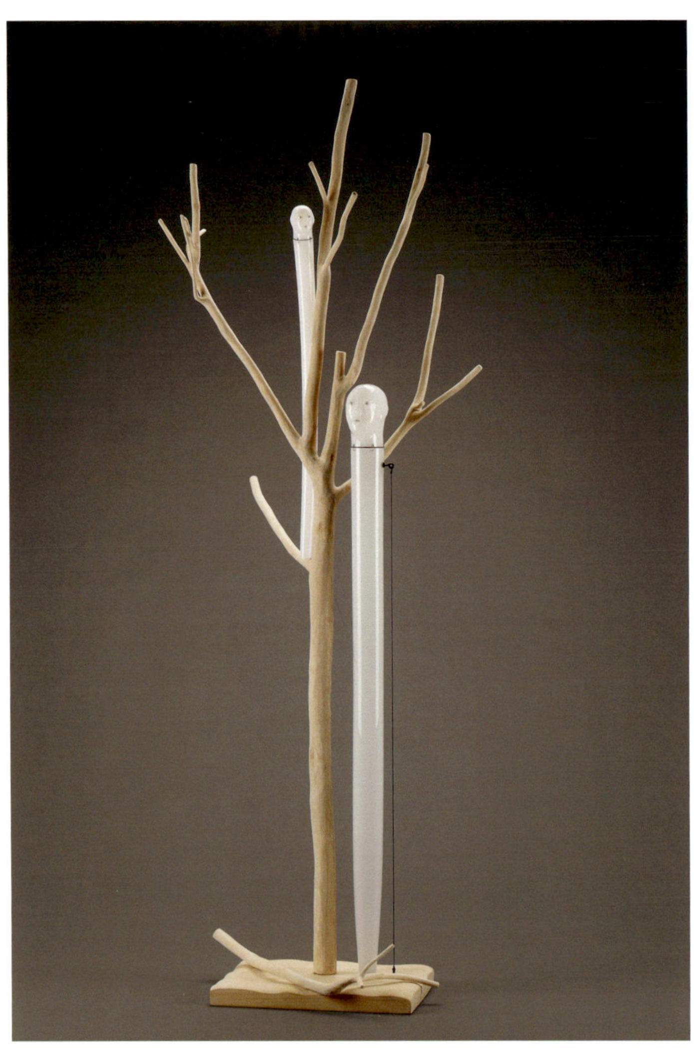

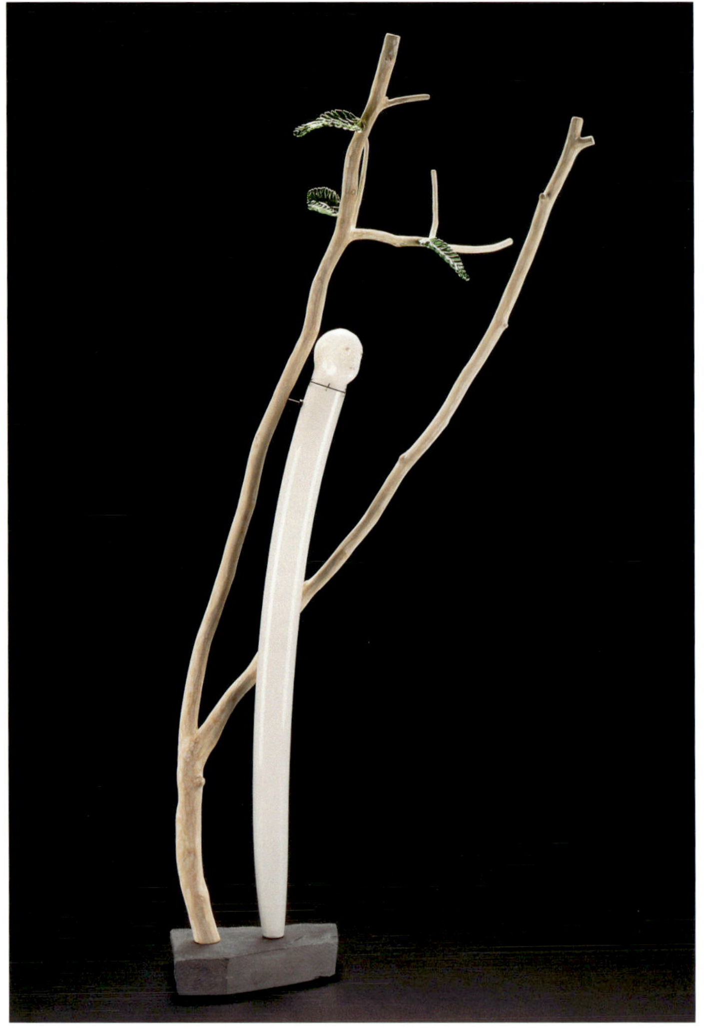

So Long As to See Far Enough, 1989
Glass, wood, paint, and steel, 73 × 28 × 21 inches

Turned Bosk, 1989
Glass, wood, paint, slate, and steel, 47 × 19 × 6 inches

Garden of Ladders, 1989 (right)
Glass, wood, paint, and steel, 74 × 36 × 16 inches

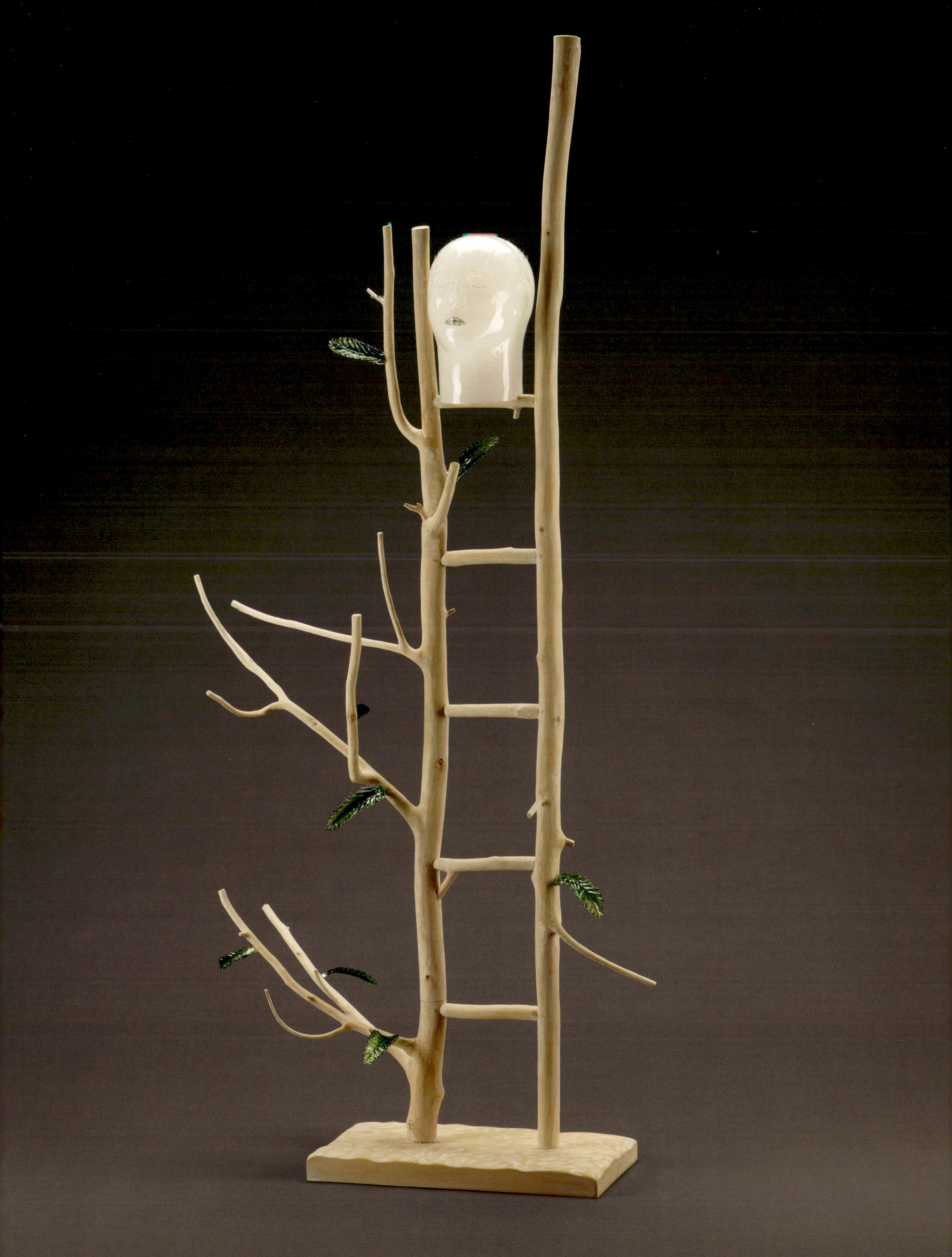

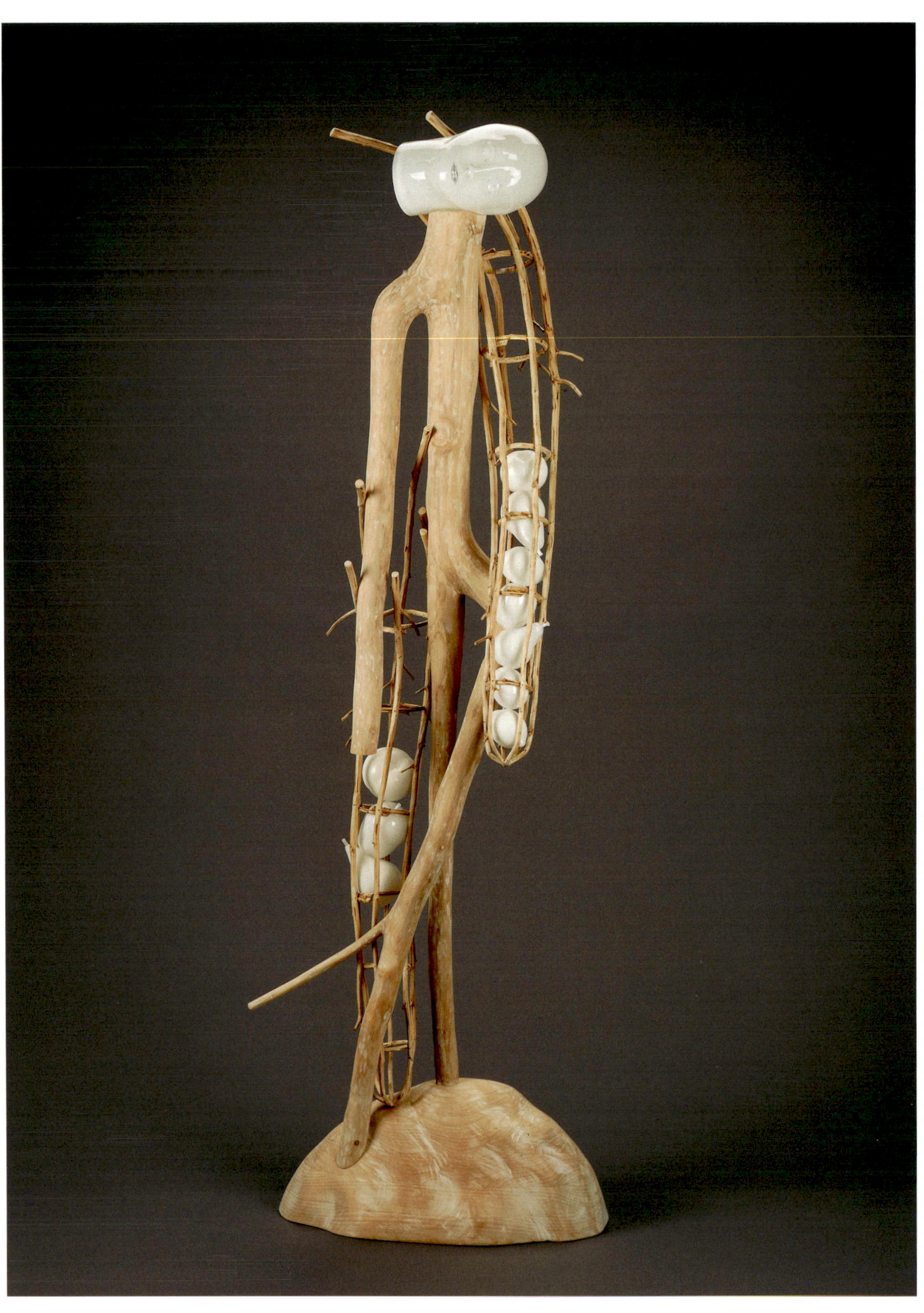

Limbed Tumbrel, 1992
Glass, wood, paint, and steel, 72 × 24 × 12 inches

Seasonal Spire, 1993
Glass, wood, paint, and steel, 82 × 46 × 23 inches

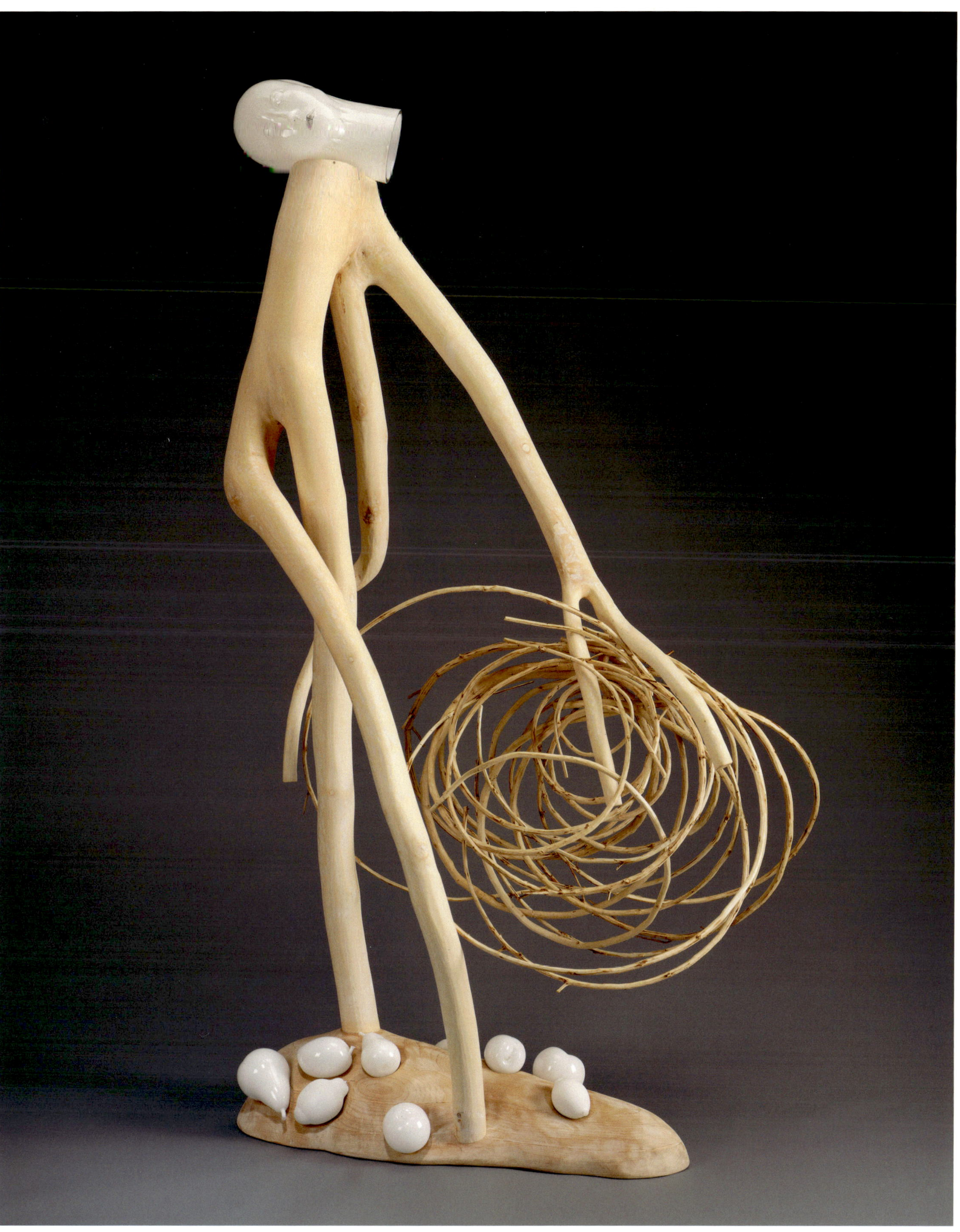

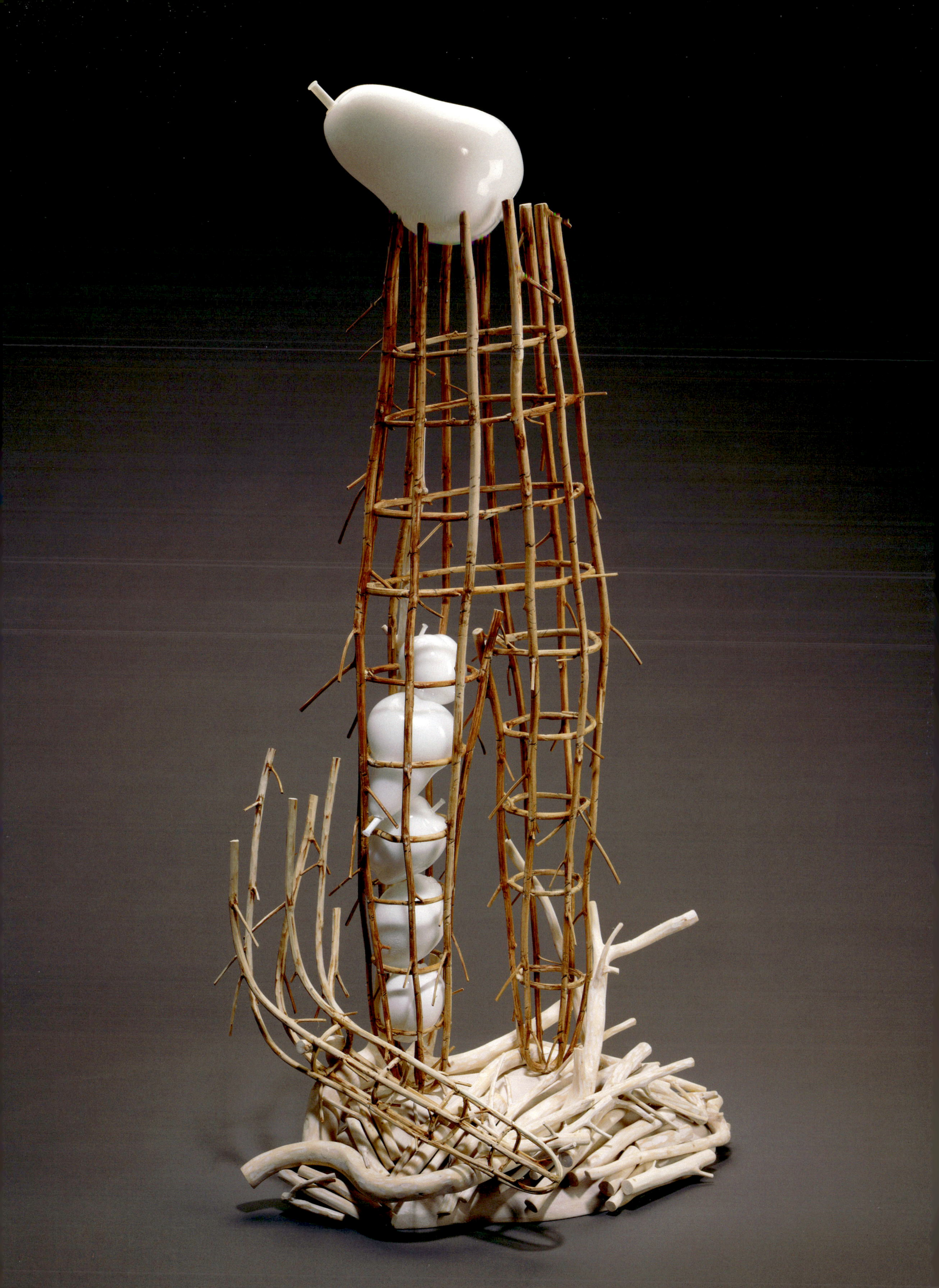

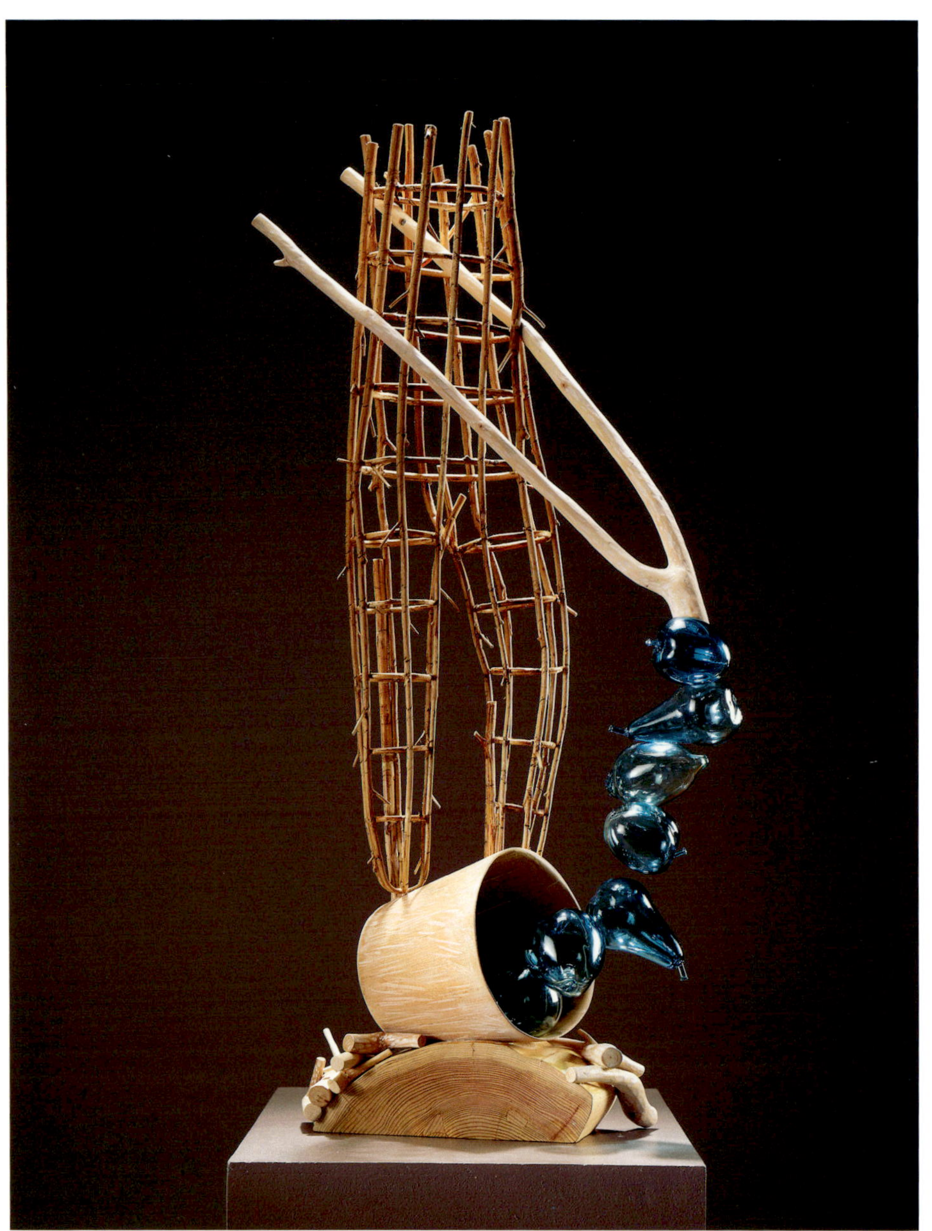

Pale Divine, 1994
Wood, glass, paint, and steel, 46 × 24 × 12 inches

Crown of Indigo, 1994
Wood, glass, paint, and steel, 52½ × 25½ × 17 inches

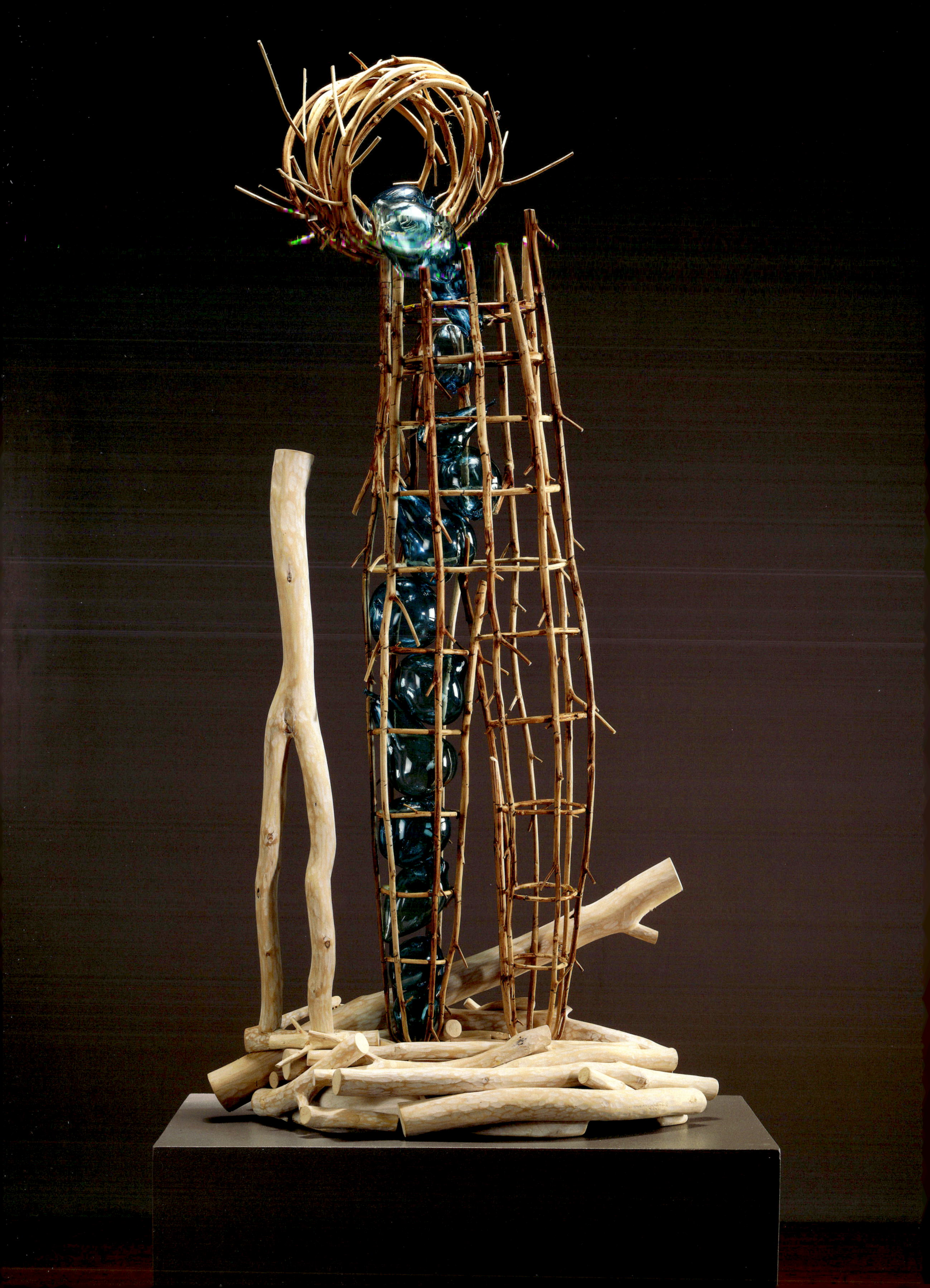

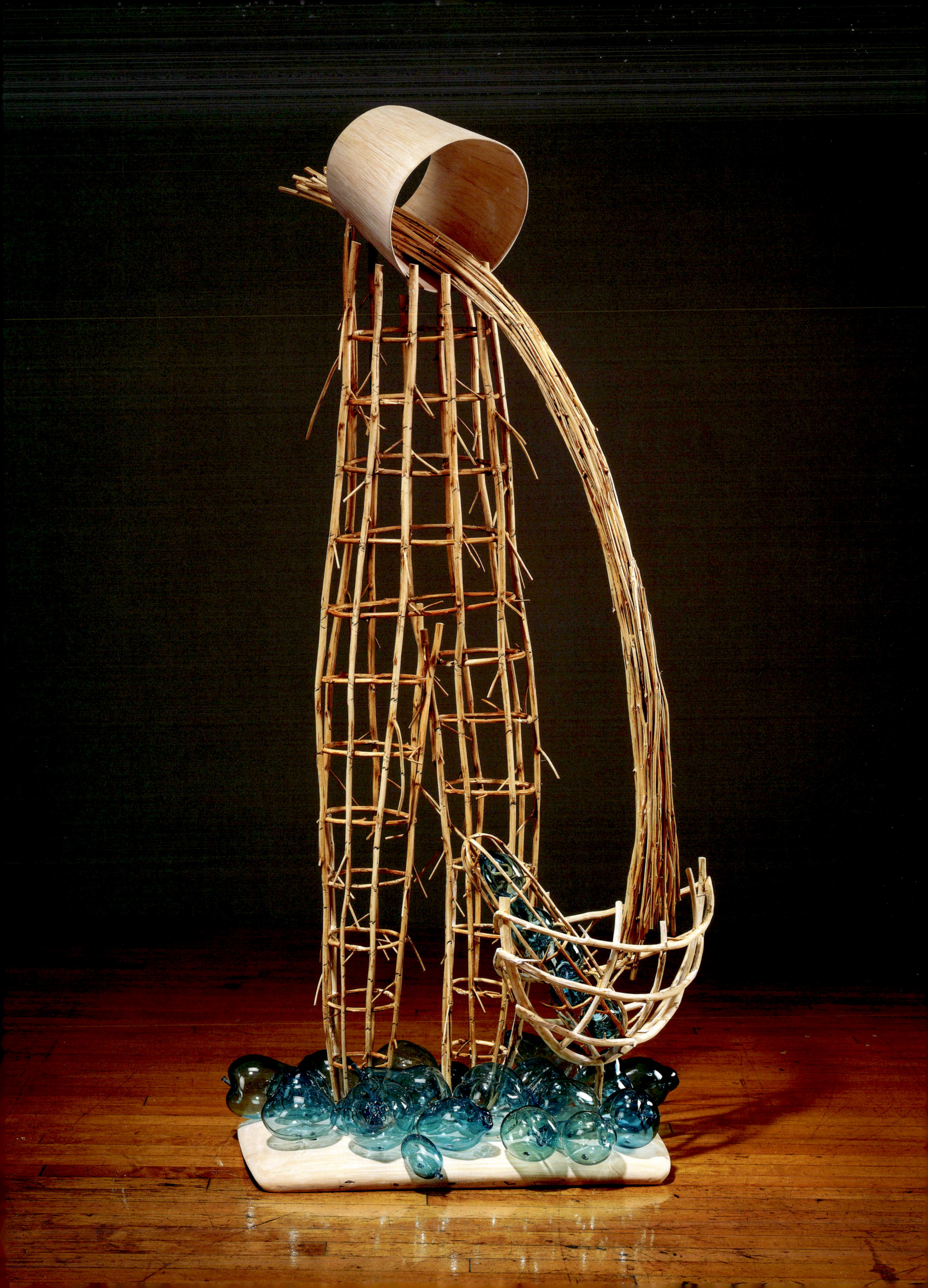

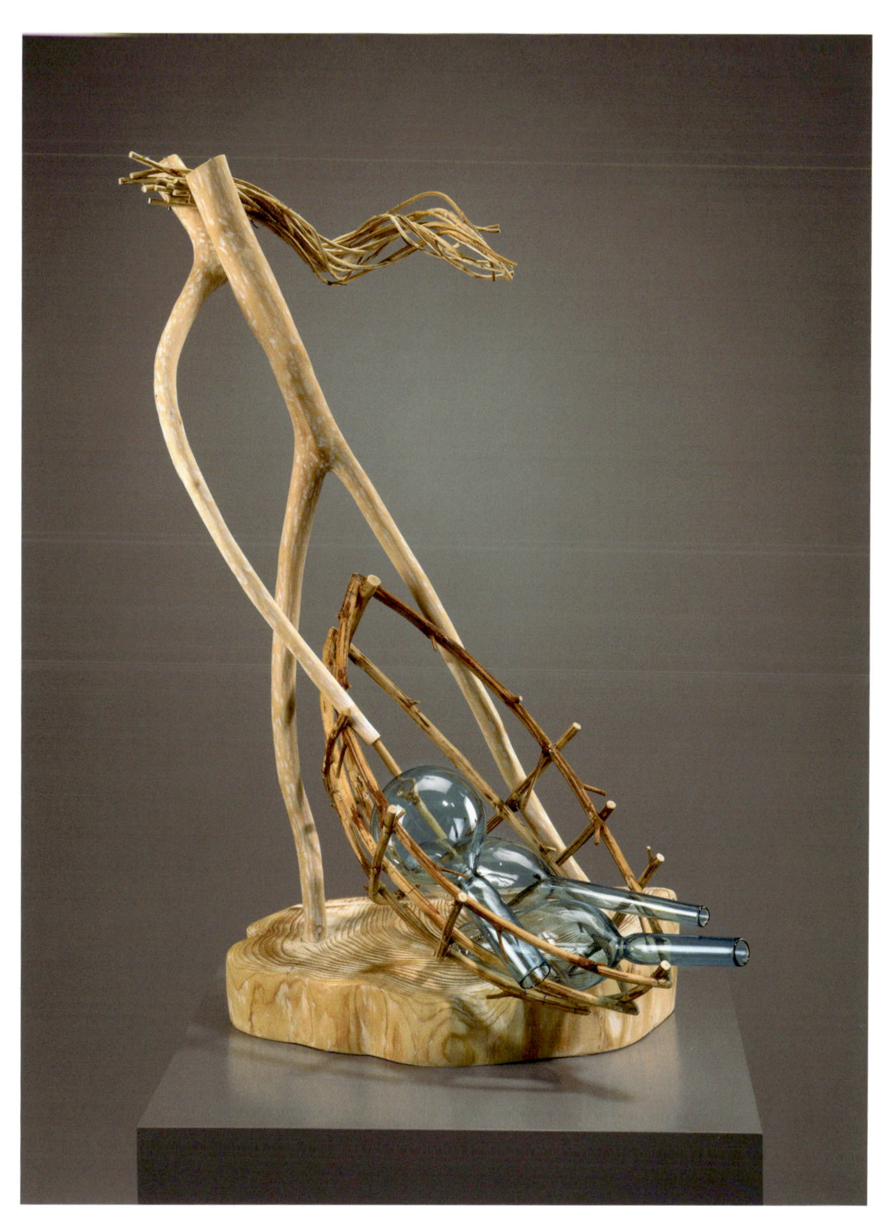

Water Catcher, 1995
Wood, glass, paint, and steel, 59 × 28 × 16 inches

Holding the Williwaw, 1996
Wood, glass, paint, and steel, 38½ × 29 × 19 inches

As Much As Measured Time, 1997
Wood, glass, paint, and steel, 48 × 30 × 18 inches

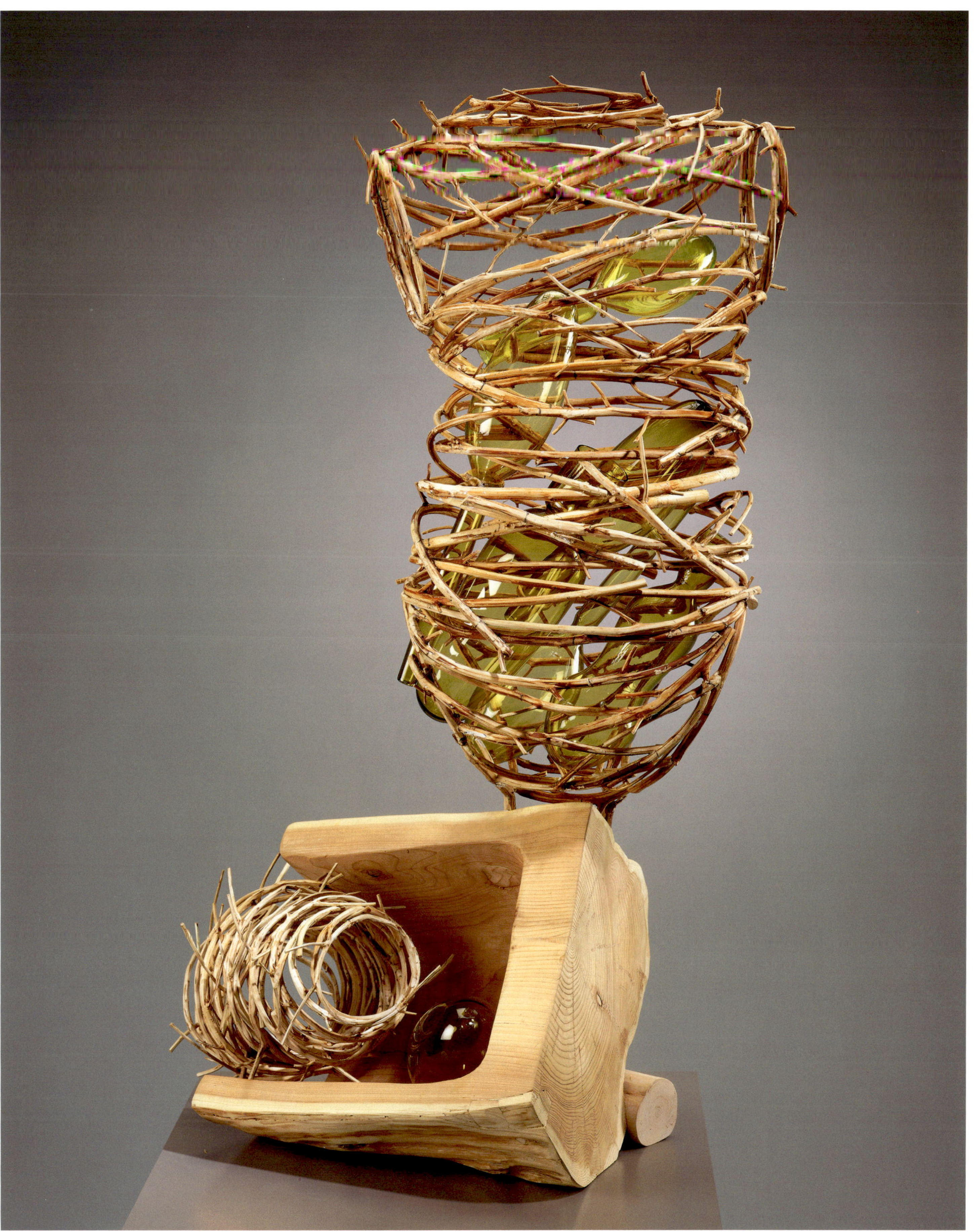

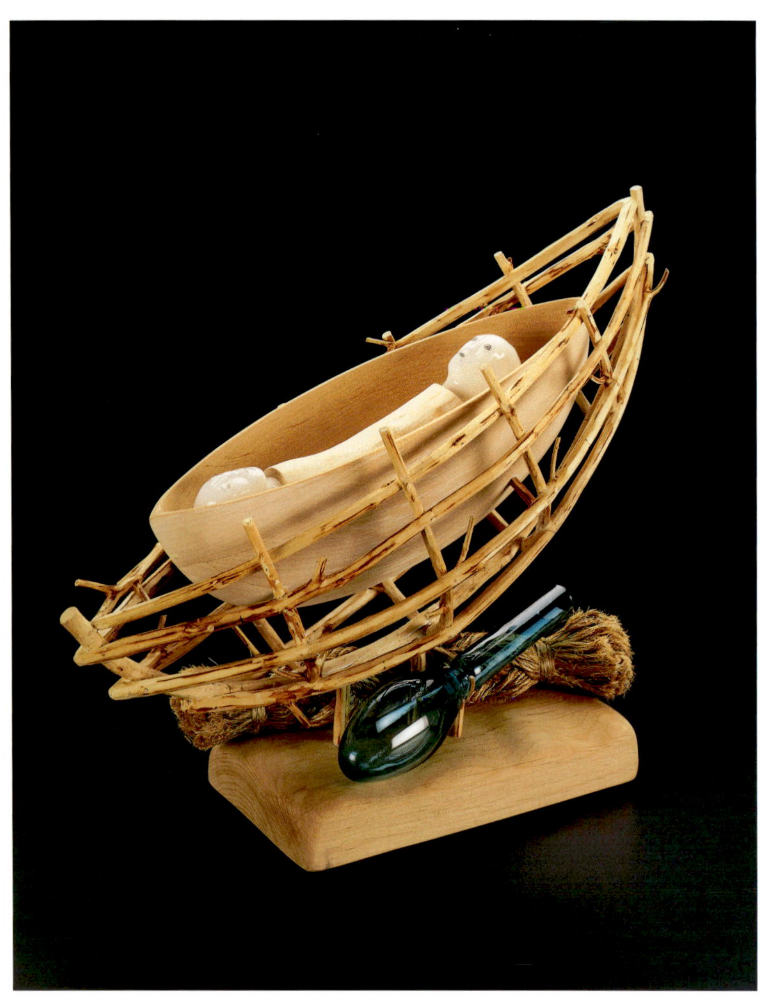

Voyage of Remembrance, 1997
Wood, glass, sisal, paint, and steel, 18 × 20½ × 8 inches

Steering Shallow Waters, 1996
Glass, wood, paint, and steel, 34½ × 24 × 11½ inches

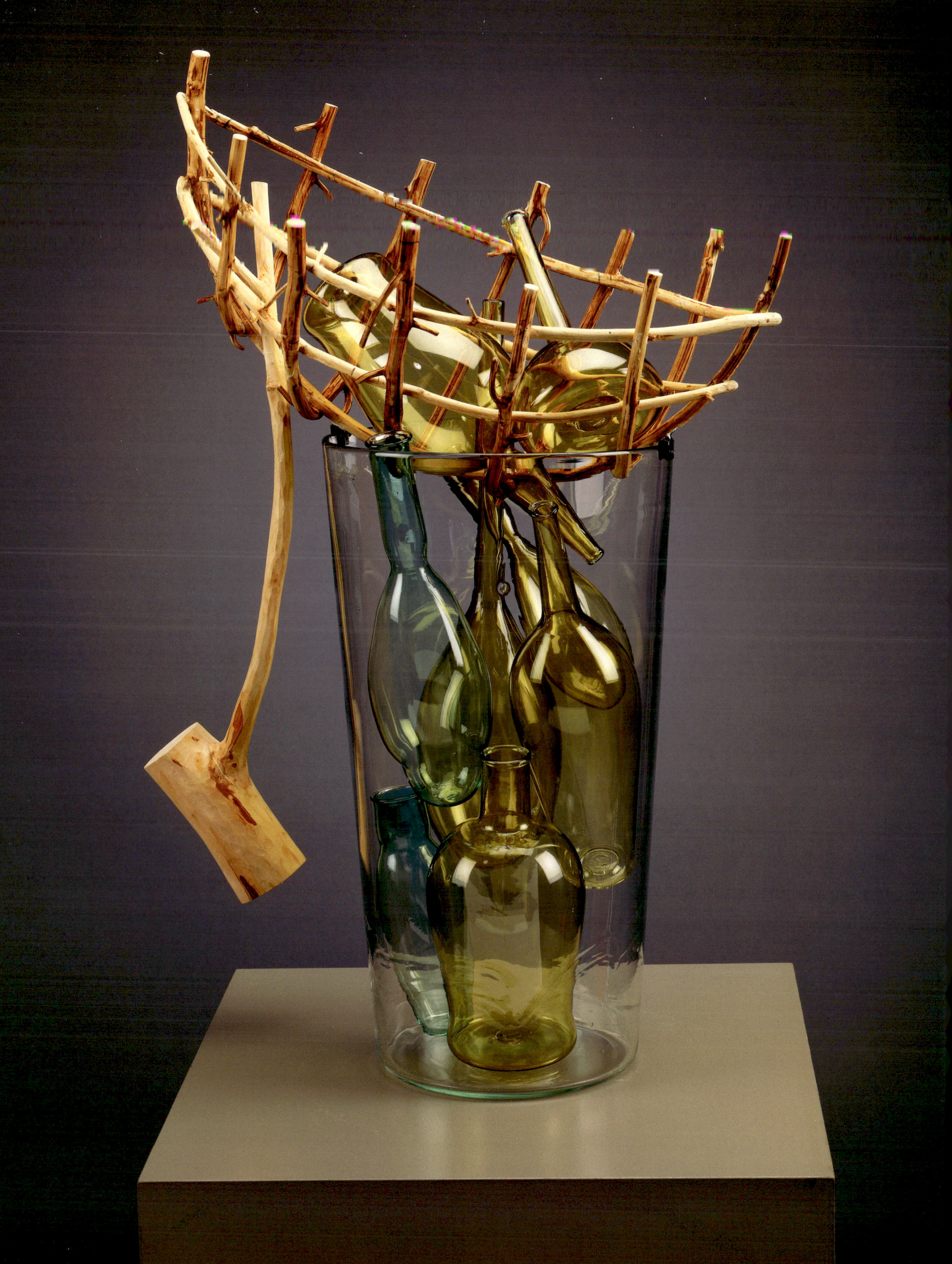

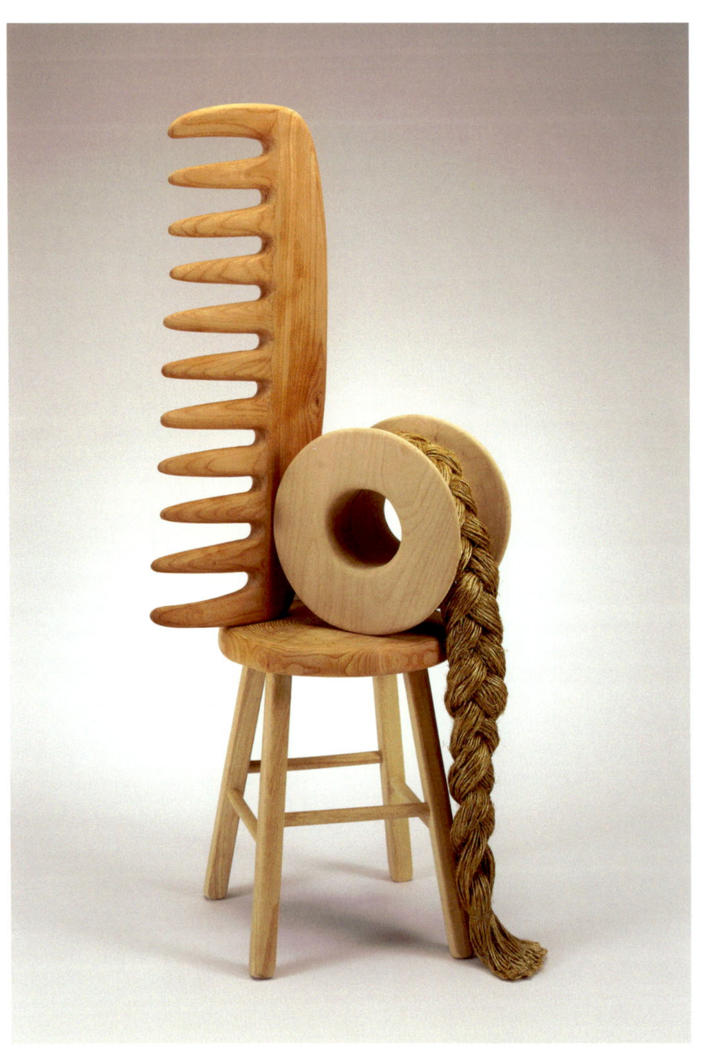

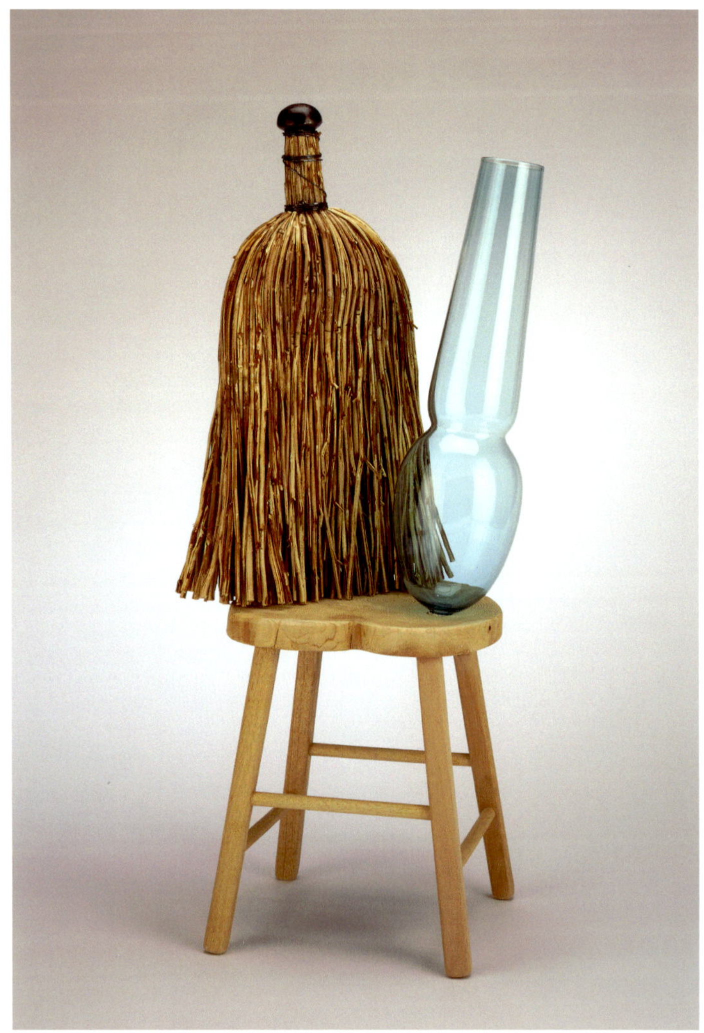

Everyday Pattern, 1998
Wood, glass, paint, and steel, 45 × 20 × 15 inches

From the Reach of Memory, 1998
Wood, sisal, paint, and steel, 47½ × 20 × 14½ inches

From the Limb of a Tree and the Water Within, 1998 (right)
Wood, glass, paint, and steel, 75 × 31 × 23 inches

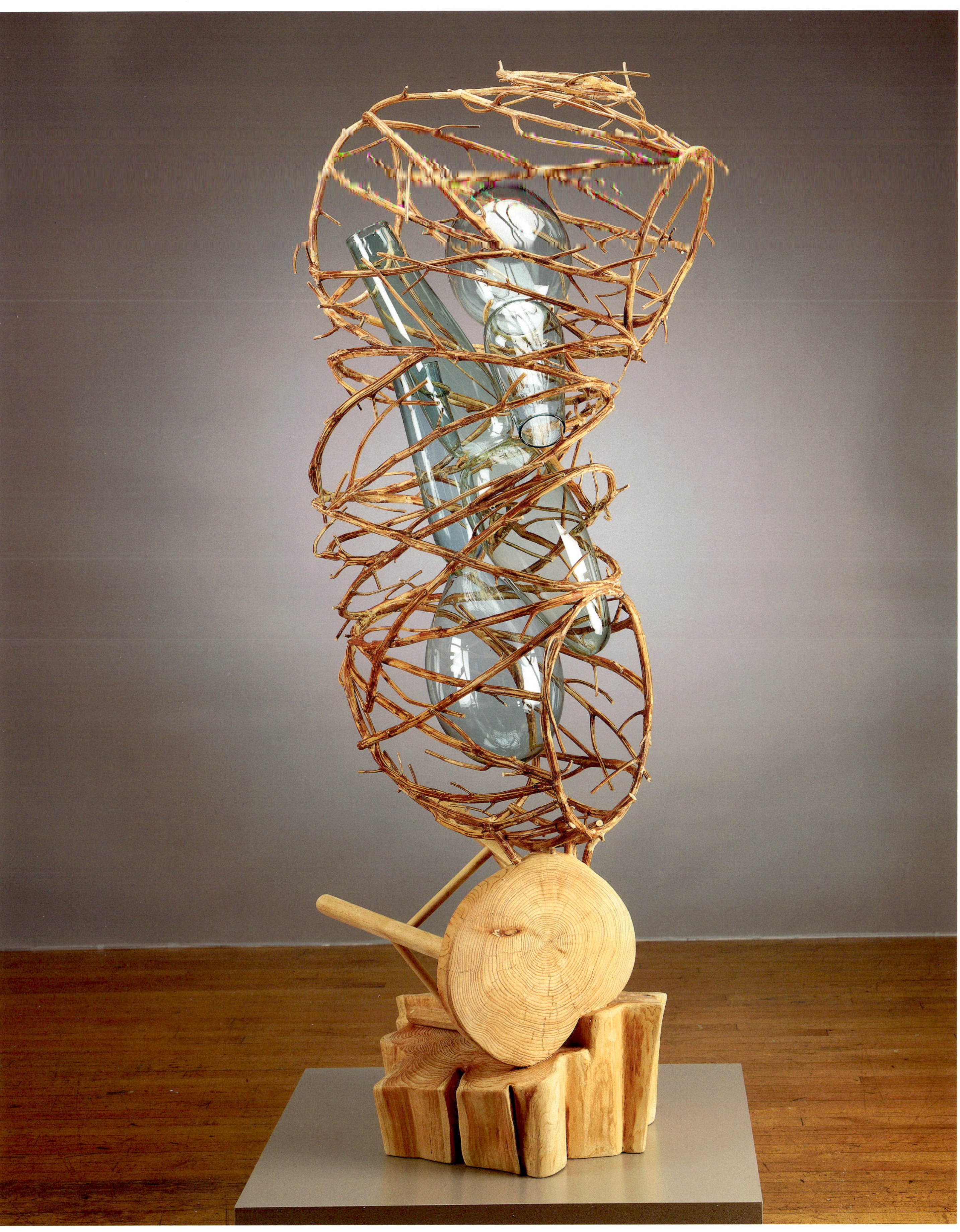

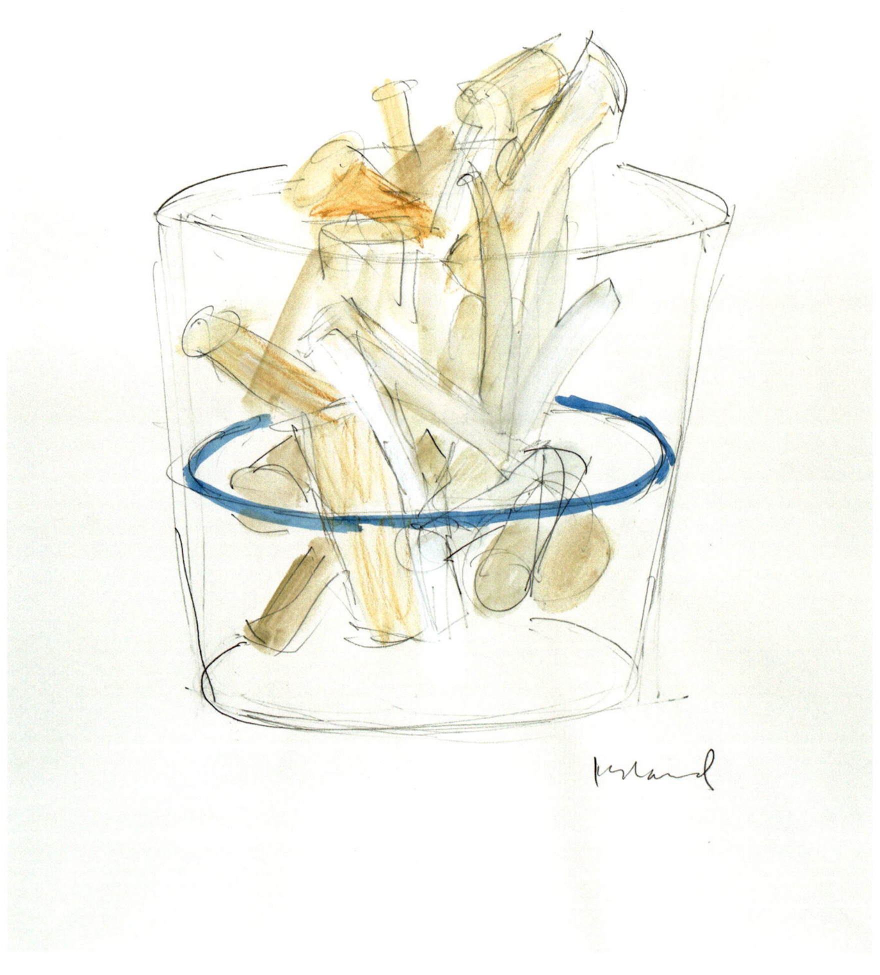

Joey Kirkpatrick, **Island**, 1998
Graphite and gouache on paper, 16¾ × 14 inches

Island, 1998
Glass, wood, paint, and steel, 19½ × 17 × 17 inches

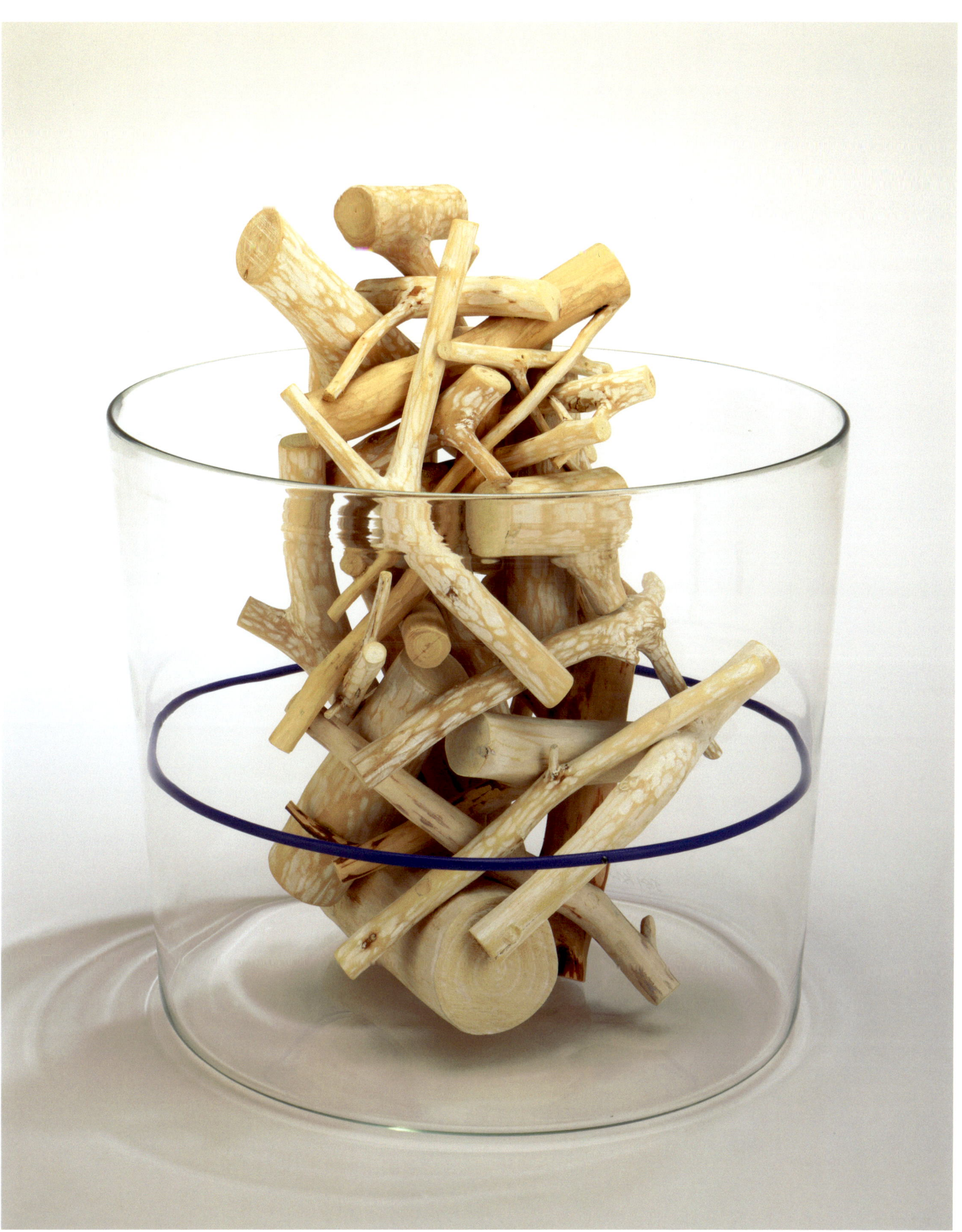

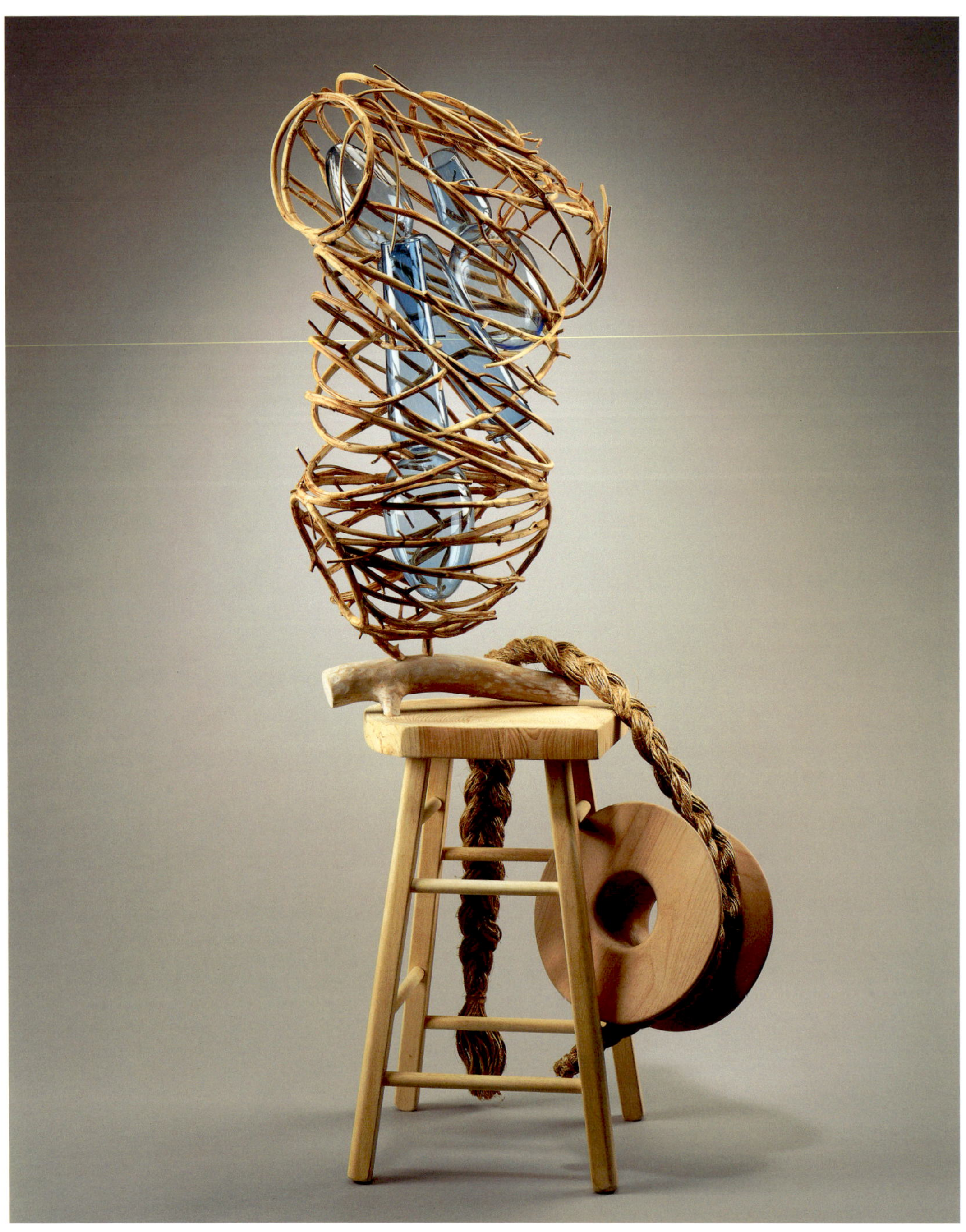

The Edge of Certainty, 2002 (right)
Wood, glass, paint, and steel, 79 × 37 × 25 inches

(following spread)
Sylvic Spheres, 1993
Wood (all *Sylvic Spheres* made into bronze in 2002), 48, 38, 74, 32 inches high

Assembling Memory, 2000
Wood, glass, sisal, paint, and steel, 58 × 25 × 21 inches

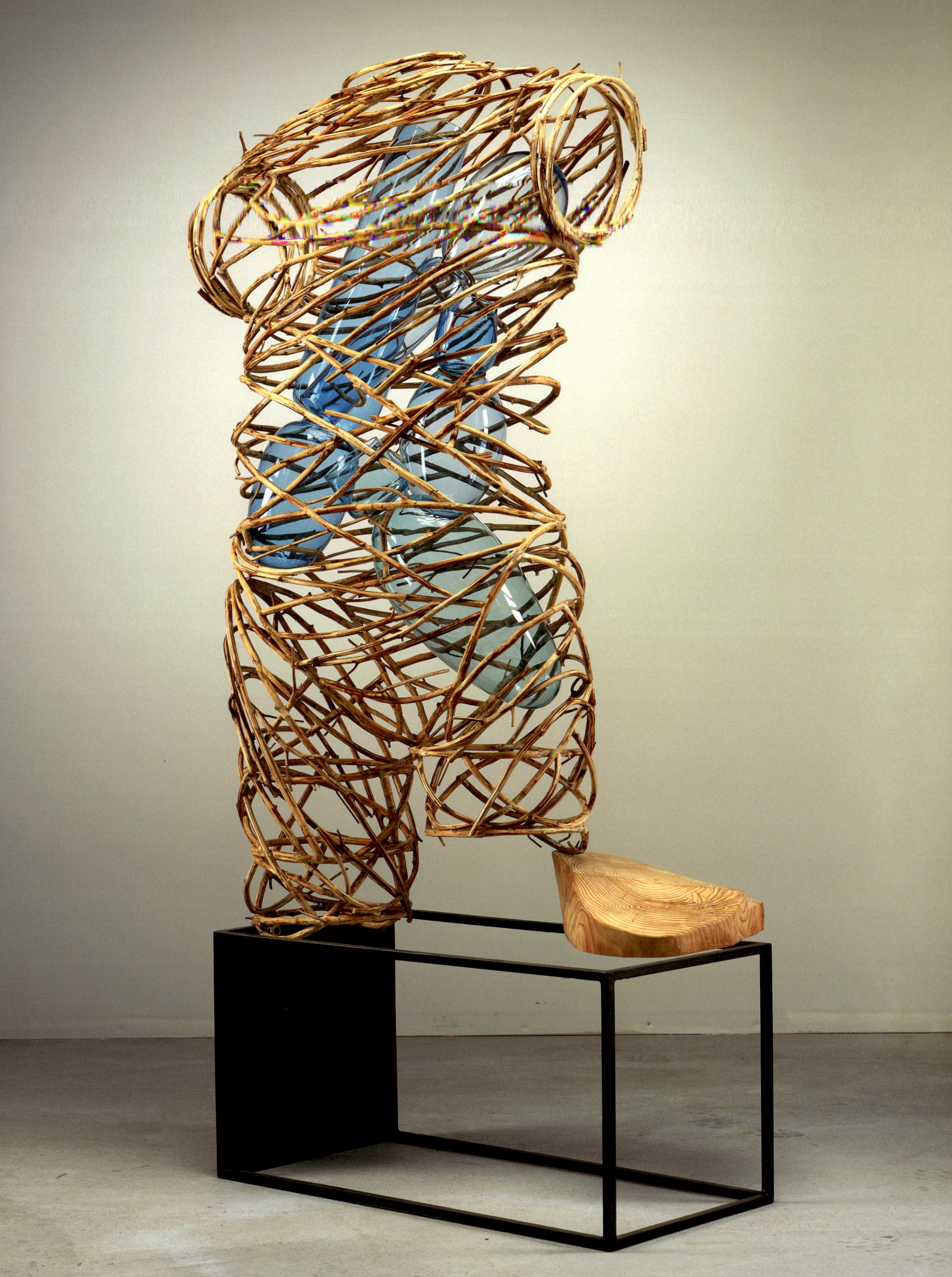

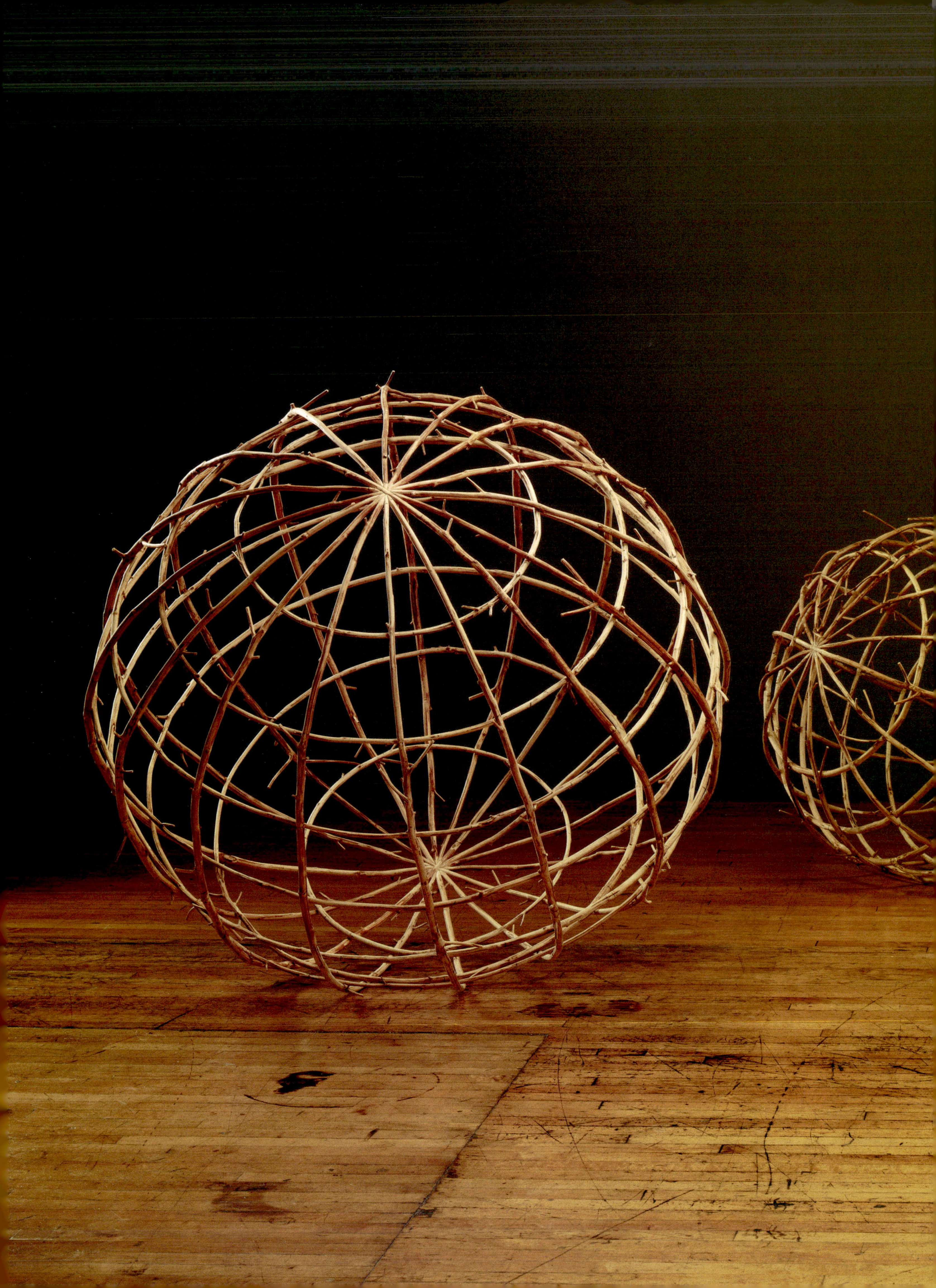

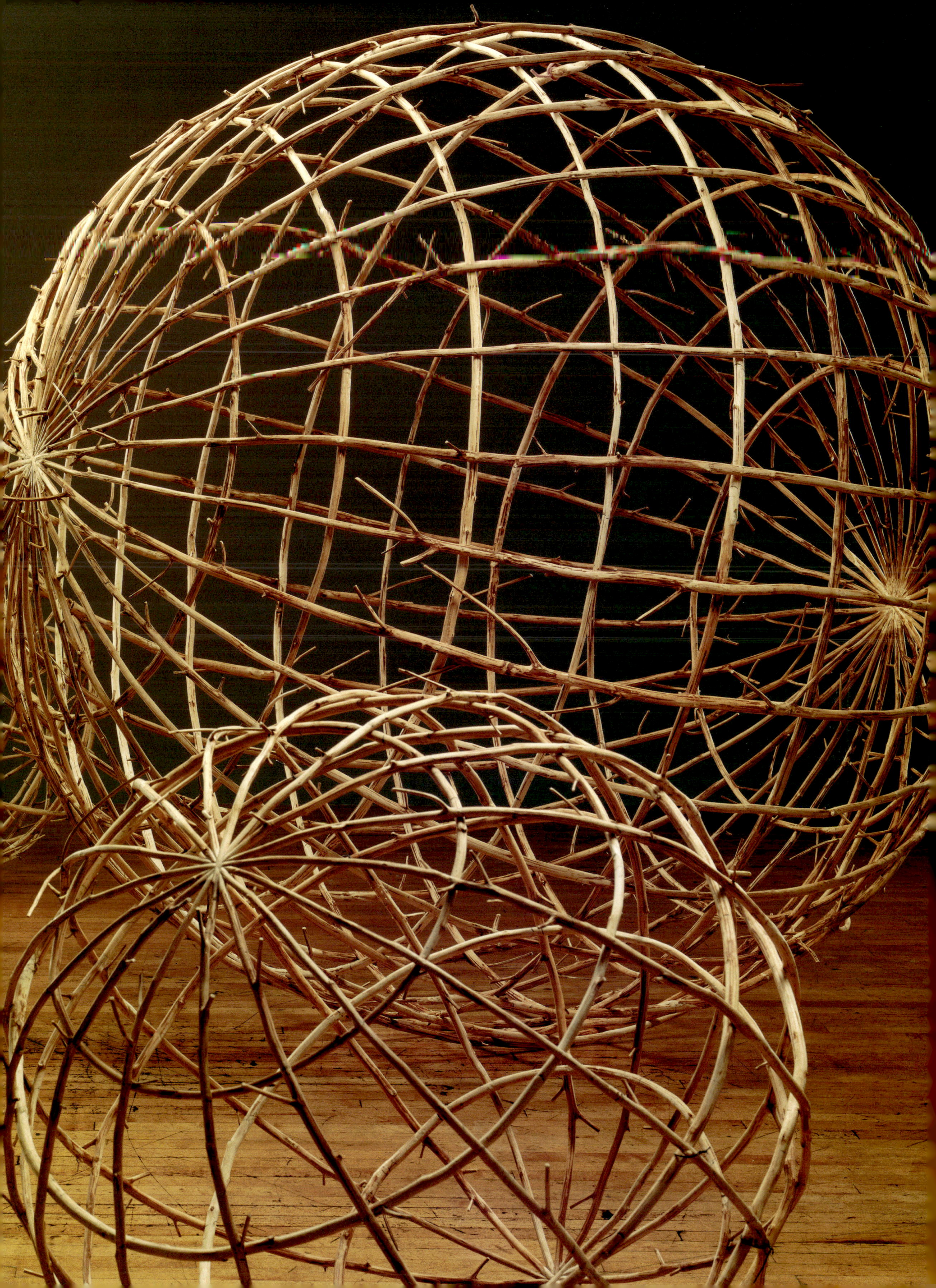

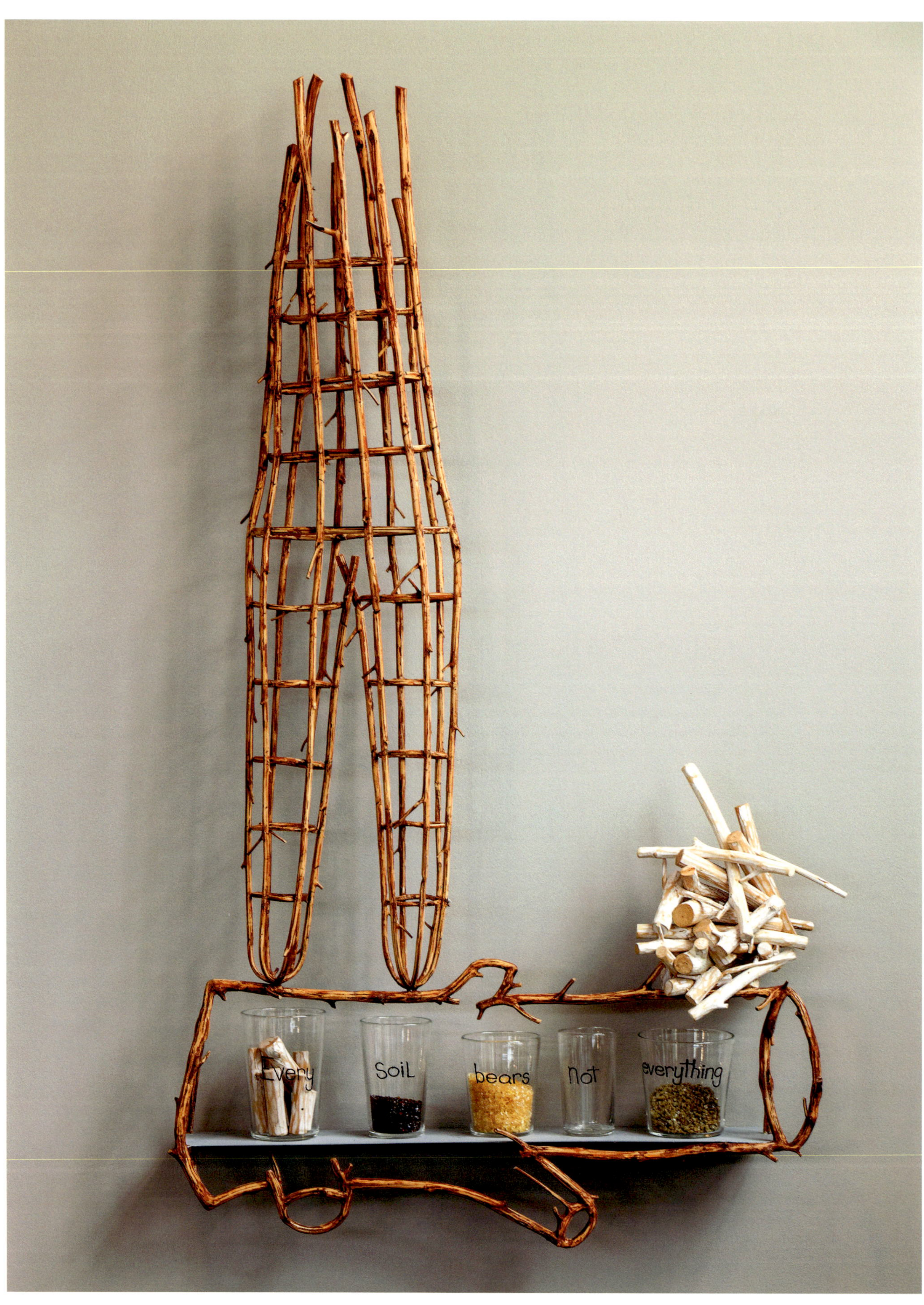

Every
Soil
bears
Not
everything

Look Upon the Vessel, 2002
Wood, glass, paint, and steel, 62½ × 23 × 9½ inches

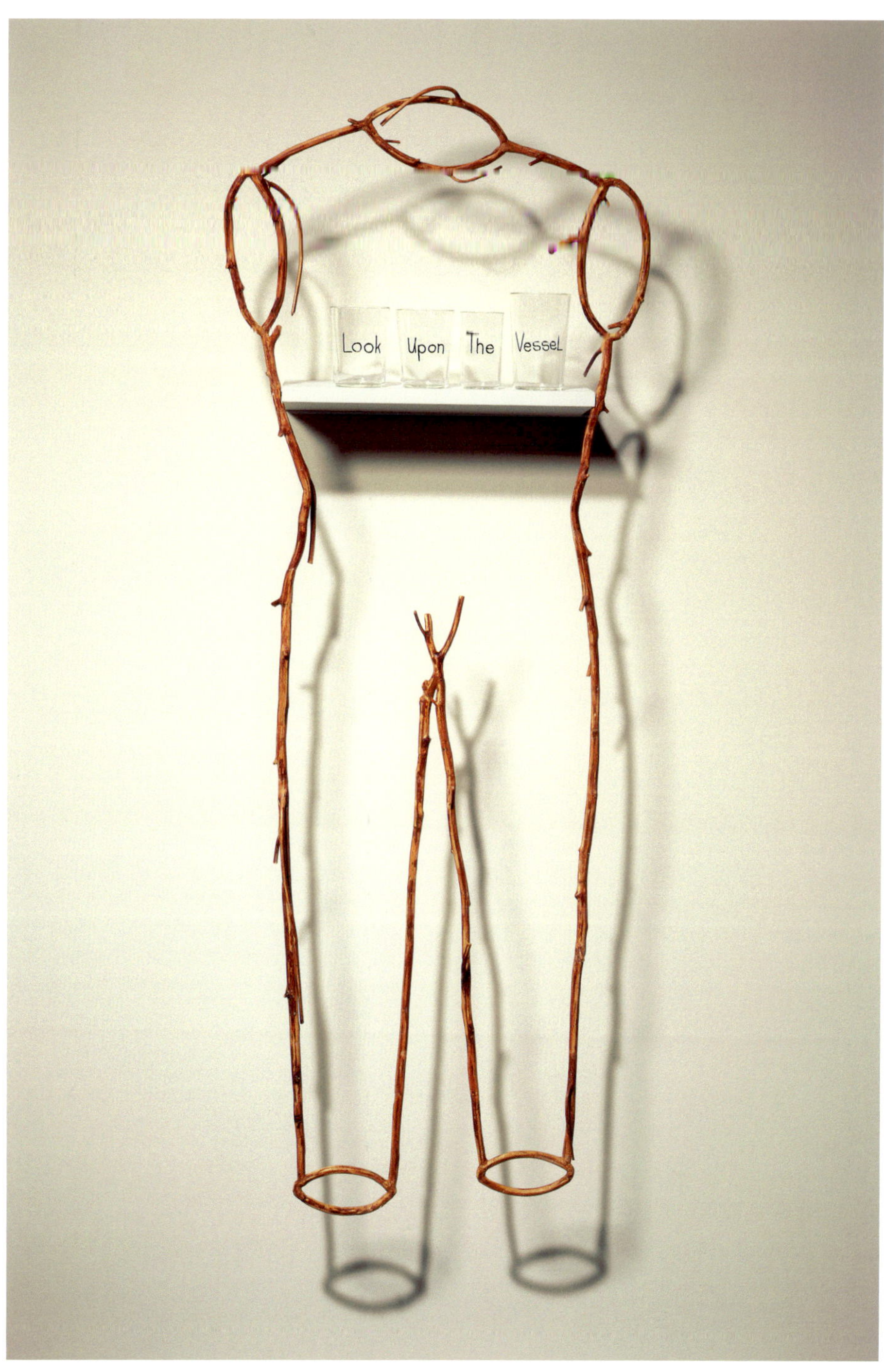

Every Soil Bears Not Everything, 2008
Wood, glass, paint, and steel, 50 × 27 × 5 inches

Look Upon the Vessel (2002) is a work made earlier than the *Woodland Drawings*, but after the wall installations based on proverbs (1998). It is a good example of how these artists explore a theme and allow it to evolve over time. In this work, the figure is made as in the *Woodland Drawings*, but housed within the chest is a shelf upon which are vessels that spell out "Look Upon the Vessel." This work overlaps three distinct themes in Kirkpatrick's and Mace's work: the "drawings in wood," proverbs, and women's work. The full saying is "Look upon the vessel for what it holds," an antiquated maxim that might urge one to regard a person's qualities beyond a superficial impression, that we might say today as "beauty is only skin deep." The artists were also intrigued by the concept that this saying implies that a woman's body is a vessel, a theme they had already considered in their work.

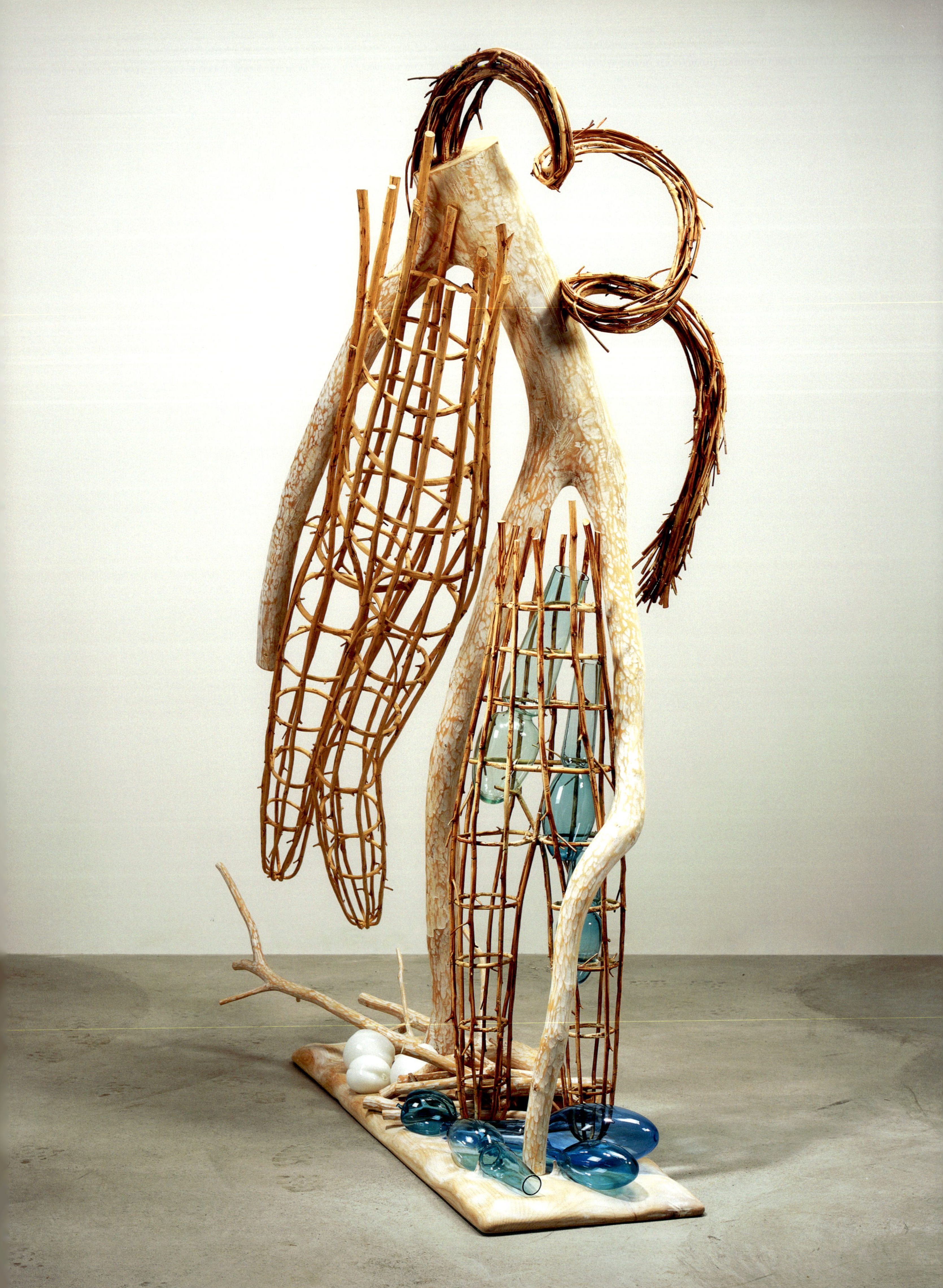

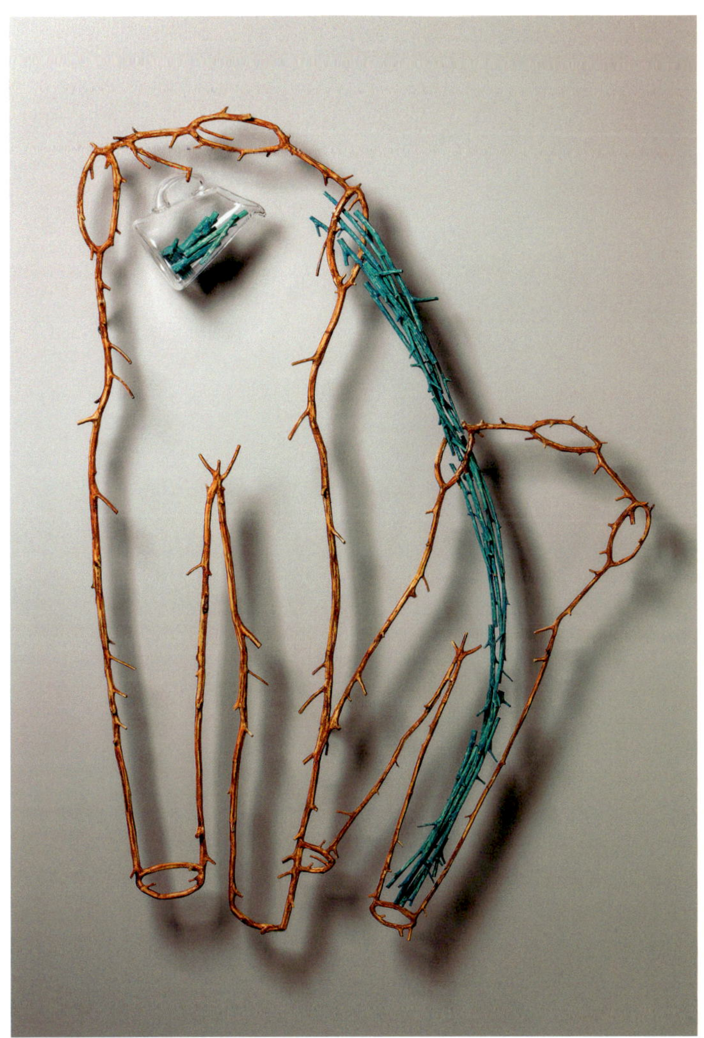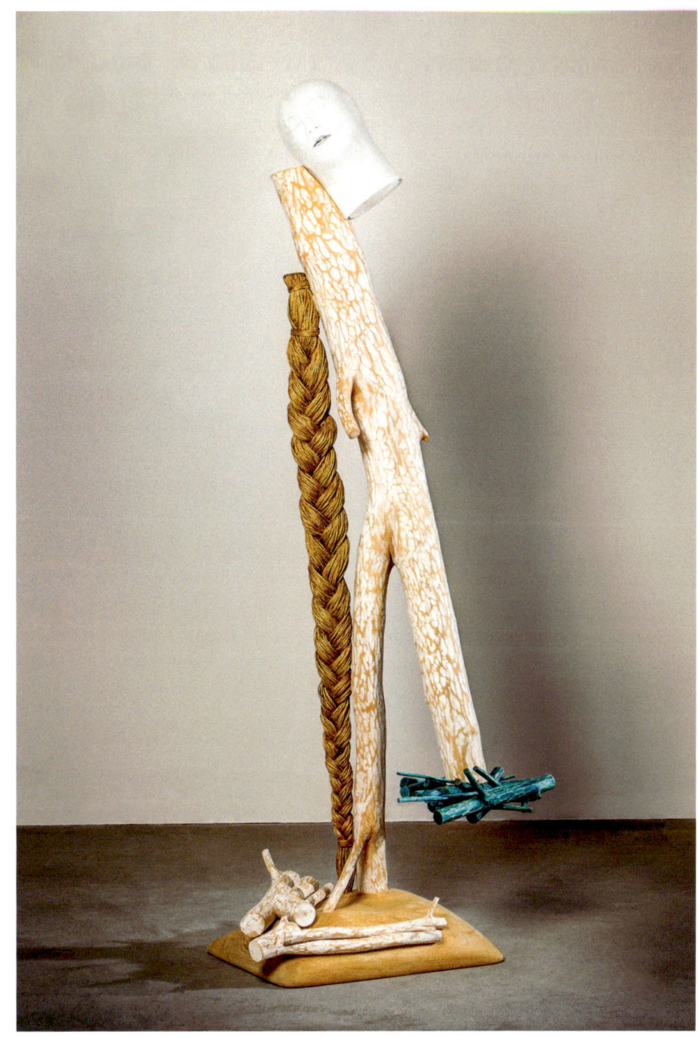

What Water Carries, 2010
Wood, glass, paint, and steel, 49½ × 35 × 4 inches

Carry Land, Carry Water, 2011 (left)
Wood, glass, paint, and steel, 78 × 65 × 30 inches

A Way Is Found, 2012
Wood, glass, sisal, paint, and steel, 58 × 22 × 14 inches

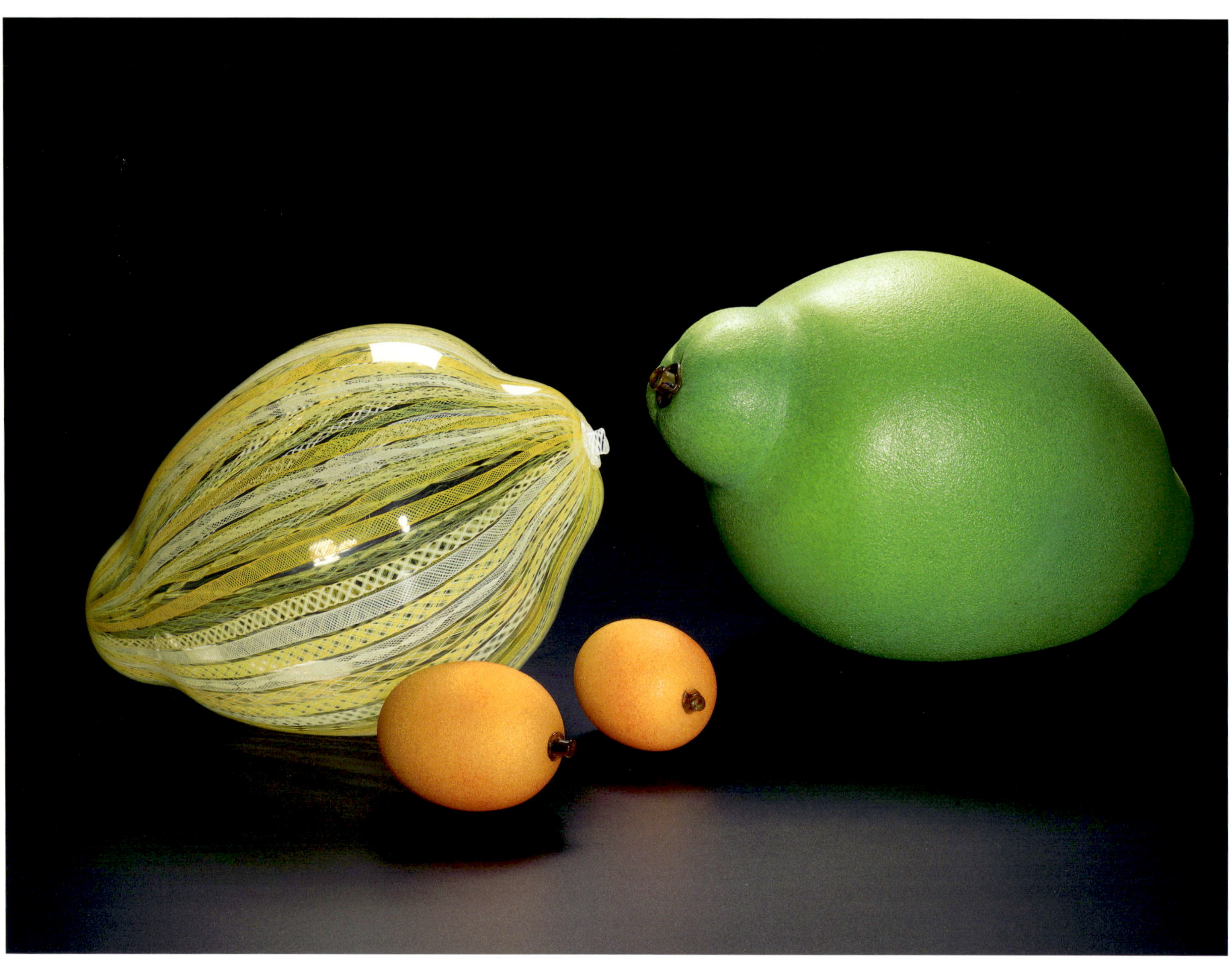

Fruit and Vegetable Grouping, 1994–2000
Glass; peach: 18½ × 20 × 21 inches

(following spread)
Fruit Still Life, 2000
Glass, wood, and paint, 26 × 45 inches

Lemon and Lime with Kumquats, 1998
Glass; lime, 11½ × 18 × 12 inches

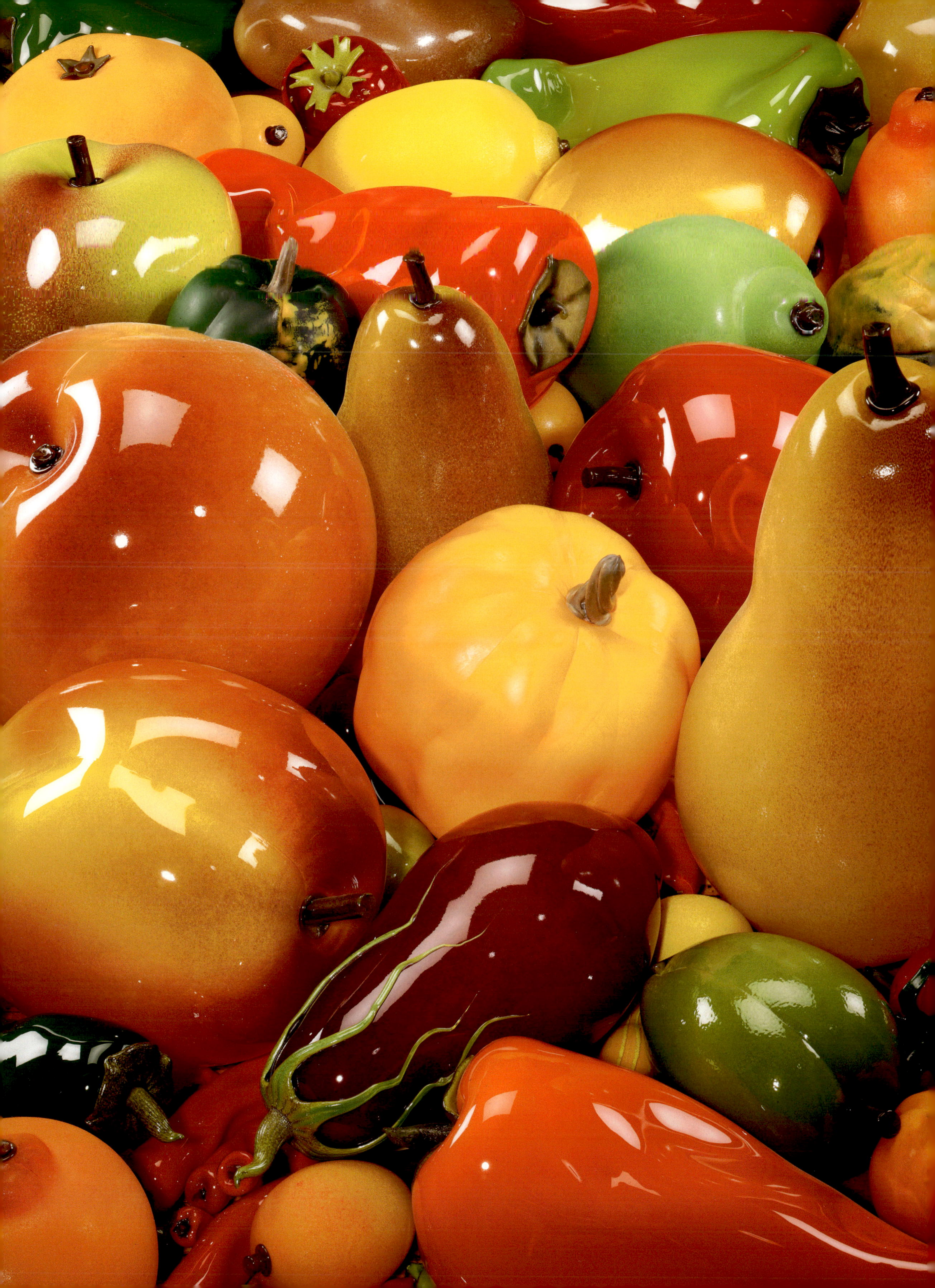

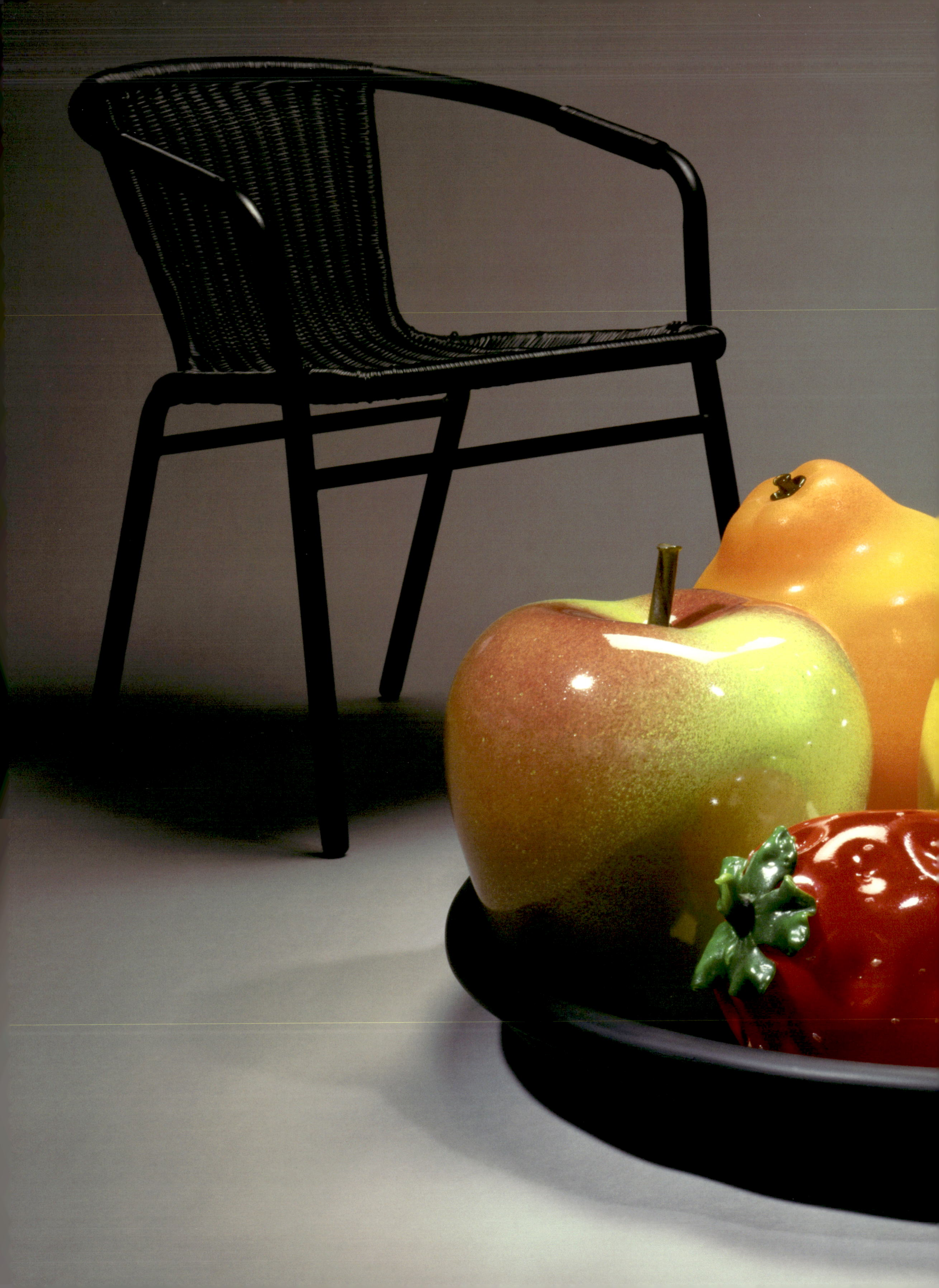

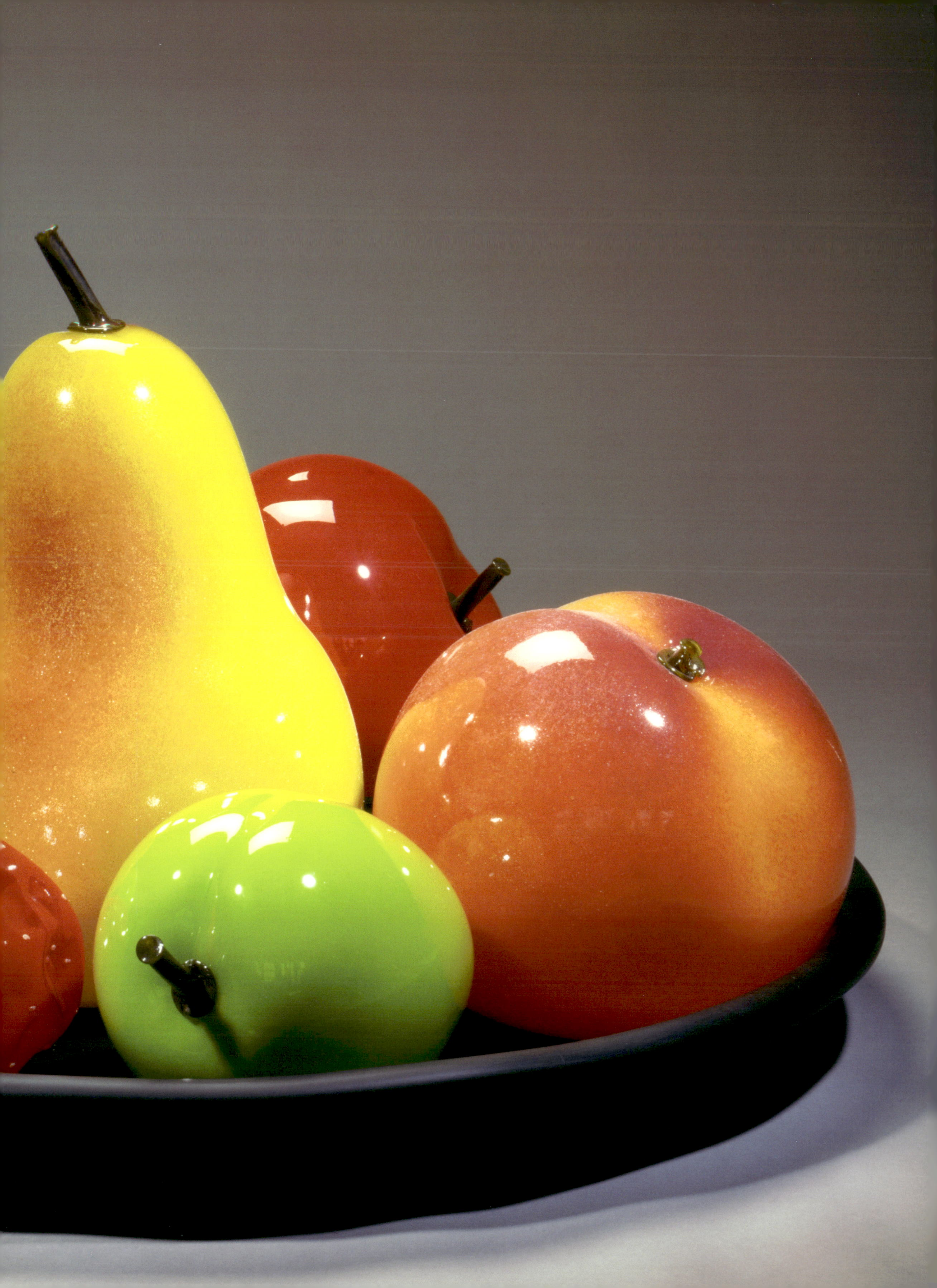

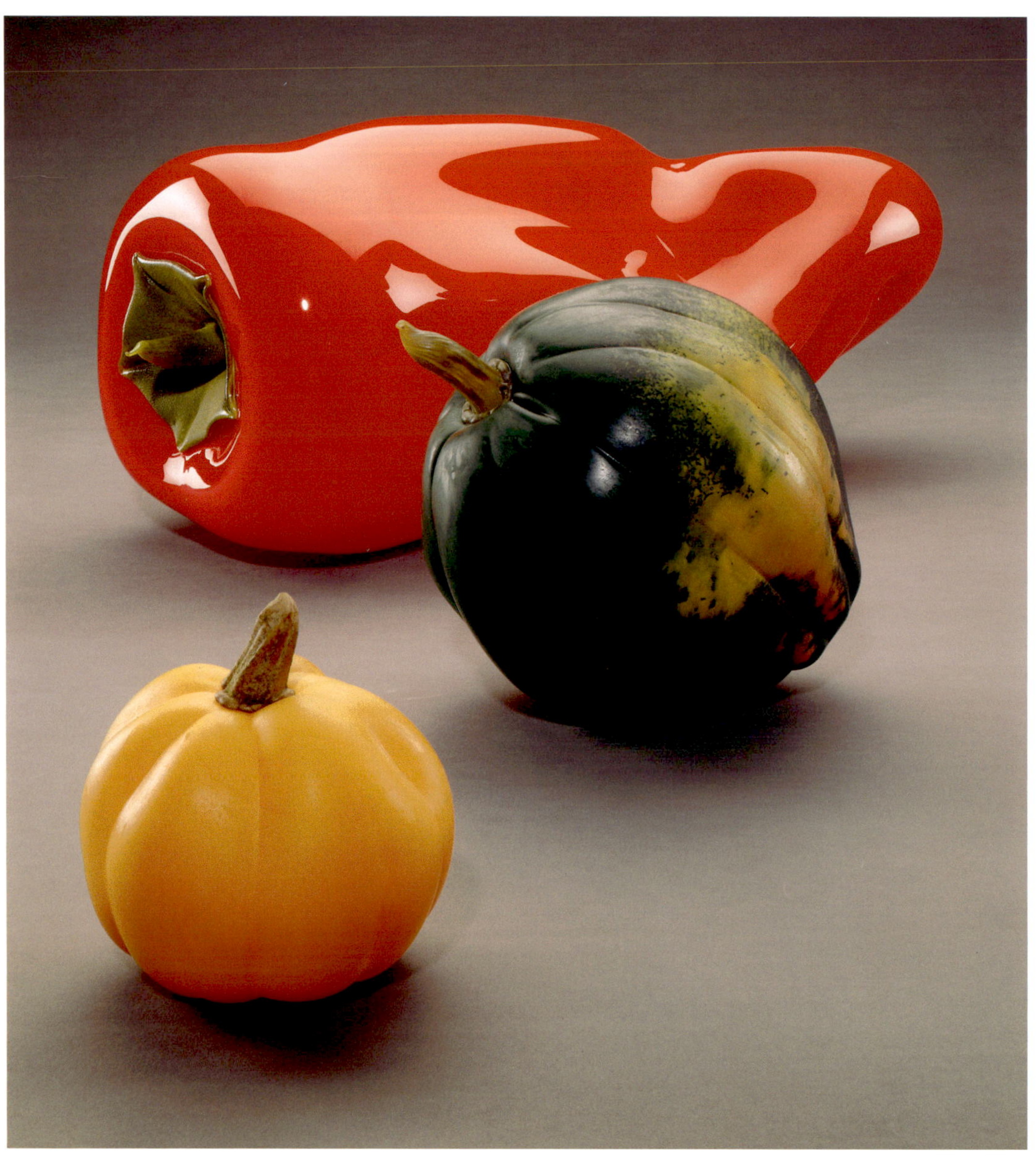

Chili Pepper and Squash with Pumpkin, 1996
Glass; chili pepper: 11½ × 27 × 12 inches

Fruit and Vegetable Goblets, 1995
Glass, each goblet approx. 9½ × 3½ × 3½ inches

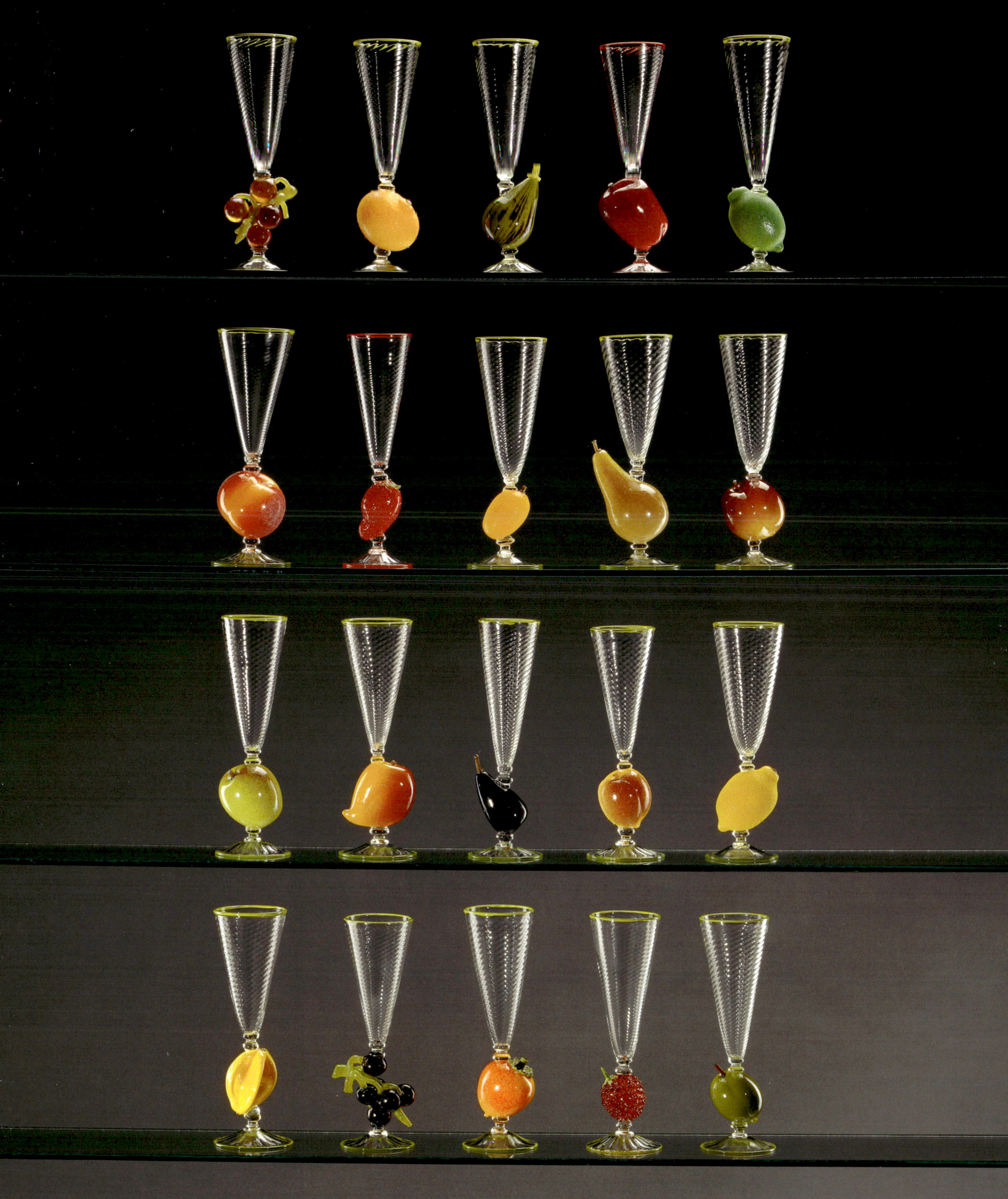

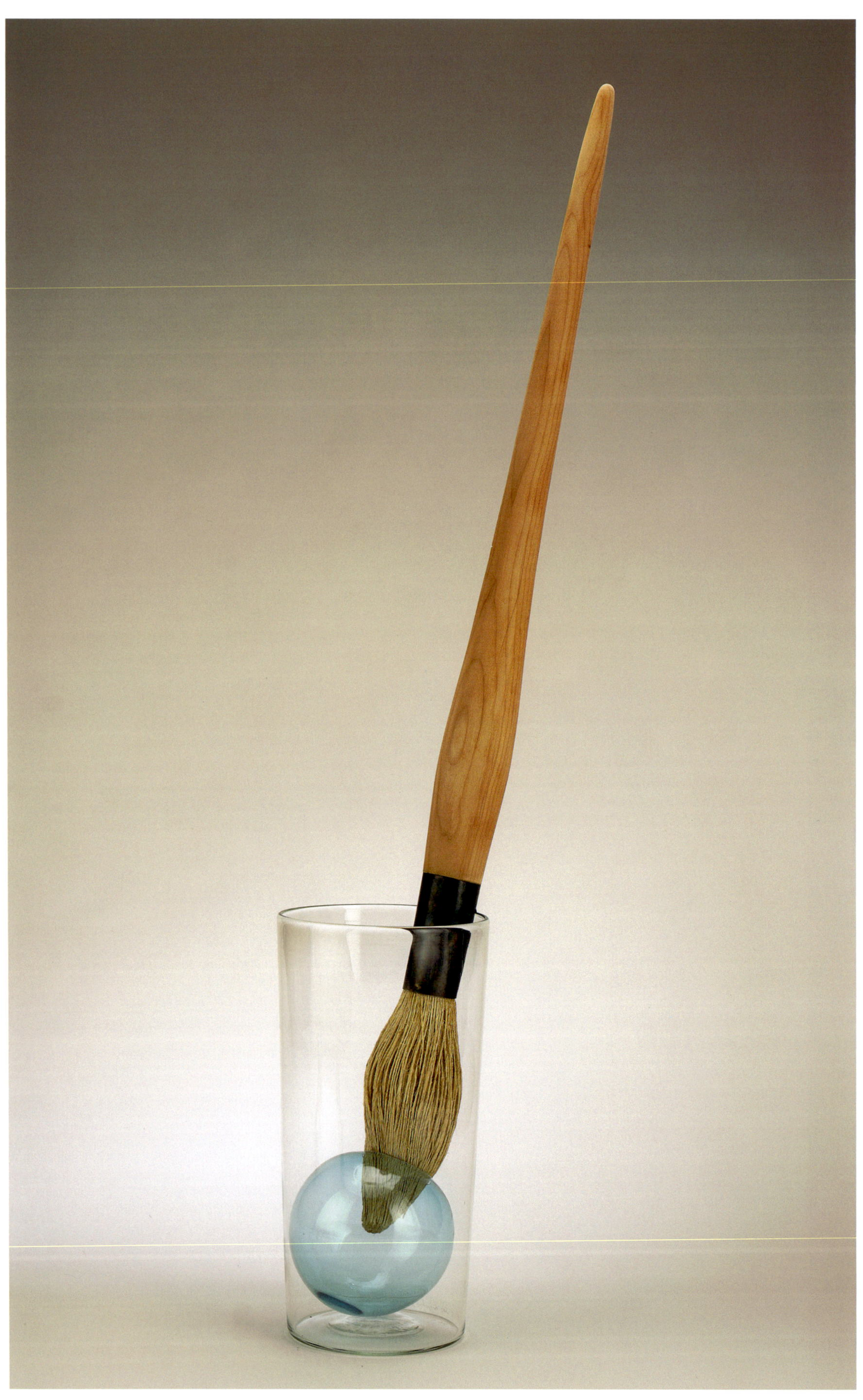

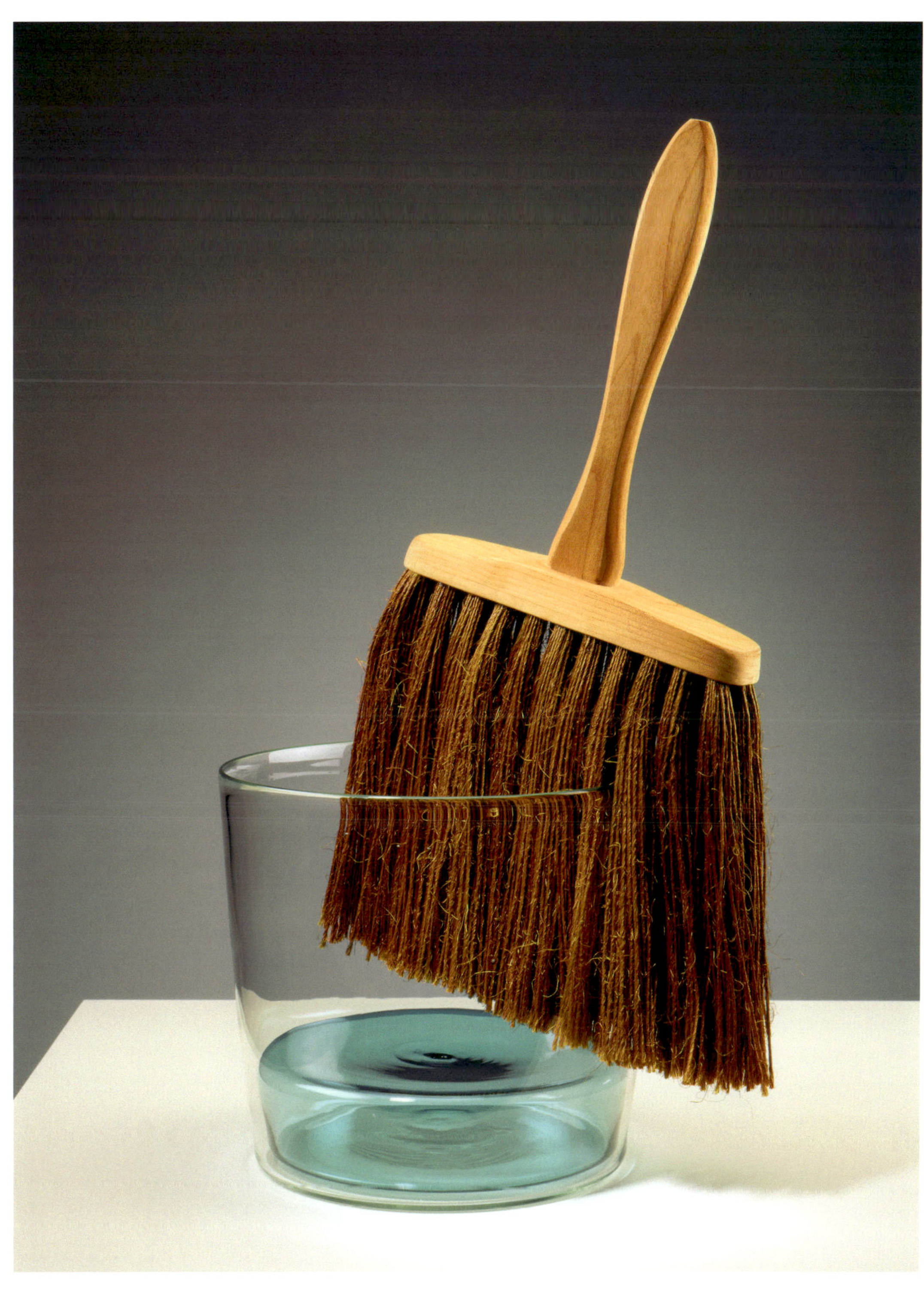

Revealing the Imagined, 1998
Glass, wood, sisal, dye, and steel, 70 × 20 × 11½ inches

Paint and Brush, 2000
Glass, wood, sisal, dye, and steel, 35 × 20 × 15 inches

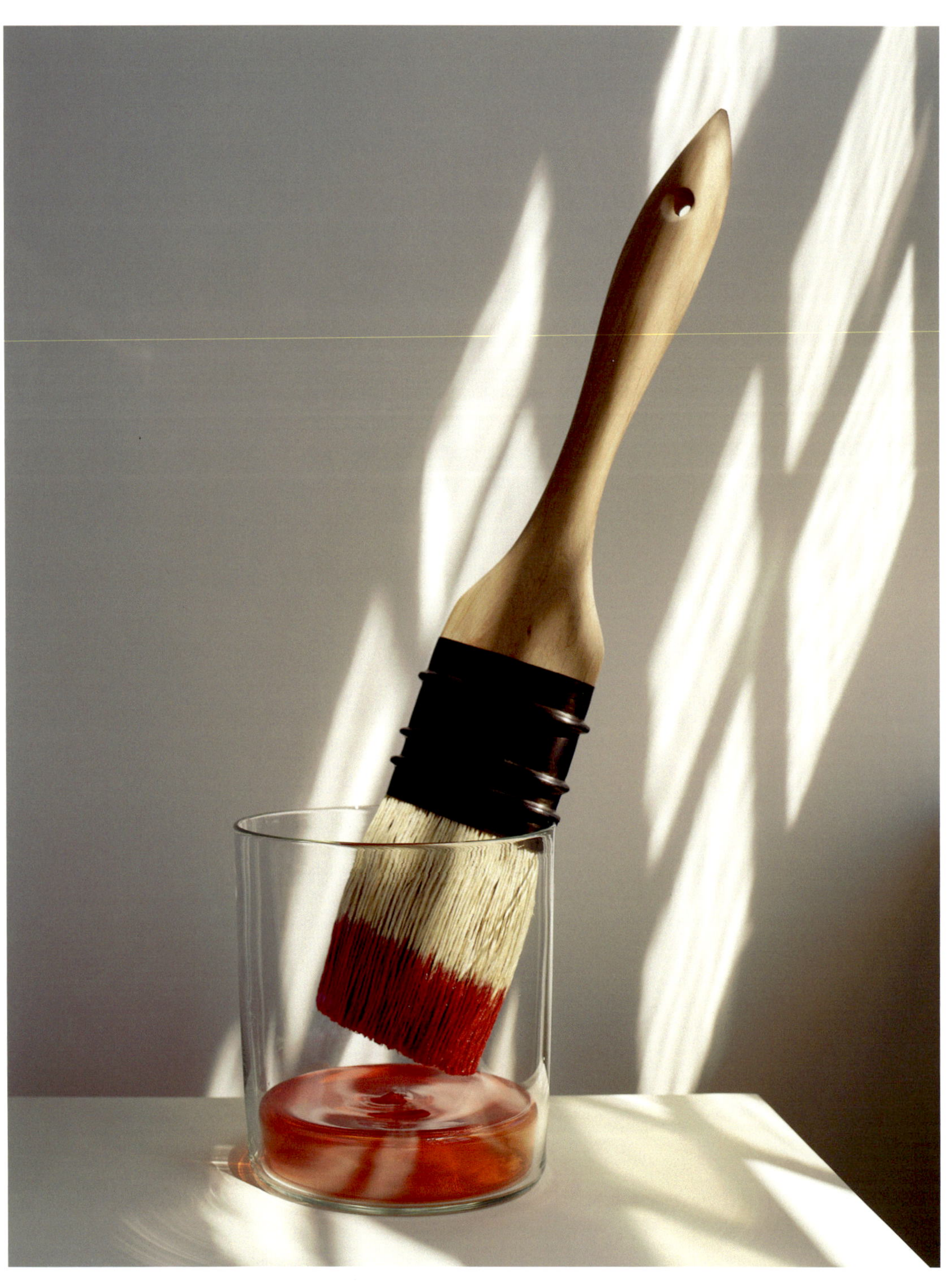

Revealing Red, 2001
Glass, wood, sisal, dye, and steel, 36 × 15 × 10½ inches

Making Before Meaning: Paintbrush Group, 2007
Glass, wood, sisal, dye, and steel; purple brush: 77 × 16 × 10 inches

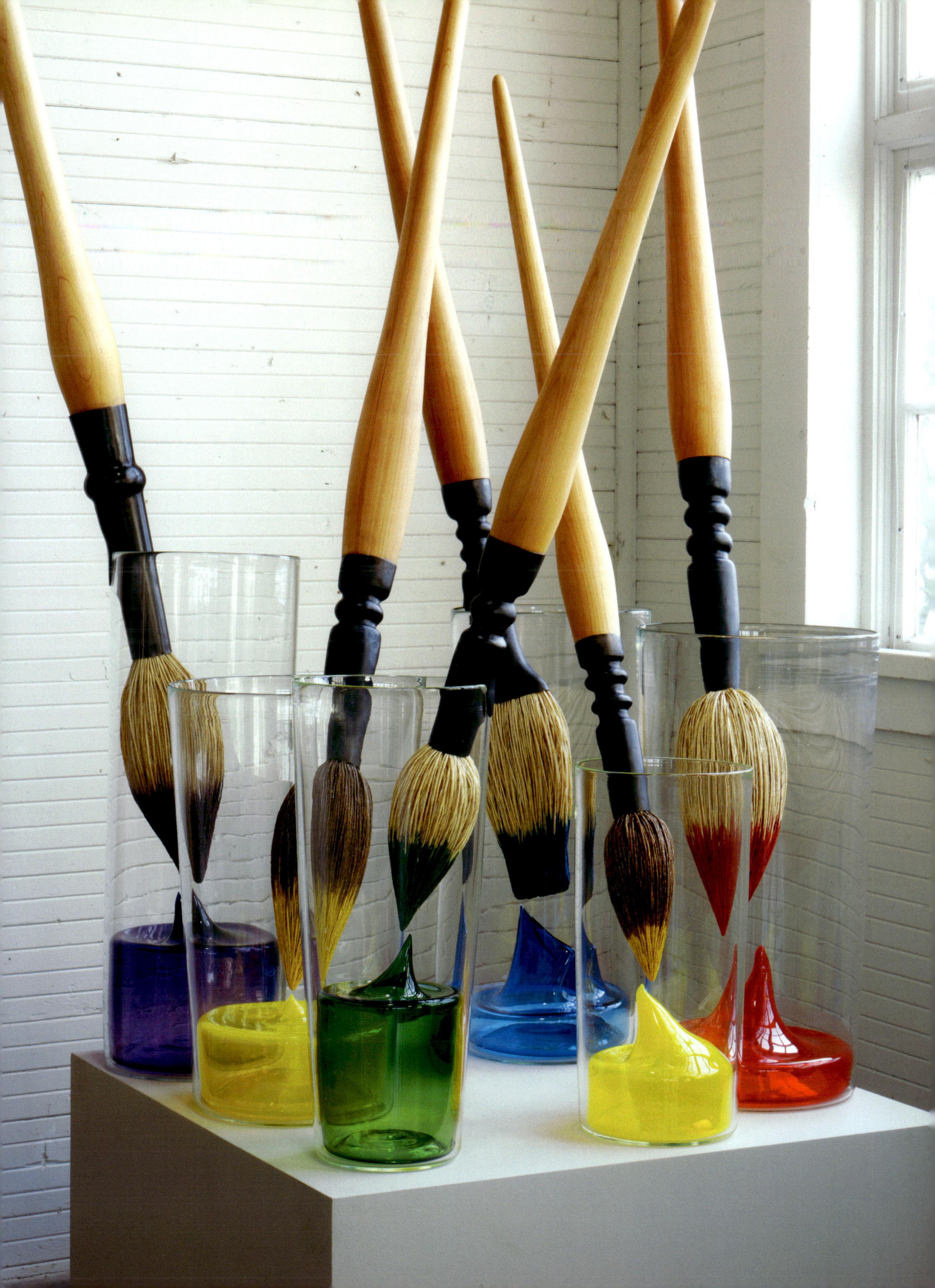

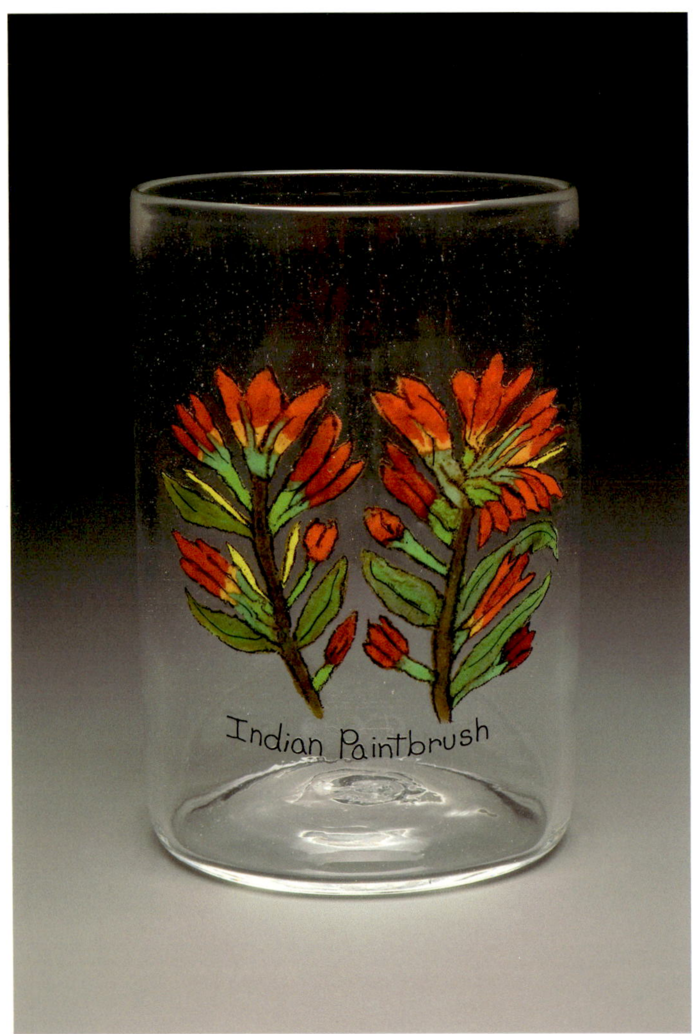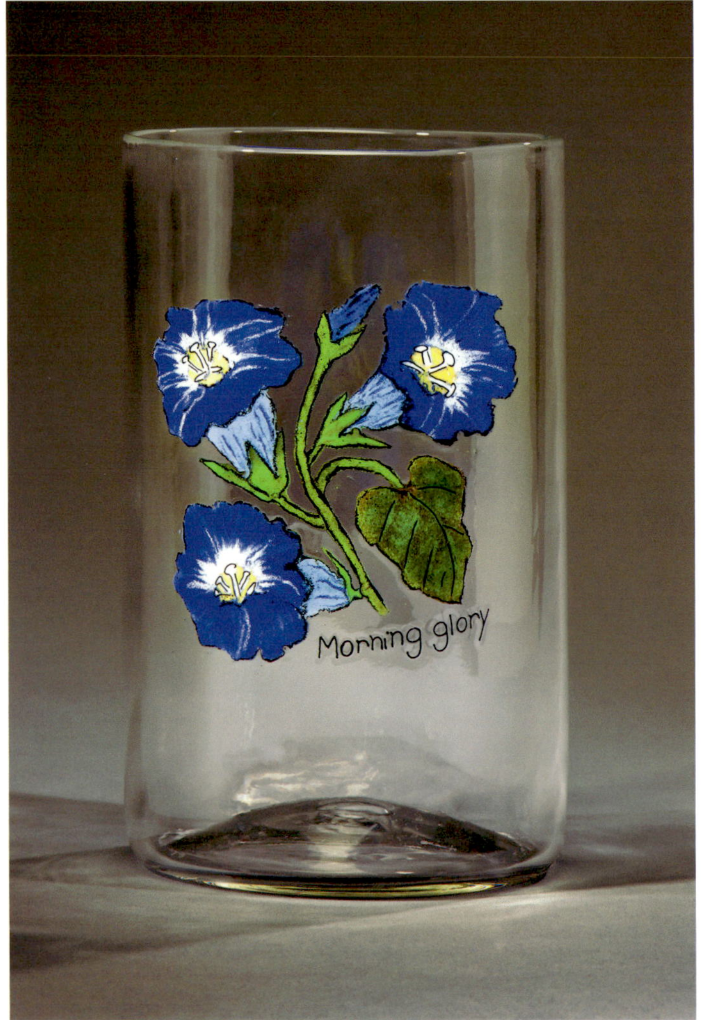

Indian Paintbrush, 2011
Glass, 9½ × 6¼ × 6¼ inches

Morning Glory II, 2010
Glass, 11 × 6¾ × 6¾ inches

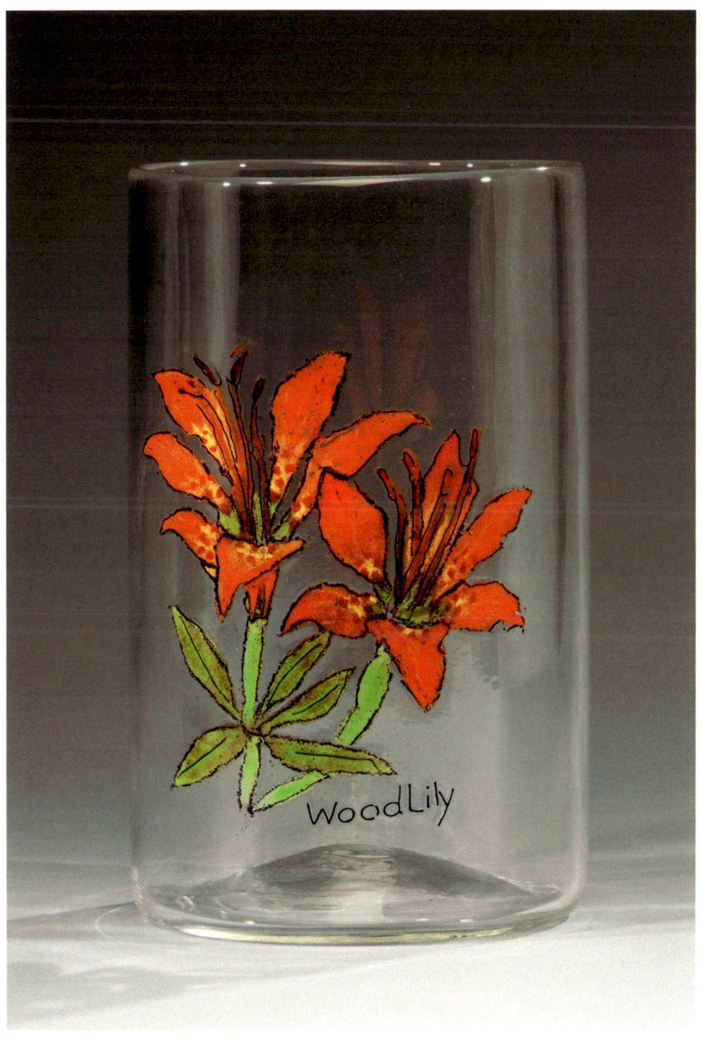

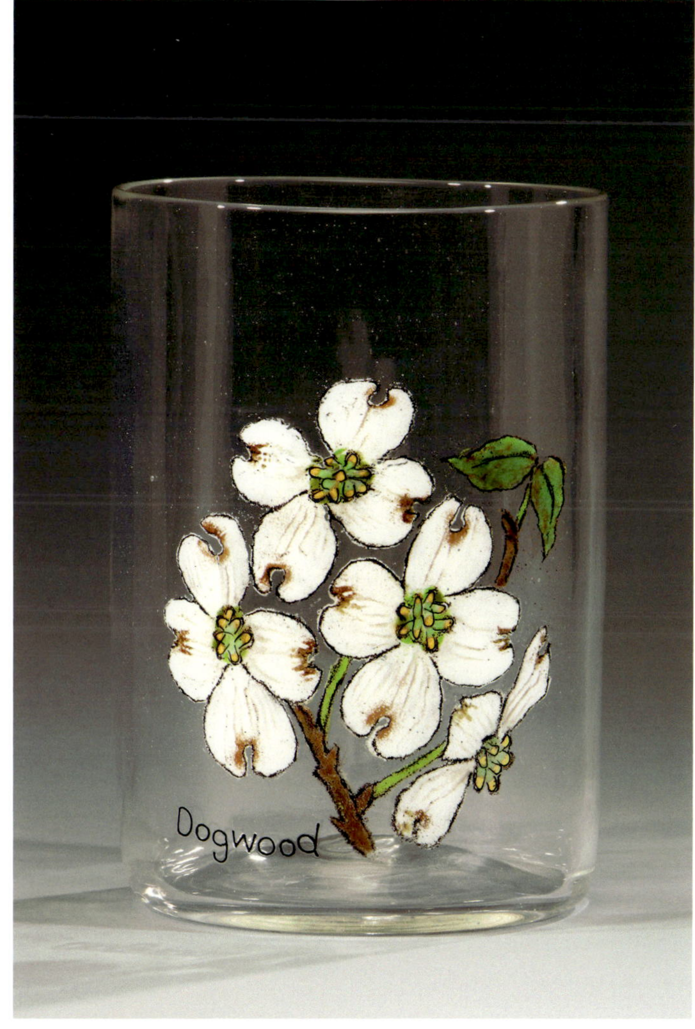

Dogwood, 2010
Glass, 8¾ × 6 × 6 inches

(following spread)
Bird Pages (details), 2003–2006

Wood Lily II, 2011
Glass, 9¾ × 6½ × 6½ inches

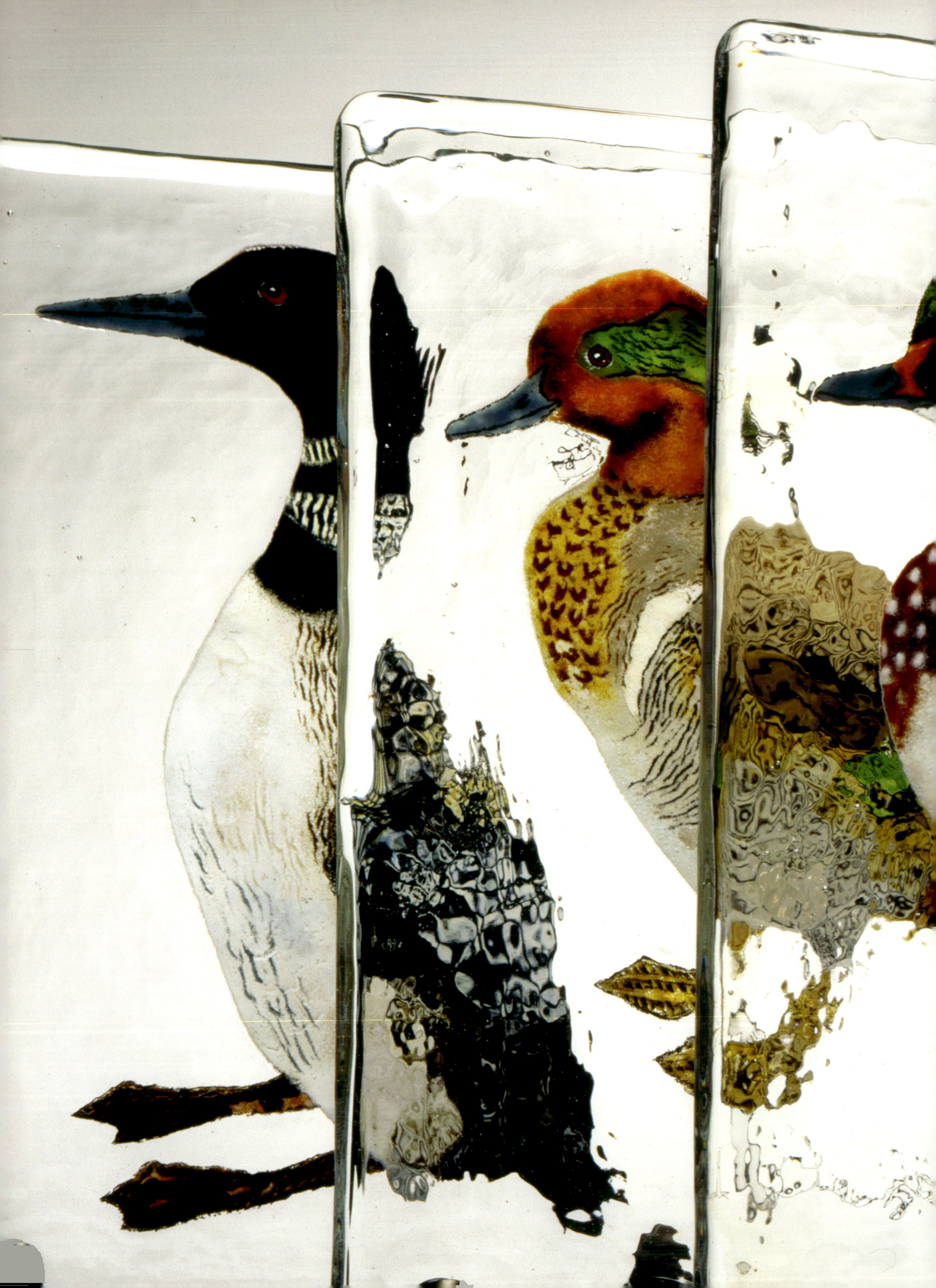

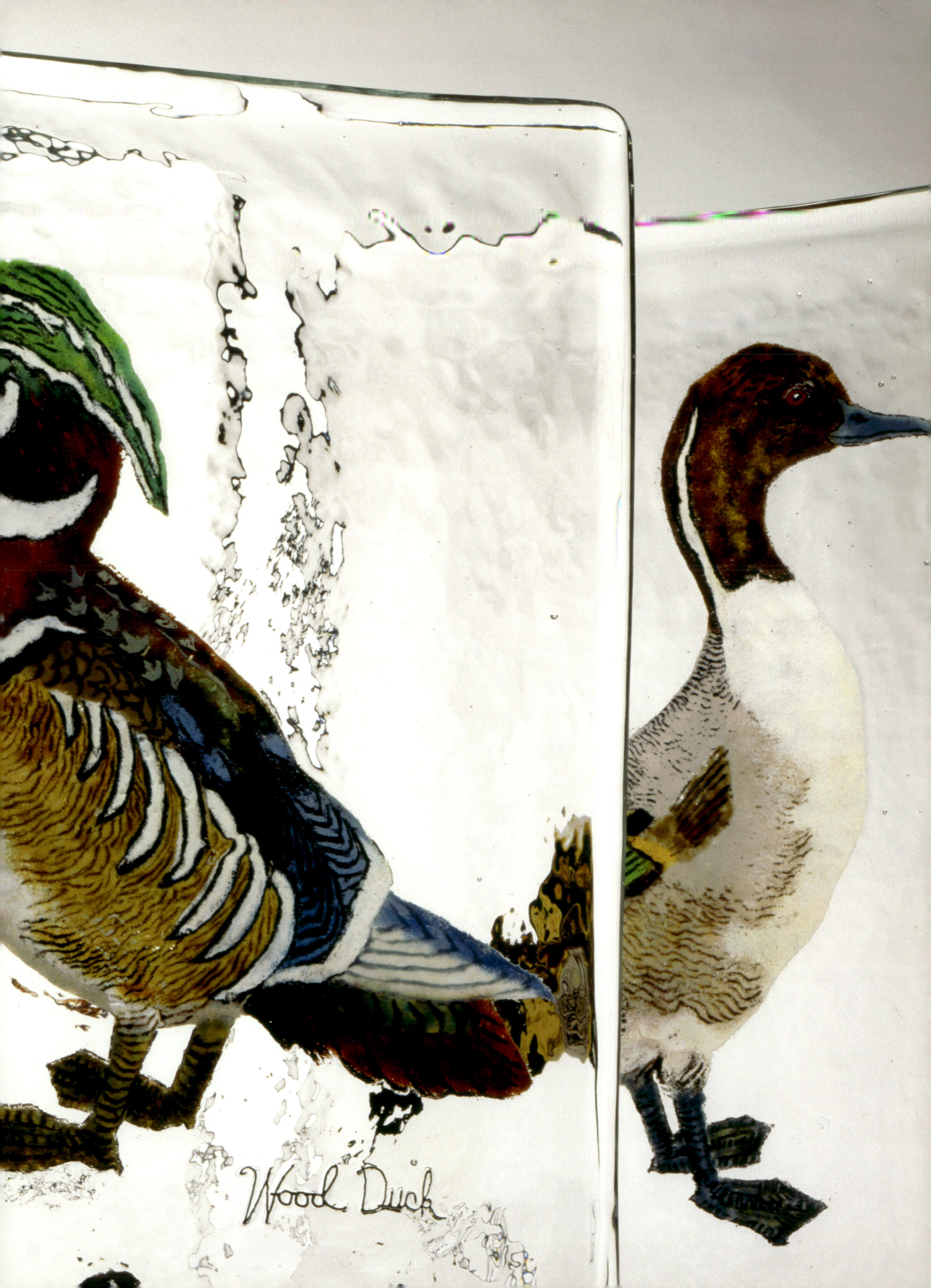
Wood Duck

Linda Tesner

Mace's Tools and Processes

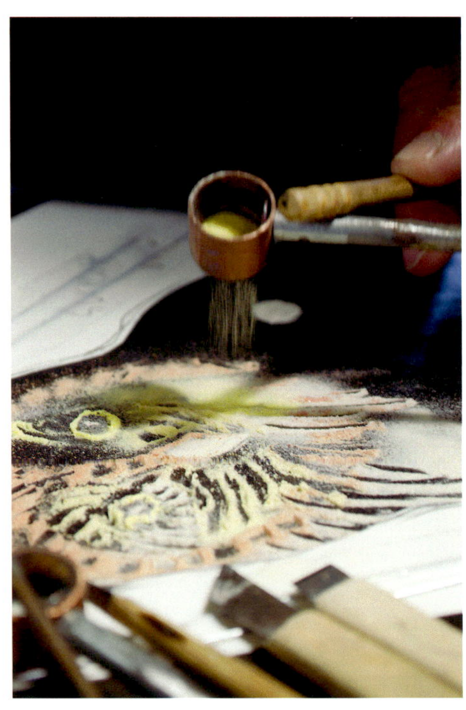

Intrinsic but mostly indiscernible components in the making of Kirkpatrick's and Mace's sculpture are the tools needed for the artists to manipulate their materials and coax them into form. The success of Kirkpatrick's and Mace's work has a backstory in Mace's ability to create the unequivocal tool or solution needed for any given studio task.

Kirkpatrick is known to say that she doesn't want to see "what holds a sculpture together," that her intention is to craft sculpture that seems to have made itself. This seamlessness very often requires Mace to fabricate components, at times using her own custom tools, to achieve a desired effect. It is not uncommon for Mace to fashion her own nuts, screws, and bolts in response to idiosyncratic sizing requirements or to cut apart different items of off-the-shelf hardware and combine them with metal elements of her own design, welding the parts together in order to make the exactly correct element for a work.

The brush ferrule on the paintbrushes in *Making Before Meaning* is a good example of how Mace makes by hand a sculptural element. First sculpting the collar in wood to the desired shape and scale, she then covered the wood carving with overlapping pieces of tape. Once removed, the tape could be laid out flat like a pattern, which Mace traced onto sheet metal. She cut the metal, rolled it, and cut darts in it to make an oversize paintbrush ferrule that appears nearly machine made. Additionally, Mace carved a void into the wood handle of each paintbrush to relieve any potential stress on the glass paint pot where the brush rests on the lip of the glass.

The paintbrush sculptures are just one example of how Mace tenaciously designs tools and works of art in such a way that imposing structural problems are elegantly resolved. When Kirkpatrick was in the process of making the glass-powder drawings for *Bird Pages: First Facts*, Mace constructed an entire set of tools with wood handles and metal blades so that Kirkpatrick could efficiently manipulate the fugitive glass powder. Mace also made thimble-sized sieves so that Kirkpatrick could sprinkle additional glass powder evenly over a drawing. Eventually, Mace designed and hand made each base for the *Bird Pages* in what was a tedious process, as the clips on each base had to be individually calibrated by hand to accommodate differing depths of the glass "page."

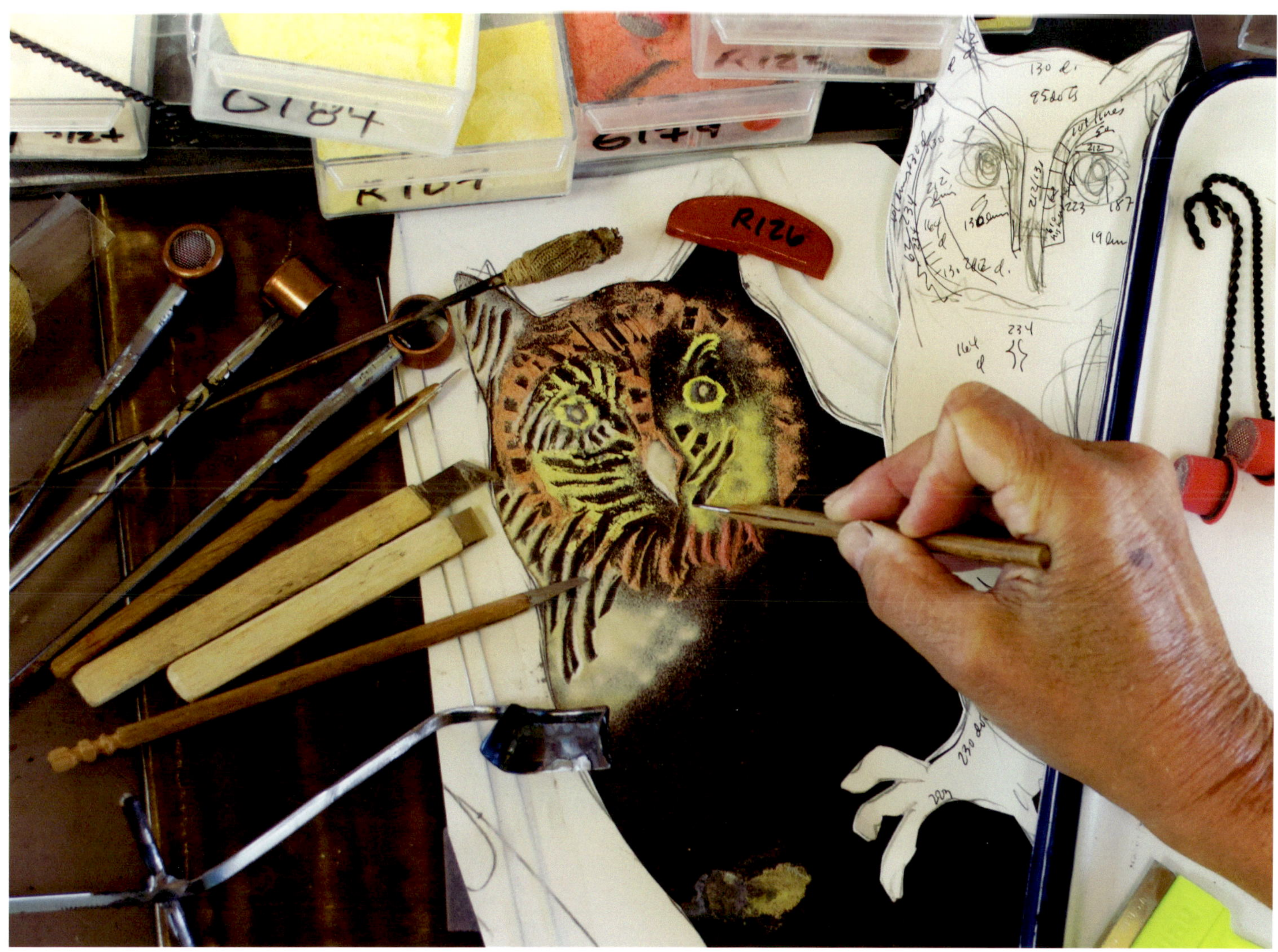

Perhaps Mace's greatest achievements in terms of puzzling through a design challenge have been the *Botanicals*. The elaborate process for drying, recomposing, and arresting the plant specimen in a hybrid composite and glass construction is unparalleled. It was only through Mace's patience and persistence that these complex and unprecedented processes were developed.

Kirkpatrick is fond of referring to Mace as a "mad scientist," since a good deal of Mace's time in the studio is spent "puttering" to refine tools and procedures. Much of Mace's conceptualization evolves through these activities, helping to drive the artists' creative process to meet the challenges they pose for themselves.

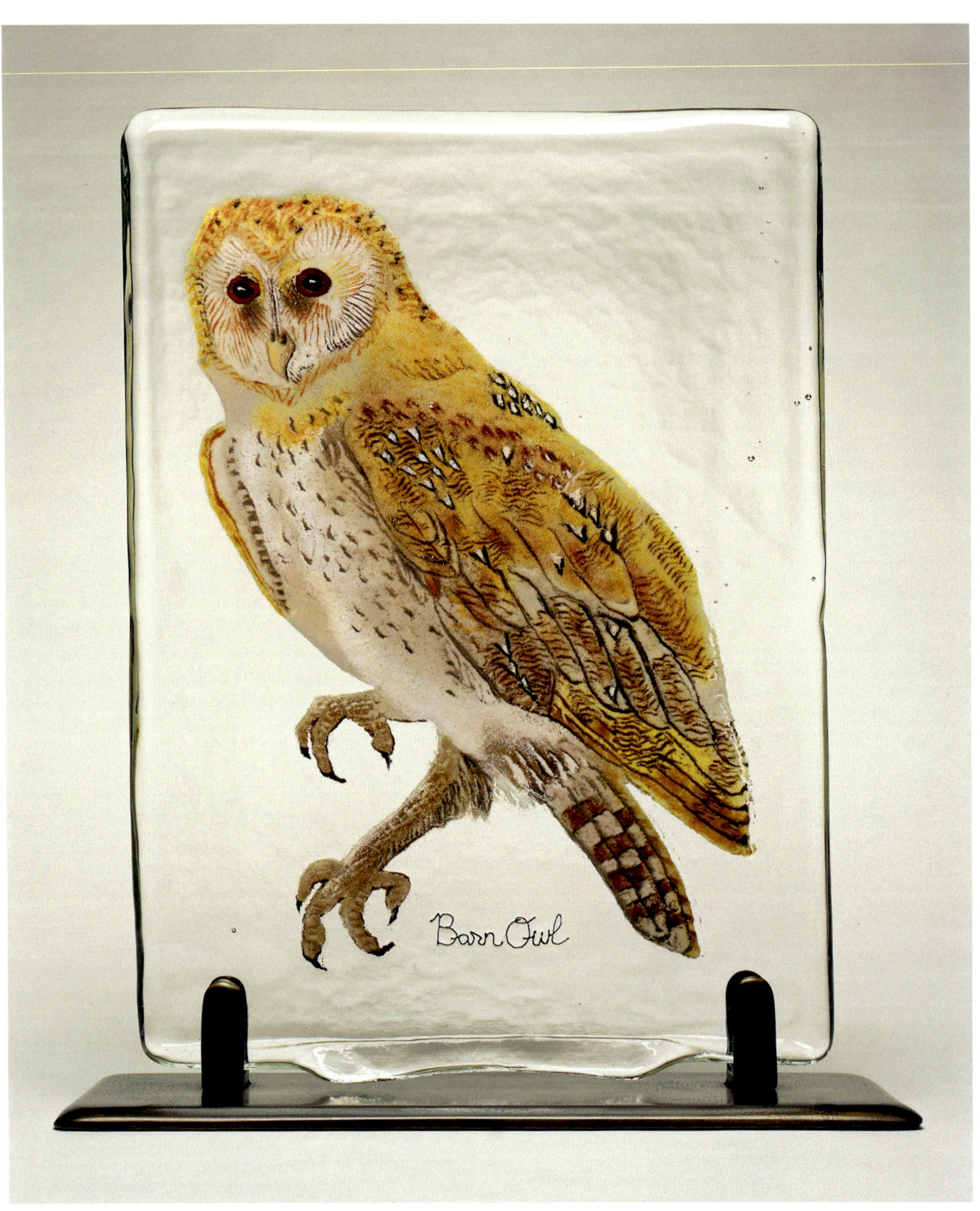

Bird Page: Barn Owl, 2004
Glass and steel, 17½ × 14 × 6 inches

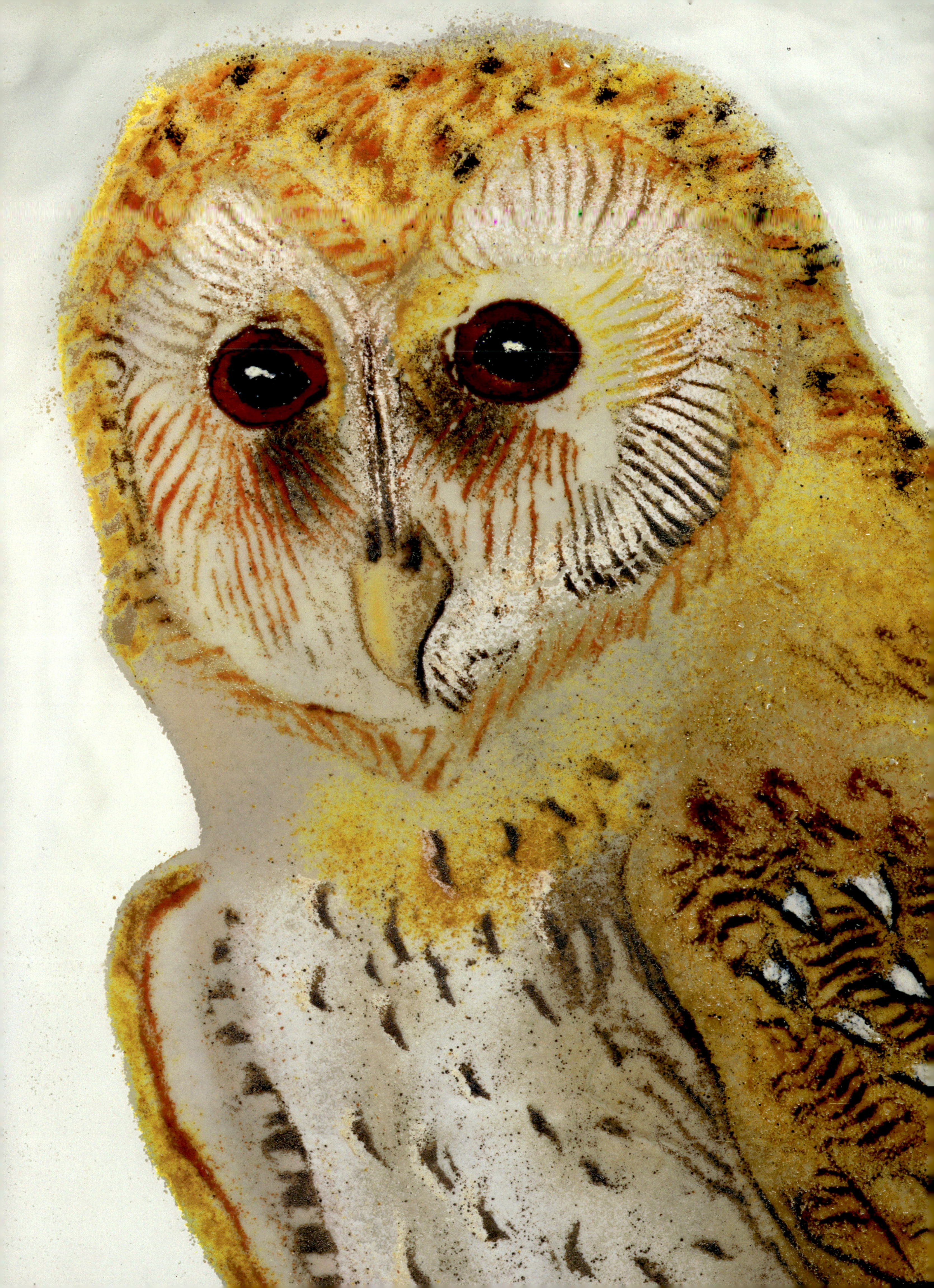

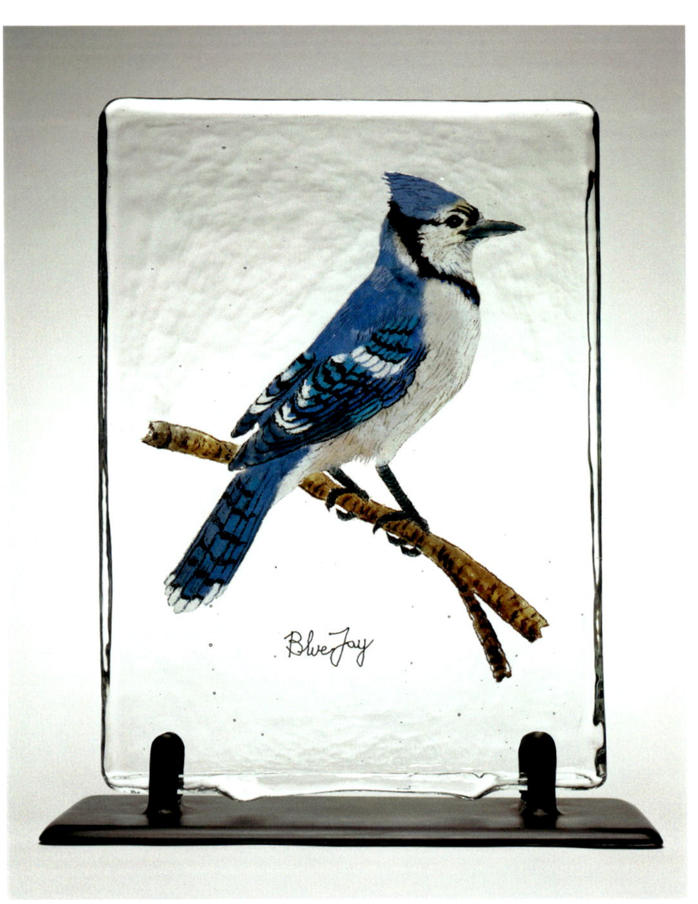

Bird Page: Blue Jay, 2006
Glass and steel, 17½ × 14 × 6 inches

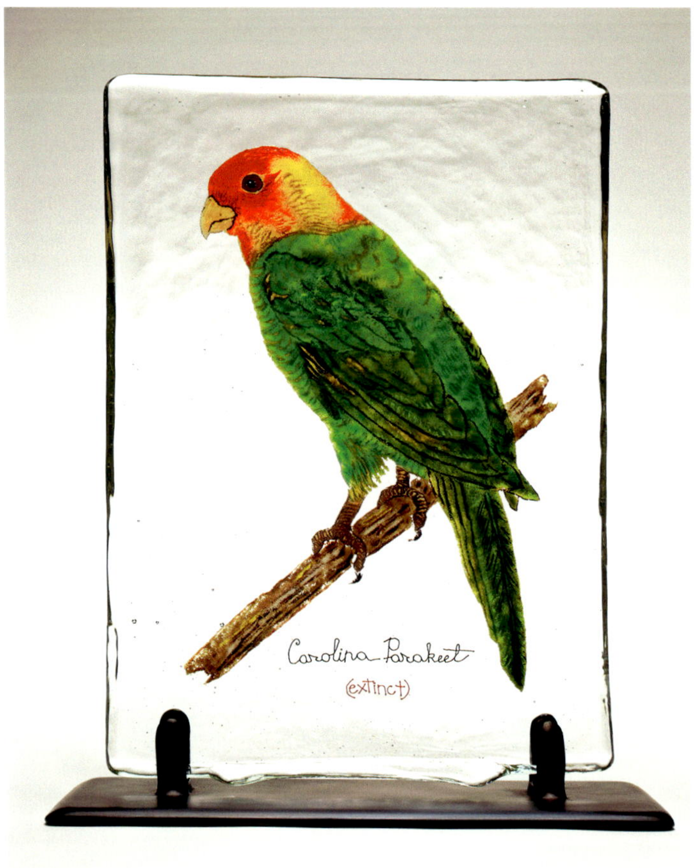

Bird Page: Carolina Parakeet, 2006
Glass and steel, 17½ × 14 × 6 inches

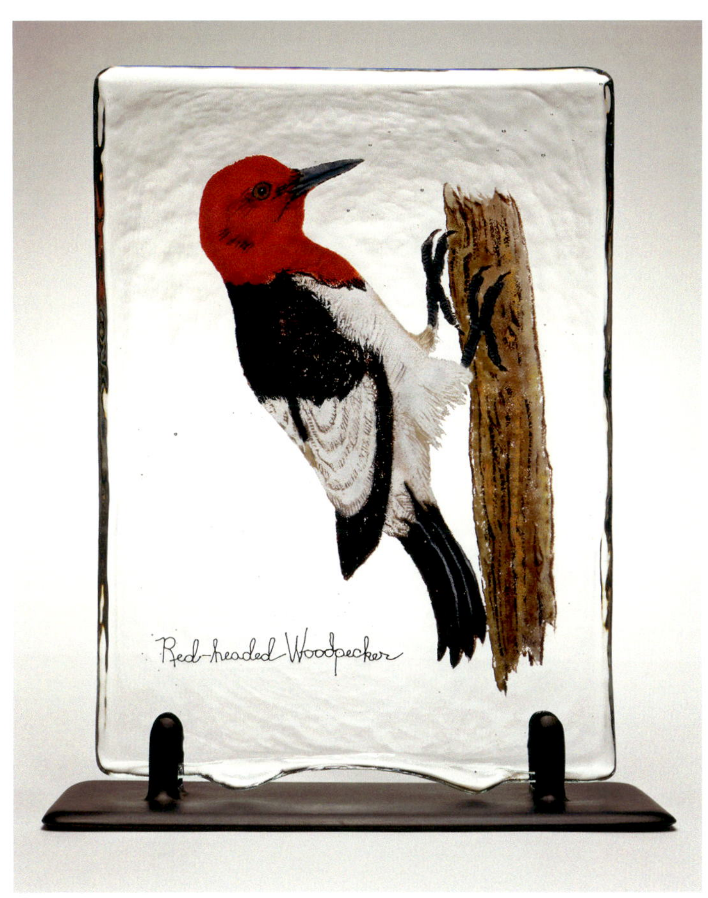

Bird Page: Red-headed Woodpecker, 2006
Glass and steel, 17½ × 14 × 6 inches

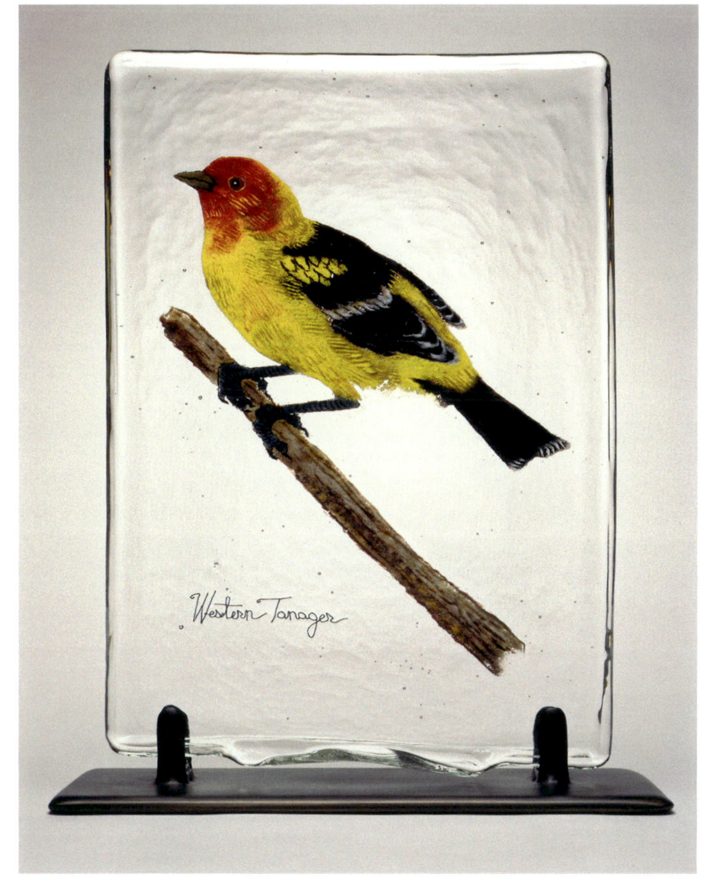

Bird Page: Western Tanager, 2004
Glass and steel, 17½ × 14 × 6 inches

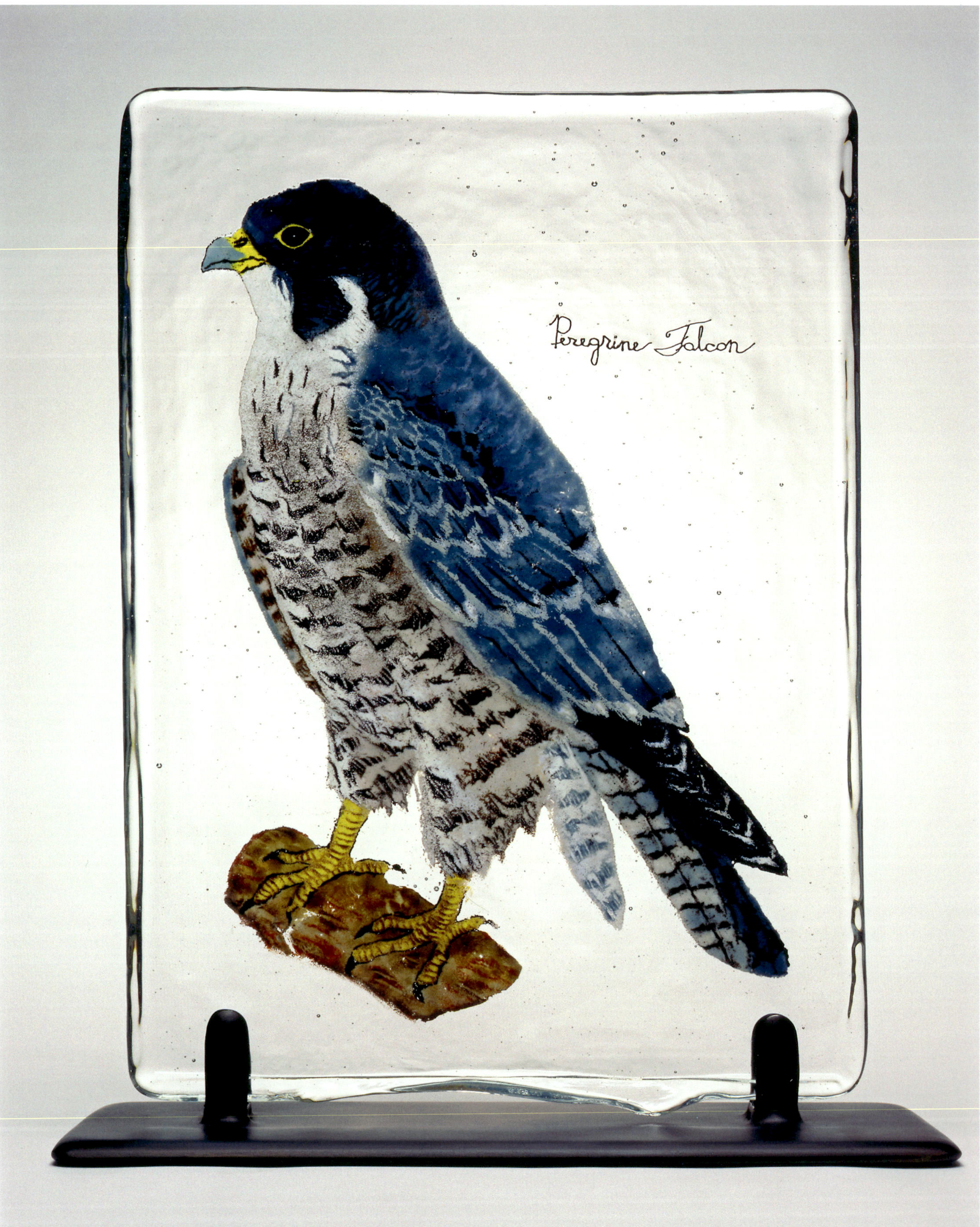

Peregrine Falcon

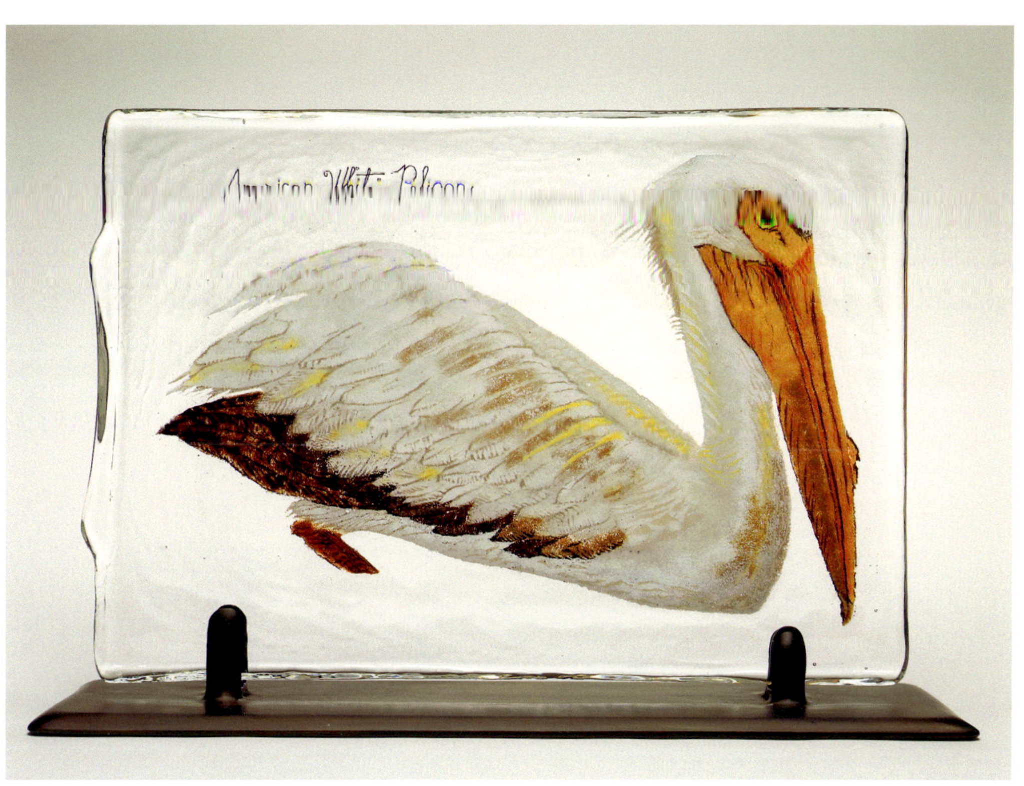

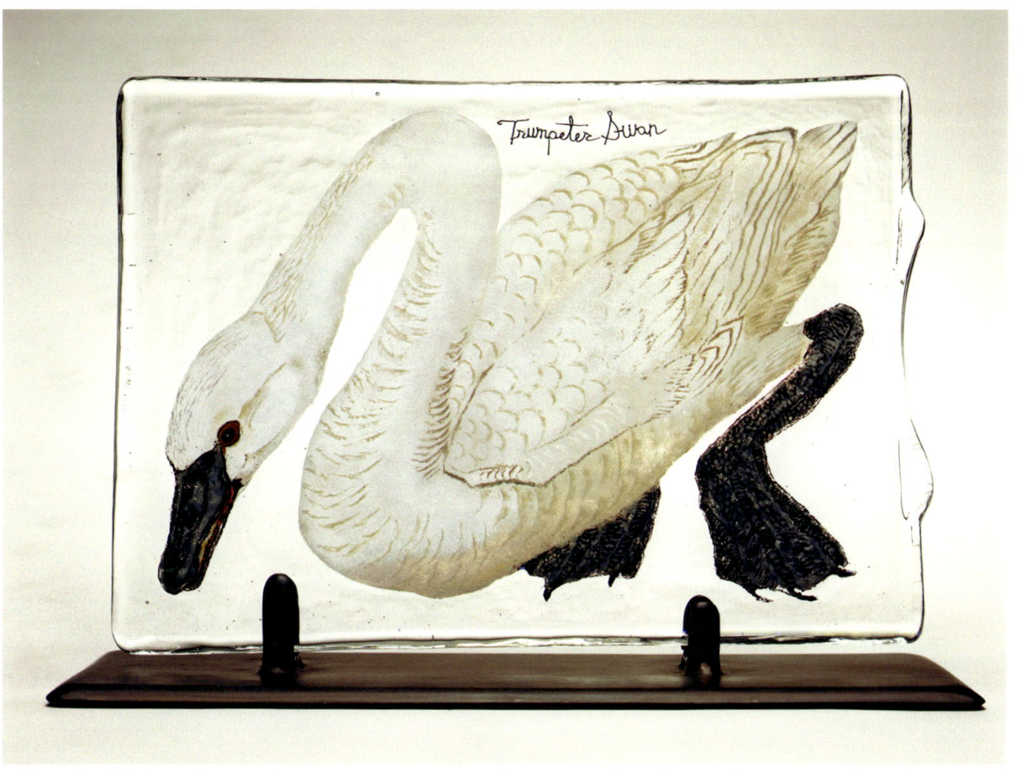

Bird Page: American White Pelican, 2006
Glass and steel, 13½ × 18½ × 6 inches

Bird Page: Trumpeter Swan, 2006
Glass and steel, 13½ × 18½ × 6 inches

Bird Page: Peregrine Falcon, 2004
Glass and steel, 17½ × 14 × 6 inches

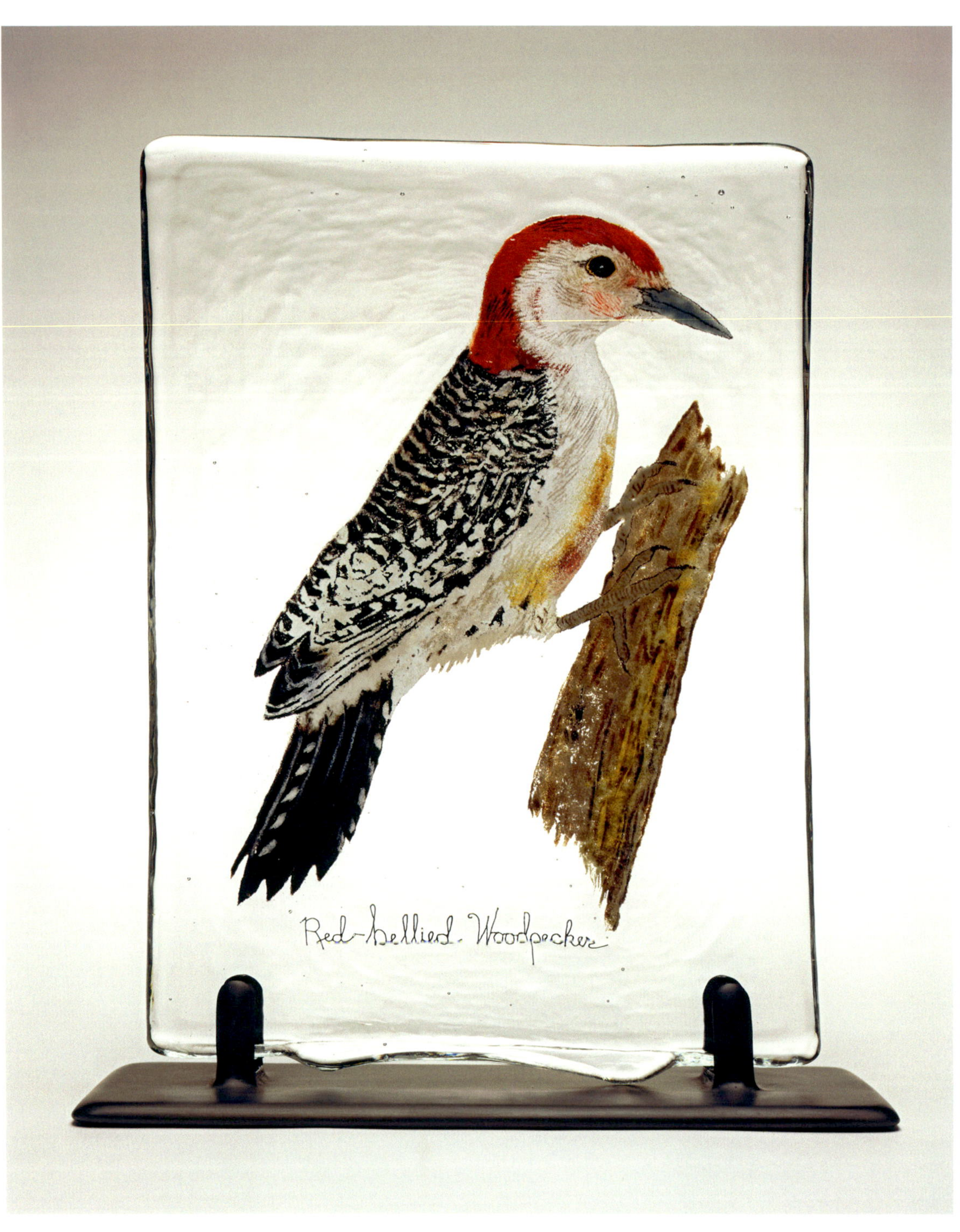

Bird Page: Red-bellied Woodpecker, 2006
Glass and steel, 17½ × 14 × 6 inches

Bird Page: Yellow-shafted Flicker, 2006
Glass and steel, 17½ × 14 × 6 inches

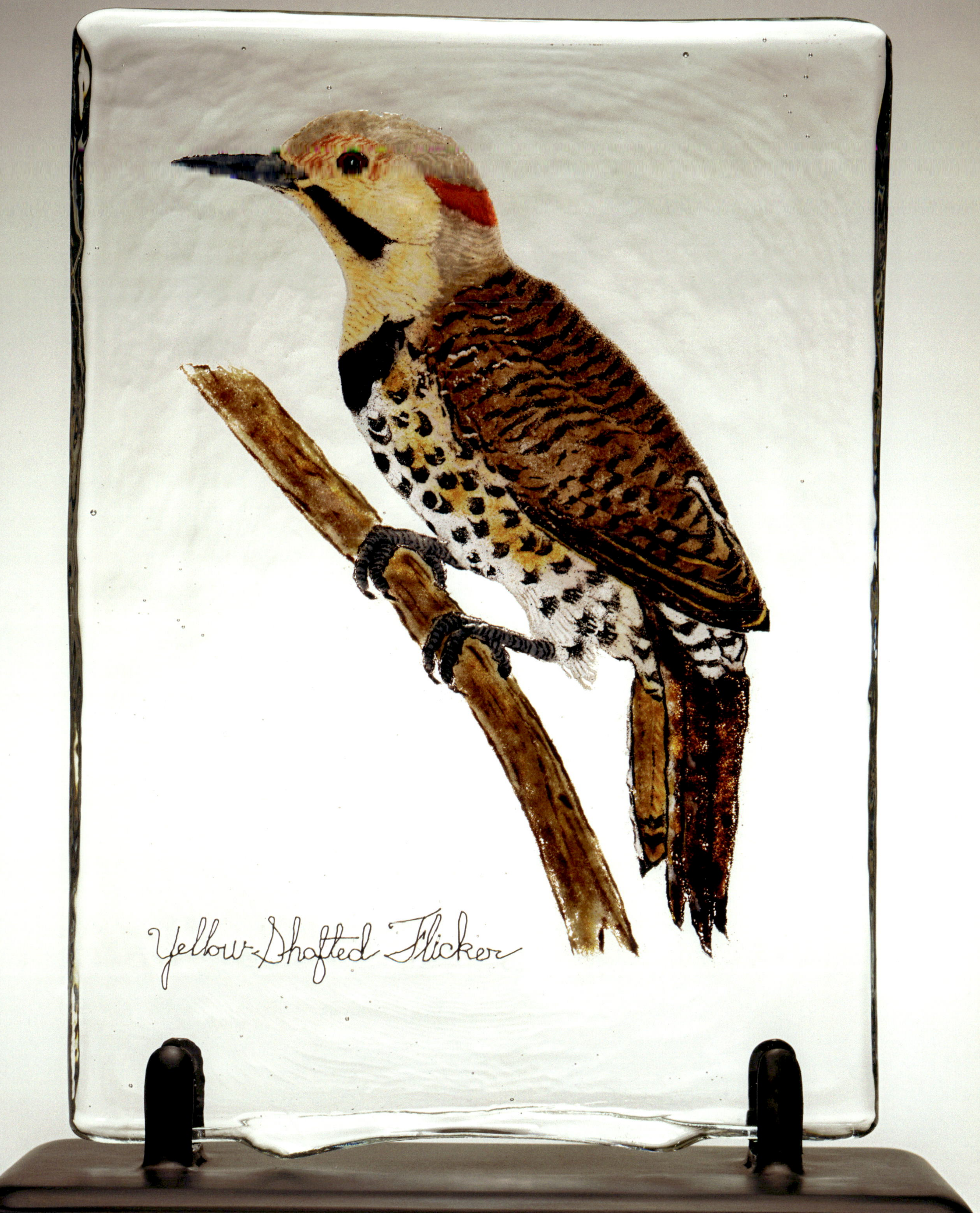

Yellow-Shafted Flicker

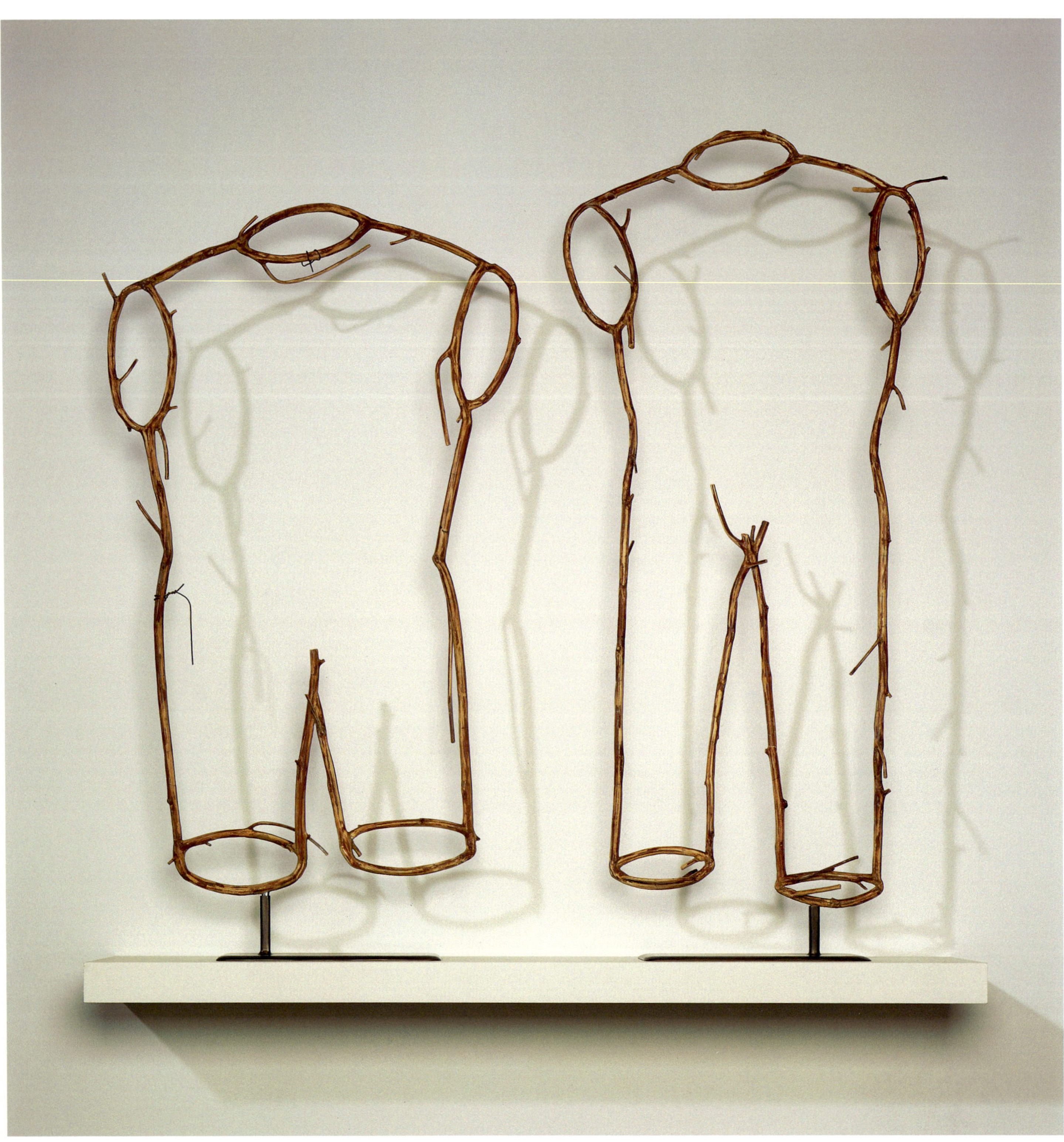

Drawing Figures: Finding Form, 2002
Wood and steel, 42 × 40 × 6 inches

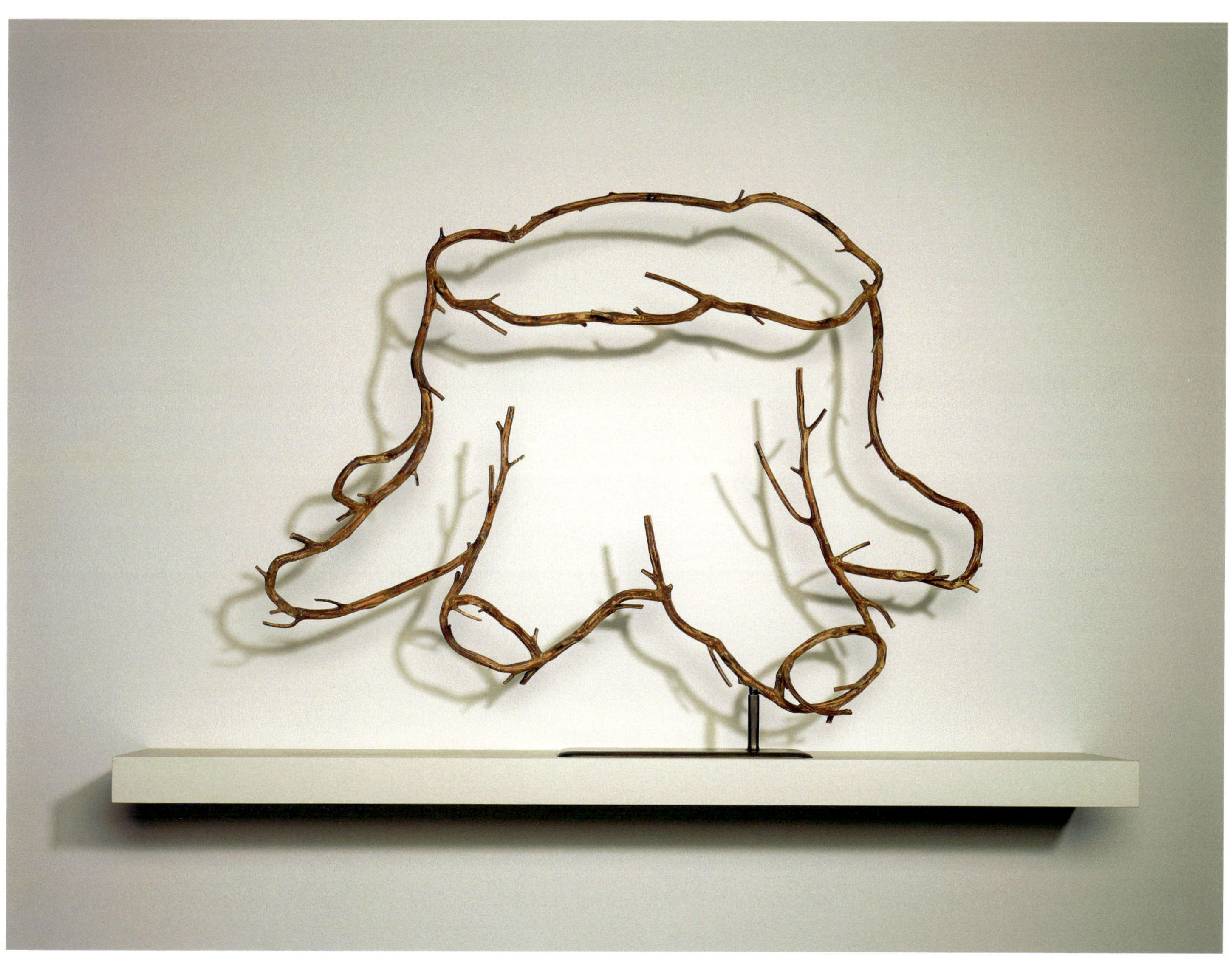

Woodland Drawing: Stump, 2003
Wood and steel, 23 × 32 × 6 inches

(following spread)
Owl and Wren, 2005
Bronze, 44 × 45 × 7 inches; 36 × 30 × 7 inches

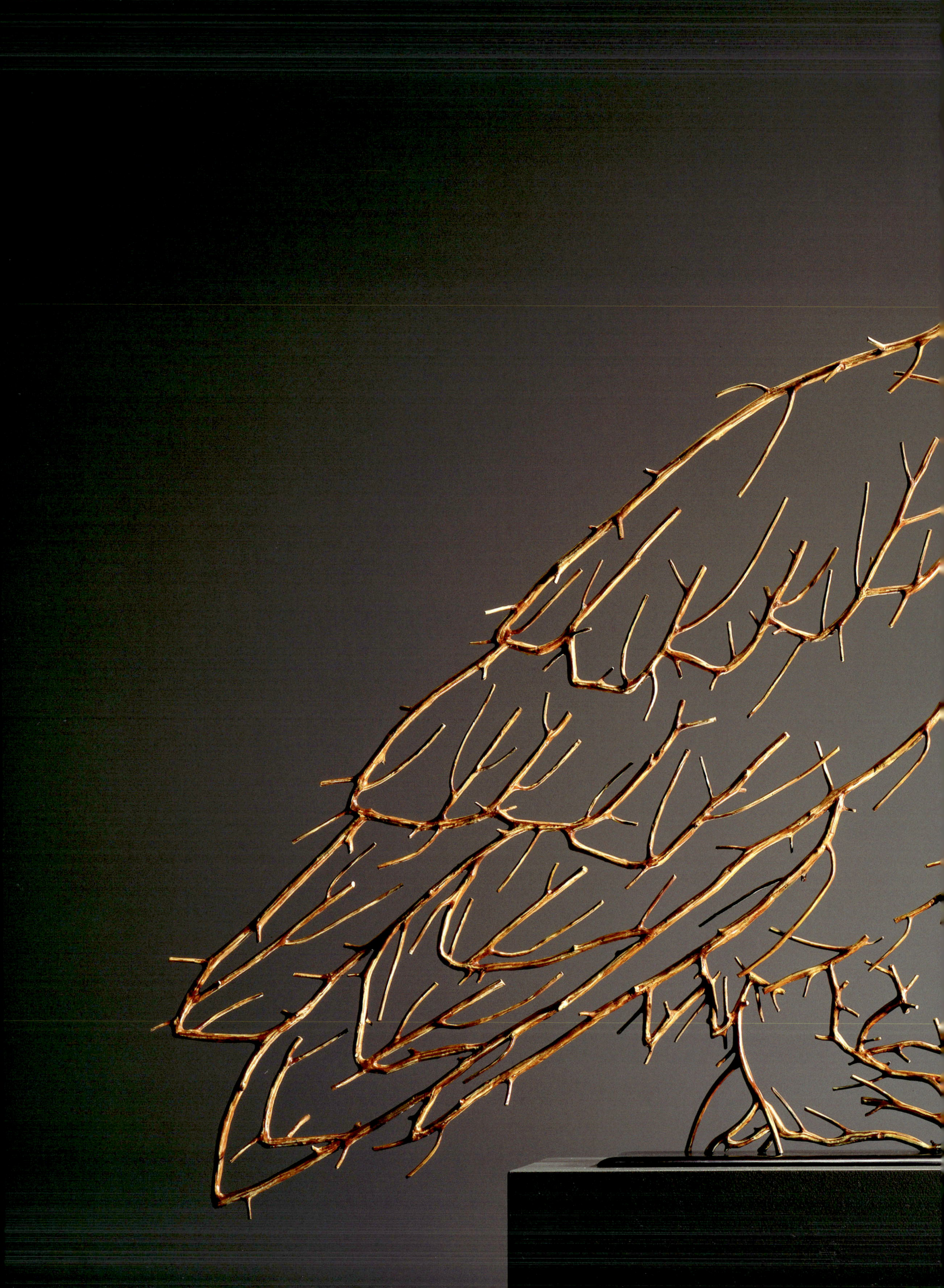

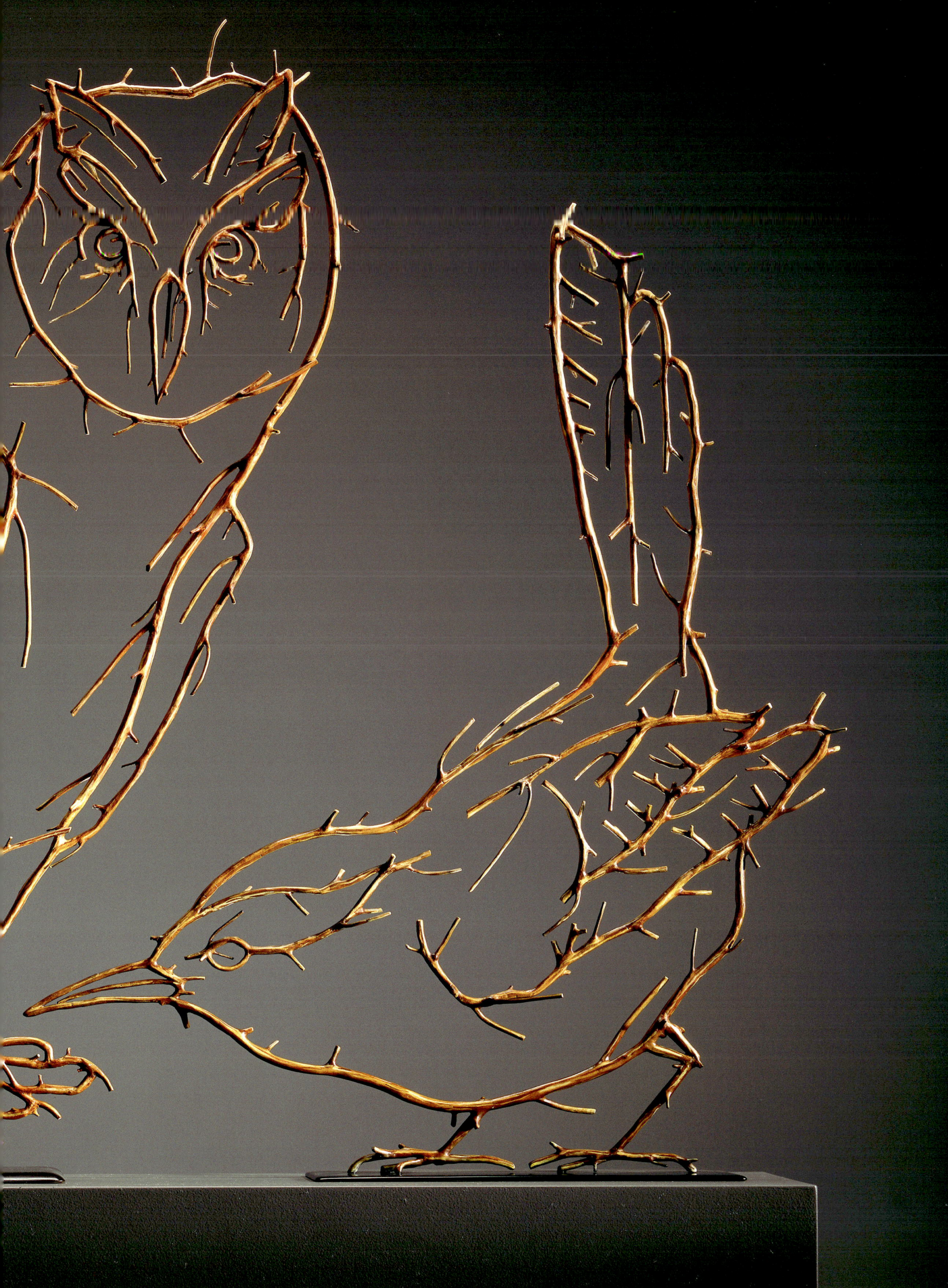

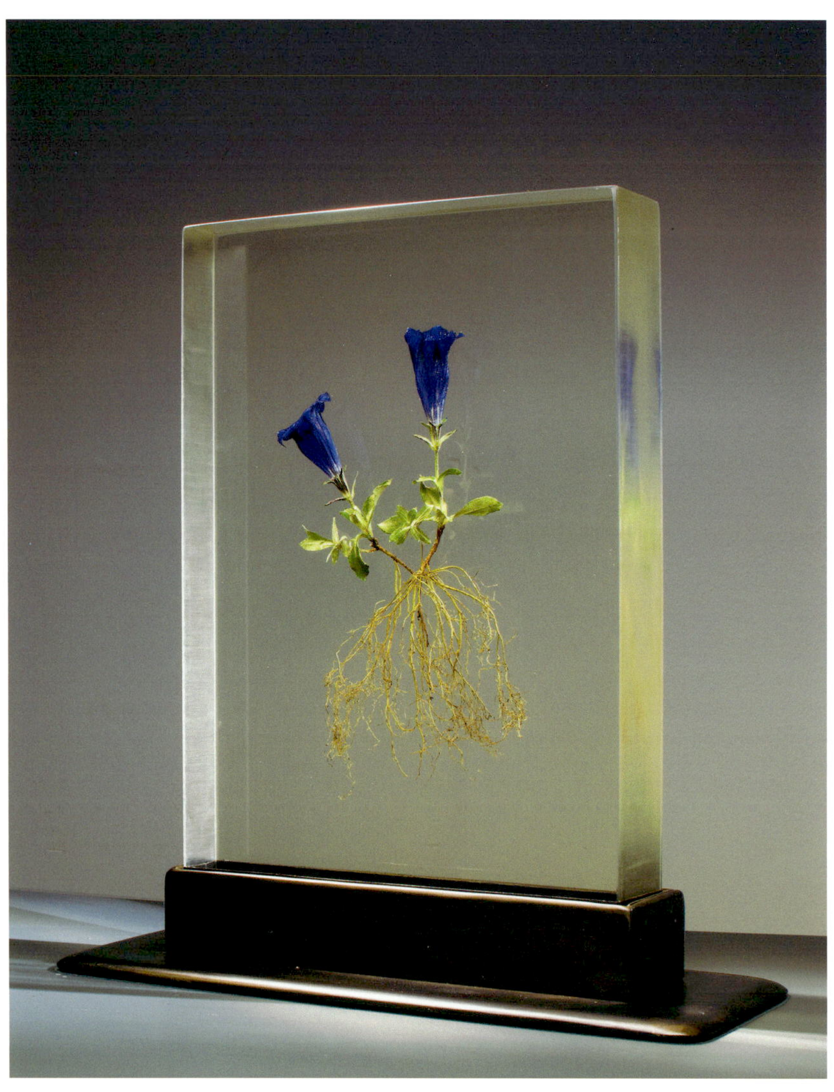

Gloxinia, 2015
Flower, composite, glass, and steel, 17 × 16 × 6 inches

Showy Lady's Slipper, 2015
Flower, composite, glass, and steel, 27½ × 20 × 8 inches

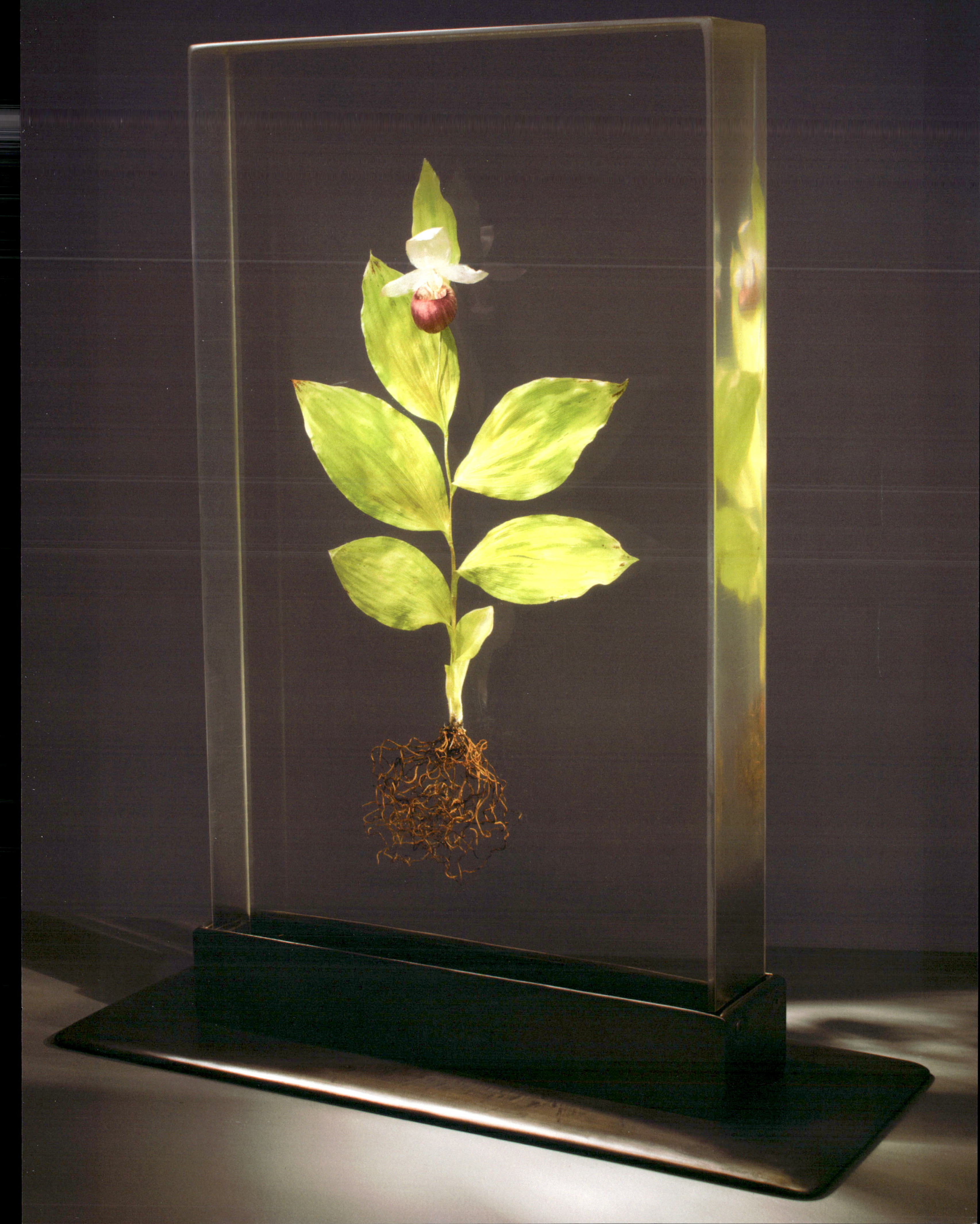

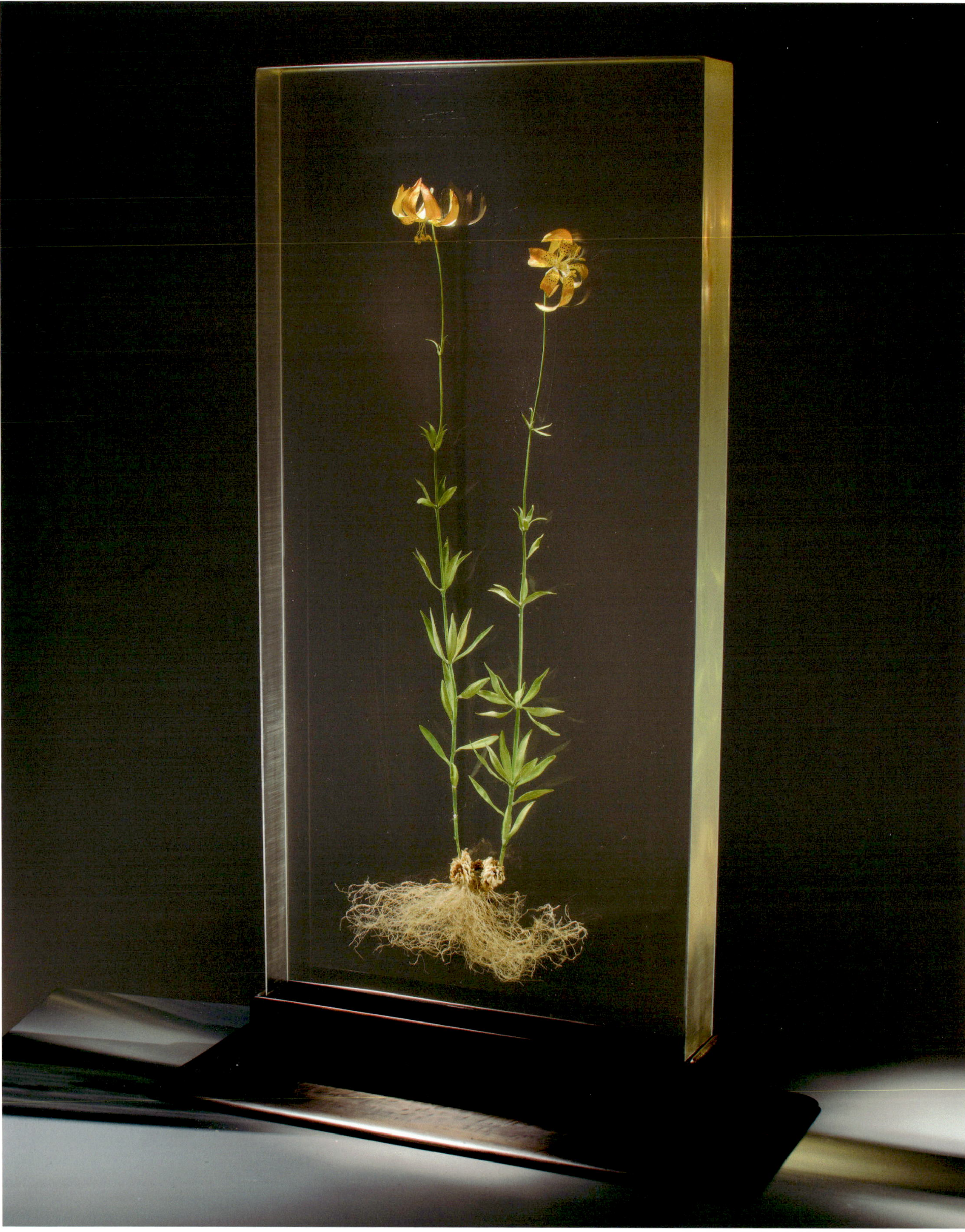

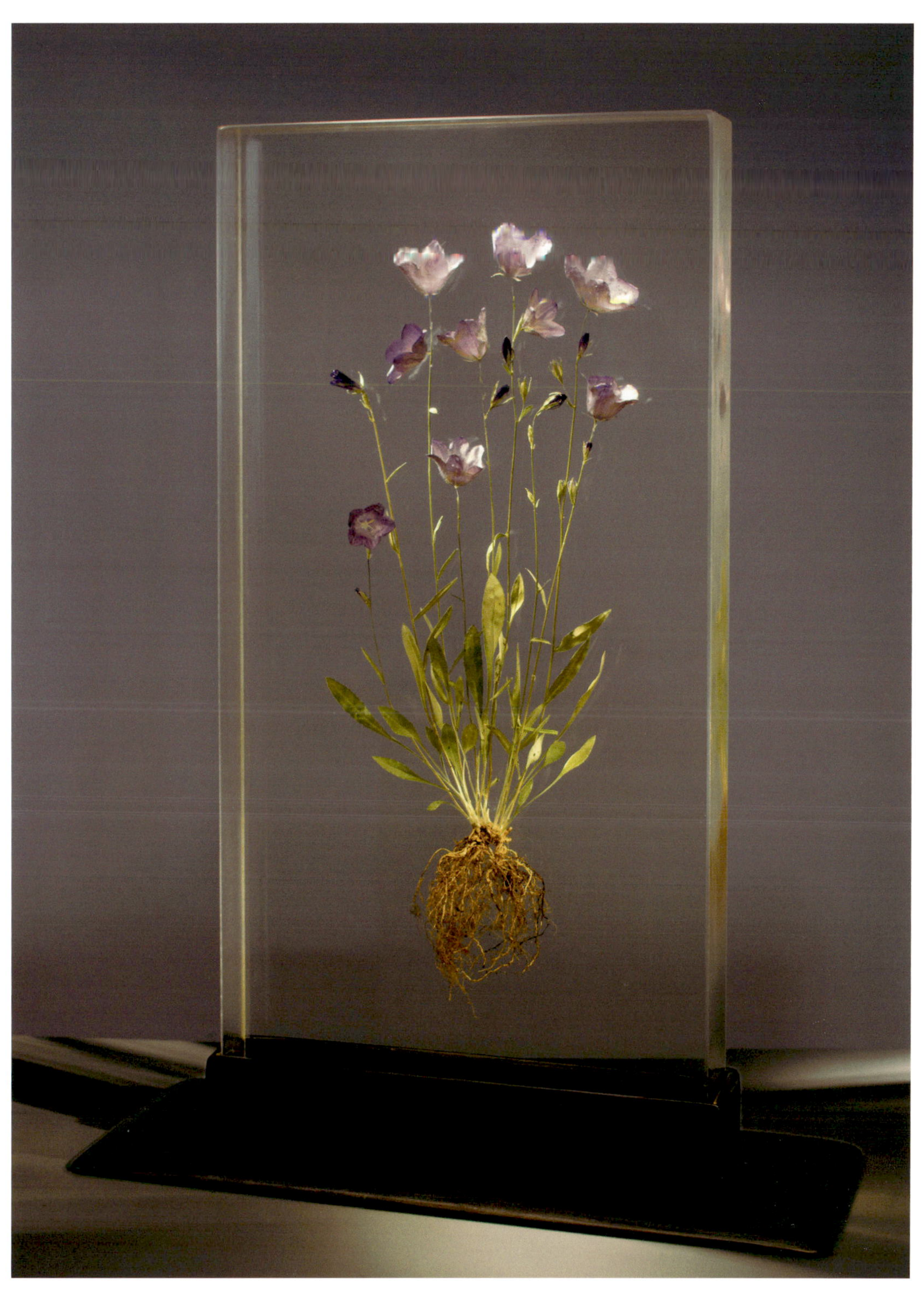

Tiger Lily, 2015
Flower, composite, glass, paint, and steel, 30½ × 19 × 8 inches

Campanula, 2015
Flower, composite, glass, and steel, 28½ × 21 × 8 inches

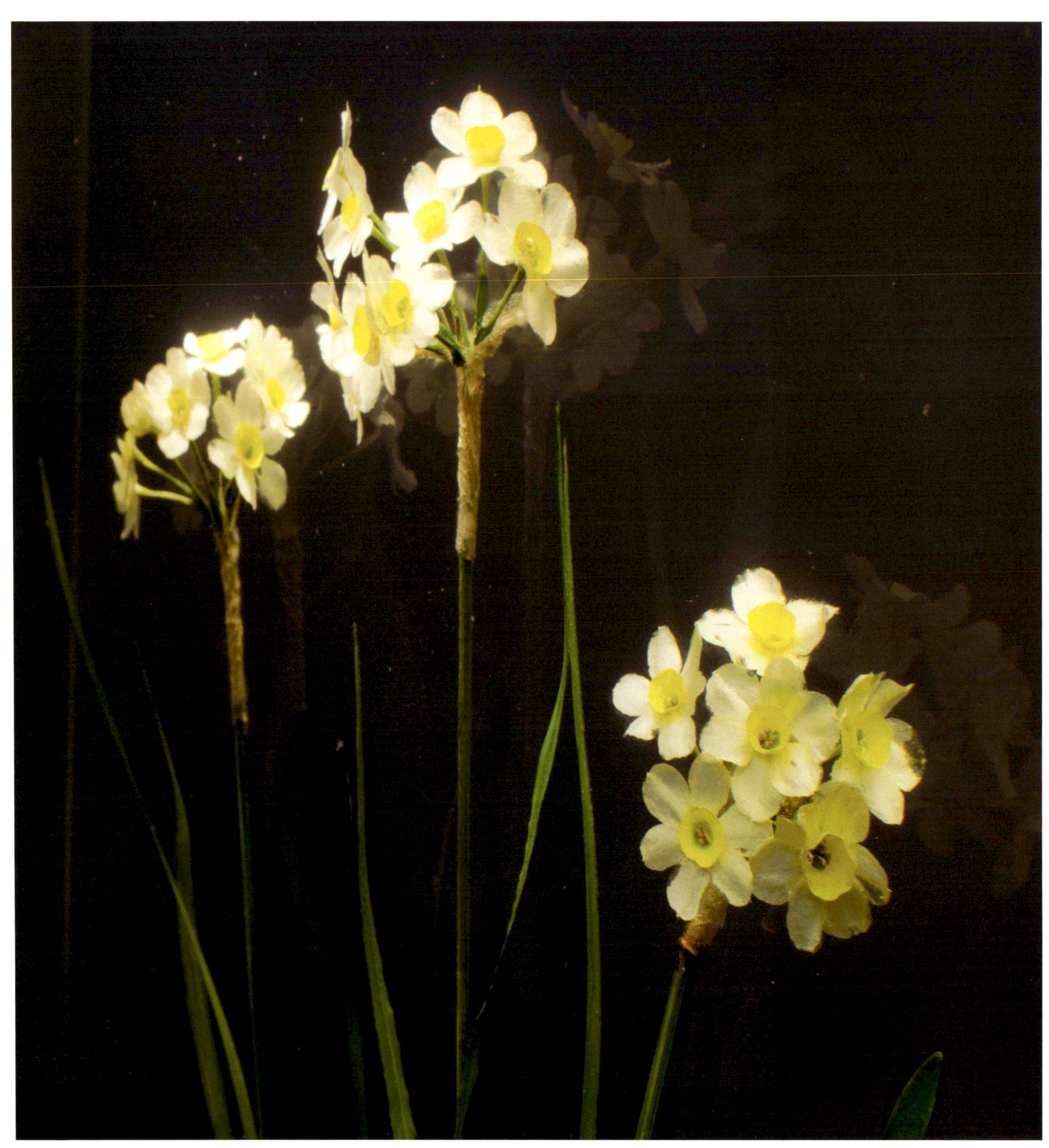

3 Bloom Tazetta, 2015
Flower, composite, glass, paint, and steel, 27¾ × 21 × 8 inches

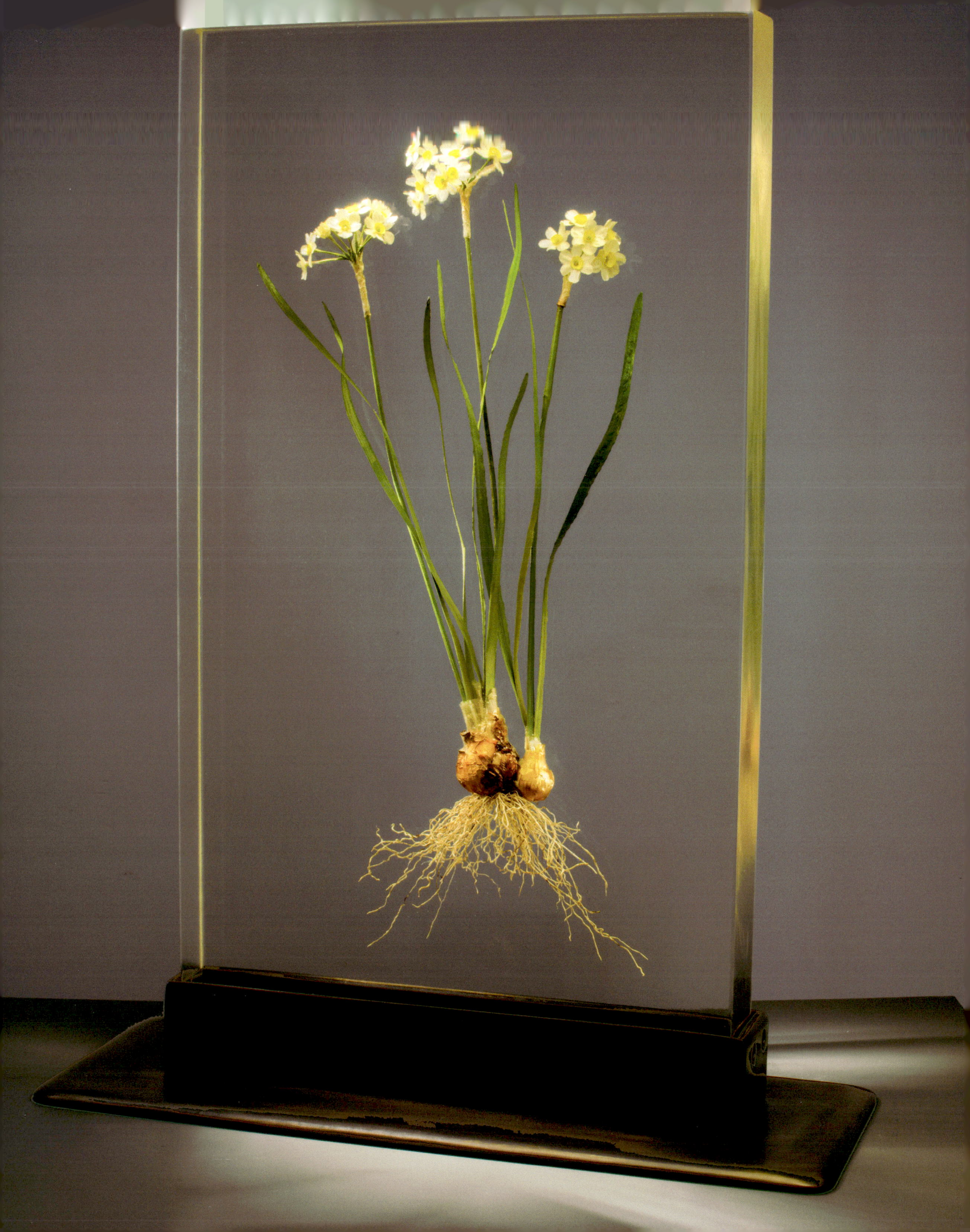

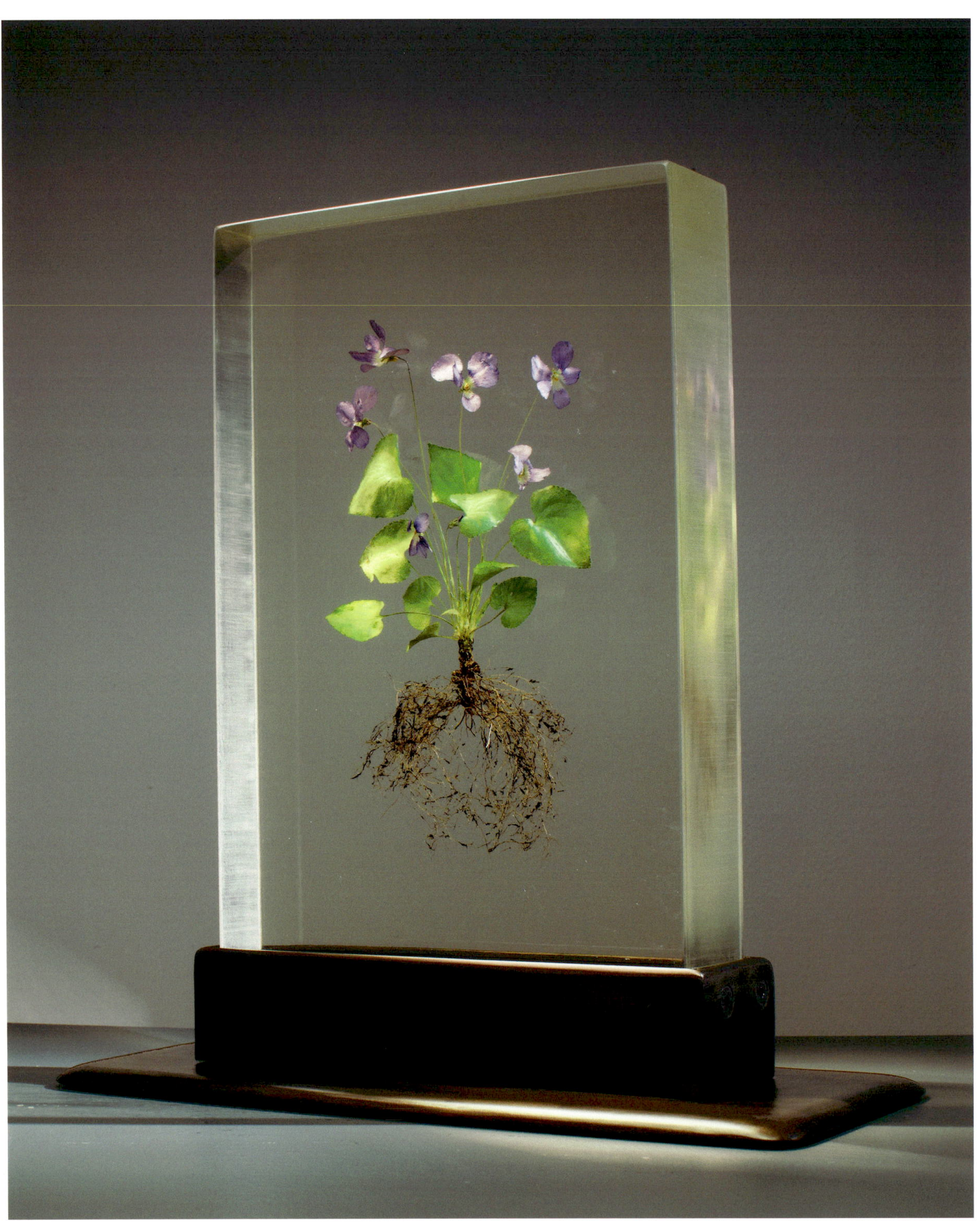

Blue Violet, 2015
Flower, composite, glass, and steel, 14¾ × 14 × 6 inches

Hoop-petticoat Daffodil, 2015
Flower, composite, glass, and steel, 18½ × 17 × 6 inches

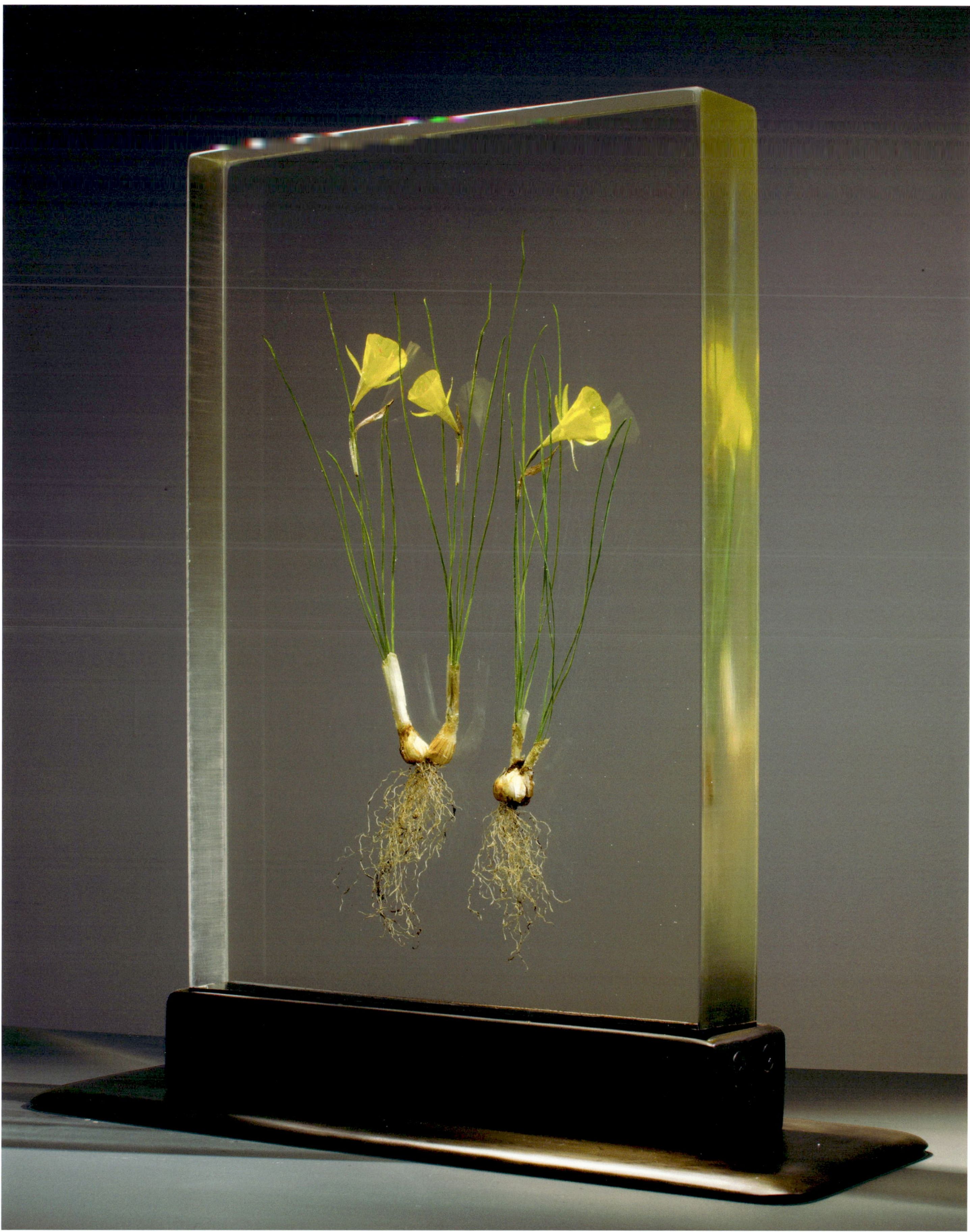

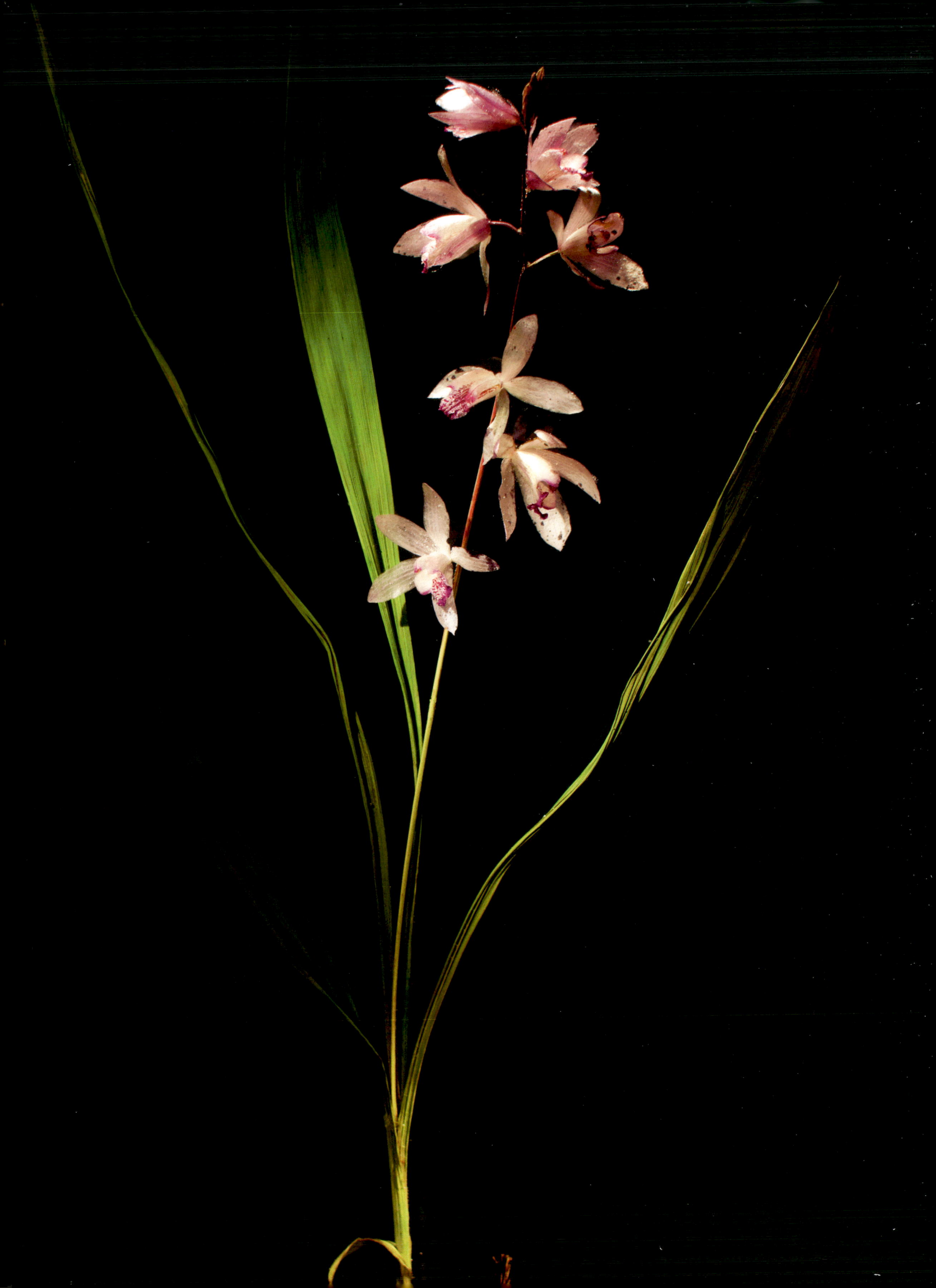

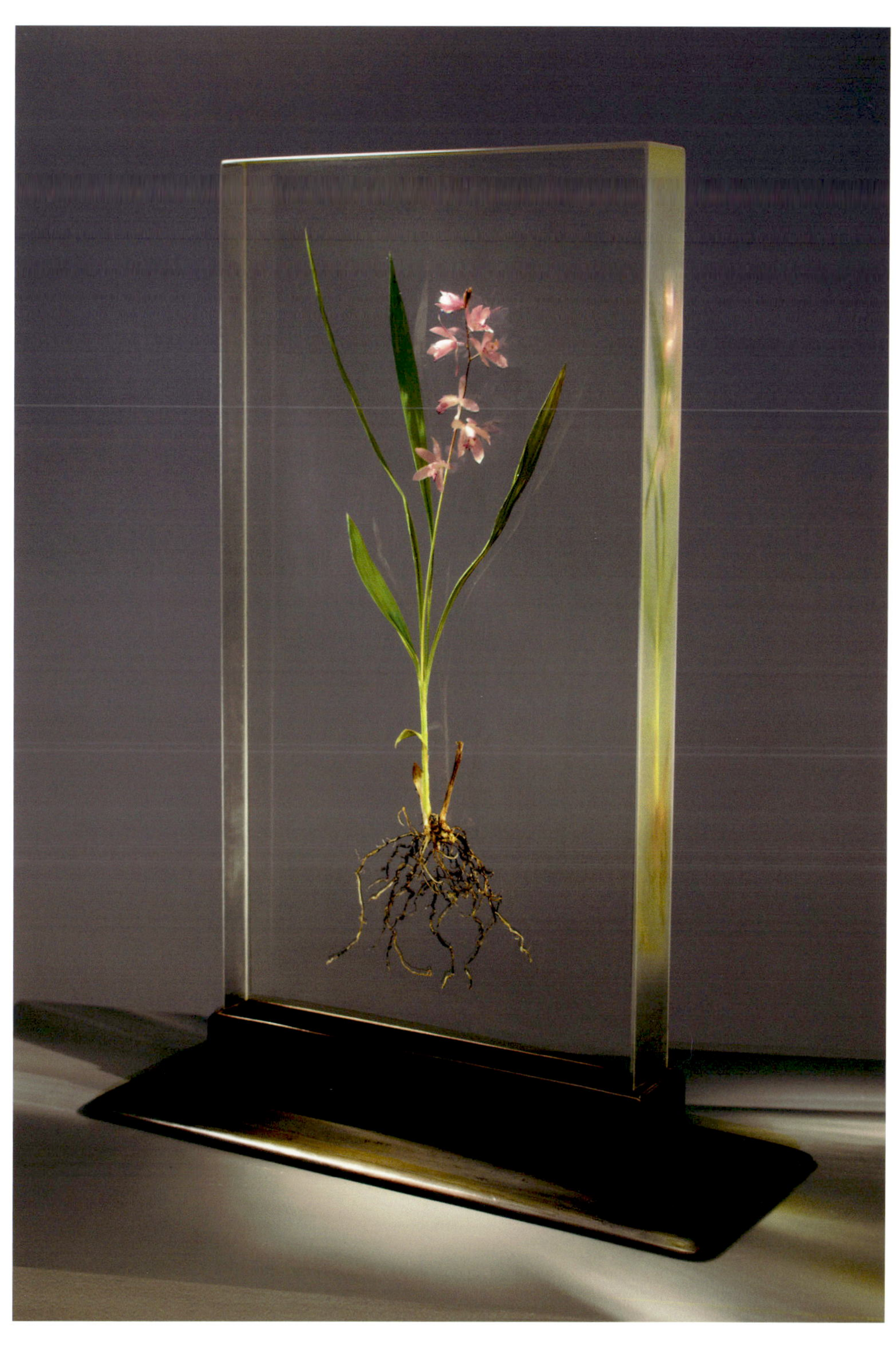

Hardy Orchid, 2015
Flower, composite, glass, paint, and steel, 27½ × 20 × 8 inches

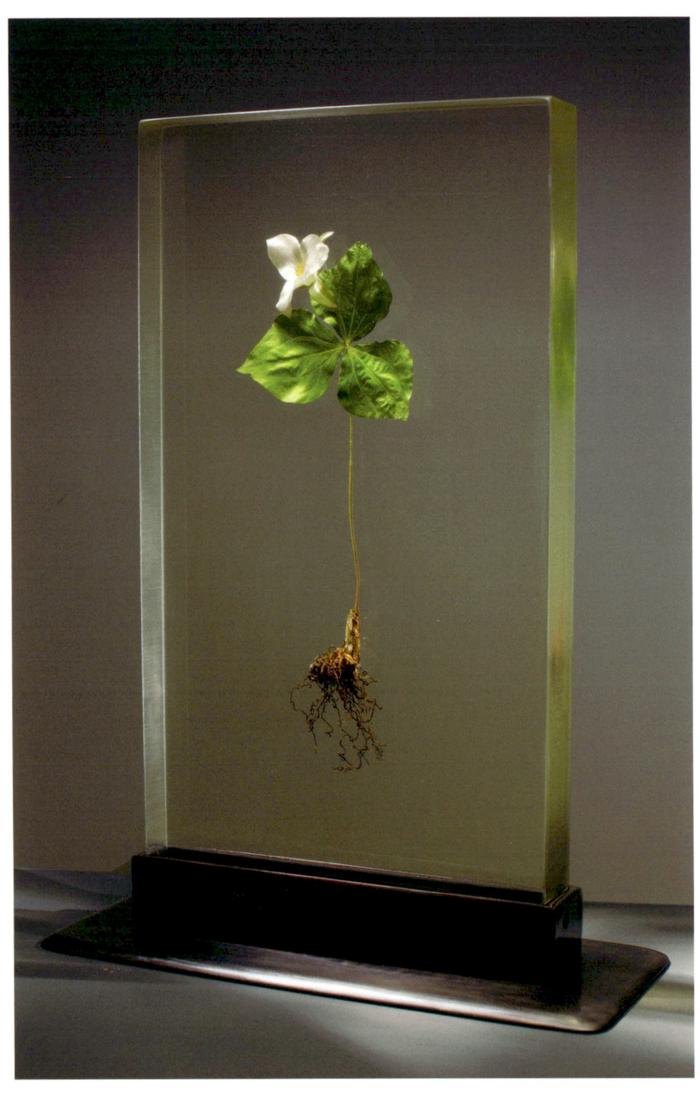

New Trillium, 2015
Flower, composite, glass, and steel, 26 × 19 × 8 inches

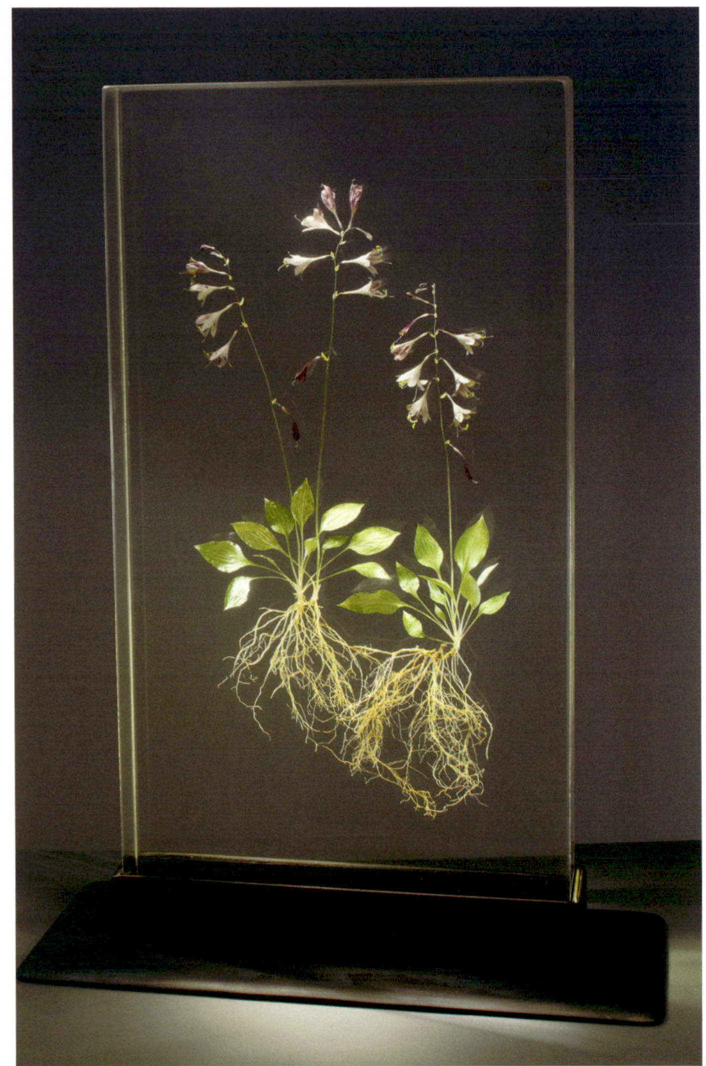

Miniature Hosta (and detail), 2015
Flower, composite, glass, and steel, 19¾ × 21 × 8 inches

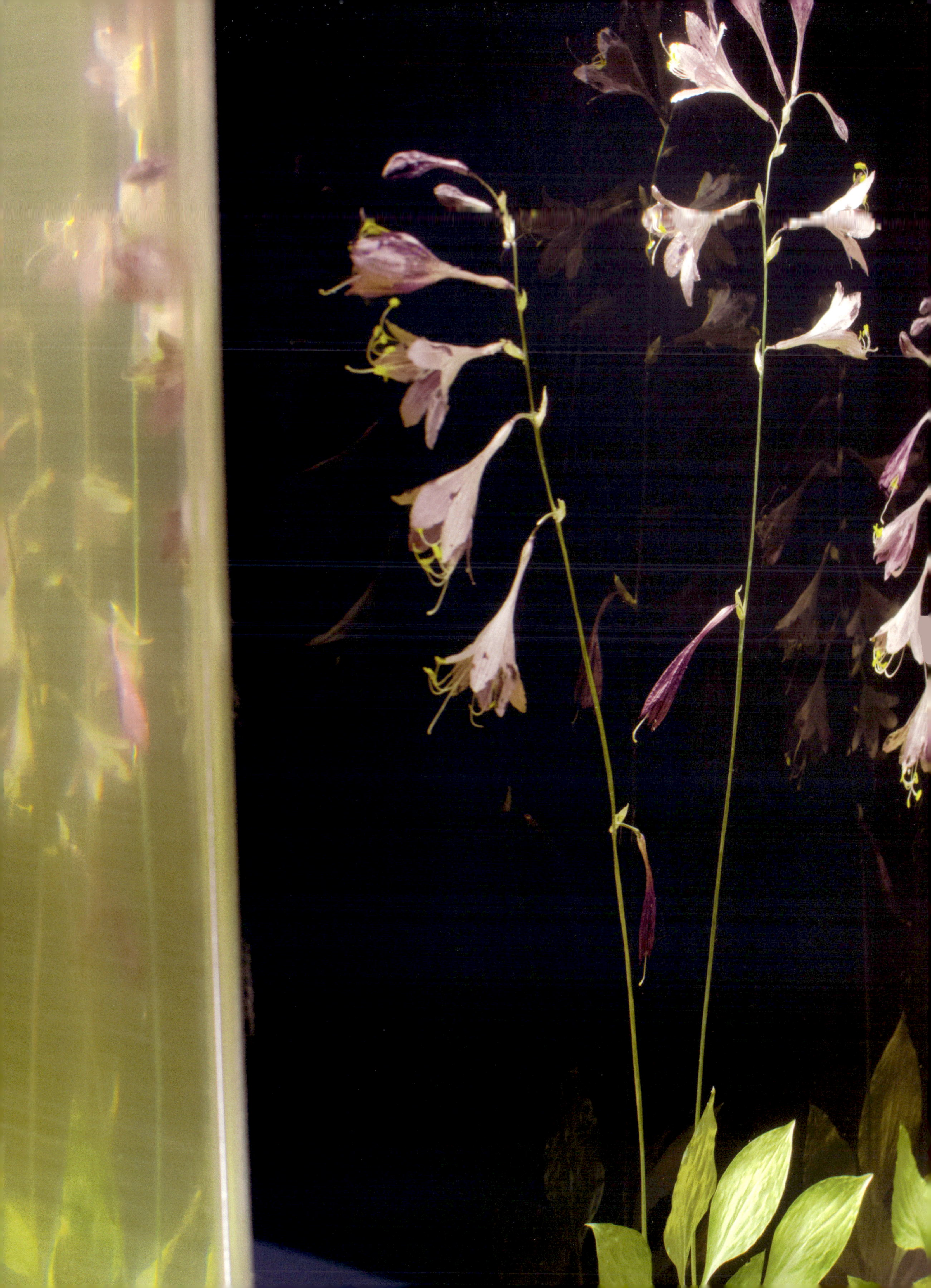

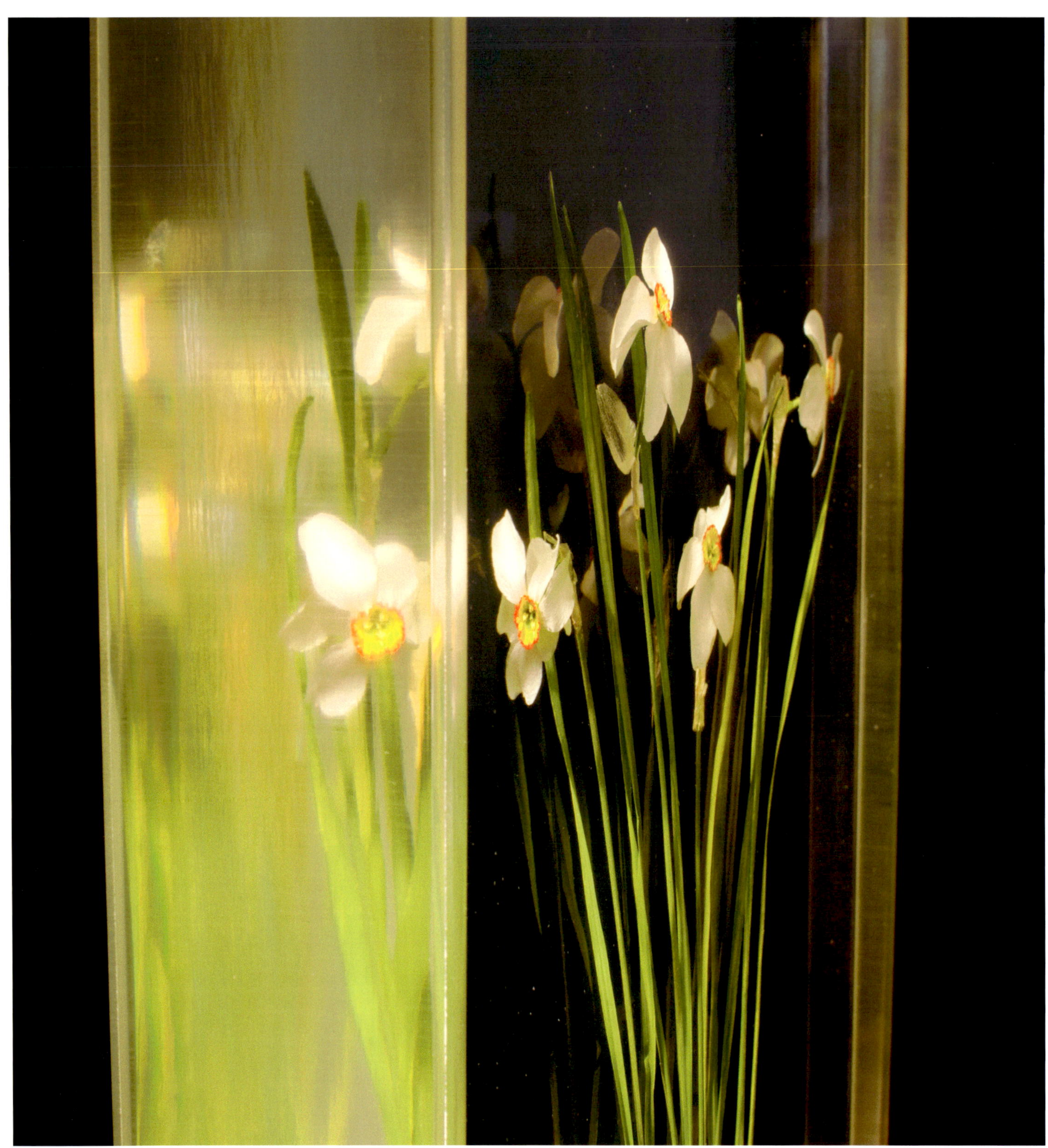

4 Bloom Poeticus Narcissus, 2015
Flower, composite, glass, paint, and steel, 25 × 20 × 8 inches

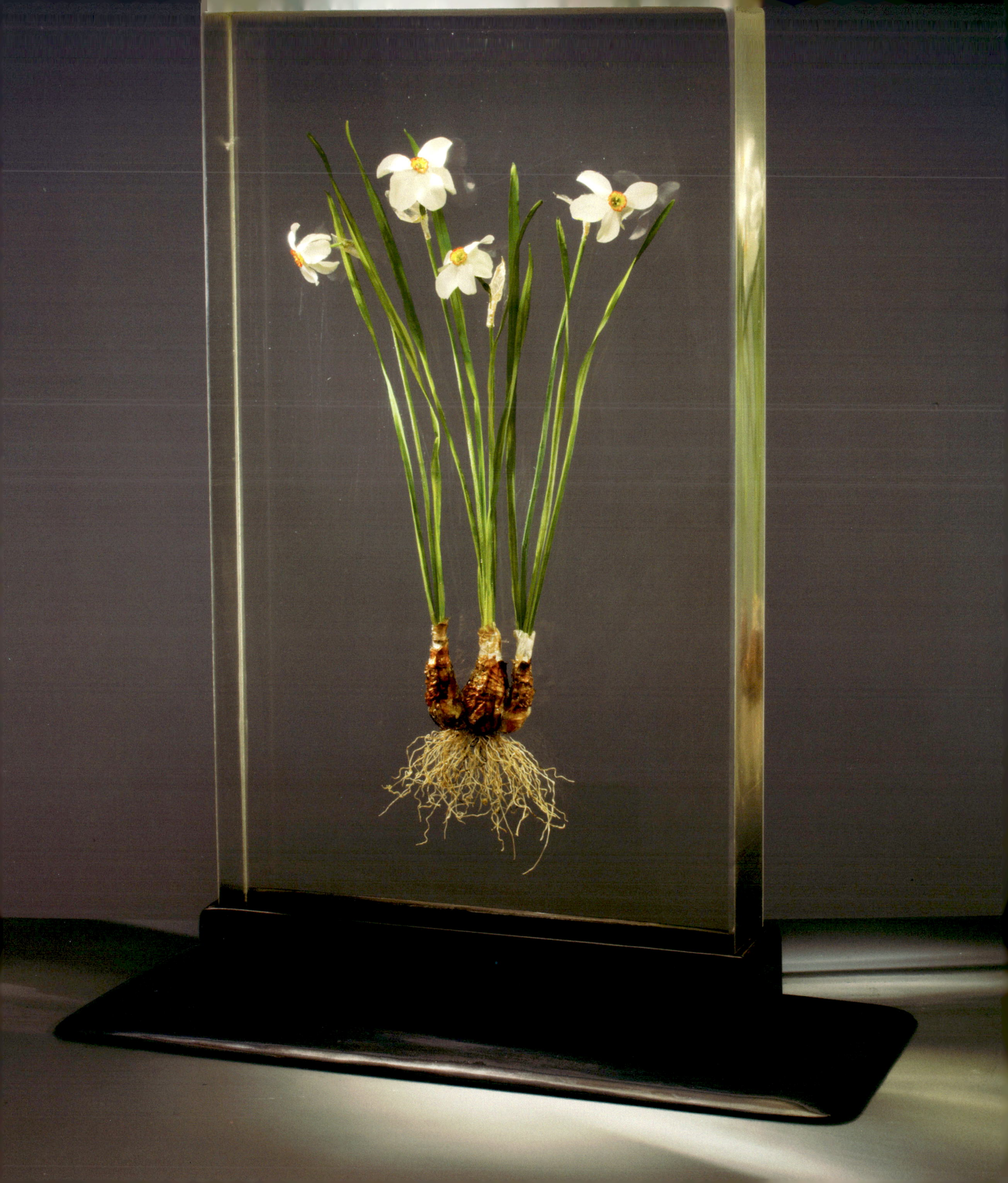

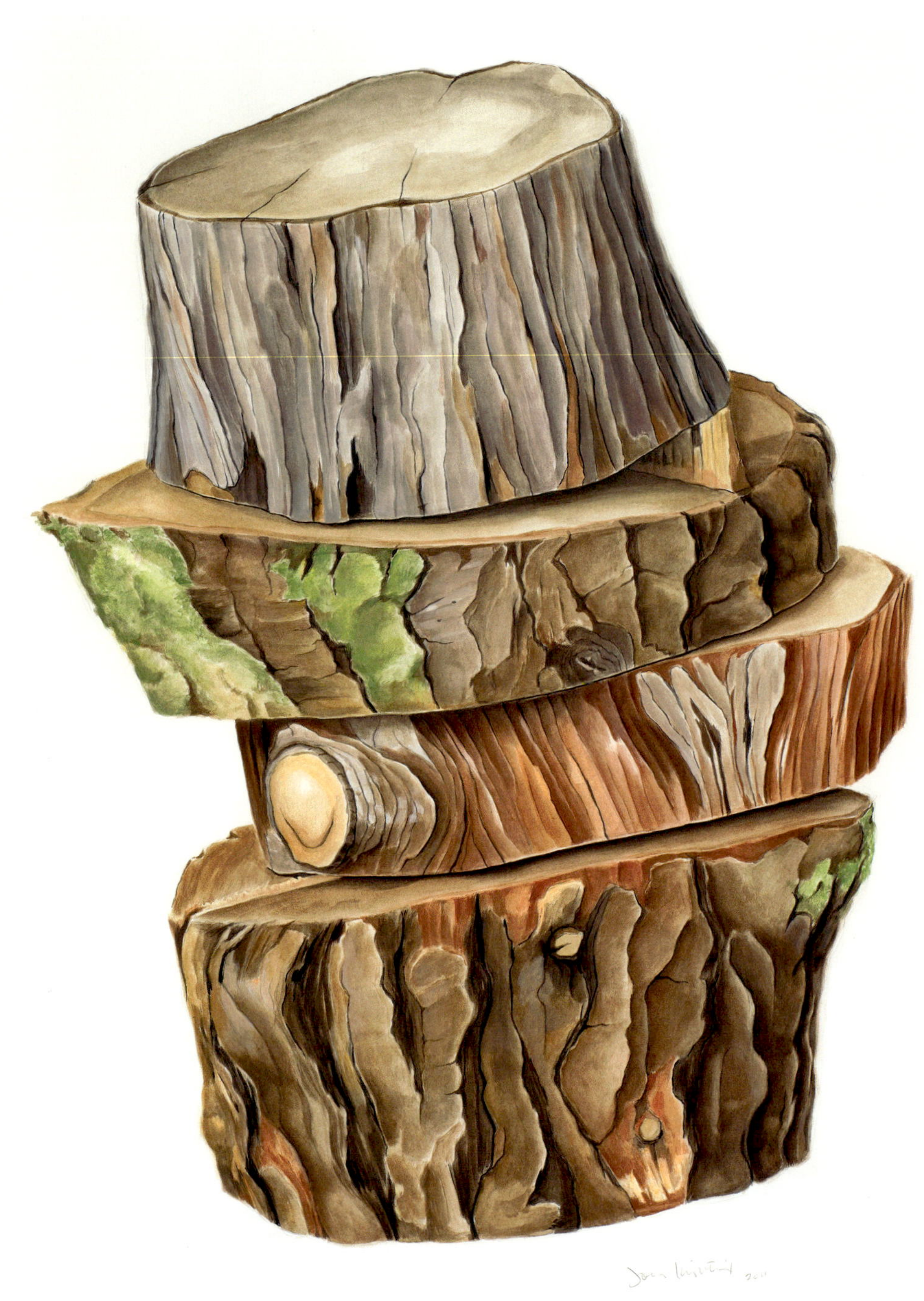

Joey Kirkpatrick, **Cordwood Stack**, 2011
Graphite and casein on paper, 45 × 35 inches

Joey Kirkpatrick, **Cordwood 5: Pine**, 2013
Graphite and casein on paper, 45 × 35 inches

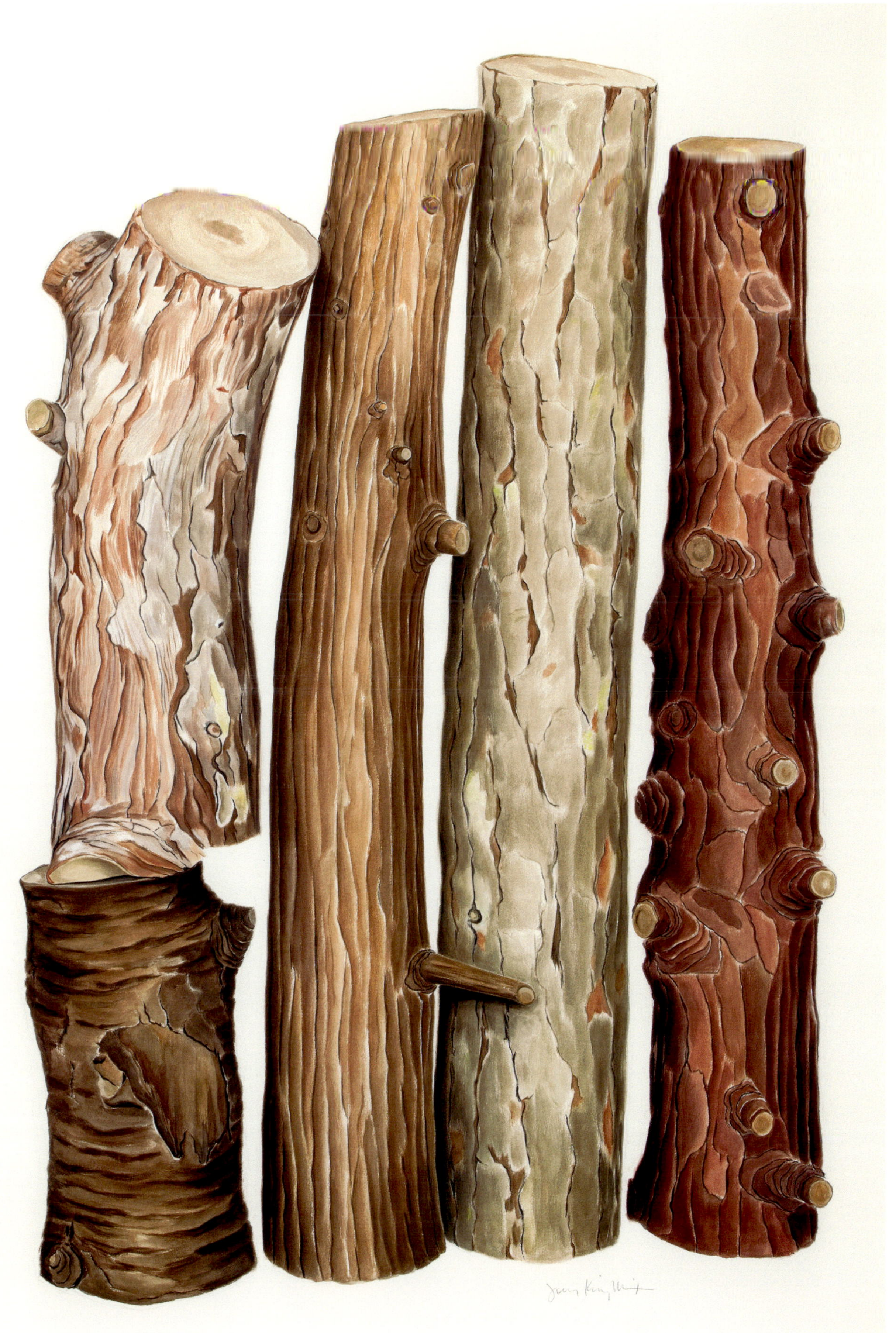

Joey Kirkpatrick, **Cordwood 5: Madrona**, 2013
Graphite and casein on paper, 53 × 40 inches

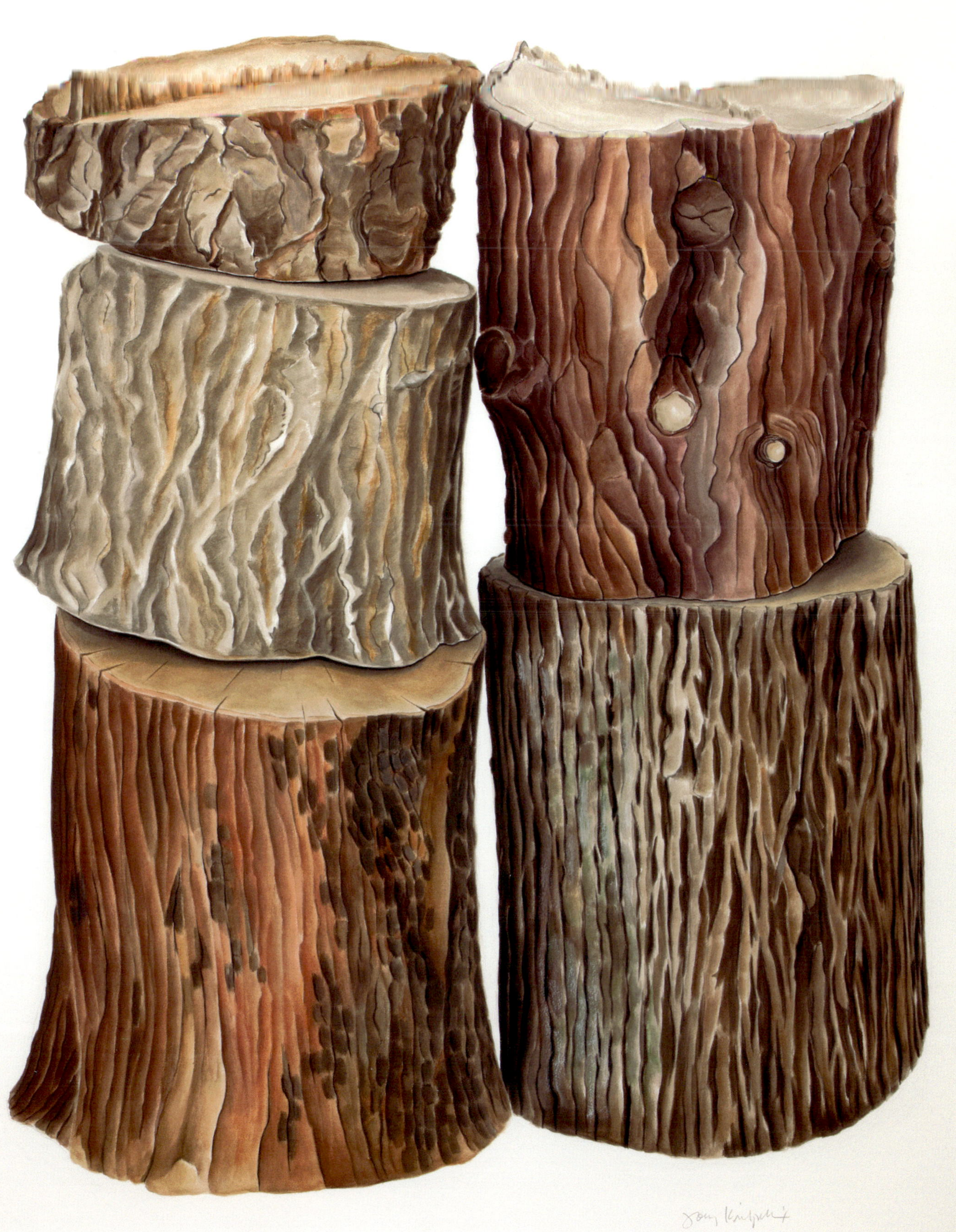

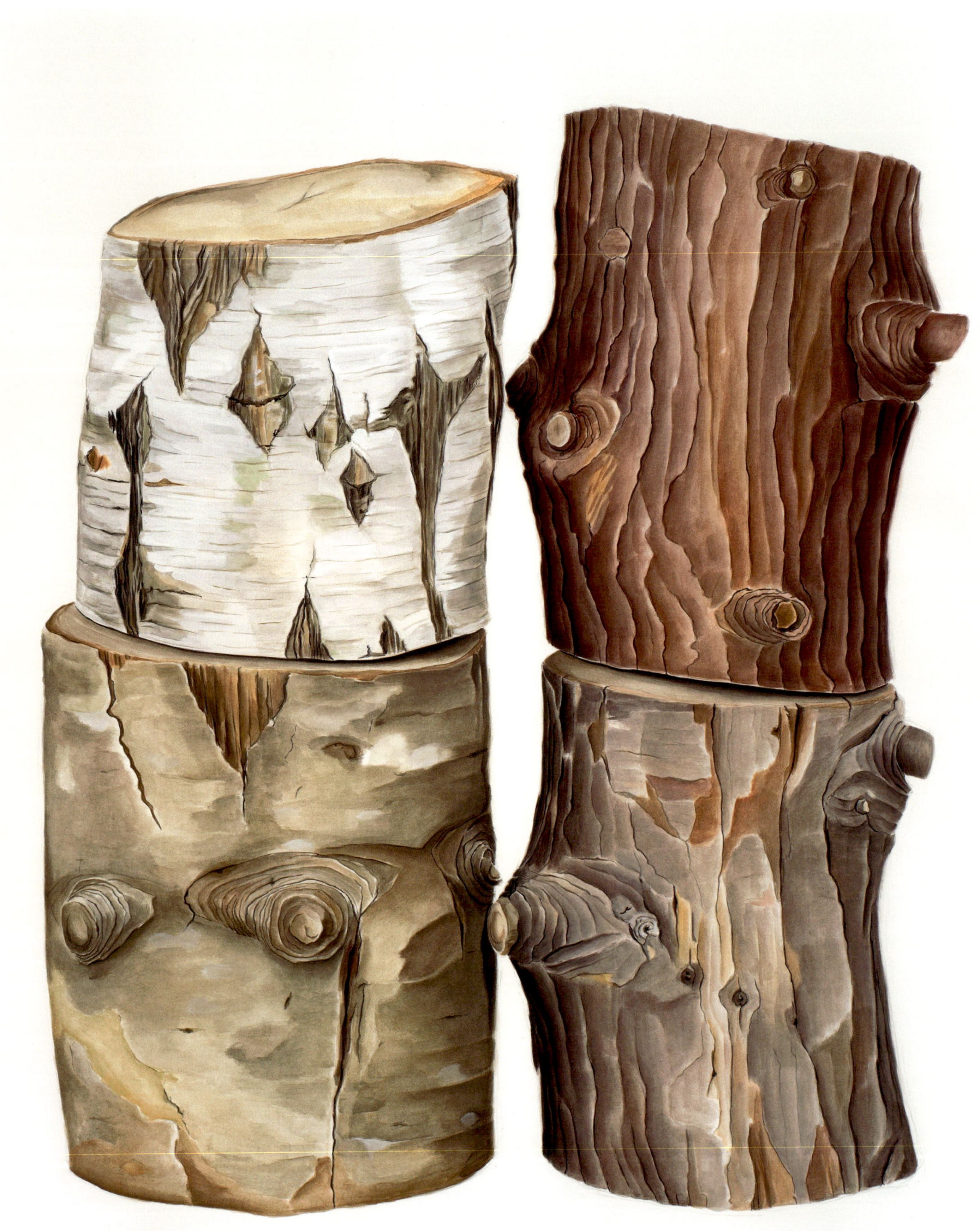

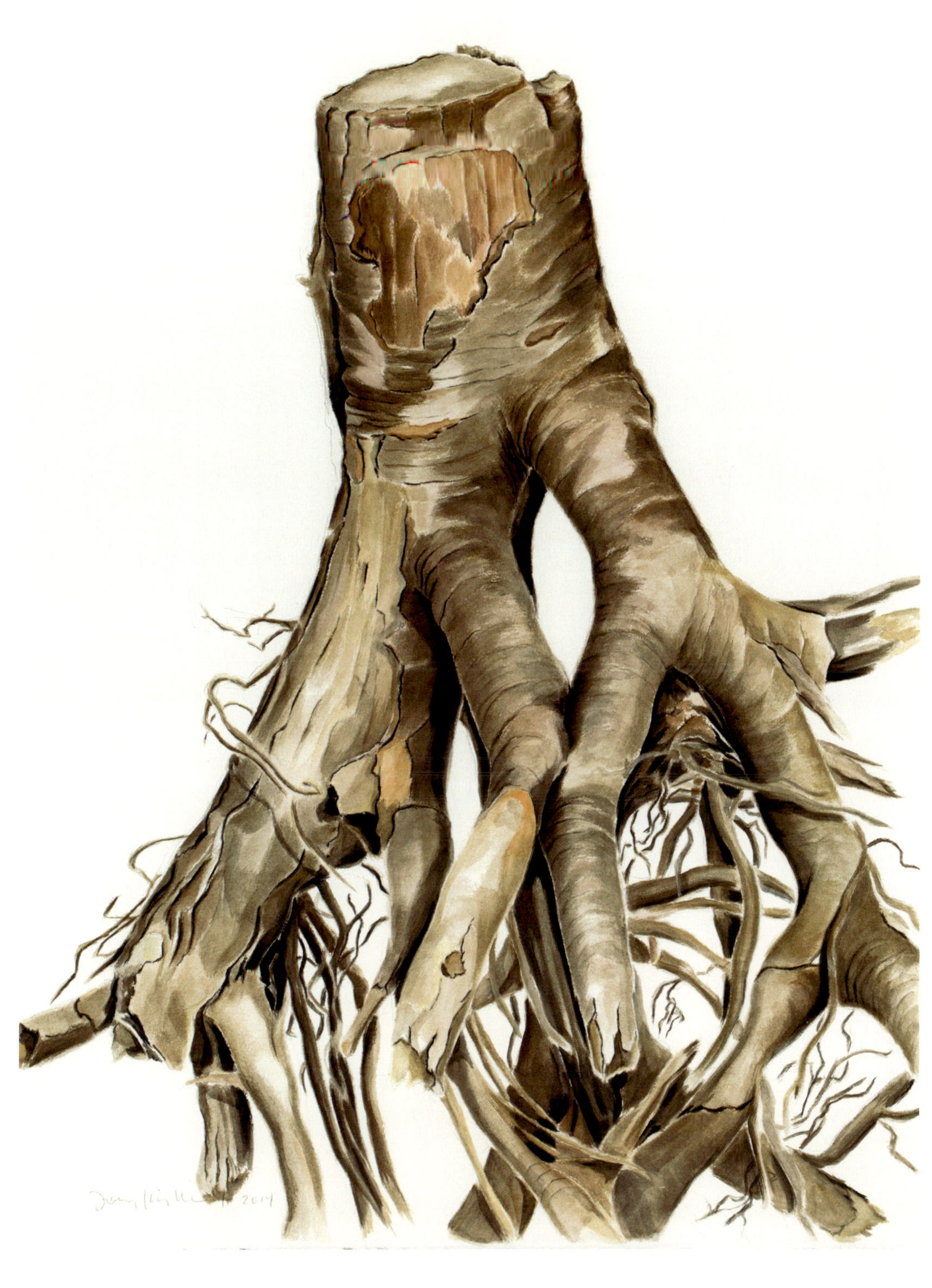

Joey Kirkpatrick, **Cordwood with Birch**, 2012
Graphite and casein on paper, 45 × 35 inches

Joey Kirkpatrick, **Root II**, 2014
Graphite and casein on paper, 40 × 28 inches

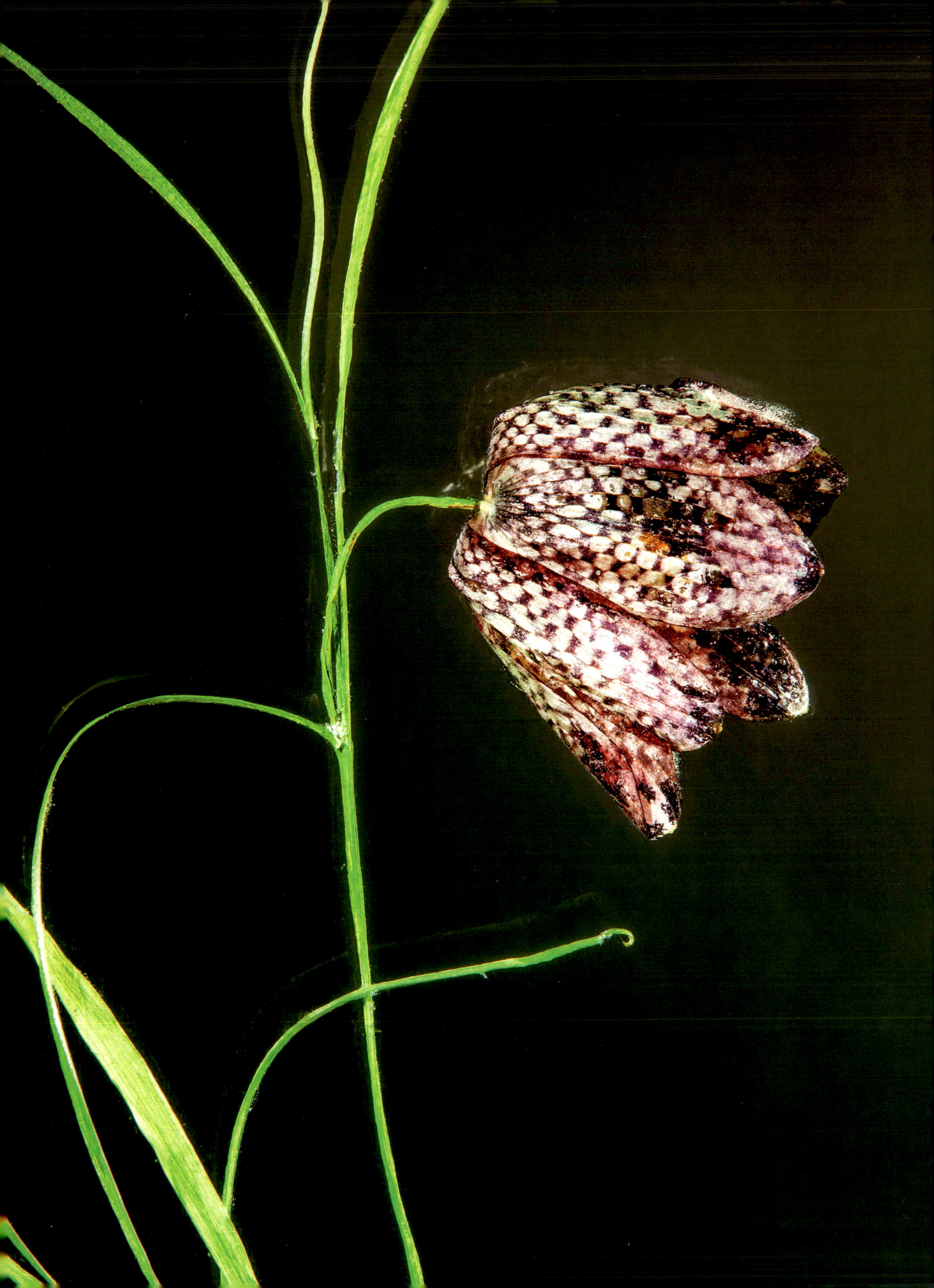

Daniel J. Hinkley

The Botanicals

I have long had a soft spot for the twinflower, *Linnaea borealis*. Named in honor of the father of modern taxonomy, Carolus Linnaeus, the species is circumboreal, a natural inhabitant of the woodlands of North America, Europe, Siberia, and northern Asia. Its prostrate, snaking stems carry evergreen leaves, shiny and tiny, and—as its common name would suggest—pairs of flowering stems, which rise from each leaf node to a height of four inches and are capped in early spring by nodding, pink bells. The flowers have always reminded me of gazelles, alert but shy. It was the very presence of this enchanting plant on a property my partner and I were considering for purchase that sealed the deal on what would become our first home and garden. In fortuitous serendipity, it was the same *Linnaea borealis* that brought me to fully understand the rigor, of both observation and execution, in the work of Joey Kirkpatrick and Flora C. Mace, while exposing my shallow comprehension of artistry in glass and pigment.

It was while being sweet-potatoed and pumpkin-pied at a Thanksgiving dinner of mutual friends that we met Kirkpatrick and Mace, calculating our petite degrees of separation, connecting our respective dots of people and places. Our common ground was a passion for the garden, of its subjects in particular—the individual components that assimilate themselves into a garden—and the marvels of birth, death, decay, and rebirth inherent to each. We lighted upon their current work, the *Botanicals*, and an invitation to visit their studio in Seattle was proffered and accepted.

At the studio, there it was, greeting me again, a length of stem of *Linnaea borealis* at its floral zenith, seized by Mace at its finest moment, floating weightless within a linear block of weighty composite and glass. "How perfectly gathered in a molten world," I doltishly thought to myself. Again, doltishly, "Simply beautiful."

Soon enough, as we accompanied the artists into the inner sanctum, the lightbulb turned on and the realization came to me of the significance of this body of work. It was at once and again Leopold and Rudolf Blaschka's glass models, capturing the improbable if not the impossible. And like a good garden made to last the ages, this work embodies passionate observation, deconstruction, resurrection, and then polish. These are not flowers frozen in time, a suggestion that would imply simple preservation. The subjects instead are

Fritillaria: Checkered Lily (detail), 2014
Flower, composite, glass, paint, and steel, 26 × 18 × 7 inches

Linnaea Borealis: Twinflower (detail), 2015
Flower, composite, glass, and steel, 13½ × 33 × 6 inches

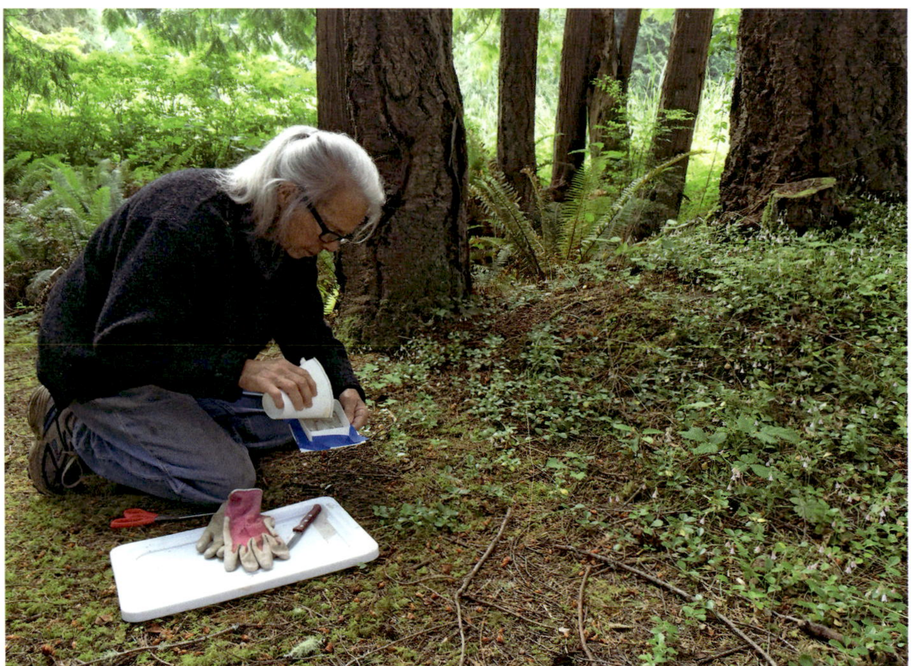

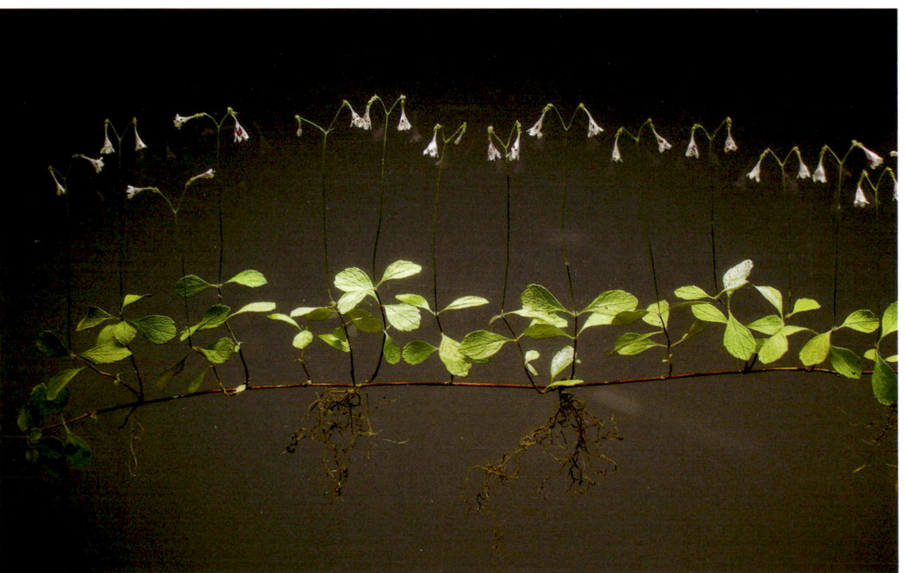

crafted by means of comprehending the mysteries embodied within each. The flowers are living still, and the clock simply slowed. Assuredly, the petals will still dehisce; the leaves abscise; the roots will extend or retract with the seasons.

Juxtaposed with Kirkpatrick's *Cordwood Paintings*, the *Botanicals* offer a continuum that is honest and apparent. The flowers simply slow the crescendo; the pieces of cut wood accelerate the demise and rebirth. Two gardeners cultivate different seasons to make one garden. Together, this work is as magical as any stand of *Linnaea borealis* in full blossom could possibly be.

Fritillaria: Checkered Lily, 2014
Flower, composite, glass, paint, and steel,
26 × 18 × 7 inches

Joey Kirkpatrick and Flora C. Mace

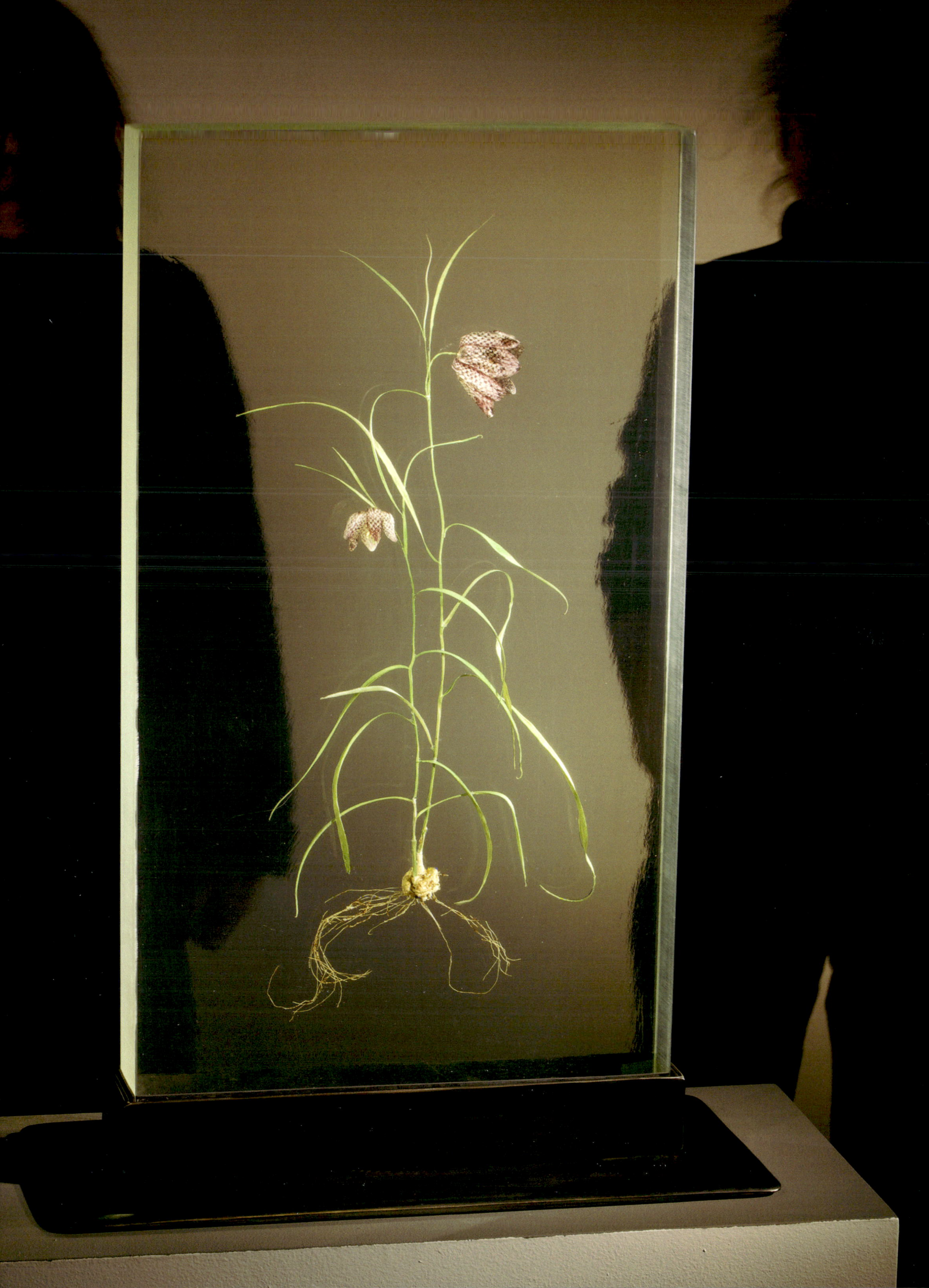

Biographies

Joey Kirkpatrick

1952	Born in Des Moines, Iowa

Education

1979	Pilchuck Glass School, Stanwood, Washington
1978-79	Graduate work in glass, Iowa State University, Ames
1975	BFA (drawing), University of Iowa, Iowa City

Flora C. Mace

1949	Born in Exeter, New Hampshire

Education

1976	MFA (sculpture/glass), University of Illinois, Champaign-Urbana
1975	Graduate work in glass, University of Utah, Salt Lake City
1973-74	Goodwill ambassador to Norway, International Farm Exchange Program
1972	BS (fine arts), Plymouth State College, Plymouth, New Hampshire

Kirkpatrick and Mace at Windcliff, Indianola, Washington.

Solo Exhibitions (collaborative work)

† An exhibition catalogue was produced but does not appear below.

2015	Museum of Glass, Tacoma
	Museum of Northwest Art, La Conner, Washington†
2013	Traver Gallery, Seattle†
2012	AMK Gallery, Toledo, Ohio
2011	Friesen Gallery, Ketchum, Idaho
2005	Museum of Art, Washington State University, Pullman
	Ronna and Eric Hoffman Gallery, Lewis and Clark College, Portland, Oregon†
2003	Hawk Galleries, Columbus, Ohio
2002	Habatat Galleries, Chicago
2000	Habatat Galleries, Boca Raton
1999	Ledbetter Lusk Gallery, Memphis
1998	Foster/White Gallery, Seattle
1997	Tempe Arts Center, Tempe
1995	Foster/White Gallery, Seattle
	Imago Galleries, Palm Desert
1994	Riley Hawk Gallery, Columbus, Ohio
1993	Brunnier Art Museum, Iowa State University, Ames
1992	Fay Gold Gallery, Atlanta
	Foster/White Gallery, Seattle
	Riley Hawk Gallery, Cleveland
1991	New Art Gallery, Paris
	Valley Museum of Northwest Art, La Conner, Washington
1988	Kurland/Summers Gallery, Los Angeles
1986	Habatat Galleries, Lathrup Village, Michigan
	Heller Gallery, New York
1985	Foster/White Gallery, Seattle
1984	Habatat Galleries, Lathrup Village, Michigan
1983	Foster/White Gallery, Seattle
	Kurland/Summers Gallery, Los Angeles
1982	Heller Gallery, New York
1981	David Bernstein Gallery, Boston
	Galerie der Kunsthandwerker, Hamburg

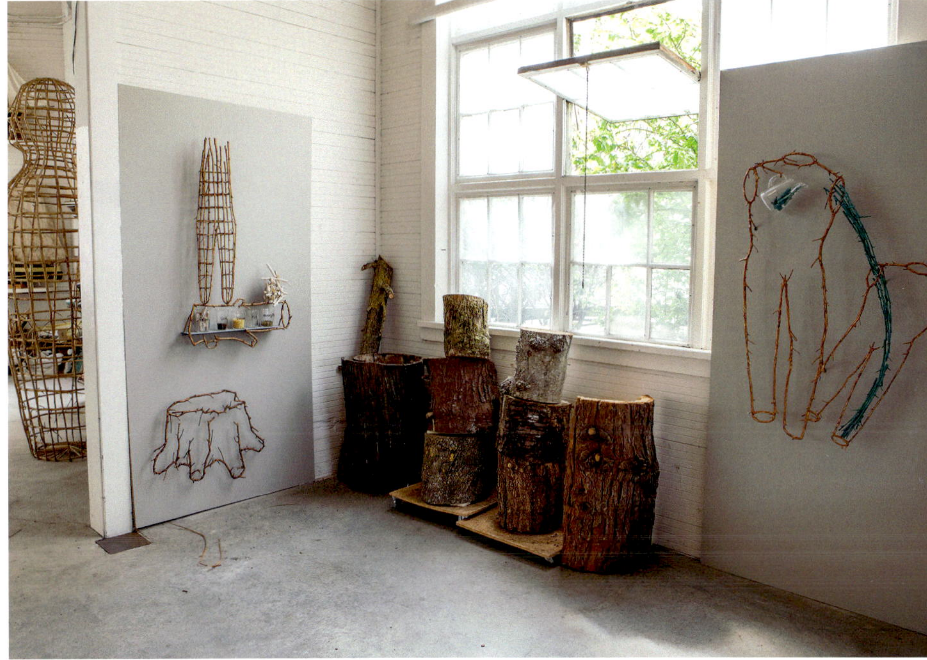

Selected Group Exhibitions (collaborative work)

* The exhibition catalogue appears in the Selected Bibliography below.

† An exhibition catalogue was produced but does not appear below.

2014   *State of the Art: Discovering American Art Now*, Crystal Bridges Museum of American Art, Bentonville, Arkansas*

2012   *Contemporary Glass Sculpture: Celebrating the 50th Anniversary of Studio Glass*, Orlando Museum of Art, Orlando†

Pilchuck: Ideas, Museum of Northwest Art, La Conner, Washington

2010   *The Secret Language of Animals*, Tacoma Art Museum, Tacoma

Women in Glass: Innovators and Visionaries, Traver Gallery, Seattle

2009   *2009 Neddy Artist Fellowship*, Tacoma Art Museum, Tacoma

Voices of Contemporary Glass: The Heineman Collection, Corning Museum of Glass, Corning, New York

2007   *Behind Glass: Creativity and Collaboration*, Arts Center, St. Petersburg, Florida

Craft in America: Expanding Traditions, Arkansas Art Center, Little Rock (traveling into 2009)†

Green Matters, Elliott Brown Gallery at SOFA Chicago, Chicago

Shattering Glass: New Perspectives, Katonah Museum of Art, Katonah, New York*

Shy Boy, She Devil, and Isis: The Art of Conceptual Craft: Selections from the Wornick Collection, Museum of Fine Arts, Boston*

2006   *Contrasts: A Glass Primer*, Museum of Glass, Tacoma*

Glass: Material Matters, Los Angeles County Museum of Art, Los Angeles*

One of a Kind: The Studio Craft Movement, Metropolitan Museum of Art, New York

A Transparent Legacy: Studio Glass Gifted to the Seattle Art Museum from the Collection of Jon and Mary Shirley, Seattle Art Museum, Seattle

Two Media/Two Expressions: An Exhibition of Contemporary Clay and Glass, Springfield Museum of Art, Springfield, Ohio

2005   *Taking Shape: Pilchuck Glass School in the '70s*, Bellevue Arts Museum, Bellevue, Washington

2004   *Transformed by Fire: Sculpture in Glass from the Collection of Becky and Jack Benaroya*, Seattle Art Museum, Seattle

2003   *Fire and Form: The Art of Contemporary Glass*, Norton Museum of Art, West Palm Beach*

2002   *Contemporary Directions: Glass from the Maxine and William Block Collection*, Carnegie Museum of Art, Pittsburgh (on view at Toledo Museum of Art, Toledo, Ohio, in 2003–4)*

Some Assembly Required, Museum of Glass, International Center for Contemporary Art, Tacoma*

2001   *Lino e Amici*, Fuller Museum of Art, Brockton, Massachusetts†

Primary Colors, Elliott Brown Gallery, Seattle

2000   *Glass: A Celebration*, Nancy Hoffman Gallery, New York

1999   *The Art of Craft: Contemporary Works from the Saxe Collection*, de Young Memorial Museum, Fine Arts Museums of San Francisco, San Francisco*

A Passion for Glass: The Aviva and Jack A. Robinson Studio Glass Collection, Detroit Institute of Arts, Detroit*

Progressions in Glass, Contemporary Art Center of Virginia, Virginia Beach

1998   *A Feast for the Eye: Food in Art*, de Young Memorial Museum, Fine Arts Museums of San Francisco, San Francisco

1997   *Earth and Air*, San Francisco Craft and Folk Art Museum, San Francisco

Glass Today: American Studio Glass from Cleveland Collections, Cleveland Museum of Art, Cleveland*

Glass Today by American Studio Artists, Museum of Fine Arts, Boston†

Heir Apparent: Translating the Secrets of Venetian Glass, Bellevue Art Museum, Bellevue, Washington*

Recent Glass Sculpture: A Union of Ideas, Milwaukee Art Museum, Milwaukee*

1996   Annual Pilchuck Exhibition: *A Tribute to Lino*, Traver Gallery, Seattle

International New Glass: Venezia aperto vetro, Museo Correr, Venice*

Invitational, Margo Jacobsen Gallery, Portland, Oregon

Studio Glass Masters, Grand Central Gallery, Tampa

1995   *Garden of Delight*, Tacoma Art Museum, Tacoma

Group Show, Anne Reed Gallery, Ketchum, Idaho

Northwest Glass: Part I, Museum of Northwest Art, La Conner, Washington

1994   *Glass Masters*, Helander Gallery, Palm Beach

World Glass Now '94, Hokkaido Museum of Modern Art, Sapporo, Japan†

1993   *Contemporary Crafts and the Saxe Collection*, Toledo Museum of Art, Toledo, Ohio (traveling into 1995)*

Formed by Fire, Carnegie Museum of Art, Pittsburgh

1992   *Artists from Pilchuck Glass School*, Sea-Tac International Airport, Seattle

Clearly Art: Pilchuck's Glass Legacy, Whatcom Museum of History and Art, Bellingham (traveling through 1995)*

Design Visions: International Directions in Glass, American Jewellery and Metalwork, Art Gallery of Western Australia, Perth*

Glass from Ancient Craft to Contemporary Art: 1962 to 1992 and Beyond, Morris Museum of Arts and Sciences, Morristown, New Jersey†

1991   *Artists at Work: Twenty-five Glassmakers, Ceramists, and Jewelers*, Cheney Cowles Museum, Spokane, and Boise Art Museum, Boise*

Frozen Moments: Glass Artists of the Northwest, Bellevue Art Museum, Bellevue, Washington

Get Real, North Miami Center of Contemporary Art, Miami†

Studio Glass: Selections from the David Jacob Chodorkoff Collection, Detroit Institute of Arts, Detroit†

World Glass Now '91, Hokkaido Museum of Modern Art, Sapporo, Japan*

1990   *Masterpieces of American Glass: The Corning Museum of Glass, the Toledo Museum of Art, Lillian Nassau Ltd.,* Steuben Glass, New York (traveling into 1991)*

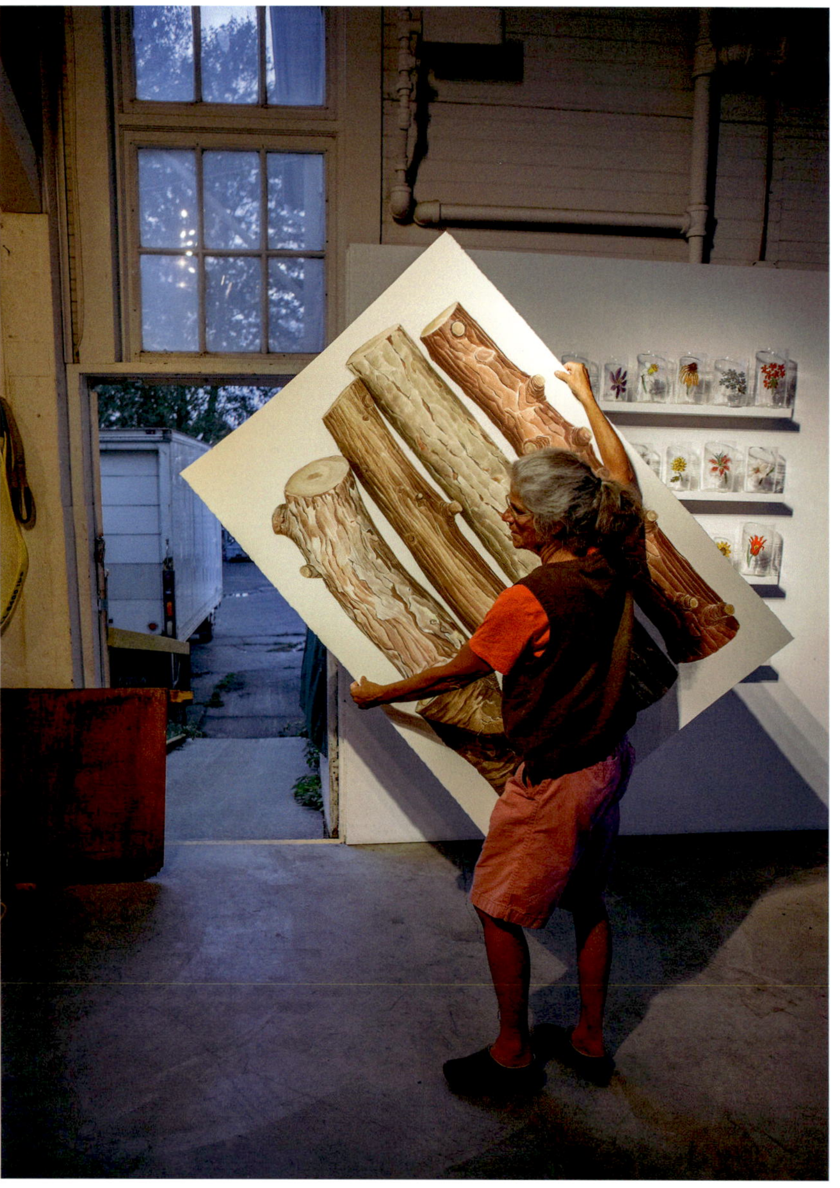

Kirkpatrick with *Cordwood 5: Pine,* 2014.

1989   *Figures of Translucence*, Documents Northwest: The PONCHO Series, Seattle Art Museum, Seattle†

Group Show, Dorothy Weiss Gallery, San Francisco

Northwest Annual, Center on Contemporary Art, Seattle

1988   Group Show, Betsy Rosenfield Gallery, Chicago

25 Years As an Art Museum, Museum Darmstadt, Darmstadt, Germany

1987   *Chicago International New Art Forms Exposition*, Chicago†

Contrasts and Reactions, Brunnier Gallery and Museum, Iowa State University, Ames

For/Four Women, Great American Gallery, Atlanta

Group Show, Betsy Rosenfield Gallery, Chicago

3+3×7: Sculpture in Glass and Works on Paper, University Art Museum, Arizona State University, Tempe*

1986   *Contemporary American and European Glass from the Saxe Collection*, Oakland Museum, Oakland, and American Craft Museum, New York (New York installation closed in 1987)†

Craft Today: Poetry of the Physical, American Craft Museum, New York (traveling through 1991)*

1985   National Glass Invitational, Owens-Illinois World Headquarters, Toledo, Ohio

Selection '85: A Benefit for the American Craft Museum, American Craft Museum, New York

World Glass Now '85, Hokkaido Museum of Modern Art, Sapporo, Japan†

1984-91   *Glass America*, Heller Gallery, New York

1983   *Contemporary American Glass Sculpture*, United States Embassy, Art in Embassies Program, Prague†

Group Show, Betsy Rosenfield Gallery, Chicago

Vicointer '83 (Vidrio contemporáneo internacional '83), Valencia, Spain

1982   *American Glass Art: Evolution and Revolution*, Morris Museum of Arts and Sciences, Morristown, New Jersey†

1981-90   Annual National Glass Invitational, Habatat Gallery, Lathrup Village, Michigan

1981   *Glaskunst '81*, Kassel, Germany†

1980-90   Annual Pilchuck Exhibition, Traver Gallery, Seattle

Selected Bibliography (in reverse chronological order)

Josslin, Victoria. "Rooted in Questions." *Glass*, no. 134 (spring 2014): pp. 42–49.

Oldknow, Tina. *Collecting Contemporary Glass: Art and Design after 1990 from the Corning Museum of Glass*. Corning, N.Y.: Corning Museum of Glass, 2014, pp. 130–131, 262.

State of the Art: Discovering American Art Now. Bentonville, Ark.: Crystal Bridges Museum of American Art, 2014.

Robinson, Joyce Henry, ed. *A Gift from the Heart: American Art from the Collection of James and Barbara Palmer*. University Park: Palmer Museum of Art, Pennsylvania State University, 2013, p. 210.

Rossi-Wilcox, Susan. *Masters: Blown Glass: Major Works by Leading Artists*. Ed. Ray Hemachandra. New York: Lark Books/Sterling Publishing, 2010, pp. 248–55.

Oldknow, Tina. *Voices of Contemporary Glass: The Heineman Collection*. Corning, N.Y.: Corning Museum of Glass in association with Hudson Hills Press, New York, 2009.

Halper, Vicki. *Contrasts: A Glass Primer*. Tacoma: Museum of Glass in association with University of Washington Press, Seattle, 2007, pp. 32–33.

Oldknow, Tina. *Shattering Glass: New Perspectives*, Katonah, N.Y.: Katonah Museum of Art, 2007, pp. 7, 34–35.

Ward, Gerald W. R., and Julie M. Muñiz. *Shy Boy, She Devil, and Isis: The Art of Conceptual Craft: Selections from the Wornick Collection*. Boston: MFA Publications, 2007, p. 48.

Fox, Howard N. *Glass: Material Matters*. Los Angeles: Los Angeles County Museum of Art, 2006, p. 56.

Dual Vision: The Simona and Jerome Chazen Collection. New York: Museum of Arts and Design, 2005, pp. 21, 94, 186.

Lynn, Martha Drexler. *Sculpture, Glass, and American Museums*. Philadelphia: University of Pennsylvania Press, 2005, pp. 52–53, 203, 210.

Lynn, Martha Drexler. *American Studio Glass, 1960–1990: An Interpretive Study*. New York: Hudson Hills Press, 2004, p. 81.

Warmus, William. *Fire and Form: The Art of Contemporary Glass*. West Palm Beach: Norton Museum of Art, 2003, pp. 72, 80–81.

Yelle, Richard Wilfred. *International Glass Art*. Atglen, Pa.: Schiffer Publishing, 2003, pp. 20, 22, 24–25, 386.

Nichols, Sarah C., and Davira S. Taragin. *Contemporary Directions: Glass from the Maxine and William Block Collection*. Pittsburgh: Carnegie Museum of Art, 2002, p. 33.

Watson, Neil. *Some Assembly Required*. Tacoma: Museum of Glass, International Center for Contemporary Art, 2002, pp. 10–11, 16–17.

Klein, Dan. *Artists in Glass: Late Twentieth Century Masters in Glass*. London: Mitchell Beazley, 2001, pp. 104–7.

Yelle, Richard Wilfred. *Glass Art from UrbanGlass*. Atglen, Pa.: Schiffer Publishing, 2000, pp. 120–21.

Micucci, Dana. "Top 100 Treasures." *Art and Antiques* 22, no. 3 (March 1999): p. 78.

Burgard, Timothy Anglin. *The Art of Craft: Contemporary Works from the Saxe Collection*. San Francisco: Fine Arts Museums of San Francisco; Boston: Bulfinch Press, 1999, pp. 114–15.

Chambers, Karen S. "A Partnership Bears Fruit." *American Style* 4, no. 4 (summer 1998): pp. 62–69.

Fike, Bonita. *A Passion for Glass: The Aviva and Jack A. Robinson Studio Glass Collection*. Detroit: Detroit Institute of Arts, 1998, p. 50.

Risatti, Howard, and Kenneth R. Trapp. *Skilled Work: American Craft in the Renwick Gallery, National Museum of American Art, Smithsonian Institution*. Washington, D.C.: Smithsonian Institution Press, 1998, pp. 50, 120.

Glueck, Grace. "In Glass, Darkly and Kissed by Light." *New York Times*, August 29, 1997, Arts and Leisure sec., pp. B1, B26.

Silver, Joanne. "Magnifying Glass." *Boston Herald*, August 15, 1997, Scene sec., pp. 12, 14.

Hawley, Henry H. *Glass Today: American Studio Glass from Cleveland Collections*. Cleveland: Cleveland Museum of Art, 1997, pp. 100–102.

Heir Apparent: Translating the Secrets of Venetian Glass. Bellevue, Washington: Bellevue Art Museum, 1997, pp. 15, 19, 23.

Recent Glass Sculpture: A Union of Ideas. Milwaukee: Milwaukee Art Museum, 1997, p. 22.

International New Glass: Venezia aperto vetro. Venice: Arsenale Editrice, 1996, pp. 122, 210.

Oldknow, Tina. *Pilchuck: A Glass School*. Seattle: Pilchuck Glass School in association with University of Washington Press, 1996. See index for page numbers.

Aronson, Margery. "Translucent and Opaque: Women and Glass." In *Modernism and Beyond: Women Artists of the Pacific Northwest*. Ed. Laura Brunsman and Ruth Askey. New York: Midmarch Arts Press, 1993, pp. 48, 50, 52–53.

Taragin, Davira S. *Contemporary Crafts and the Saxe Collection*. Ed. Terry Ann R. Neff. New York: Hudson Hills Press; Toledo, Ohio: Toledo Museum of Art, 1993, pp. 59, 180, 199.

Waldrich, Joachim. *Who's Who in Contemporary Glass: A Comprehensive World Guide to Glass Artists, Craftsmen, Designers*. 1st ed. Munich: Joachim Waldrich, 1993.

Bell, Robert. *Design Visions: International Directions in Glass, American Jewellery and Metalwork*. Perth: Art Gallery of Western Australia, 1992, p. 42.

Herman, Lloyd E. *Clearly Art: Pilchuck's Glass Legacy*. Bellingham: Whatcom Museum of History and Art, 1992, pp. 36, 44, 82–83.

Chambers, Karen S. *Trompe l'Oeil at Home: Faux Finishes and Fantasy Settings*. New York: Rizzoli, 1991, pp. 32–33.

Miller, Bonnie J. *Out of the Fire: Contemporary Glass Artists and Their Work*. San Francisco: Chronicle Books, 1991, pp. 50–53.

World Glass Now '91. Sapporo: Hokkaido Museum of Modern Art, 1991, pp. 76–77, 218.

Biskeborn, Susan. *Artists at Work: Twenty-five Glassmakers, Ceramists, and Jewelers*. Seattle: Alaska Northwest Books, 1990, pp. 10–15.

Spillman, Jane Shadel, and Susanne K. Frantz. *Masterpieces of American Glass: The Corning Museum of Glass, the Toledo Museum of Art, Lillian Nassau Ltd.* New York: Crown Publishers, 1990, pp. 70, 86.

Miller, Bonnie J. "Double Vision." *American Craft* 49, no. 5 (October 1989): pp. 40–45.

Frantz, Susanne K. *Contemporary Glass: A World Survey from the Corning Museum of Glass*. New York: Harry N. Abrams, 1989, pp. 83–84.

Klein, Dan. *Glass: A Contemporary Art*. New York: Rizzoli, 1989, pp. 38–39, 48, 75.

Heineman, Ben W., Sr. *Contemporary Glass: A Private Collection*. Chicago: Falcon II Press, 1988, pp. 50–51.

Gedeon, Lucinda H., and Dianne Cripe, eds. *3+3×7: Sculpture in Glass and Works on Paper*. Tempe: University Art Museum, Arizona State University, 1987, pp. 15–19.

Smith, Paul J., and Edward Lucie-Smith. *Craft Today: Poetry of the Physical*. New York: American Craft Museum and Weidenfeld and Nicolson, 1986, p. 99.

Hammell, Lisa. "The Highly Skilled Teamwork behind the Master Craftsman." *New York Times*, August 29, 1985, pp. C1, C6.

Chambers, Karen S. "Flora Mace and Joey Kirkpatrick: Partners in Glass." *New Work* (New York Experimental Glass Workshop, New York), nos. 23–24 (summer–fall 1985): pp. 8–9.

Hollister, Paul. "Gefühle personifiziert: Arbeiten von Flora Mace und Joey Kirkpatrick/Personification of Feelings: The Mace/Kirkpatrick Collaboration." *Neues Glas* 1 (Jan.–March 1984): pp. 14–19.

Glowen, Ron. "Renewing the Vessel." *Artweek*, December 17, 1983, p. 4.

Selected Public and Corporate Collections

Art Museum, Arizona State University, Tempe

The Boeing Collection, The Boeing Company World Headquarters, Chicago

Broadfield House Glass Museum, West Midlands, United Kingdom

Brunnier Art Museum, Iowa State University, Ames

Cleveland Museum of Art, Cleveland

Corning Museum of Glass, Corning, New York

Davis Wright Tremaine, Bellevue and Seattle

Dayton Art Institute, Dayton

Detroit Institute of Arts, David Jacob Chodorkoff Collection, Detroit

de Young Memorial Museum, Fine Arts Museums of San Francisco, San Francisco

Glasmuseet, Ebeltoft, Denmark

Hokkaido Museum of Modern Art, Sapporo, Japan

Huntington Galleries, Huntington, West Virginia

JPMorgan Chase Art Collection, New York (Joey Kirkpatrick)

Kitazawa Museum of Art, Suwa, Nagano, Japan

Leigh Yawkey Woodson Art Museum, Wausau

Lowe Art Museum, University of Miami, Coral Gables

Mayo Clinic, Rochester, Minnesota

Metropolitan Museum of Art, New York

Microsoft Corporation, Redmond, Washington

Mobile Museum of Art, Mobile

Montgomery Museum of Fine Arts, Montgomery

Musée des Arts Decoratifs, Lausanne, Switzerland

Museum of Art, Washington State University, Pullman

Museum of Arts and Design, New York

Museum of Fine Arts, Boston

Museum of Fine Arts, St. Petersburg, Florida

Museum of Glass, Tacoma

Palm Springs Art Museum, Palm Springs

Pilchuck Glass School, Stanwood, Washington

Portland Art Museum, Portland, Oregon

Prescott Collection of Pilchuck Glass at U.S. Bank Centre, Seattle

Racine Art Museum, Racine, Wisconsin

Seattle Art Museum, Seattle

Sheraton Hotel Collection, Seattle

Smithsonian American Art Museum and the Renwick Gallery, Smithsonian Institution, Washington, D.C.

Speed Art Museum, Louisville

Tacoma Art Museum, Tacoma

Toledo Museum of Art, Toledo, Ohio

Washington Art Consortium

Honors and Awards

2009   Neddy Artist Fellowship Finalists

2006   Interviewed for the Archives of American Art, Smithsonian Institution, Washington, D.C.

2005   Elected to American Craft Council of Fellows

        Design Achievement Award, Seattle Design Center and Seattle Homes and Lifestyles

2001   Libenský Award, Pilchuck Glass School, Chateau Ste. Michelle, Woodinville, Washington

Professional Appointments

2001   Artists-in-Residence, Pilchuck Glass School, Stanwood, Washington

1996   Visiting Faculty, Toyama City Institute of Glass Art, Toyama, Japan (Flora C. Mace)

1994   Faculty, Haystack Mountain School of Crafts, Deer Isle, Maine (Flora C. Mace)

        Guest Lecturers, Palm Springs Desert Museum, Palm Springs

1993   Visiting Faculty, University of Hawaii, Honolulu

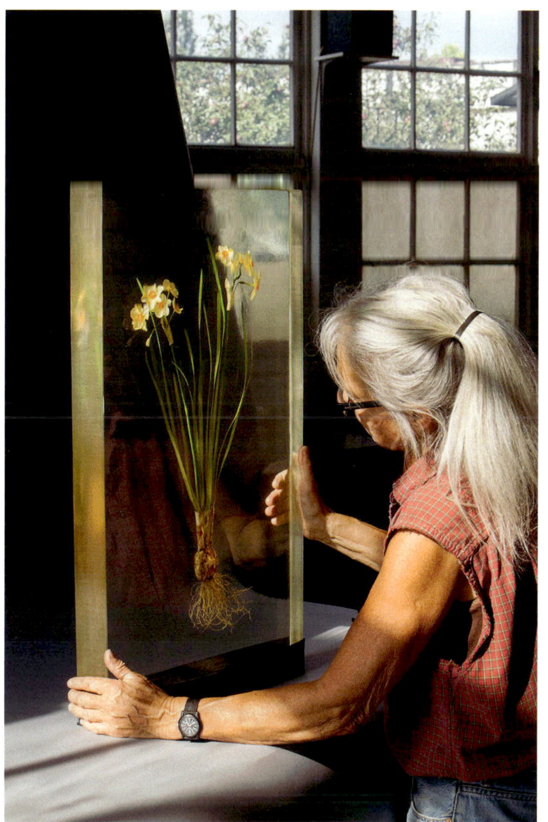

Mace with *Tazetta Botanical,* 2014.

1991-2006   Trustee, Pilchuck Glass School, Stanwood, Washington (Joey Kirkpatrick)

1987   Artists-in-Residence, Pilchuck Glass School, Stanwood, Washington

        Guest Lecturers, Harbourfront Studios, Toronto; National College of Art, Crafts, and Design, Konstfack, Stockholm; and San Francisco State University, San Francisco

1986-90   Faculty, Pilchuck Glass School, Stanwood, Washington (summers)

1985   Faculty, Haystack Mountain School of Crafts, Deer Isle, Maine

        Guest Lecturers, *Nordisk Glas '85*, Reykjavík

        Visiting Faculty, J. & L. Lobmeyr Factory/School, Vienna

1984   Artist-in-Residence Assistants (to Italo Scanga and Christopher Wilmarth), Pilchuck Glass School, Stanwood, Washington

1981-83   Faculty, Pilchuck Glass School, Stanwood, Washington (summers)

1981-82   Faculty, University of Illinois, Champaign-Urbana (Flora C. Mace)

1981   Guest Instructors, University of California, Los Angeles

1980   Artists-in-Residence, Pilchuck Glass School, Stanwood, Washington, and Rhode Island School of Design, Providence

Acknowledgments

This book project has been at once thrilling and a bit frightening, as we measured the speedy passing of many years of work and life. It is now very rewarding to see the project come together, and we are extremely grateful for the contributions of many people.

Linda Tesner envisioned this book long before we could. She worked through many fits and starts with a gentle but persistent determination to bring it to life. We thank her for her intelligent essay, written with a great understanding of our relationship to our work.

Many thanks to Patricia Kirkpatrick, a regular collaborator in our lives, who dared to interview us! Patricia was able to make the important connections between our interests and the personal history that we each bring to our work. Her questions were at once thoughtful and challenging enough to help us better understand our own path.

We offer our gratitude to Mark Doty for visiting us at the studio and writing about our work in a way that placed it in new landscapes. Thank you as well to Dan Hinkley, your words added a unique view from your garden to ours.

The long days in the studio were often made easier, more interesting, and certainly more fun by the good help of so many who interrupted their own studio practice to make a commitment to our work. We thank Nancy Callan, Pat Davidson, Paul DeSomma, Katherine Gray, Catherine Hobbs, Kris Kirkpatrick, Tracy Kirkpatrick, Nancy Mace, William Morris, Jon Ormbreck, Rich Royal, Dan Spitzer, Paula Stokes, Boyd Sugiki, Randy Walker, Karen Willenbrink, and Lisa Zerkowitz.

After our work was done, Claire Garoutte, Russell Johnson, Scott Leen, Mike Seidl, Robert Vinnedge, and Ann Welch brought their imagination and technical skills to the photography of our work.

Many thanks are extended to Ed Marquand, Jeff Wincapaw, Melissa Duffes, and the Marquand staff for their patience and the very beautiful design of this book, as well as to Laura Morris for her careful editing.

Pilchuck Glass School has played an integral part in our development as artists. We remember and appreciate so many staff members, teachers, and supporters from around the world, whom we have crossed paths with again and again.

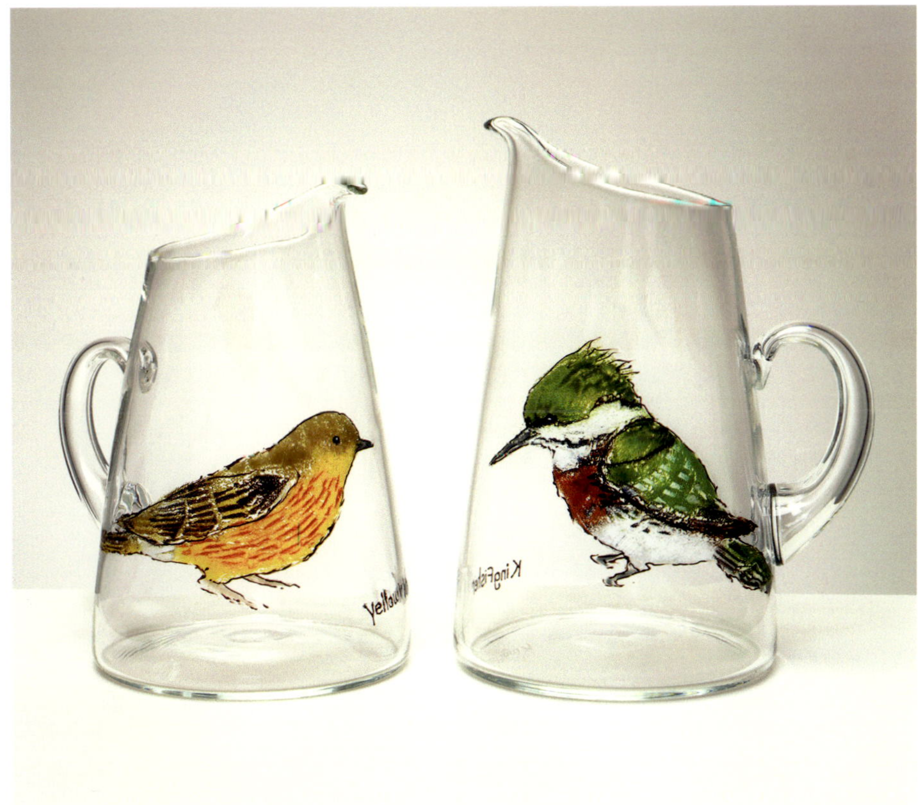

Winged Vessels: Yellow Warbler
and *Kingfisher*, 2002
Glass, 10 × 7¾ × 6 inches; 11 × 8½ × 6¼ inches

We especially thank our dear friends Marsha McCroskey, Paula Stokes, and Ann Welch, who have supported us in so many ways for a very long time.

We deeply appreciate the enthusiasm of the following people who have supported our work through the years and, with their contributions, have also helped to make the production of this book a reality: Eve and Chap Alvord, Rebecca Benaroya, Leslie and Michael Bernstein, Fay and Phelan Bright, Leslie and Dale Chihuly, Michèle and Larry Corash, Sara Jane and William Dehoff, Tana and James Kirkpatrick, Carolyn and Robert Kitchell, Colleen and John Kotelly, Alison and Glen Milliman, Barbara R. Palmer, Francine and Benson Pilloff, Joyce and John Price, Chris Rifkin, Dorothy Saxe, Jon Shirley, Patricia and Samuel Smith, Paula Stokes and John Sullivan, and George R. Stroemple, as well as the staff of the Museum of Glass, Tacoma.

We remember with great affection and appreciation the late Italo Scanga, our friend, mentor, and muse. And it is with much gratitude that we thank Dale Chihuly, whose example and generosity inspired and enriched our journey as artists.

With the publication of this book, we also remember Virginia Kirkpatrick, Joey's mother, who at every turn encouraged and delighted in not only her daughter's success and artistic pursuits but also those of her "fifth daughter, Flora." The many hours she spent setting the table for us for play school, art projects, and the library in the back room are where our journey began.

We dedicate this book to our sisters with love.

Joey and Flora

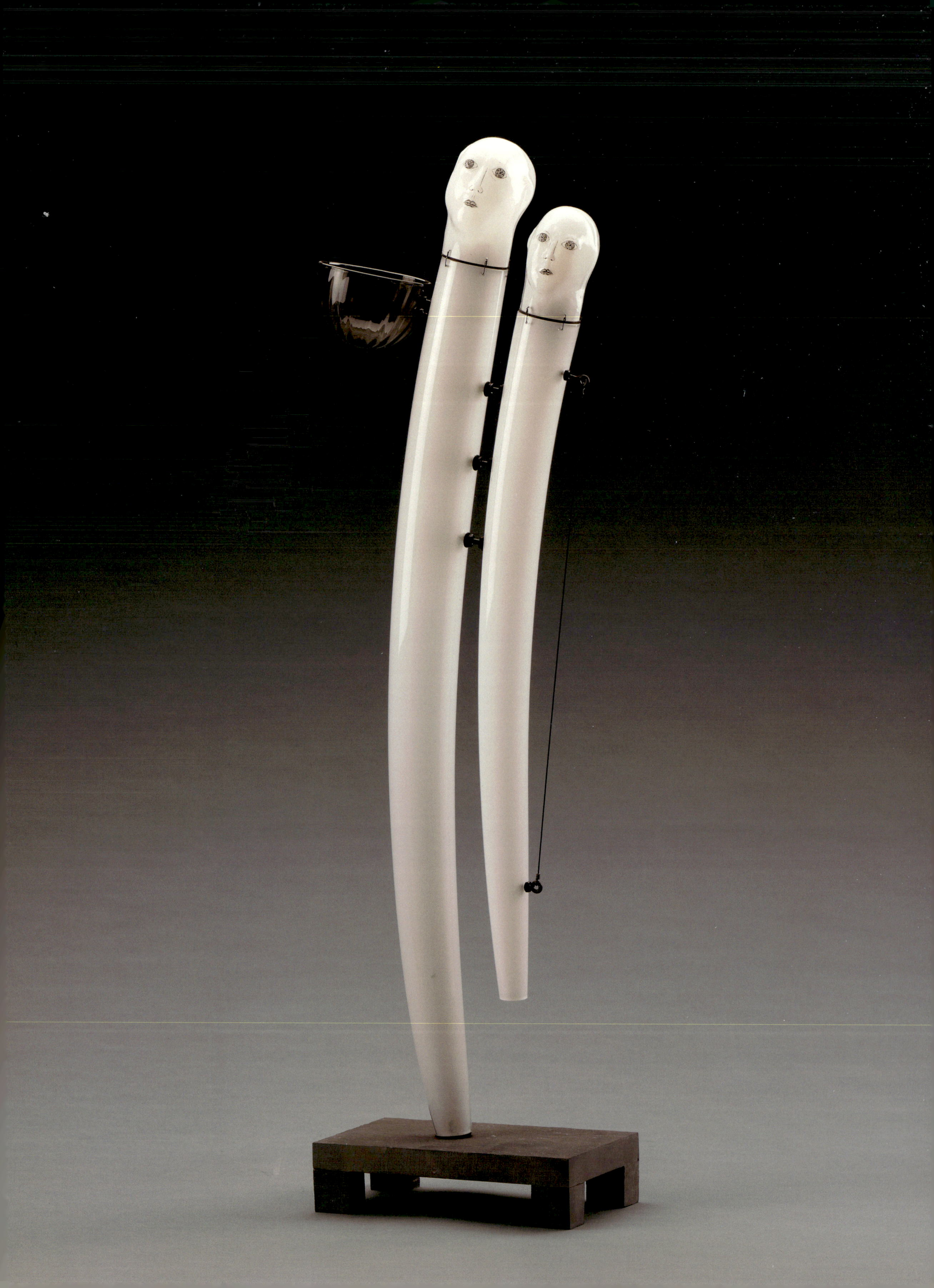

Contributors

Mark Doty is the author of eight books of poems, four volumes of nonfiction, and *The Art of Description*, a handbook for writers. His new and selected poems, *Fire to Fire*, won the 2008 National Book Award. Among his writings on the visual arts is *Still Life with Oysters and Lemon*, a book-length meditation on Dutch still life painting, objects, and intimacy. He has taught at many universities, including Stanford University, the University of Iowa, Columbia University, Rutgers University, and New York University.

Daniel J. Hinkley, with Robert Jones, founded and ran Heronswood Nursery for almost twenty years. Devoted to introducing rare plant species to American gardeners, Hinkley undertook many international journeys to gather seeds. A contributing editor to *Horticulture Magazine*, he has written books and articles for gardening magazines, spoken to diverse audiences, and consulted for popular television programs. Hinkley has received the American Horticultural Society's Liberty Hyde Bailey Award for lifetime achievement and the Royal Horticultural Society's Veitch Memorial Medal.

Patricia Kirkpatrick is the author of *Odessa*, which received the 2013 Minnesota Book Award in Poetry, *Century's Road*, and *Plowie: A Story from the Prairie*. Her work has appeared in such places as *Poetry*, *The Threepenny Review*, and *She Walks in Beauty*. She has been awarded fellowships from the National Endowment for the Arts and National Endowment for the Humanities and has taught writing in many universities. Her interviews with American writers are published widely.

Linda Tesner is director and curator of the Ronna and Eric Hoffman Gallery of Contemporary Art at Lewis & Clark College, Portland, Oregon. Previously, she was assistant director of the Portland Art Museum and director of the Maryhill Museum of Art, Goldendale, Washington. The author of numerous exhibition catalogues and monographs, Tesner serves on the Public Art Advisory Committee of the Regional Arts and Culture Council, Portland.

Foregather, 1985
Glass, slate, and steel, 32 × 10 × 5 inches

Credits

All works are by both artists unless otherwise specified.

p. 12: *Neither Two a Stranger*, Barbara Billings and Ernest Vogel

p. 14: *Sheep Bowl*, private collection

p. 23: *François*, Kathryn Kendall

p. 28: *Harp*, Capper Heffernan

p. 29: *Figure Shoring*, private collection

p. 31: *Wire Drawing on Glass,* Ginger and Parks Anderson

p. 32: *Waterborne*, Carolle Baskin

p. 34: *Nature's Palette*, Oakland Museum of California, Oakland, Promised gift of Dorothy and George Saxe

p. 37: *Water's Edge, Year's Round*, Museum of Arts and Design, New York

p. 39: *Braided to Great Effects*, Speed Art Museum, Louisville

p. 40: *Spooled Torso, So Made*, Museum of Fine Arts, Boston, Promised gift of Anita and Ronald Wornick

p. 43: *Still Life with Pear*, Toledo Art Museum, Toledo, Ohio

p. 47: *Ten Birds*, Alison and Glen Milliman

p. 51: *Woodland Voices*, Michele and Kyle Peltonen

p. 61: *Cordwood 4: Cherry I*, JPMorgan Chase Art Collection

p. 73: Untitled, Patricia Kirkpatrick

p. 75: *Celestial Eclipse*, Rebecca and Jack Benaroya

p. 84: *Beaked Vessel: Barred Owl*, Alison and Glen Milliman

p. 85: *Single Iris*, Kirsten Feldman and Hugh Frater

p. 89: *Figure*, private collection

p. 91 left: *Two Figure Drawing*, Robert Minkoff

p. 92 top right: *Figure with Child*, George R. Stroemple; bottom: *Two Women on a Ladder*, George R. Stroemple

p. 104: *The Conversation*, Dale and Doug Anderson

p. 105 left: *Double Doll on Blue*, The Metropolitan Museum of Art, New York; right: *Wishing Will*, private collection

p. 111: *Personal Sonata*, Colleen and John Kotelly

p. 113: *Foretold Journey*, Fay and Phelan Bright

p. 117: *Garden of Ladders*, private collection

p. 118: *Voyage Carrier*, Sara Jane and William Dehoff

p. 119: *Cargo*, private collection

p. 120: *Tidal Eclipse*, Palm Springs Art Museum, Palm Springs

p. 121: *The Juggler*, private collection

p. 122: *Crossing*, Rebecca and Jack Benaroya

p. 123: *Passage*, Seattle Art Museum, Seattle, Gift of Mary and Jon Shirley

p. 125: *Century's Rounding*, private collection

p. 126 left: *So Long As to See Far Enough*, Chris Rifkin; right: *Turned Bosk*, Michèle and Larry Corash

p. 127: *Garden of Ladders*, Toledo Museum of Art, Toledo, Ohio

p. 128: *Limbed Tumbrel*, Seattle Art Museum, Seattle, Gift of Mary and Jon Shirley

p. 129: *Seasonal Spire*, Francine and Benson Pilloff

p. 132: *Pale Divine*, Seattle Art Museum, Seattle, Gift of Mary and Jon Shirley

p. 133: *Crown of Indigo*, Barbara and Warren Poole

p. 134: *Water Catcher*, de Young Memorial Museum, San Francisco, Partial gift of Dorothy and George Saxe

p. 135: *Holding the Williwaw*, Sara Jane and William Dehoff

p. 137: *As Much As Measured Time*, private collection

p. 138: *Voyage of Remembrance*, Dale and Doug Anderson

p. 140 left: *From the Reach of Memory*, Francine and Benson Pilloff

p. 141: *From the Limb of a Tree and the Water Within*, Myra and Hal Weiss

p. 144: *Assembling Memory*, de Young Memorial Museum, San Francisco, Partial gift of Dorothy and George Saxe

pp. 146–47: *Sylvic Spheres*, private collection

p. 151 right: *A Way Is Found*, private collection

p. 154–55: *Fruit Still Life*, Chateau Ste. Michelle, Woodinville, Washington

p. 158: *Revealing the Imagined*, Sara Jane and William Dehoff

p. 160: *Revealing Red*, Chris Rifkin

p. 161: *Making Before Meaning: Paintbrush Group, Big Yellow*, Kathleen and Allen Shoup; *Green*, private collection; *Blue*, Renee and Carl Behnke; *Little Yellow*, Fay and Phelan Bright; *Big Red*, private collection

p. 174: *Bird Page: Red-bellied Woodpecker*, David Thomsen

p. 175: *Yellow-shafted Flicker*, private collection

p. 177: *Woodland Drawing: Stump*, Susan and Furman Moseley

p. 180: *Gloxinia*, Daniel Wolf

p. 186: *Blue Violet*, Robert Dedman Family

p. 187: *Hoop-petticoat Daffodil*, private collection

p. 190 left: *New Trillium*, private collection

p. 192: *4 Bloom Poeticus Narcissus*, Barbara R. Palmer

p. 197: *Cordwood 5: Madrona*, Alison and Glen Milliman

p. 198: *Cordwood with Birch*, Katy McCoy and Phil Vogelzang

p. 203: *Fritillaria: Checkered Lily*, private collection

p. 211 left: *Winged Vessel: Yellow Warbler*, Colleen and John Kotelly

p. 212: *Foregather*, Capper Heffernan

Reproductions of all other works are courtesy of the artists.

We have done our best to credit collections, individuals, and reference sources as accurately as possible. Any errors or omissions are the responsibility of the artists, and we apologize for them.

Library of Congress Control Number: 2015947318
978-0-692-39713-8

Distributed by University of Washington Press
www.washington.edu/uwpress

Published by Marquand Books, Inc., Seattle
www.marquand.com

Edited by Laura Morris
Designed by Jeff Wincapaw
Typeset in Adagio by Maggie Lee
Proofread by Elissa Griesz
Color management by iocolor, Seattle
Printed and bound in China by Artron Art Group

Photography Credits

Dick Busher: pp. 12, 28, 114–15
Claire Garoutte: pp. 20, 70 (top), 80
Russell Johnson: p. 49
Warren Jagger: p. 15
Scott Leen: jacket front and back, pp. 54, 64, 82–83, 86–87, 148–49, 151, 162–63, 200, 203, 205, 206, 209
Mike Seidl: p. 55
Robert Vinnedge: pp. 2, 4, 8, 14 (bottom), 17, 19, 22, 23, 27, 31–37, 39, 40, 42–44, 45 (left), 48, 51, 52, 73 (bottom), 75, 79, 84, 90–95, 100–09, 111, 113, 116–41, 143–47, 150, 152–61, 164–65, 168–79, 211
Ann Welch: pp. 56, 59, 85, 166–67, 180–93, 202 (bottom), 204